*Collector's Illustrated
Encyclopedia of the
American Revolution*

Collector's Illustrated Encyclopedia of the American Revolution

George C. Neumann and Frank J. Kravic

Drawings by George C. Woodbridge

Stackpole Books

COLLECTOR'S ILLUSTRATED ENCYCLOPEDIA OF THE AMERICAN REVOLUTION

Copyright © 1975 by
George C. Neumann and Frank J. Kravic

Published by
STACKPOLE BOOKS
Cameron and Kelker Streets
Harrisburg, Pa. 17105

Printed in the U.S.A.

Library of Congress Cataloging in Publication Data

Neumann, George C
    Collector's illustrated encyclopedia of the American Revolution.

    Bibliography: p.
    1. United States—History—Revolution, 1775–1783—Collectibles—Dic-
tionaries. I. Kravic, Frank J., joint author. II. Woodbridge, George C. III. Title.
NK806.N37   973.3'075   75-6897
ISBN 0-8117-0394-0

Contents

Preface

In the midst of our nationwide Bicentennial celebration it is unfortunate that most Americans have only a vague impression of the man who made it all happen—the common soldier on both sides who persevered so remarkably from 1775 to 1783. Fundamental to this clouded image is the fact that we know amazingly little about the day-to-day personal life of these soldiers. Their military handbooks, diaries, letters, etc. are available, but it was not customary to describe personal effects in writing. Identification of materials which did survive has been further complicated by great numbers of handmade uniforms and accoutrements created for the Centennial festivities in 1876. The result has been a multitude of improvised opinions leading to many common misconceptions.

There is still insufficient knowledge to prepare a final study on the subject. Our work is presented as a pictorial summary at the current levels of information to help historians and collectors more correctly understand and identify items associated with the officer and enlisted man in the field. To keep this coverage within practical bounds, our subjects have been limited primarily to their personal effects, i.e. clothing, weapons, accoutrements, tools, and living accessories.

The three creators of this book have attempted to combine their primary areas of research to reach this objective, i.e. George C. Neumann's studies of weapons and accoutrements, Frank J. Kravic's extensive archeological material and period document collection, and artist George C. Woodbridge's broad knowledge of uniforms and clothing. To achieve maximum authenticity every effort has been made to illustrate items not based on "hand me down" identification, but verifiable in reliable records or matched to properly excavated material. The archeological sources are mostly campsites of both sides in the Revolution as well as the French and Indian War (under the assumption that its basic equipment was reused during the War for Independence). The majority of these sites are in the northeast—particularly the Champlain Valley and Hudson River areas.

In an effort to present the full spectrum of personal items found among excavated material, our illustrations vary from fine chinaware to standard equipment of issue. It should be remembered that most of this material could have been used by irregulars, militia, or professional "line" troops. When an object is not specifically dated, it has been selected as representative of this period.

Since proper archeology remains our most authentic source for identifying these accessories, Frank Kravic has contributed an additional chapter describing methods for preserving artifacts, as well as other collectable material.

Particular thanks are also extended to the Brigade of the American Revolution for permitting us to photograph typical uniformed members from among its regiments. All three of us are active participants in this organization and consider it a leader in authenticity among groups recreating the Revolutionary War soldier.

It is impossible to list here all of the individuals who so generously helped to make this book possible, but many are noted with appreciation under illustrations of material from their collections. Special acknowledgment is also extended to the following individuals:

To Elaine Salls, Robert Nittolo, and Edward Charol for their enthusiastic encouragement and help.

To Harold L. Peterson, Michael Cleary, Richard Gerding, David Hervey, Marvin K. Salls, Wm. Richard Gordon of the Valley Forge Historical Society; Craddock R. Goins, Jr. at the Smithsonian Institution; Susan Finley and the National Society of Colonial Dames of America in Connecticut who maintain the Webb, Deane, Stevens Museum (Wethersfield, Ct.); and John H. G. Pell and Jane M. Lape of Fort Ticonderoga.

To Richard Ryan of the Nassau County (N.Y.) Museum; Edward and Joan W. Friedland; Philip H. Dunbar at The Connecticut Historical Society; Robert W. Fisch, West Point Museum; Richard J. Koke, of the New-York Historical Society; Donald Fangboner, New Windsor Cantonment (N.Y.); Peter Blum of The Soldier Shop; Carroll V. Lonergan; Phil Snyder; William M. Wigham, Brigade of the American Revolution; Marie Absalon at Morristown National Historical Park; John Fortier, Fortress Louisbourg (N.S.); Kenneth A. Hinde and Lawrie Rufe of the Mercer Museum, Bucks County Historical Society; Christine Meadows, The Mount Vernon Ladies Assn.; Craig W. C. Brown, at the First Corps of Cadets Museum, Boston; Donald G. Herold, from the Charleston Museum, S.C.; Jacob Grimm, of the Fort Ligonier Memorial Foundation; Mark Sextant and Kathy Flynn, Peabody Museum of Salem, Mass.; Willard C. Cousins; Wayne and Wanda Daniels; Martin Retting; Lynn Glaser; David Currie; William McInerney; and Clyde Risley of Imrie/Risely Miniatures.

To Robert Ekenstierna, G. Gedney Godwin, Paul Weisberg; William W. Jeffries, the U.S. Naval Academy Museum; John H. Mead of the Trailside Museums, Interstate Park Commission (N.Y.); Vivian F. Buckle at the Thomas Jefferson Memorial Foundation; Loring Chandler; Thomas Williams, Williamsburg, Va.; Col. Joshua E. Henderson at the Armed Forces Institute of Pathology; Scott Bishop; Lee Hanson of the Fort Stanwix National Monument, Rome, N.Y.; Col. Vernon S. Allen, Varnum Military and Naval Museum, East Greenwich, R.I.; Michael Winey and Bruce Bazelon of the Pennsylvania Historical and Museum Commission; William H. Bradford, Washington Headquarters, Newburgh, N.Y.; and Richard DeAngelis.

George C. Neumann
Frank J. Kravic
George C. Woodbridge

1

ABATIS (see "Fortifications, Field.") **ACCOUTREMENTS:** Generally defined as a soldier's personal equipment excepting clothes and weapons. Thus the wide variety of cartridge boxes, pouches, belts, scabbards, canteens, knapsacks, powder horns, etc. are all included in this category and will be further defined under separate headings. Despite official specifications for most of these items they varied greatly especially among American forces—reflecting the sparse industry in the colonies, attrition in the field, and the lengthy supply routes from Europe. (1) A list of required arms and accoutrements for Massachusetts troops in 1775 from the journal of Arthur Harris of Bridgewater, i.e. "Each Soldier to provide himself with/ A Good Fire Arm/ A Steal or Iron Ram Rod & Spring for Same/ A Worm Priming Wire & Brush/ A Bayonet fitted to his Gun/ A Scabard & Belt Therefor/ A Cuting Sword or Tomahawk or Hatchet/ A Pouch Containing a Cartridge Box that will Hold/ fifteen Rounds of Cartridges as Least/ A Hundred Buck Shot/ A Jack Knife & Tow for Wadding/ Six flints, one pound of Powder/ forty Leaden Balls fitted to the Gun/ A Knapsack & Blankett/ A Canteen or Wood Bottle to Hold 1 Quart."

Source: William H. Guthman.

2

3

(2) A portrayal of how diversified an American line company looked after a period in the field. ADZ (see "Tools, Hand.") **ALMANAC** (see "Books.") **AMMUNITION** (also see "Artillery," "Gunpowder," "Cartridge Boxes," "Grenades," "Horns," "Hunting Bag," "Molds," "Pouches, Bullet"): Basically a round projectile fired by black powder out of weapons ranging from hand guns to heavy cannon. It was normally made of lead for hand arms and iron for artillery. Most were solid, although mortars and howitzers fired hollow "shells" which contained a fuse leading to an internal powder charge for exploding among the enemy. (3) A cross-section of the great variety of artillery shell and solid shot excavated from colonial sites (these 1758–1778). They vary from 7" to 2" in diameter and reflect the supply problem, especially among the Americans, who were forced to employ a diverse collection of cannon sizes. (cont.)

Sources: 2—Brigade of the American Revolution, photo by Michael Cleary; 3—Frank J. Kravic.

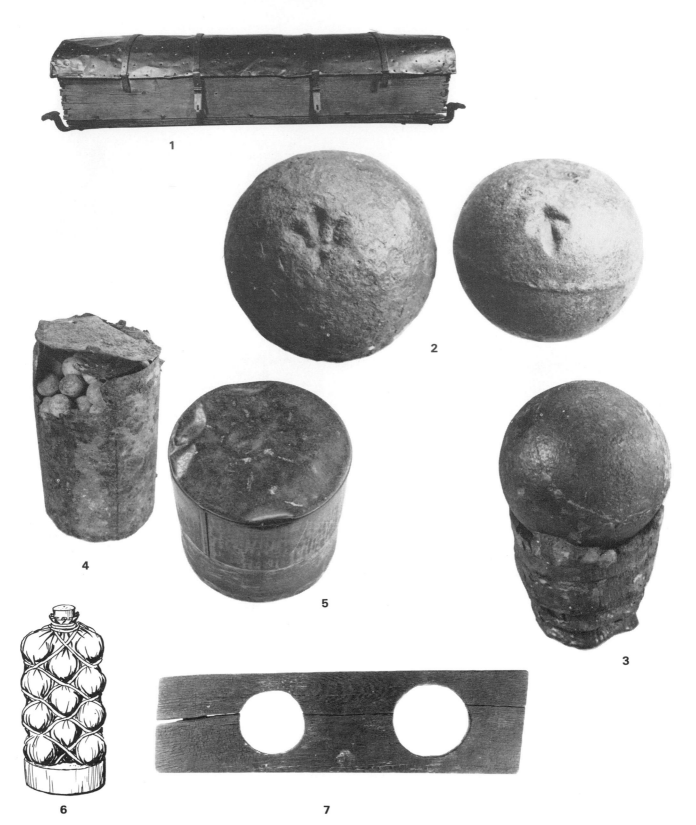

AMMUNITION (cont.) (1) The wood and iron body of an American high-wheeled French type Gribeauval Caisson for transporting artillery ammunition. (2) Cannon balls marked with the French fleur-de-lis (left) and an English broad arrow (both from a 1759–1777 British Champlain Valley camp). (3) Solid cannon shot on a wooden sabot; the ball was originally attached by two crossing straps of tinned iron; horizontal channels around its tapering base helped attach a powder bag—thus creating a complete charge (similar fixed cannister and grape loads were also used). The sabot was usually reserved for rapid fire, as most shooting employed a separate projectile and powder bag (normally of flannel). (4) A cannon cannister load, i.e. the tinned container was filled with musket size lead balls for anti-personnel use; 6¼″ x 3½″. (5) Larger cannister load (wooden base, tin nailed to sides; 5½″ dia.). (6) Grape shot having a flat iron or wooden base and center pole surrounded by iron balls, covered with cloth and tied; mostly fired by large cannon against sizable targets. (7) A wooden shot gauge to verify the ball's maximum diameter; from the Valcour Island gondola, *Philadelphia*, 1776; for 9 and 12-pound shot.

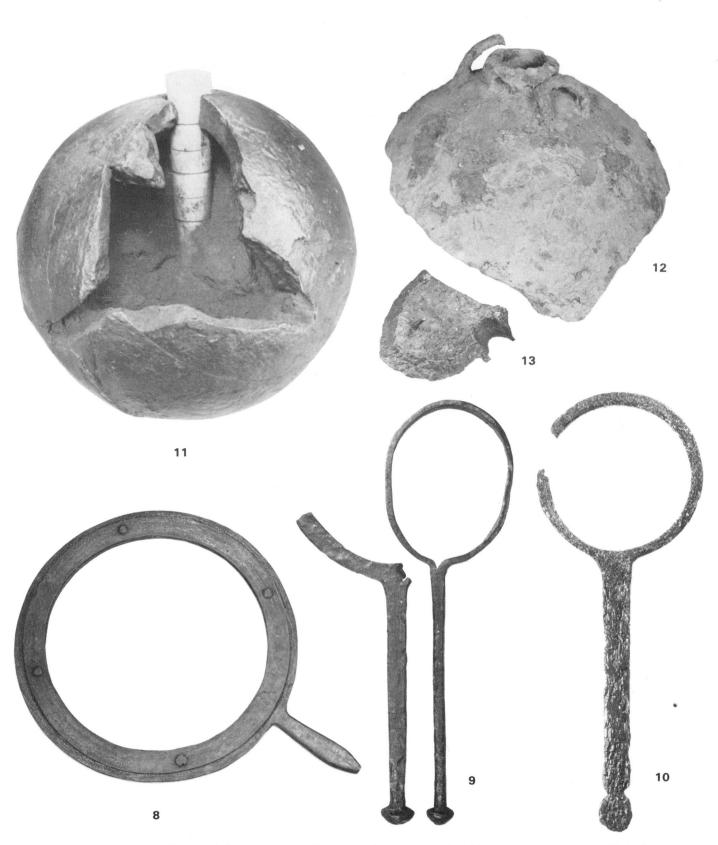

(8) Iron cannon gauge; 8″ internal dia. (9) Excavated remains of shot gauges (British camp, c. 1759–1777). (10) An iron 12-pounder shot gauge; from the American gondola, *Philadelphia,* 1776. (11) A cannon shell opened to show its internal cavity filled with black powder and the hollow wooden fuse. Shells were usually fired by mortars or howitzers and designated by their diameter—solid shot was identified by its weight. (12) An excavated fragment of a large 13″ mortar shell (fired c. 1759) showing the raised lip for its fuse and two side handles. (13) A shell fragment having a nail driven through a small hole or flaw as a plug (an illegal practice). (cont.)

Sources: 1—Morristown National Historical Park; 2, 9, 12, 13—Frank J. Kravic; 3, 4, 11—Fort Ticonderoga Museum; 5—Washington's Hdq., Newburgh; 7, 10—Smithsonian Institution, Dr. Philip K. Lundeberg Collection; 8—George C. Neumann.

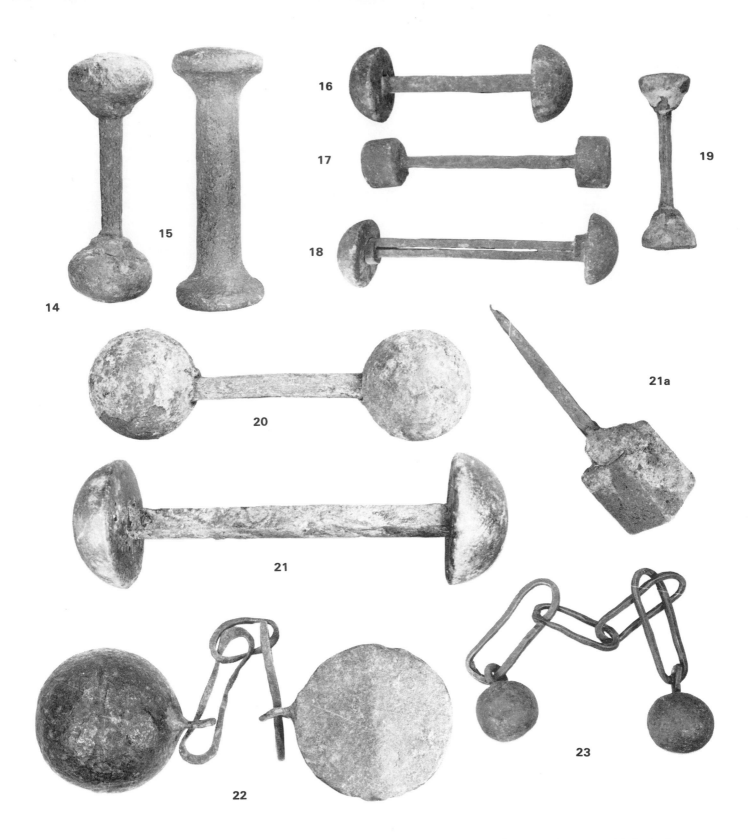

AMMUNITION (cont.) (14–21) Types of cannon "bar shot" which rotated in flight to damage a ship's rigging or disrupt formations of men; the lengths shown are 9¼" to 17". Note the two sliding bars in #18 to spread in flight ("expanding bar shot"). (21a) The remains of one of a group of four sectioned bar shot loaded together to divide after firing. (22) Chain shot with a split ball for use against personnel and ship's rigging. (23) A chain shot having two solid balls.

Sources: 14, 15, 20, 21—Frank J. Kravic; 16, 17, 18, 19, 21a, 23—George C. Neumann; 22—Don Troiani.

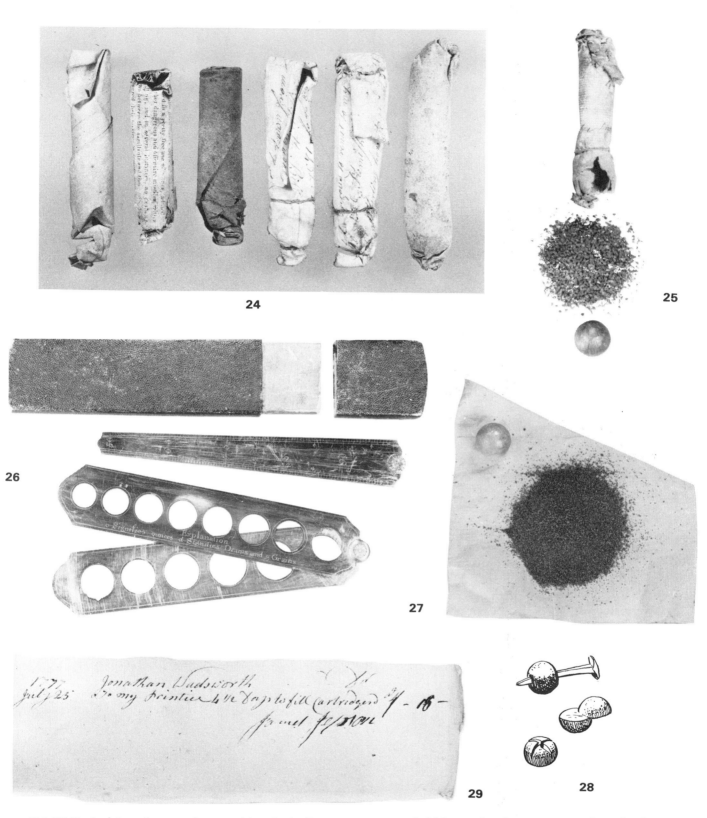

(24, 25) Typical American musket cartridges including newspapers and old letters for the paper wrapping; the three at left contain only powder (to allow use with the variety of ball diameters employed by the colonials). The standard cartridge included a premeasured amount of black powder, plus a round lead bullet (and often some smaller ones, i.e. "buck and ball"). Many militia and riflemen also used buckshot and loose charges. British cartridges of brown paper were normally tied at the bottom with pack thread, the French were pasted—while the Americans copied both. (27) A common cartridge paper pattern (about 6" x 5½") plus the black powder and lead bullet. (26) An English tapered musket ball bore gauge and a bullet sizer which also lists "ozs., grains, and drams" of powder for each size; the case is 6¾" long. (28) Mutilation bullet types (as found in the camps of both forces). (29) The troops were often issued the ingredients to produce their own cartridges. Others came from large and small contractors; this is a 1777 receipt for a tradesman's "prentice" making cartridges.

Sources: 24—George C. Neumann; 25, 26—Edward Charol; 29—Frank J. Kravic.

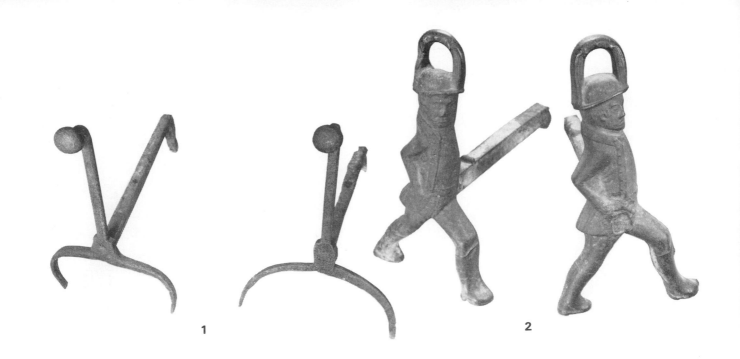

1

2

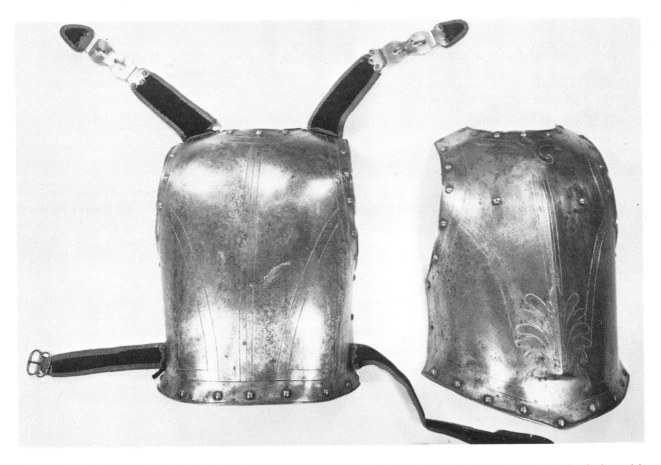

3

ANDIRONS (also see "Firebacks"): Semi-permanent camps with huts often disclose articles with which the soldiers would have been familiar at home—especially at sites near populated areas. Fireplaces, for example, not only yield the expected iron pots and kettles, but also various accessories including andirons. Both brass and iron designs were used (iron most popular). (1) Iron, first half of the 18th century. (2) Soldier pattern, c. 1750–1780. The troops also placed iron bars between rocks, and even used cannon bar shot to help draft their fires. **ANVILS** (see "Blacksmithing.") **ARMOR:** By the time of the American Revolution the wearing of body armor had almost disappeared except for specialized troops. (3) French back and breast plates as used by engineer officers working close to enemy works in daylight; the straps are velvet with gold and silver embroidery, c. 1750–1760.

Sources: 1—The Conn. Historical Society; 2—Frank J. Kravic; 3—Edward Charol.

4

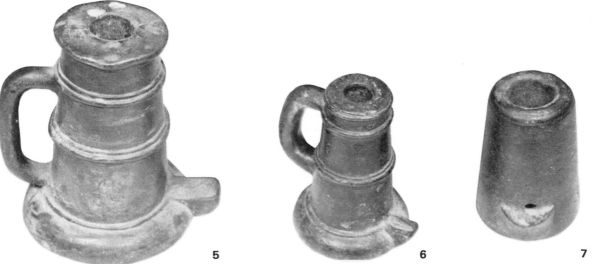

5　　　　　　　　　　　　　　　6　　　　　　　　　　7

(4) A corselet worn by John Paul Jones during naval combat as a protection against splinters and small arms fire; weight: 11½ lbs. **ARTILLERY** (also see "Ammunition," "Linstocks"): (5–7) These small portable saluting cannon (also used for powder testing) were popular in Europe and other parts of the world during the 17th and 18th centuries. Note the touch holes at the base (2 at left are brass), and the crude iron version (7) which is believed to be American; heights (l to r) 8″, 6″, 5⅜″. Although artillery served in a traditional siege capacity at such sites as Boston, Charleston, and Yorktown, its greatest use in the Revolution was as a tactical field weapon employed to protect an army during deployment and to prepare for its advance by firing into enemy formations. Barrels were made from both iron and brass (bronze). (cont.)

Sources: 4—U.S. Naval Academy Museum; 5, 6, 7—George C. Neumann.

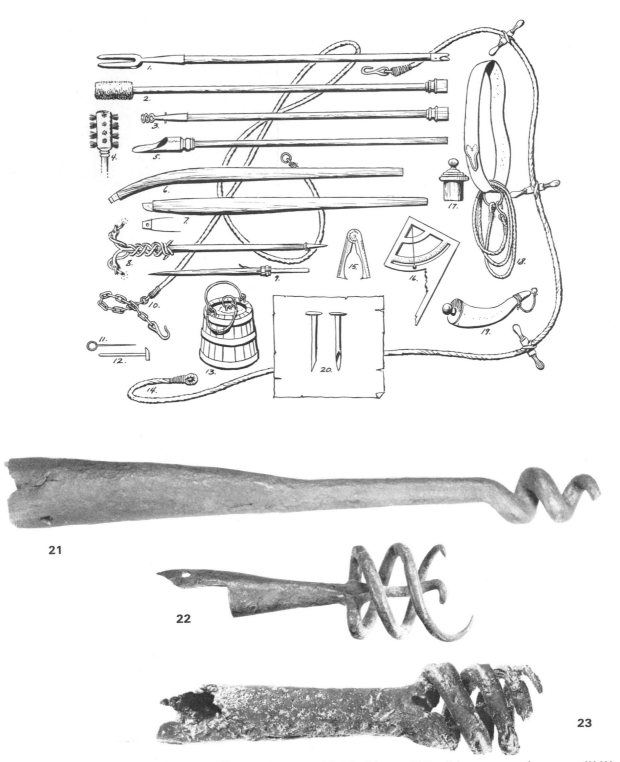

21

22

23

ARTILLERY (cont.) (1–20) English type artillery implements: (1) A fork lever. (2) English sponge and rammer. (3) Worm and rammer. (4) Sponge. (5) Powder Ladle. (6, 7) Handspikes. (8) Linstock, a pole arm holding a smoldering slow match rope. (9) Portfire (new—for rapid fire), a wooden holder ("stock") with a fast burning flare-like "quick match." (10) Drag rope and prolonge. (11) Priming wire. (12) Small hammer. (13) Water bucket (French type). (14) Drag rope. (15) Gunner's callipers. (16) Gunner's quadrant. (17) Tompion to close muzzle. (18) Cross belt or Bricole— shows drag rope (also see "Belts" #51, p. 80). (19) Priming powder horn. (20) Primer tubes of tin (often common reeds) filled with a quick-match mixture for rapid fire. (21) A single arm worm. (22) Double arm worm with a center searcher. (23) Double arm worm; from the American gondola, *Philadelphia* (1776). There were *three basic types of artillery in the Revolution:* First, "guns" or regular cannon to shoot either solid shot as single balls, or multiple type anti-personnel ammunition, e.g. cannister and grape. They were designated by the weight of their solid shot, and the wide array employed included 1, 2, 3, 4, 6, 9, 12, 18, 24, and 32-pounders. Their range often exceeded 2,000 yards, but most field use was restricted to under 500 yards or below 250 yards for cannister. The most popular against infantry were 3, 4, and 6-pounders.

Sources: 21—George C. Neumann; 22—Fort Ticonderoga Museum; 23—Smithsonian Institution, Dr. Philip K. Lundeberg Collection.

23a

24

28a

25

26

27

28

Second, mortars, which fired in a low velocity high trajectory with exploding shells for siege conditions; they were known by the diameter of their shells, which included: 4½", 5½", 8", 10", 13", and 16" sizes. Third, howitzers; these were short-barreled cannon having a trajectory between that of a gun and mortar—which could do double duty with shells into fortifications, or cannister and grape against troops in the open. Since they fired shells like mortars, howitzers were designated by the ammunition's diameter, e.g. 4½", 5½", and 8". Both British and American artillerymen generally wore blue coats with red facings. (23a) A typical field gun on a travel carriage showing the usual double trail and dished wheels. Note its wedge-shaped "quoin" under the breech for adjusting elevation (also see #33, p. 19). A light field carriage called a "galloper" was also used with 1½, 2, and 3-pounders; this employed a pair of shafts for a single horse instead of the normal trail. (24) Iron priming wires for clearing the touch hole and piercing the powder bag; 13¼" to 16⅜" long. (25) French priming wires in a leather case with strap; 17" long. (26) A central European gunner's level. (27) A sponge showing the remains of its original lamb's skin covering. (28) Wooden rammer end. (28a) Powder horn engraving of a field gun attached to a limber with two horses in tandem. (cont.)

Sources: 23a—Brigade of the American Revolution, photo by Michael Cleary; 24, 25—Fort Ticonderoga Museum; 26—Edward Charol; 27, 28—Frank J. Kravic; 28a—Harold L. Peterson.

17

29

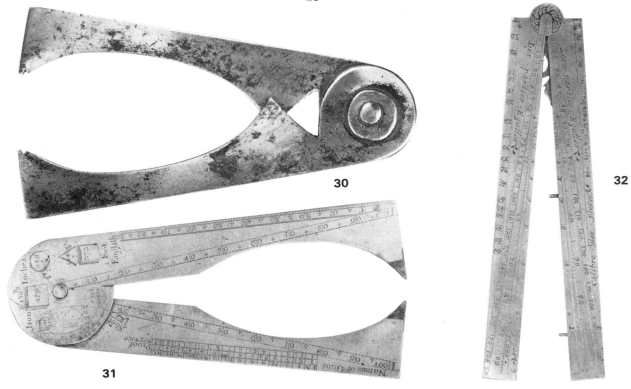

30

31

32

ARTILLERY (cont.) (29) A silver British gunner's set marked, "Tho Wright Maker to His Majesty Geo II^D"; (l to r) callipers, gauge and angle finder, carrying case, parallel rule, engraved calculator. (30) American iron gunner's callipers. (31) English gunner's callipers of brass. (32) French artillerist's brass gauge and angle finder.

Sources: 29—William H. Guthman; 30, 32—George C. Neumann; 31—Edward Charol.

33

34

(33) A 6-pounder field gun. The original British bronze barrel, marked "W. Bowen—Fecit 1756," was captured by the Americans at Saratoga in 1777; it has a 4' 6" length, 3.66" bore, and weighs 555 lbs. The reconstructed carriage includes the two canvas-covered ammunition side boxes used in battle (holding 21 rounds) and an elevating screw under the breech. Field cannon were usually transported by hired civilian drivers using horses or oxen. On the battlefield they were maneuvered by the cannoneers employing drag ropes. The full crew for an American or British 6-pounder numbered 14 or 15 men. (34) Heavy French siege guns as employed at Yorktown. (cont.)

Sources: 33—E. Norman Flayderman; 34—Yorktown National Historical Park.

35

36

ARTILLERY (cont.) (35) A British 8″ bronze howitzer barrel made by William Bowen in his foundry at Woolwich in 1758. It is mounted on a reproduction carriage. Cannon beds and carriages were normally made of oak, and occasionally chestnut or walnut; beech or elm were favored for the wheels. Most iron barrels and fittings received coats of black paint; the English carriages were painted a standard "lead gray." American artillery originally followed the British, but did have some in red and generally adopted the French practice of blue by the war's end. (36) An American receipt at Cambridge for 10″ carcasses (an incendiary projectile) case shot, and quick match; it is dated in April 1776.

Sources: 35—West Point Museum; 36—Frank J. Kravic.

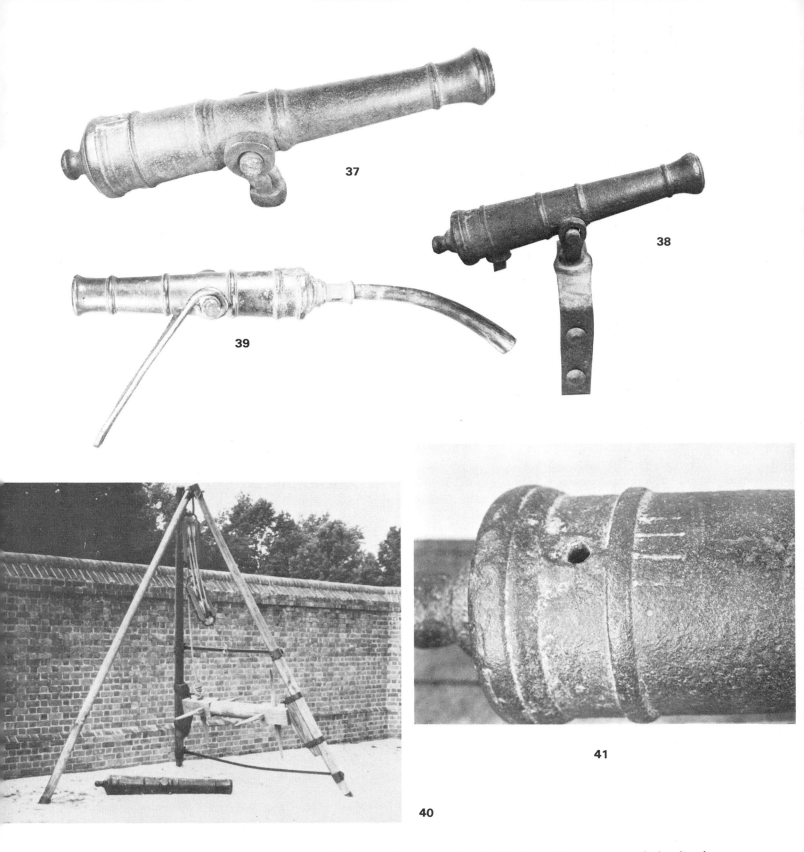

37

38

39

40

41

(37–39) Small swivel guns were popular aboard ships, small boats, and in fortifications. They were mostly fired with multiple loads against personnel; (37) 31½" long with a 1⅞" bore. (38) A length of 19", and a 1⅛" bore. (39) Has a wooden "monkeytail" tiller; 14½" less handle. The bore is 1⅛". (41) A close-up of the breech on #38 (used by Americans at Lake Champlain) showing the touch hole, an area where earlier British markings were erased, and four chisel marks apparently to designate gun #4. (40) A tripod "gin" used to mount cannon barrels. (cont.)

Sources: 37—Frank J. Kravic; 38, 41—George C. Neumann; 39—Edward Charol; 40—Colonial Williamsburg.

42

43

ARTILLERY (cont.) (42) A 9-pounder waist gun with an original naval or garrison type carriage—on the raised American gondola, *Philadelphia,* sunk at Valcour Island in 1776. (43) A battery of reproduced field guns illustrating the variety of sizes the Americans were forced to use.

Sources: 42—Smithsonian Institution, Dr. Philip K. Lundeberg Collection; 43—Brigade of the American Revolution, photo by Michael Cleary.

(44) A 10″ bronze mortar on its fixed bed. (45, 46) A 4½″ English iron mortar; 13½″ long, it includes a shaped touch hole and the typical raised Royal Cypher ("GR 2" for King George II) under a crown. (47) A small 2⅛″ bore mortar used to throw grenades or minor size shells; 7¼″ overall.

Sources: 44—Yorktown National Historical Park; 45, 46—Frank J. Kravic; 47—Edward Charol.

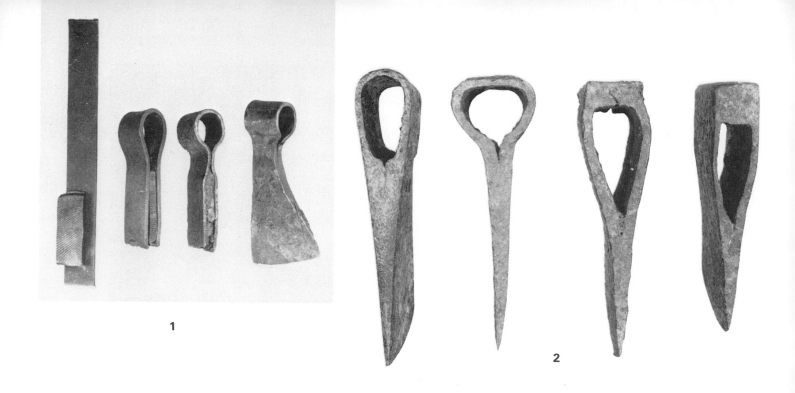

1

2

3

AXES (also see "Halberd Tomahawks"): Many heads are found in the discard heaps of Revolutionary War camps, and careful examination of dated sites shows a gradual though not complete change in axe styles during the war. In the 17th and early 18th centuries most axes were simply made from an iron bar bent around a removable form to shape the handle's eye (1). The two ends of the heated bar were then hammered together where they met to create the blade. As the century progressed, ears were added pointing back along the handle to better weight the axe and strengthen the eye; but the preponderance of weight still remained below the haft causing a sideways shift or wobble. To cure this the colonists shortened the blade and added to the poll above the handle—leading to the square poll pattern which still predominates today. The practice of adding a steel cutting edge to the soft iron head (see #1) was apparently not widespread until late in the 1700s, as few excavated specimens include one; however, all 18th century patterns have been found in the camps. The smaller axe sizes (also called "hatchets," "belt axes," and "tomahawks"); generally followed the patterns of the larger felling axes.

Sources: 1—by Heinrich Schreiber; 2, 3—Frank J. Kravic.

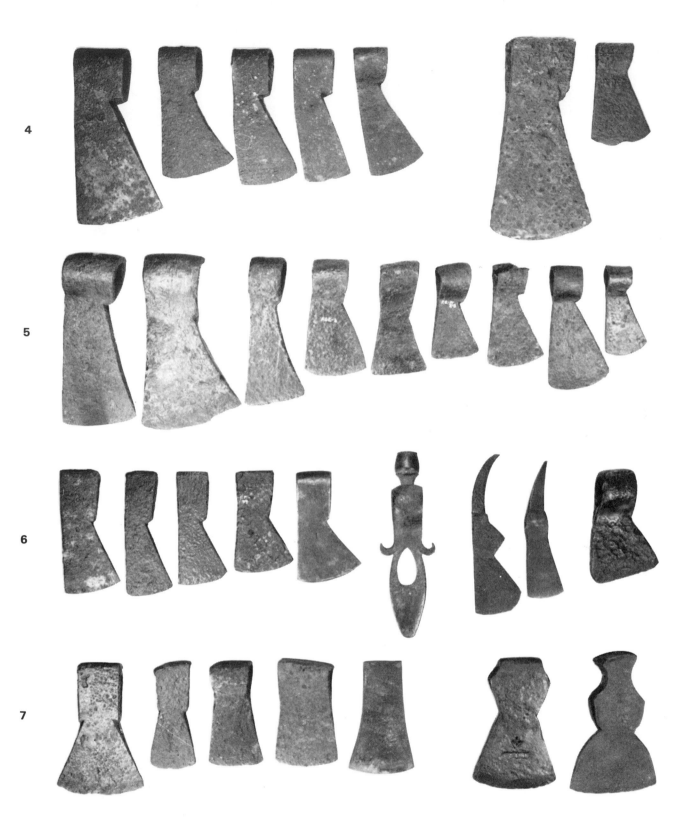

(2) Typical patterns: the two at left are round poll designs illustrating an oval (far left) and round eye; those to the right show the American 18th century evolution toward the final raised square poll and shortened blade form at the far right (all of these from Hudson and Champlain Valley sites). (3) Common straight handles; The third one down is a spiked head form, the fourth a small 9½″ long hatchet for trimming light game; at the bottom is a British naval boarding axe, circa 1750–1850. All heads on this page have been recovered from military excavations. (4) This row depicts the round poll pattern; the five at left include oval eyes, the two to the right incorporate inverted tear-shaped eyes. (5) All round eyes; note the simple but rare incised decoration on the third from the right. (6) Inverted tear eyes, the three at the far left have military rack number markings; notice too the pipe spontoon tomahawk; c. 1740–1780. (7) All have oval eyes in this row; the three at the left (and the second from the right) are marked with the British broad arrow. (cont.)

Source: Frank J. Kravic.

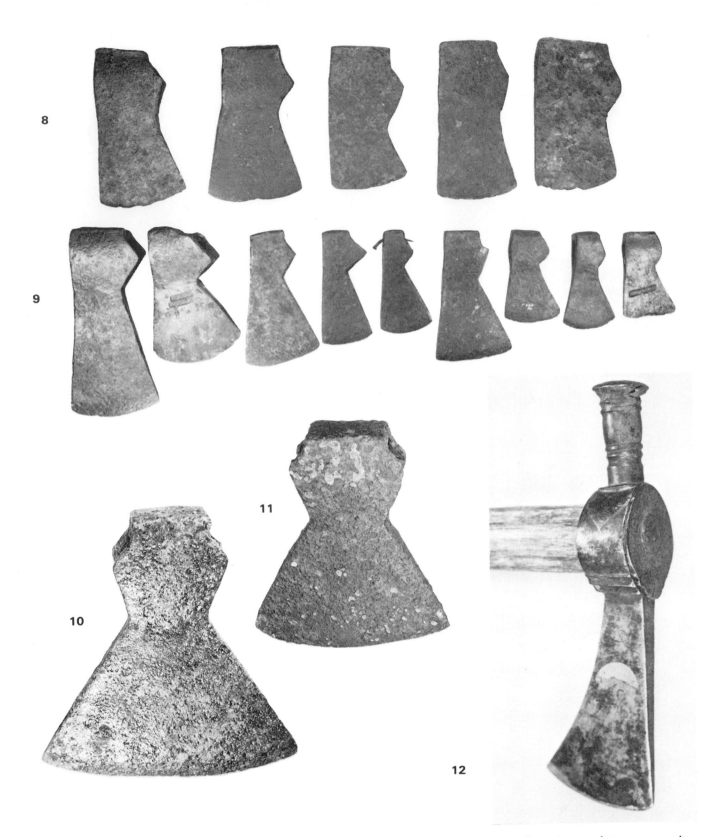

AXES (cont.) (Row 8) Larger camp axes, 6″ to 9″ high; all have the heavy squared poll, an inverted tear eye, and simple ears. (9) Square polls with eared patterns and tear-shaped eyes; the second from the left is stamped "TIS-DALE" (the maker), while the second from the right was marked with a cold chisel, "C N 20 48"; the head at the far right came from a Pennsylvania regimental campsite of 1775–1776. (10, 11) Large felling axes; 10″ and 8″ tall. (12) An iron hammer poll tomahawk, 5¾″ in height.

Sources: 8, 9, 10, 11—Frank J. Kravic; 12—William H. Guthman.

26

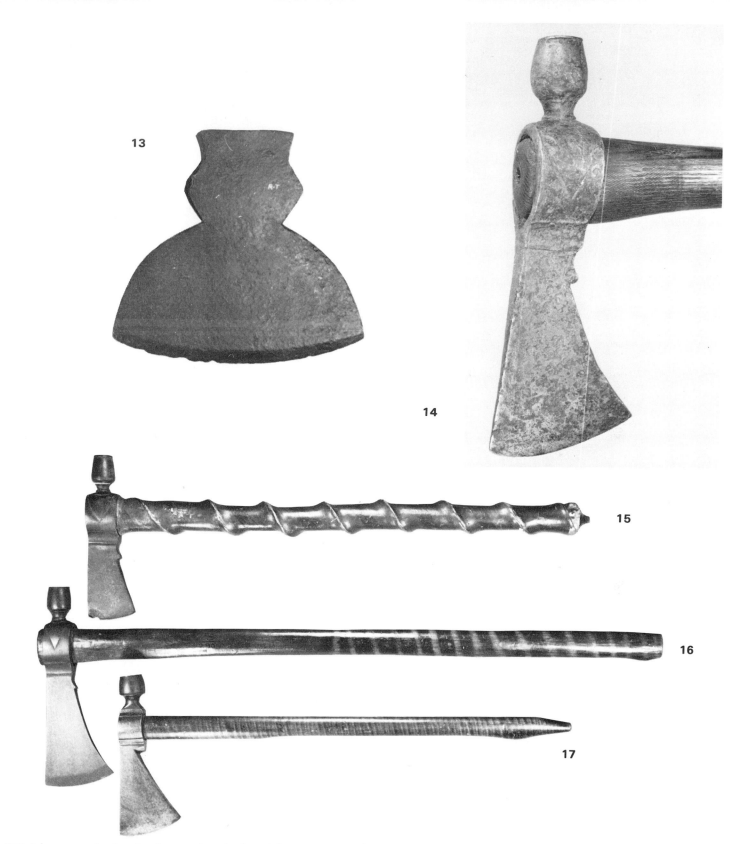

(13) A large axe for hewing beams, i.e. the bevel for its cutting edge occurs only on one side; 9″ tall. (14) An English pipe-headed trade tomahawk. A great favorite on the frontier, it combined a small axe blade with a pipe bowl; the handle was drilled or burned through the center to function as the stem. Also note the front clean-out hole; this head measures 8⅛″ high, circa 1740–1800. (15) A British pipe tomahawk trade head mounted by northeastern American Indians with a spiraled maple handle ("haft"); c. 1750–1775, 22¾″ long. (16) An English pipe tomahawk, c. 1760–1775 with a long straight 27½″ chestnut handle. (17) A pipe pattern showing evolution toward the later lower wider bowl and straight flared blade profile; the haft is curly maple; c. 1775–1800; 19¾″ in length.

Sources: 13—Frank J. Kravic; 14—George C. Neumann; 15, 16, 17—David Currie.

27

BADGES (see "Decorations," "Plates, Uniform.") **BALE SEALS** (see "Seals, Bale.") **BARRELS, URNS:** The cooper's trade was put to good use during war time. Food and goods had to be shipped to and by the armies and, in the process, taken aboard ships or bounced on wagons over poor roads. Some were made with much skill while others were quickly and carelessly assembled. Hoops were formed from split saplings or metal. The latter ones were also reused to create useful items by the troops, and such specimens as pot hooks, broilers, etc. are recovered from their camps (see "Cookingware"). (1) A shipping or storage barrel with sapling bands, circa 1750–1880. (2) Typical powder keg construction which continued well into the 19th century, c. 1770–1860. (3) A salt barrel, c. 1750–1820. (4) A powder barrel with copper hoops (i.e. no sparks) reconstructed from excavated remains at Fort Ligonier, c. 1758–1766; 17½" high. (5) The large style pottery urn commonly used to hold both dry and liquid stores; 32" tall.

Sources: 1, 3—Frank J. Kravic; 2—George C. Neumann; 4—Fort Ligonier; 5—Mercer Museum, Bucks County Historical Society.

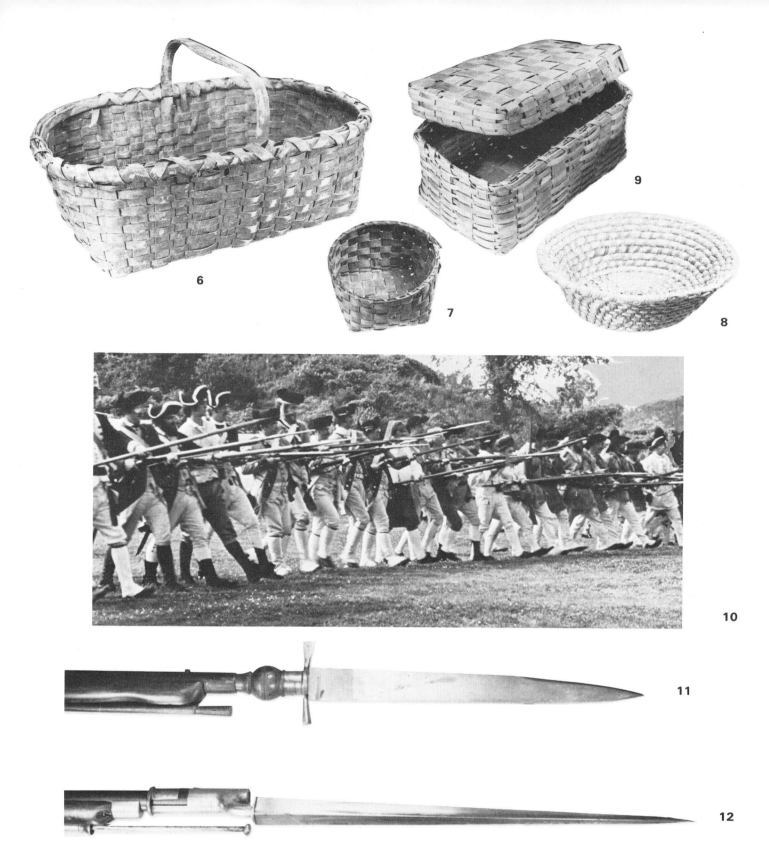

6

9

7

8

10

11

12

BASKETS (6–9): While rarely surviving in the soil, enough basket fragments have been found to indicate their common use in the camps. Abundant and practical in civilian life, they were readily available—woven or bound from numerous native materials such as split saplings, rushes, and reeds; #8 is a straw basket. While difficult to date because they changed little over the years, those illustrated here are common types of the 1750–1850 period. **BATTLE** (see "Tactics, Battle.") **BAYONETS** (also see "Belts, Frogs, Scabbards," "Tactics, Battle"): Despite history's preoccupation with firearms in this period, the ultimate infantry weapon on the battlefield was actually the bayonet. It changed the inaccurate slow firing musket into a spear at close quarters and was traditionally employed in disciplined attacks by massed formations (see #10). The construction was a long steel blade offset by a thin neck from a cylindrical socket which slid over the muzzle. It was attached by a fixed barrel stud sliding through a segmented slot in the socket. (11) An early (c. 1680–1700) plug bayonet with its tapering handle pushed into the muzzle. (12) A typical Revolutionary War period socket bayonet having the neck always projecting out to the right of the barrel in fixed position. (cont.)

Sources: 6, 7, 8, 9—Frank J. Kravic; 10—Brigade of the American Revolution; photo by Richard Gerding; 11, 12—George C. Neumann.

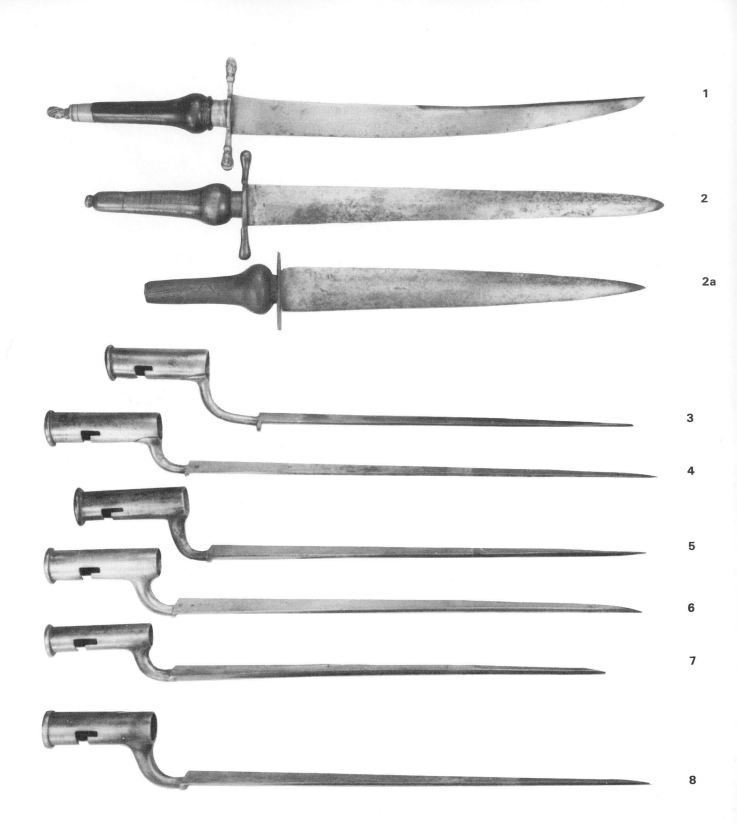

1

2

2a

3

4

5

6

7

8

BAYONETS (cont.) (1) An English "plug" bayonet, circa 1700; the tapered handle was pushed into the gun muzzle; its brass fittings include molded head finials; length 17¾". (2) European plug pattern having brass furniture; 17" long. (2a) American plug, circa 1700–1740 with iron mountings; 14½" overall. **BRITISH BAYONETS** (3–8): (3) Early socket style, c. 1710–1720; it incorporates a long neck with a raised lip at the socket junction; 19" long. (4) The early Brown Bess musket pattern, c. 1720–1740; it now incorporates a shorter neck and longer blade (vs. #3); 22" total length. (5) A midcentury variation with the neck's raised lip gone but its attachment is still at the socket's front edge; 20½" long. (6) The common Brown Bess style, c. 1730–1820; note the heavy neck set back from the end of the socket; 21¼" overall (the typical socket is 4", blade 16¾"–17"). (7) The carbine variation, i.e. a smaller diameter socket for the .65 cal. bore carbine vs the .75 cal. normal British musket; circa 1757–1790; length, 19⅞". (8) A fusil bayonet requiring a smaller socket size for those light officer muskets; 17¼" long.

Source: George C. Neumann.

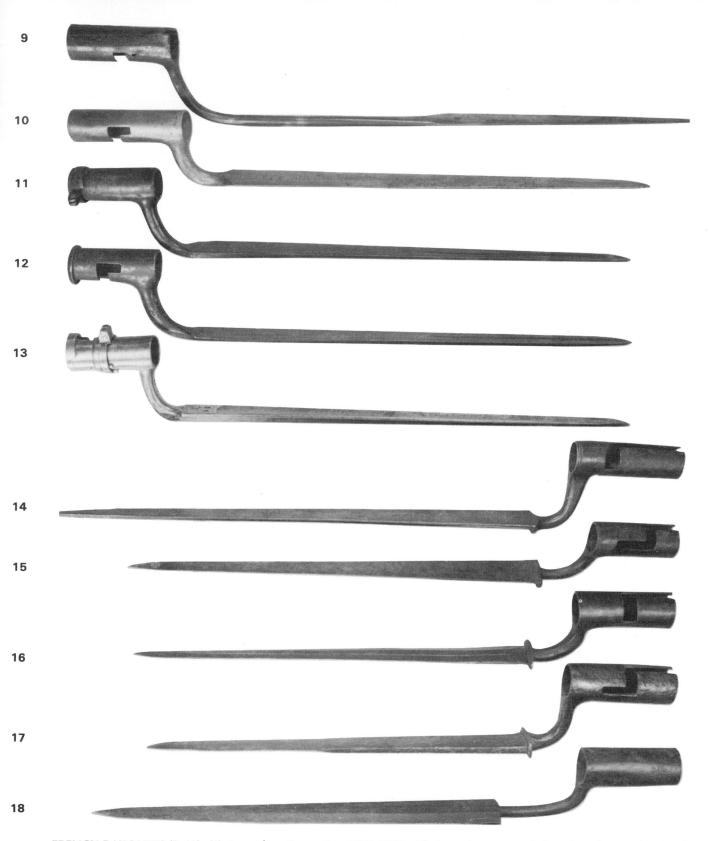

9

10

11

12

13

14

15

16

17

18

FRENCH BAYONETS (9–13): (9) An early pattern, circa 1690–1710 with the unique extended neck and spear tip; 19¼″ in length. (10) Circa 1754; a short neck plus slope-shouldered triangular blade; it measures 18″. (11) This c. 1763–1773 design introduced a rear rotating ring to secure the barrel stud after it entered a short socket slot; 17⅜″ long. (12) In 1774 a rear raised ring was added to the socket for snapping under a short spring catch projecting from under the muzzle; length, 17½″. (13) Model 1777; a new design which introduced a rotating locking ring in the center of its socket; 17½″ overall. **GERMAN-DUTCH BAYONETS** (14–18): (14) The Prussian type that includes a characteristic squared neck; 19″ long. (15) Pattern having a blade similar to the British, i.e. triangular with concave surfaces on the two bottom sides; length, 16½″. (16) A horizontal blade (3 facets each on the upper and lower faces) extends from an oval crossguard at the end of its neck; 16⅜″ overall. (17) Like #16 with a rectangular blade; 16″ long. (18) A faceted blade similar to #16 but adding a long neck without the crossguard; 17⅝″ in length. (cont.)

Source: George C. Neumann.

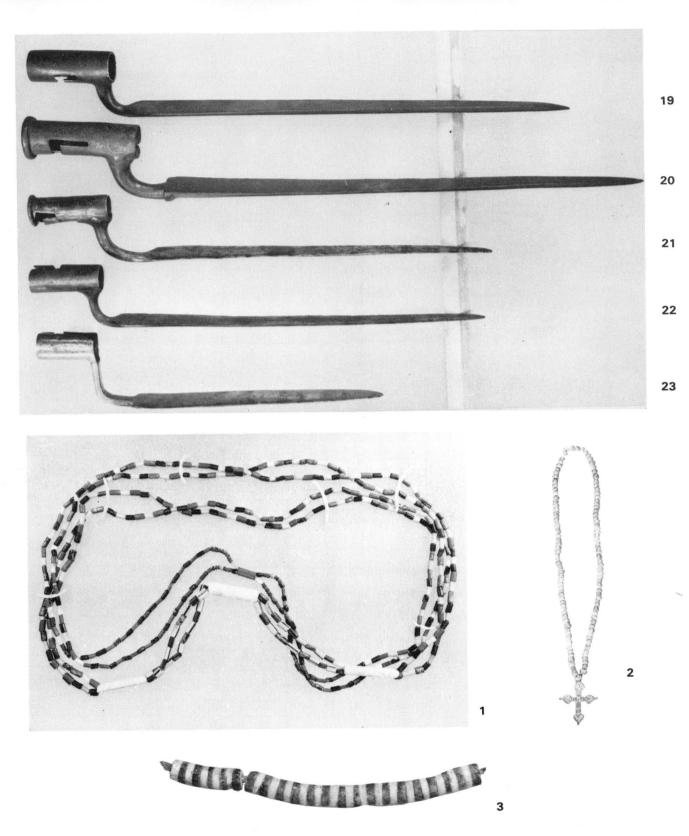

BAYONETS (cont.) (19) Spanish bayonet, c. 1752–1800; 18½″ long. (20–23) **AMERICAN BAYONETS:** (20) A crude copy of the Brown Bess pattern; 20¾″ overall. (21) 15⅝″ length. (22) 15⅜″ long. (23) A weak abbreviated example measuring 11⅝″. **BEADS, INDIAN TRADE** (also see "Trade Ornaments, Indian"): Since the earliest contacts between Europeans and Indians, one of the most desired trade items was beads. The use of native shells and stones palled against the gaudy colors achieved in glass and ceramics, which, by the 1700s, were being shipped world-wide by Venetian and Dutch bead makers. Illustrated here are typical 17th and 18th century beads traded on the American continent. Some are solid colors while others were formed by placing colored glass tubes and shapes around a central core of glass before fusing the parts. (1) A necklace of tubular beads, bone, and sections of broken pipe stems recovered from an Indian gravesite. (2) Indian bead necklace with a cross. (3) Indian wampum made from shaped and pierced shell pieces strung on natural fiber; from Conn., 17th century.

Sources: 19–23 George C. Neumann; 1—George Juno; 2—Edward Charol; 3—Frank J. Kravic.

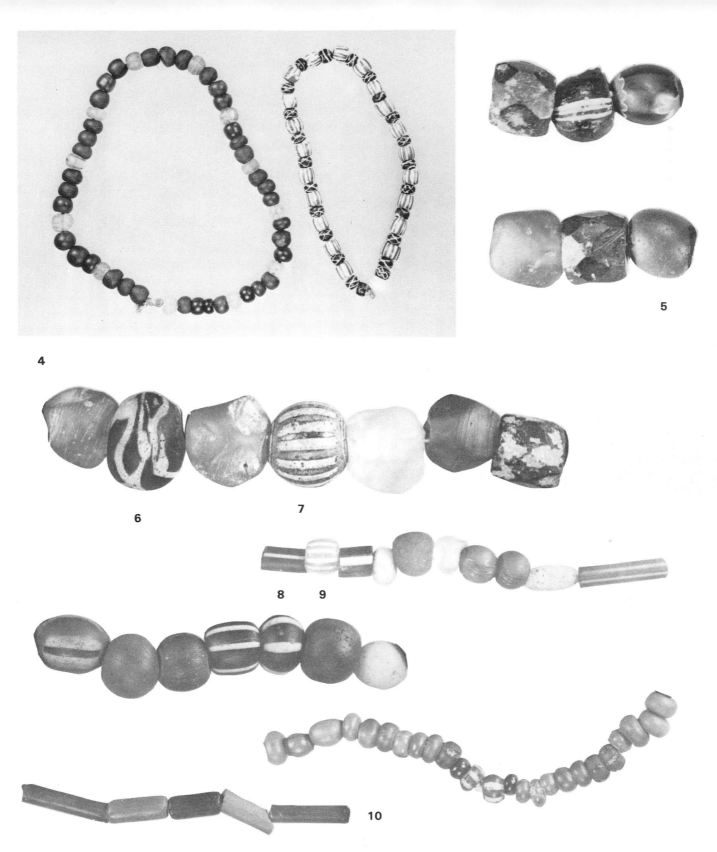

(4) (at right) Bead Necklace, c. 1680–1710; alternating the black and white polychrome "web" pattern with blue, red, and white striped oval beads; (left) c. 1750, translucent deep blue and colorless glass beads. (5–10) Various popular trade patterns of the 17th and 18th centuries that include: (5) Translucent blue. (6) Polychrome, having many layers built around a central core. (7) A candystripe oval design. (8) Striped tubular. (9) Gooseberry shape with stripes. (10) Tubular monochrome beads.

Sources: 4—The Authors; 5–10 George Juno Collection, excavated by Derrick Gagnon.

BEDS: While common soldiers could expect little to sleep on other than that provided by nature, the officers lived far more comfortable lives. Since they were normally provided with wagons for personal gear, folding beds were customarily included. (1) Covered by heavy linen ("tow") and fitted with removable headboards, this bed—which folds only once—would probably have added a tow mattress filled with straw. The headboard dowels pivot on a single nail so as not to break during travel. (2) Folding camp bed of walnut used by General George Washington; note the attachments for a canopy. (3) Number 2 above in a folded position for transport. (4) A field cot employed by General Peter Gansevoort, 3rd Rgt., Continental Line. **BELLS** (see next page): Most permanent camps would be populated with domestic animals as long as food was in adequate supply. Many military sites did not have large refuse deposits, but employed small scattered locations. Even prevailing winds do not seem to have received much consideration; the Light Infantry Redoubt garbage dump at Crown Point, N.Y. (1759–1776) for example, was just 25 feet to the west of the entry gate. Free running chickens, pigs, and other animals would readily forage the day's refuse.

Sources: 1—Frank J. Kravic; 2, 3—Mt. Vernon Ladies' Assn.; 4—Smithsonian Institution.

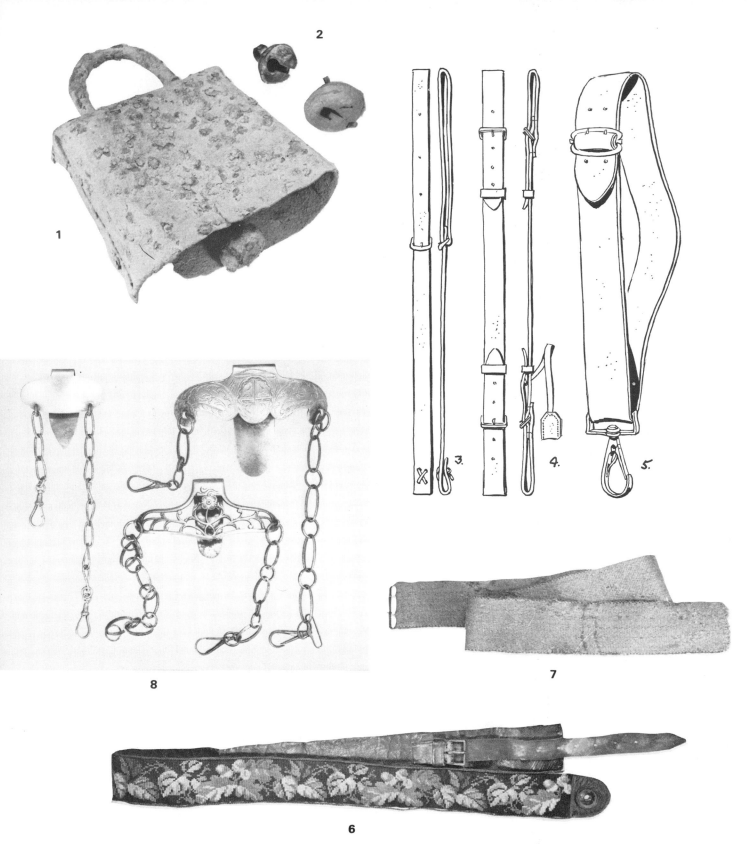

BELLS (cont.) Garden areas were also set aside to supply fresh vegetables for the soldiers and camp followers. (1) This cowbell was discovered in the refuse pile of a French and Indian War campsite of New York's Champlain Valley. Made of hammered iron, the rope-holding loop continues through the top of the bell and hooks onto the iron clapper. (2) Small trade bells (see "Trade Ornaments, Indian"). **BELTS, FROGS, SCABBARDS** (also see "Buckles," "Canteens," "Cartridge Boxes," "Horns," "Hunting Bags," "Knapsacks"): (3) A musket sling as used by British and Americans; usually of buff leather plus brass furniture. (4) German pattern sling of red bridle leather with brass buckles; note the frizzen cover to prevent accidental discharge when loading. (5) A typical cavalry shoulder cross-belt (normally buff leather) with a snap hook to attach on the ring of a carbine's side bar (see "Carbines"); the trooper fired his weapon and dropped it to dangle while he drew his sword or pistols for close quarter fighting. (6) A civilian jaeger rifle strap from Pennsylvania; it includes crewel designs and leather backing. (7) American red wool waist belt (2½'' wide). (8) Metal carriers used by officers and civilians to secure their swords by simply hooking them over the waist belt. (cont.)

Sources: 1, 2—Frank J. Kravic; 6—Edward Charol; 7—J. Craig Nannos; 8—George C. Neumann.

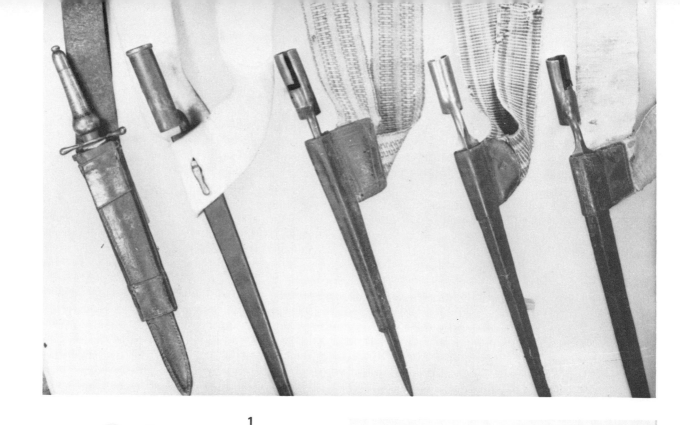

1

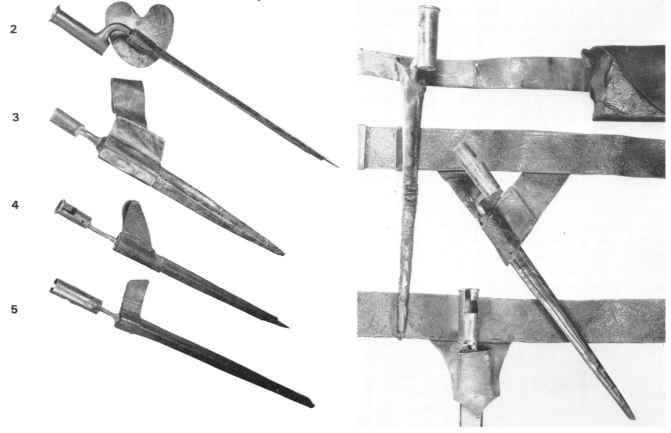

2

3

4

5

6

BELTS, FROGS, SCABBARDS (cont.) The soldier's suspensory equipment was attached to either a waist or shoulder belt. The waist belt predominated during the French and Indian War, but in the Revolution the shoulder version became the more popular. Most regular troops employed buff leather—although the hard pressed Americans were also forced to use harness leather, linen, and even rope. (1) Left to right: First, a plug bayonet, circa 1700, in its two-part sheath on a leather strap; second, an American cross-belt (over the right shoulder) of buff leather with a dark scabbard attached by a brass stud (British style); the remaining three are typical American linen cross-belts with leather frogs sewn to the bayonet scabbard. (2) A heart-shaped frog with waist belt loops behind; the scabbard is sewn to the frog. (3) A leather waist belt loop has replaced the original linen shoulder strap. (4, 5) Simple belt loop patterns. (6) American variations of frogs and scabbards sewn directly to the waist belt; all circa 1750–1810.

Source: George C. Neumann.

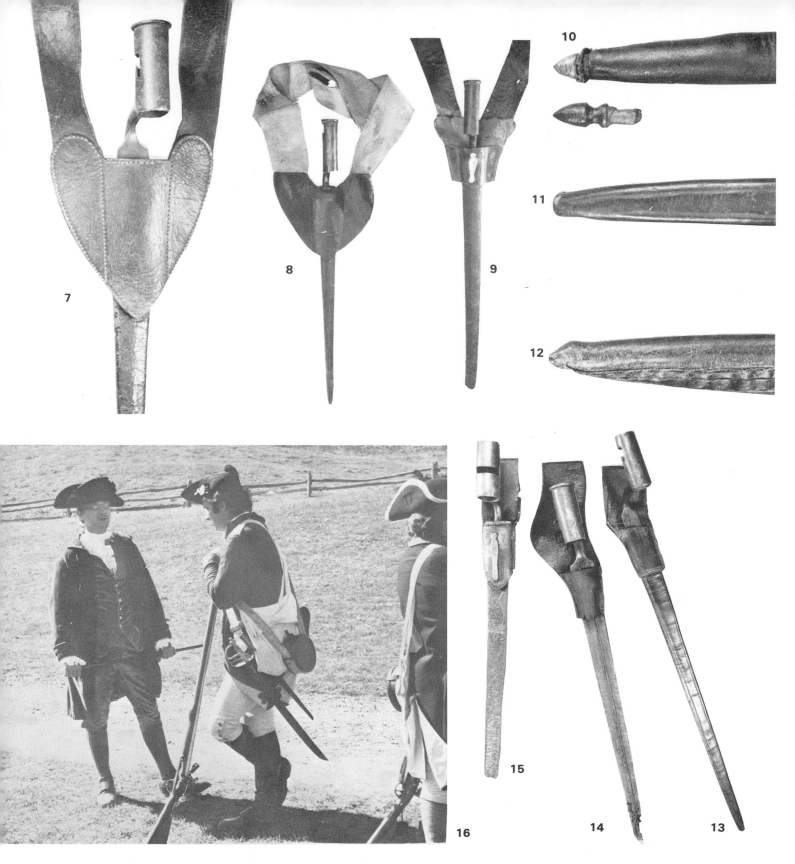

(7, 8, 9) Wide American bayonet frog patterns using linen or leather shoulder cross-belts. (10) The tip of a British bayonet scabbard, the brass stud (excavated specimen adjacent to it) projects below the leather which is tied with twine around its narrow neck. (11, 12) Typical scabbards of the colonists omit the metal tips. (13, 14, 15) Simple sliding waist belt loop-frog styles maintain the bayonet in a vertical position; circa 1760–1810. (16) Continental infantryman wears a shoulder belt having a double frog which supports a sword ("hanger") and bayonet. (cont.)

Sources: 16—Brigade of the American Revolution, photo by Michael Cleary; remainder, George C. Neumann.

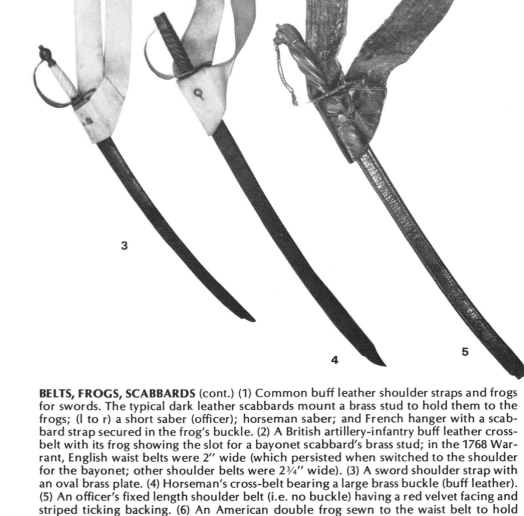

BELTS, FROGS, SCABBARDS (cont.) (1) Common buff leather shoulder straps and frogs for swords. The typical dark leather scabbards mount a brass stud to hold them to the frogs; (l to r) a short saber (officer); horseman saber; and French hanger with a scabbard strap secured in the frog's buckle. (2) A British artillery-infantry buff leather cross-belt with its frog showing the slot for a bayonet scabbard's brass stud; in the 1768 Warrant, English waist belts were 2″ wide (which persisted when switched to the shoulder for the bayonet; other shoulder belts were 2¾″ wide). (3) A sword shoulder strap with an oval brass plate. (4) Horseman's cross-belt bearing a large brass buckle (buff leather). (5) An officer's fixed length shoulder belt (i.e. no buckle) having a red velvet facing and striped ticking backing. (6) An American double frog sewn to the waist belt to hold both a sword and bayonet; circa 1775–1800.

Sources: 1, 3, 4, 6—George C. Neumann; 2—The Charleston Museum (S.C.); 5—William H. Guthman.

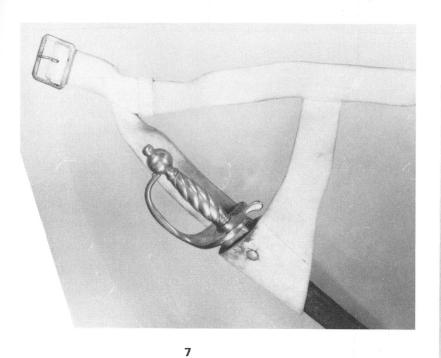

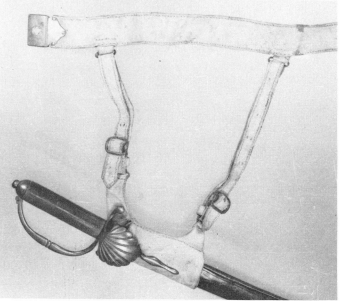

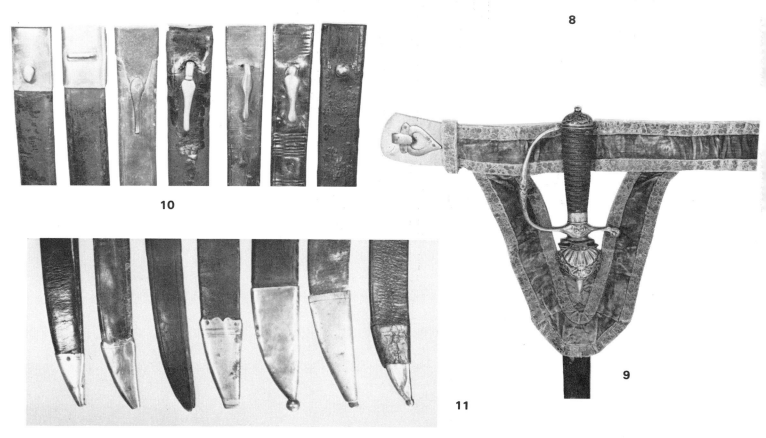

(7) Infantry buff leather waist belt plus a suspended frog (for either sword or bayonet)—popular in the French and Indian War and early Revolutionary period. (8) A buckskin waist belt with the supporting straps having buckles for height adjustment. (9) A buff leather officer's belt-frog covered by green velvet and embroidered tape; circa 1730–1750. (10) Typical scabbard studs for attachment to a frog (l to r): American, French, 2 German, 3 British. (11) Sword scabbard tip patterns (l to r): 2 British, American, British, French, 2 German; note the Germanic practice of leather covering the upper part of the brass tip.

Source: George C. Neumann.

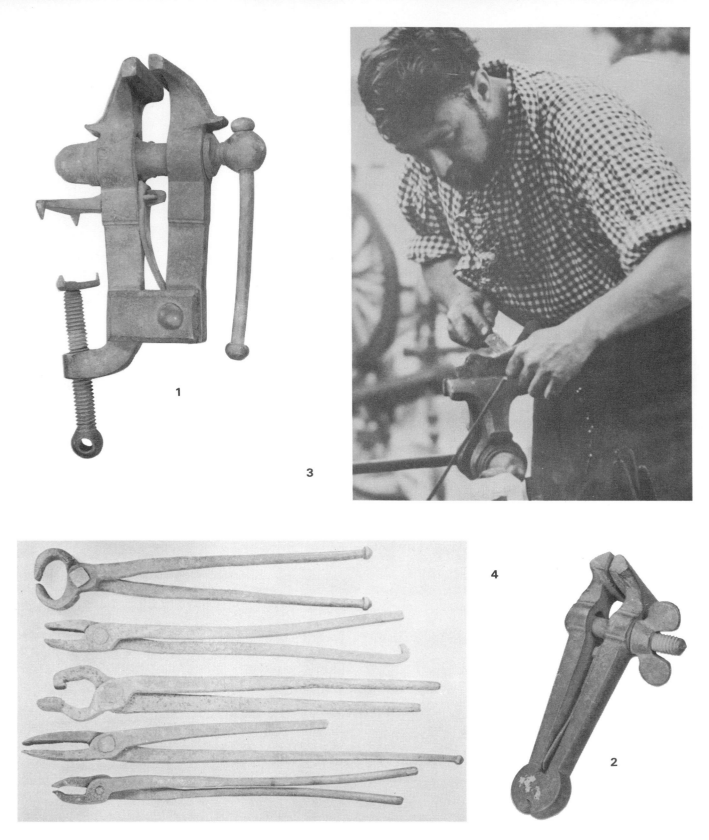

BELT AXE (see "Axes.") **BEVERAGES** (see "Drinking Ware.") **BILL HOOK** (see "Fascine Knives.") **BLACKSMITHING** (also see "Horse Equipage," "Tools, Hand"): The blacksmith was indispensable in an 18th century camp. His ability to "work" iron was in constant demand to repair, as well as to create weapon parts, nails, axes, tools, fittings, utensils, etc.; he required a forge, bellows, anvil, and metalworking tools plus accessories which could be employed on a locally constructed facility or from a wheeled "traveling forge" in the field. (1) A portable bench vise. (2) Hand vise. (3) The blacksmith at work. (4) Common blacksmith tools (often made by the smith himself).

Sources: 1, 2—George C. Neumann; 3—Brigade of the American Revolution; photo by Michael Cleary; 4—Marvin K. Salls.

(5) A "post" type bench vise; 38¼" high. (6) Anvils were used primarily for forging and welding; this is a double horn style with a six-sided chamfer post; 23¾" above the wood. It is believed to have been the property of the Remington family prior to moving to Ilion, N.Y. in the late 18th century. (7) Small stump anvil; 9½" high; from a 1760–1780 camp. (8, 9) Two anvils of the period; the insert is a removable cutting chisel, or "hardie" (also see #10). (11) An ingot of pig iron from the "Hibernia" Furnace north of Morristown, N.J.; about 32" long. **BLANKETS AND BEDDING** (also see "Beds," "Fabrics"): The variety of patterns and colors found in 18th century blankets were only limited by the imagination of the family weavers. Localities were often called upon to supply blankets for their own men in the army, and the town, in turn, purchased them from the homes of its people. (12) A request to the Selectmen of the town of Sommers, Conn. for five blankets to be issued to new men just inducted into the "Continental Service." (cont.)

Sources: 5, 6, 8, 9, 10—Marvin K. Salls: 7, 12—Frank J. Kravic; 11—Morristown National Historical Park.

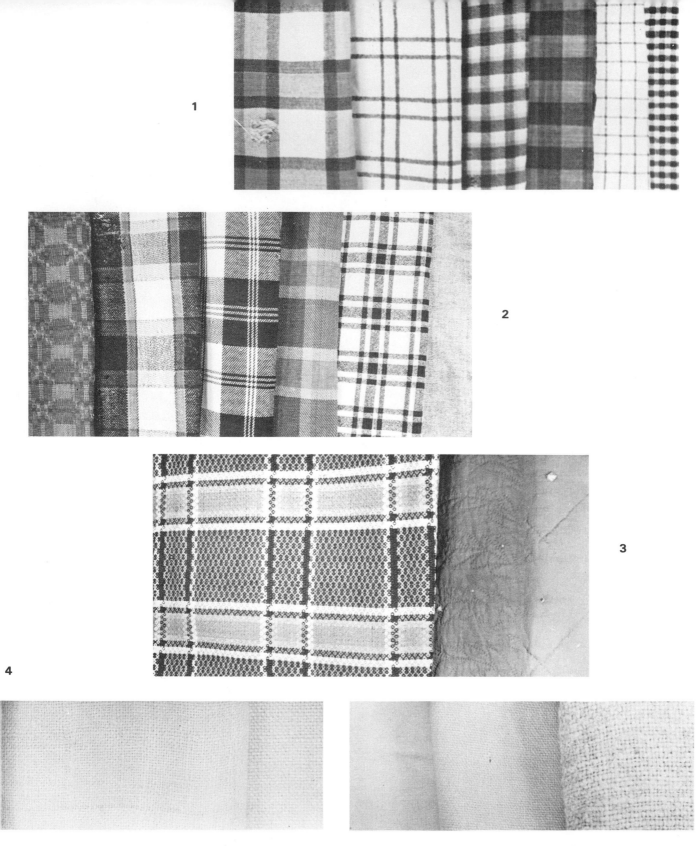

BLANKETS (cont.) Since the usual limit in width for home looms was about 32″ at this time, most blankets were made of two pieces sewn together; their length was entirely optional. The thread was commonly two-ply as is visible in most weaves, and their patterns remained with minimum change until the mid 1800s. Almost all American blankets of the 1700s were made of wool or linen. (1, 2) Wool and, or linen plaid blankets, all homespun of 1 or 2-ply weft and warp in various patterns. The colors include blue, white, red, brown, orange, and green; circa 1750–1830. (3) Two heavy blankets; at the left is the linen "Canadian" style. (4) A close-up of three linen sheets. (5) Two wool sheets (at left) plus a coarse tow mattress cover.

Source: Frank J. Kravic.

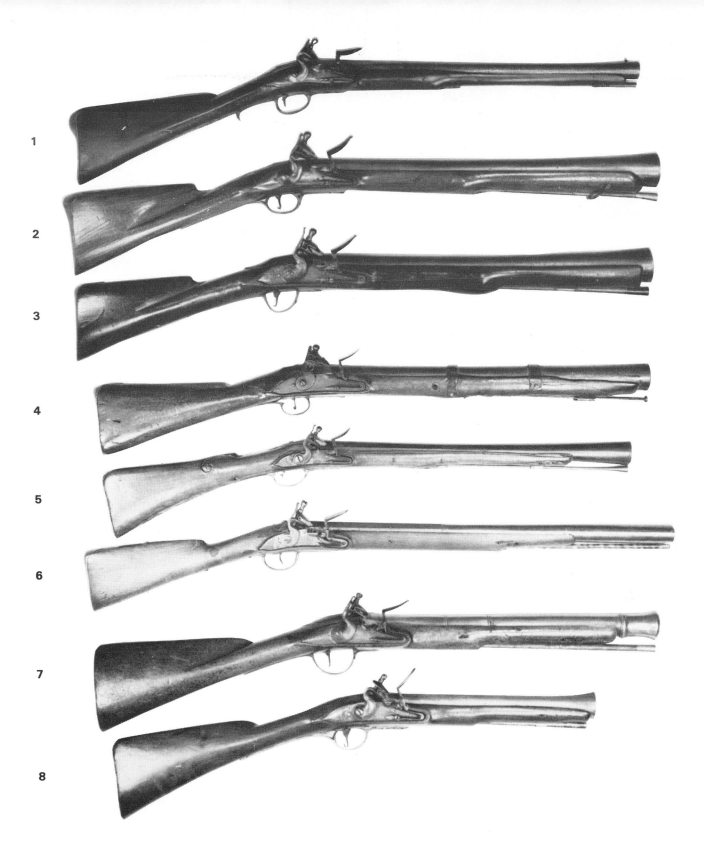

BLUNDERBUSSES: These were short large-bore shoulder firearms popular with civilians for close defense using multiple bullets or small shot. The military favored them primarily aboard ship during crowded deck fighting, or on land in special situations for sentry duty, signaling, or crowd control; some American light dragoons also carried them due to a shortage of carbines. Their flared muzzle aided in loading but did little to affect the shot pattern as subsequent tests have shown. (1) British musketoon; circa 1690–1710; 22″ barrel. (2) An English military blunderbuss with Long Land pattern musket type furniture and a 22⅞″ flared iron barrel; circa 1735–1745. (3) American (probably for naval use), using a salvaged lock and barrel from a pattern like #2; c. 1775–1783. (4) A colonist's crude blunderbuss having an early European lock and nailed iron straps to secure the 23″ round barrel; circa 1750–1780. (5) A French Mediterranean type, c. 1750; it mounts a 22½″ iron barrel. (6) French style semi-military pattern having an oval muzzle on a 26″ barrel; circa 1730–1750. (7) British brass "cannon barrel" style by Collumbell; c. 1740. (8) English, c. 1770–1780; a semi-military example employing a short 12⅛″ bell-muzzled barrel.

Source: George C. Neumann.

7

8

532 Tucker (Josiah, *Dean of Glocester*, Tract V: the Respective Pleas and Arguments of the Mother Country and the COLONIES distinctly set forth. 8° (152 pages), 2s 6d Glos., 1775
533 A Series of Answers to certain Popular Objections against separating from the REBELLIOUS COLONIES. 8°, new half sheep, 5/ Glos., 1776

TRACT V.

THE RESPECTIVE PLEAS AND ARGUMENTS OF THE MOTHER COUNTRY, AND OF THE COLONIES, DISTINCTLY SET FORTH;

And the Impossibility of a COMPROMISE OF DIFFERENCES, OR A MUTUAL CONCESSION OF RIGHTS, PLAINLY DEMONSTRATED. WITH A PREFATORY EPISTLE TO THE PLENIPOTENTIARIES of the late CONGRESS at PHILADELPHIA.

BY JOSIAH TUCKER, D.D. DEAN OF GLOCESTER.

GLOCESTER: PRINTED BY R. RAIKES, AND SOLD BY T. CADELL, IN THE STRAND, AND J. WALTER, CHARING-CROSS, LONDON. M.DCC.LXXV.

[PRICE ONE SHILLING.]

10

In CONGRESS, 29th March, 1779.

CONGRESS judging it of the greatest importance to prescribe some invariable rules for the order and discipline of the troops, especially for the purpose of introducing an uniformity in their formation and manœuvres, and in the service of the camp:

ORDERED, That the following regulations be observed by all the troops of the United States, and that all general and other officers cause the same to be executed with all possible exactness.

By Order,

JOHN JAY, PRESIDENT.

Attest.

CHARLES THOMPSON, Secretary.

9

BOOKS (also see "Periodicals," "Tactics, Battle"): (1) Typical military texts and guides for the formal linear warfare of the 18th century. Virtually every officer had one for reference; they included such English authors as Bland, Cuthbertson, Kane, Barrisse, Simes, and General Wolfe—as well as the Americans: Pickering, Windham, and finally von Steuben. (2, 3) A small pocket almanac with a common multicolored embossed soft cover. (4) German military intelligence summary of all European armies and navies, e.g. the fold-out lists all British regiments; Liepzig, 1780. (5) American-owned Bible printed in London, 1707. (6) An 18th century Psalm Book as would have been carried in the field. (7, 8) Suede leather-covered muster book of Captain Spurr's Company in Col. Nixon's Regt.; the page shown has 29 men acknowledging wages received after Burgoyne's surrender—of which 12 had to sign with an "X." (9) Introductory page from the first printed edition of the American von Steuben military manual; it was published by Styner and Cist in Philadelphia, 1779. (10) Many pamphlets were published in the years prior to the Revolution offering arguments, conciliation plans, and religious concerns to both sides regarding independence; this one from England's Glocester in 1775 offers a plan to the Continental Congress even as the fighting erupts.

Sources: 1, 2, 3, 5–8—George C. Neumann; 4—Edward Charol; 9, 10—Frank J. Kravic.

BOSUN'S PIPE (see "Naval.") BOTTLES (also see "Canteens," "Corkscrews," "Drinking Ware"): Fragments of liquor bottles are universal to Revolutionary War campsites. They were used and reused to hold various liquids from wine to olive oil, and remains of styles that show a wide difference in period are often discovered together—suggesting their continued employment until broken. Dating usually relies upon the shape, treatment of the pontil, and tooling of the lip. Bottlemaking was a minor industry in 18th century America, as England and Holland were the centers of production. The Dutch lagged in some refinements adopted by England, which further confuses accurate dating. Most common to Revolutionary War excavations is the cylinder shape—a form that persisted well into the 19th century. During the 1770s the pontil on the bottle's base was ground relatively smooth, the string rim of applied glass below the lip appeared quite distinct though crude, and the lip itself showed little forming beyond a smoothing of the surface.

The normal evolution progressed successively from the early "squat" form to the "bell," "porter," and "cylinder." Large quantities of square "case" bottle fragments are also found in camp debris. This was a long surviving shape; early ones usually had crude features of the lip and rim, or a rough open pontil.

Source: Frank J. Kravic.

(1–5) Squat or "onion" liquor bottles; chronologically c. 1680–1720. (6–8) Bell bottles, circa 1720–1750. (9, 10) The porter style, from about 1740–1770. (11–15) Cylinder bottles—the most common form found in Revolutionary War period camps; c. 1760–1785. (16–23) French wine and sack bottles dating circa 1730–1780. (24–28) Case bottles from about 1740–1780; they were blown into a mold and could easily be carried in a compartmented case (see page 49). (29) A hand painted liquor bottle. (30, 31) Glass seals as applied to bottles since the 17th century to identify consumers, merchants, or trade names. Note these details: (1–11, 16–27, 29) All have open-pontils and string rims; (12–15, 28) An improved pontil, string rim, and tooled lip. (cont.)

Source: 1–30—Frank J. Kravic.

BOTTLES (cont.) (1–6) Variations in bottle bases: (1) A rough unimproved pontil (i.e. not ground smooth). (2) Like #1, but with a high conical "kick up" base. (3) The four marks were left by a quadrafoil pontil iron. (4) This rough pontil mark has been ground smooth. (5) A sand pontil; note the rough texture in the ground area. (6) Bottles blown into a mold often show marks on their base from the mold's air release slots. (7, 8) A fine liquor chest having leather plus iron fittings on the exterior, and a green felt lining. Scratched on the shoulders of its four bottles are "Rum," "Brandy," "Whiskey," and "Gin"; the label reads, "THOMAS PLAYFAIR," Trunk & Camp Equipage To His Majesty, No 17"; the dimensions are 12" h. x 11" w. x 11¼" d. (9) An English oak liquor chest, c. 1750; it measures 11½" high and wide, 16" long.

Sources: 1–6 Frank J. Kravic; 7, 8—William H. Guthman; 9—Webb, Deane, Stevens Museum, Wethersfield, Ct., N.S.C.D.A.

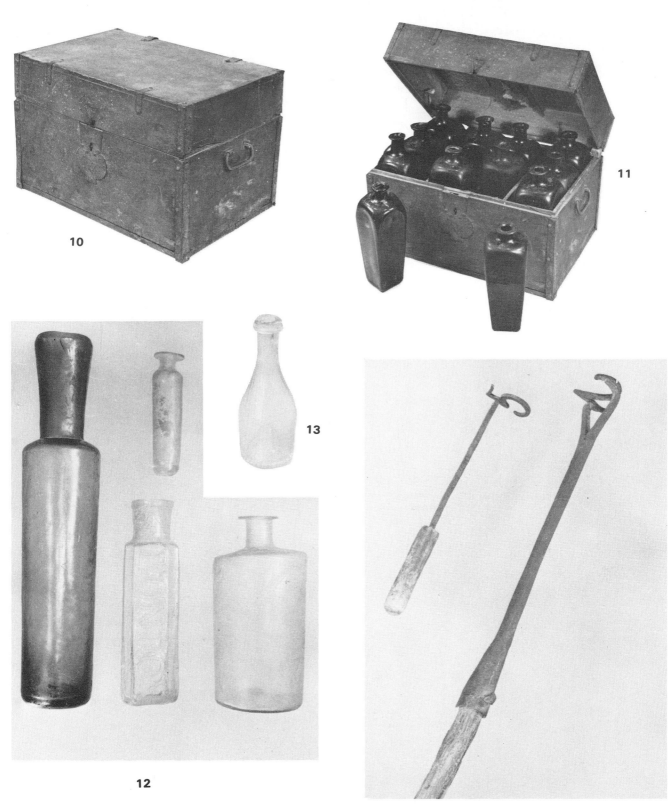

(10, 11) A typical American liquor chest of wood with iron edging (painted green); it is compartmented for 12 case bottles. (12) Various small bottles and vials employed for medicines and oils; circa 1750–1820. (13) Ribbed mold lines are visible here as well as a crude lip; medicine type vial, midcentury. **BRANDING IRONS:** Shaped in colonial script or block numbers, branding irons were mostly used to identify state and government property. For example, one excavated from Crown Point, N.Y. in a British refuse area (c. 1759–1775) has the number "17" in block figures, and some Connecticut muskets were branded "CC" on the stock (Colony of Connecticut) in 1775–1776. (14) A small light iron of the type for marking leather and wood; the large "2" would have been used on cattle, heavy packing cases, etc.

Sources: 10, 11—George C. Neumann; 12, 13, 14—Frank J. Kravic.

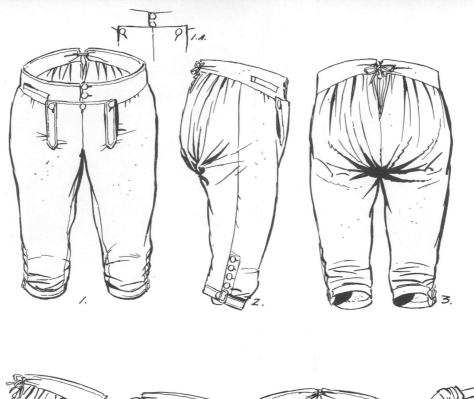

BREECHES, OVERALLS, TROUSERS (also see "Buckles," "Infantry," "Leggings," "Seamen"): The three primary forms of men's leg covering were the knee-length "Breeches," the full-length "Overalls" (buttoned at the ankle), and open-bottomed "Trousers." They all normally had a wide buttoned flap (or "fall") just below the front waistband, and an adjustable tie-string opening in the rear. It was customary to favor wool in the winter and linen in the summer, but buckskin, old tent canvas, and ticking were also prevalent. Most linen was left unbleached—although some was colored with vegetable dyestuffs to achieve earthy blues, browns, greens, and some striped patterns. Their normal construction was tight fitting to the leg, but allowed a baggy seat in the rear so that the body filled it when sitting instead of causing the knee binding experienced in modern styles. (1–3) Knee breeches (civilian and military) showing the typical front "fall" (also variation #1.A), waistband, pocket, buttons, plus buckles at the knees. (4) Overalls (also called "gaitored trousers" or "sliders"), mostly for military use by both American and European troops. (5) Trousers, as worn by both civilians and soldiers; they were also used to cover breeches and overalls for fatigue work or added warmth.

9

8

(6) A seaman's popular loose trousers with two legs (in addition, he often wore a crude kilt, i.e. sail canvas wrapped around the waist and tied with rope. (7) Indian leggings (worn, too, by many whites on the frontier); generally used in winter, they include the common breechcloth, a waist belt for supporting the leggings, and cloth or leather knee garters; usually in varied colors of wool, they were sewn down the side to provide the wide flaps. (8) A variety of leg wear among American troops. (9) A Pennsylvania Loyalist regiment wearing trousers. **BROOMS, BRUSHES:** When in camp with huts or frame buildings, the troops improvised brooms for cleaning. Among the most popular types at the time were (11, 13) the "birch broom" (or "Indian broom") which came from shaving one end of a birch or hickory stick, bending down the resulting shreds, and tying them as shown; (14) A "hickory twig" broom. (12) Small birch brush for use in cooking and cleaning; 10" long. (10) A brush left on Long Island by Hessians; it is painted with German words still faintly visible.

Sources: (8, 9) Brigade of the American Revolution; photos by Michael Cleary and Richard Gerding; 11, 12, 13—The Conn. Historical Society; 10—Nassau County (N.Y.) Museum; (14) Webb, Deane, Stevens Museum, N.S.C.D.A.

BUCKETS, PAILS: Changing little over the years, wooden buckets with their iron or wooden bands were common in camps. Large tinned iron specimens have also been excavated, as well as fragments of leather versions with iron bails. (1) A covered grain or flour bucket. (2, 3, 4) Open wooden types having nailed wooden binding straps. (5) One using iron bands. (6) Reconstructed tin plated buckets from excavated examples; heights (excluding bails and lugs): 9¼″ and 7½″ ; circa 1758-1766. (7) Typical well bucket. All of these are representative of the 1750–1850 period.

Sources: 1–5 Frank J. Kravic; 6—Fort Ligonier; 7—Webb, Deane, Stevens Museum, N.S.C.D.A.

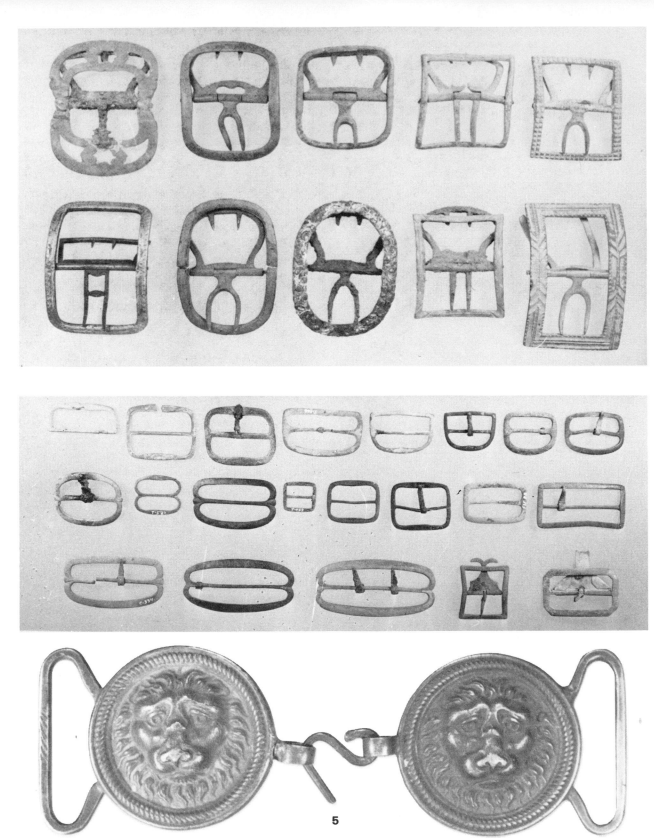

BUCKLES (also see "Belts, Frogs, Scabbards," "Footwear," "Plates, Uniform," "Spurs," "Stocks"): The reliance on buckles was prodigious in the 18th century; their use included shoes, belts, suspension straps, stocks, breeches, spurs, weapon slings, harness, etc. Although most military types were of cast brass with iron or brass tines ("keepers"), camp sites have revealed the use of large numbers of civilian patterns—especially for shoes. Common material for these included pewter, cast silver, iron, cut steel, and brass—plus tin, silver, or pewter over an iron or brass base. The majority are classified as double (i.e. with a center bar), or single framed. (1) Shoe buckle variations found in campsites, circa 1757–1777. (2, 3, 4) Excavated military belt and shoulder strap buckles (both American and English); the frames are all of brass except the iron example second from the right at the bottom; most of the iron tines have rusted away. (5) An English brass sword belt clasp. (cont.)

Sources: 1–4—Frank J. Kravic; 5—Edward Charol.

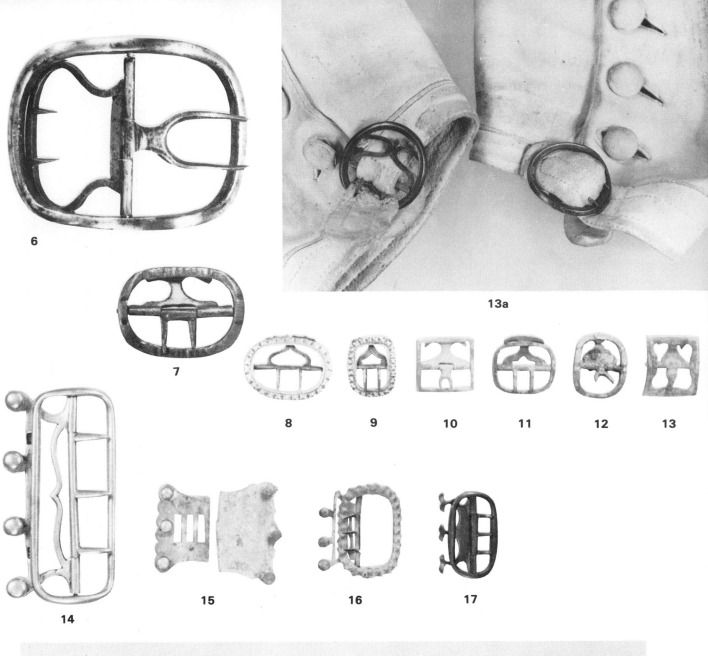

BUCKLES (cont.) (6) A typical plain military shoe buckle. (7–13) Buckles as used on knee breeches. (13a) Buckskin breeches with the steel buckles still attached. Stock Buckles (14–17): (14) An enlarged view of a silver English pattern, (15) Popular British military clasps of sheet brass, (17) Plain brass, American; it used wings for attachment instead of the common studs, (18) Single frame iron examples excavated from 1775–1777 camps—as used on cartridge boxes, harness, and other leather straps.

Sources: 6, 7—G. Gedney Godwin; 8, 13a, 14, 17—George C. Neumann; 9–13, 15, 16, 18—Frank J. Kravic.

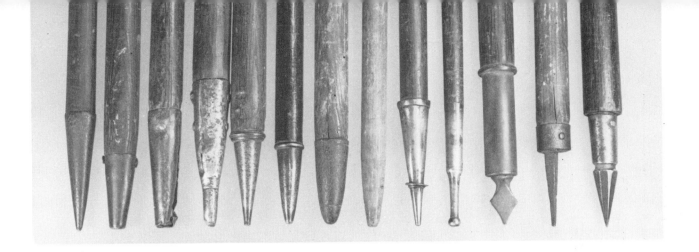

1

2

3

4

5

BULLET POUCHES (see "Pouches, Bullet.") **BULLETS** (see "Ammunition," "Molds.") **BUTT CONES** ("Ground Irons"): A butt cone was the metal tip added at the bottom of the wooden staff ("haft") on a pole arm. Made mostly of iron, and occasionally brass, its purpose was to prevent wear and, when needed, to help anchor it in the ground against a charge by horsemen. Naval pikes usually left the wood exposed to prevent deck damage. (1) Types of butt cones used by both Americans and Europeans. **BUTTONS** (also see "Breeches," "Coats," "Molds," "Waistcoats"): Row #2 (l to r) A button of the French "Troupes de la Marine" (Louisbourg, c. 1748–1758). The remaining buttons on this page are accurate reproductions; Row #2 (contd.), Royal Provincials, 1776–1783; 20th Regt. of Foot, 1776–1777; American Artillery, c. 1775–1783;. Row #3: 2nd Conn. Regt. 1777–1783; 3rd Mass. Line, 1779–1783; Butler's Rangers, 1777–1783; American Artillery (waistcoat), 1775–1783; 5th Conn. Rgt. c. 1777–1781; A New York Rgt., c. 1775–1778;. Row #4: Boston Rgt., c. 1776–1778; 27th Rgt. of Foot, c. 1775–1778; USA Continental button, c. 1775–1783 (most common marked American soldier's button found); 10th Mass. Line, 1777–1783; Row #5: 38th Rgt. of Foot, 1775–1783; Royal Rgt. of Artillery, late or post Revolution, c. 1780–1800; 60th Rgt. "Royal Americans," 1761–1783; The King's 8th Rgt., 1774–1784. (cont.)

Sources: 1—George C. Neumann; 2—Fortress Louisbourg; All other buttons from The Soldier Shop.

6

7

8

9

BUTTONS (cont.) Following the French and Indian War it became common to wear the regimental designation on various accoutrements. This included buttons which often bear the number of the regiment as well as descriptive initials or special insignia. The easiest to make, and the most common in the American Army were pewter, lead, or brass buttons cast in a mold which also provided an integral eyelet. British regiments often favored gilded or silvered buttons in keeping with regimental colors. Yet many other varieties are recovered including plain pewter specimens, brass one and two-piece constructions, some with wire eyelets soldered on, plus buttons having brass fronts and bone or wood backs. It is not uncommon to find a wide variety in a single site as the soldiers, hard pressed for replacement, had to make do. Rows #6– #8 are reproductions struck from excavated originals. (Row 6; l. to r.) British 37th Regt.; American 18th Regt., pre-1777; American, pre-1777; variation of the English 37th Regt.. (Row 7; l. to r.) Rhode Island Regiment; British 53rd Regt.; English 26th Regt., c. 1780–1800; British marine and naval pattern. (Row 8) Left, an English 64th Regt. button believed made in America; right, a British officer's example fom the 17th Regt.

Sources: 6–8 The Soldier Shop; 9—George C. Neumann

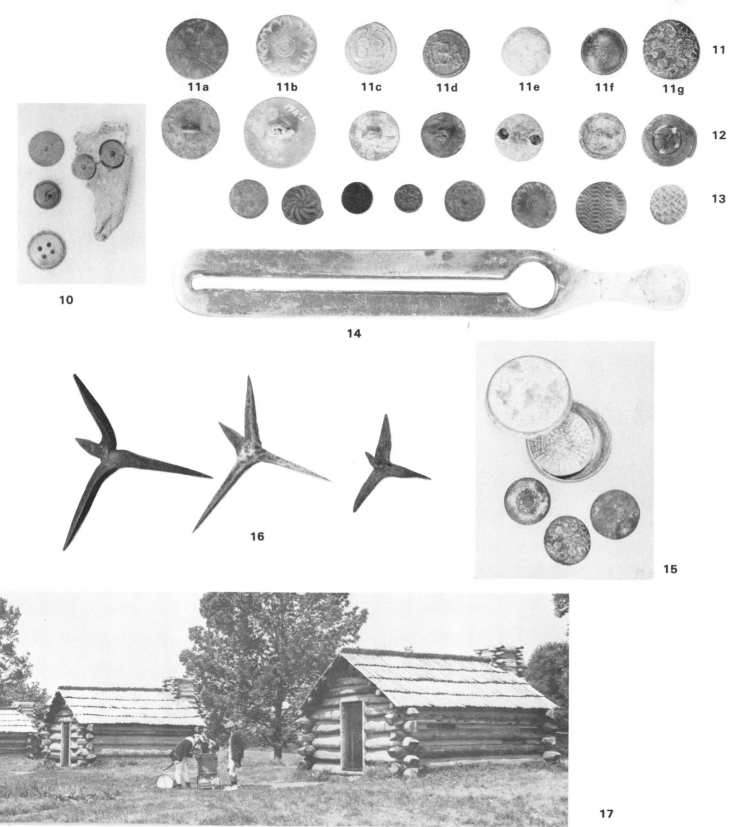

(9) Typical civilian buttons as found in abundance on American campsites. These are made from brass, tinned iron, wood, pewter, and silver-plated brass; note that several include the popular cut or punched designs; (10–13) *Buttons excavated from military sites, c. 1755–1783:* (10) Top right, a segment of bone with two buttons cut from it; left, top to bottom, a bone button back and bone matrix; a complete button having a backing of bone and a brass loop; a common 4-hole bone type. (11a) Plain brass. (11b) Pewter, with a design. (11c) Pewter, the British 62nd Regt. (11d) USA button (11e) A 2-piece pewter example with holes in the base to release gas while cooling (French site, Champlain Valley, N.Y.) (11f) Brass. (11g) A brass face washed with gold, plus a bone backing; dyed green, it includes linen cross loops. (12) Typical backs of the button types above them in Row #11. (13) Civilian styles. (14) A brass shield to protect the uniform while cleaning the buttons. (15) Brass compass case reused to hold three buttons (Champlain Valley). **CALTROPS:** Small anti-personnel and anti-horse weapons having four sharpened points so that when scattered on the ground or under water at fords one lethal spike was always pointed up. (16) Left, made by cutting and bending one piece; the others had two sections welded at the center. **CAMPS:** (also see "Tents"): Typical huts used in winter camps. (cont.)

Sources: 10–13, 15—Frank J. Kravic; 14—Edward Charol; 16—George C. Neumann; 17—Valley Forge State Park (Penn.).

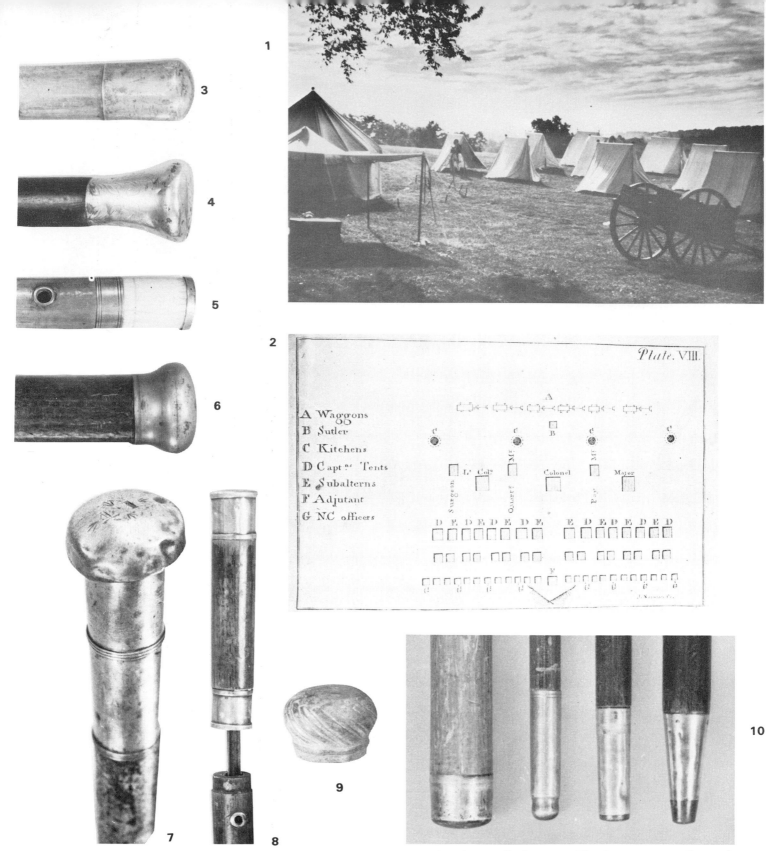

CAMPS (cont.) Military camps were set up under a very formal and controlled pattern. The Quartermaster General fixed the line of encampment with specific positions for each regiment or battalion, arranged as they formed in order of battle. The wagons, kitchens, sutler, officers and men—whether in huts or tents—each had a firm location. The key for this layout was the "color line" where colors were massed along with the drums and often the officers' spontoons. (2) The order of encampment for one battalion, from von Steuben's American manual. **CANES:** Canes were commonly carried by civilians and officers. It was considered part of a gentleman's dress and also served as a means of protection—often concealing a sword or dagger blade, or a weight for use as a club. (3) A silver head. (4) Silver head with engraved designs and a lead weight inside. (5) An ivory top including silver bands; signed, "J Moseley 1773." (6) Popular abbreviated bulbous-shaped head. (7) Silver-headed cane of Gov. Joseph Talcott (Conn.); engraved, "I T" (note, "J" was written as an "I" at this time). (8) A silver-banded dagger cane; blade 11". (9) Excavated head; English camp. (10) Common tips which often included a steel or brass plug at the bottom to minimize wear.

Sources: 1—Brigade of the American Revolution; photo by Michael Cleary; 2, 3, 4, 8, 10—George C. Neumann; 5—Robert Nittolo; 6, 9—Frank J. Kravic; 7—The Conn. Historical Society.

1

2

3

4

5

6

CANNON (see "Artillery.") CANTEENS: As with most accoutrements, a wide variety of portable beverage containers saw service. The European troops normally favored tin canteens (tinned iron), usually with cloth covers. Americans also used tin, as well as glass, leather, and even gourds—but mostly wood. The soldier's canteen was usually carried on his left hip suspended from a linen or leather strap (also rope) over the right shoulder. Small ones were often secured in the knapsack, blanket roll, or haversack, while the large type commonly used in the fields by farmers— which were pressed into service during militia duty—frequently rode in wagons or were carried by handles. (1) Tinned iron canteen (note loops on side for shoulder cord); 6'' high (less spout), 3'' thick at base; used by Abraham Van Vlaack, Jr., Dutchess County Militia (N.Y.), 1777. (2, 3) Reproductions of British tin specimens as excavated from Fort Ligonier, c. 1758–1766; 7.6'' and 8.4'' high with neck. (4) Tinned German canteen of Lieb Regt.; excavated in New York City; 7¾'' high, 5¾'' across. (5) Rendering of scrimshaw on a tin canteen recovered from Champlain Valley site, circa 1757–1777. (6) Variety of canteens as worn by Revolutionary War troops; American light infantry company shown. (cont.)

Sources: 1—Washington's Hdq., Newburgh; N.Y. 4—New-York Historical Society; 5—Frank J. Kravic; 6—Brigade of the American Revolution; photo by Richard Gerding.

CANTEENS (cont.) (1–4) Wooden barrel type construction (usually of white oak, pine, or cedar), with the side staves secured by interlocking wooden hoops (mostly of willow, hickory, or ash); their diameters: (1) 7″, (2) 5⅜″, (3) 6¾″; painted red, (4) 7⅛″. (5) Triangular shape bound by split hickory saplings; 7″ high. (6, 7) A wooden style held by iron hoops—which gained acceptance toward the end of the war; #7 has both faces expanded to cover the ends of the staves; note too the iron keepers between the hoops to secure a shoulder strap (leather keepers were also used). Diameters: (6) 6½″, (7) 7″ . The above canteens would be typical of those used in America from 1750 to 1870.

Sources: 1–4, 6, 7—George C. Neumann; 5—Robert Nittolo.

60

(8–11) Another practice was to hollow out a piece of wood and then drive two heads into the openings when dry—before expanding and sealing after soaking (also see "swiglers" on page 62): (8) 5⅜" diameter, painted green; it shows strap keepers and repairs for a crack by the spout . (9) 4¾" dia. (10) 6" dia. (11) Hollowed out, but iron bands have been added against splitting; 5¾" dia. (12–14) A single rim pattern popular in New England from the 1760s until the 1840s. The rim is held by pegs or iron nails and normally includes a round hole or spout instead of a raised rim. (12) Two sizes, 4⅜" dia. and 7⅜" dia.; note the iron holders for its linen shoulder strap. (13) An unusual oval shape (8¾" x 6½" x 2⅞") that mounts a leather carrying strap. (14) An interesting example, 8⅛" x 2¾", carved on one side with a heart and "Hear Is my Heart/And hear Is my hand/When this you Se/Remember me 1777"; on the reverse side, "September the 25/1777/ May the Heavens/protect Poor Souls/that We are/Samuel Richmon" (a member of the 8th Conn. Line Regiment). (15) A common gourd was often employed by many of the colonists—especially the militia; 15½" high. (cont.)

Sources: 8–12—George C. Neumann; 13-Madison Grant; 14—Edward Charol; 15—Mercer Museum, Bucks County Historical Society.

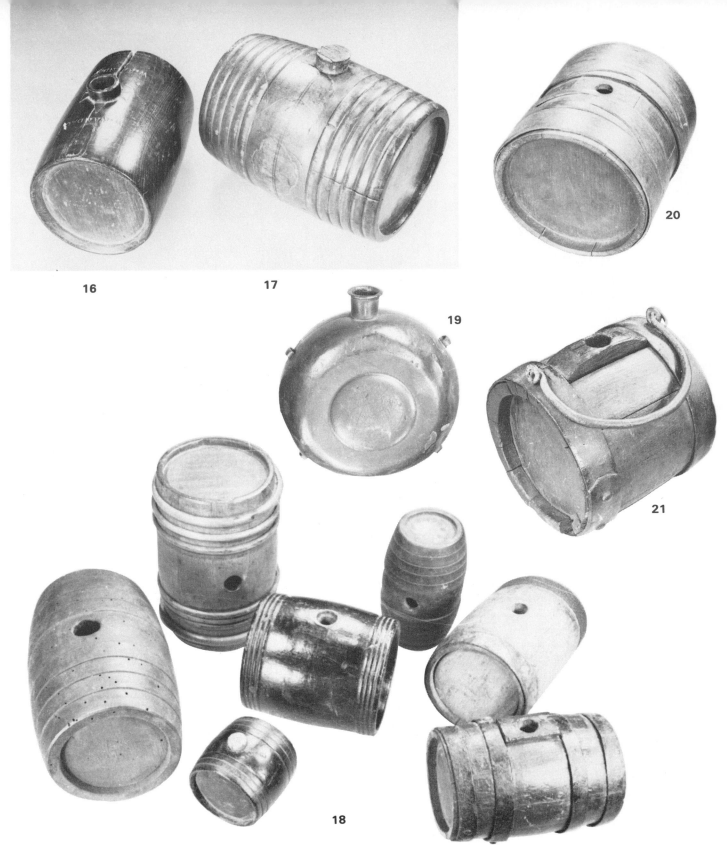

16

17

19

20

21

18

CANTEENS (cont.) (16–18) Small elongated civilian "rundlets," "rum kegs," or "swiglers," usually made from hollowed and lathe-turned logs plus the insertion of flat ends; they were popular from about 1750–1850. (16) 6½" long with pewter spout. (17) 7¼" in length; it includes turned decorative channels. (18) Various sizes from 6½" to 2⅜" in length; note the banded stave types bound by split saplings or iron bands. (19) A pewter canteen, 4⅜" dia.; made from molding two porringers. (20) A large extended barrel style having staves secured by four lapped wooden bands; 6¾" long. (21) A common type carried by farmers into the fields and undoubtedly used by militia and irregulars during the War for Independence; iron handle and bands, 6½" in length.

Source: George C. Neumann.

22

21a

23

24

(21a) A hand blown glass water bottle carried by Robert Bradford of Haddam, Conn.; 10⅞" high. (22) Leather flask which probably enclosed a glass or ceramic bottle; excavated at Fortress Louisbourg. (23) American soldiers wearing wooden canteens. (24) A large "wagon" style canteen with a flattened wooden base to act as a stand; it mounts iron straps, a pewter spout, and is painted red; marks of the British broad arrow and "BO" (Board of Ordnance) are also included; 10¼" diameter. (cont)

Sources: 21a, 24—George C. Neumann; 22—Fortress Louisbourg; Dept. of Indian and Northern Affairs, Parks, Canada; 23—Brigade of the American Revolution, photo by Michael Cleary.

CANTEENS (cont.) (25–27) Large "wagon" or civilian "field" type canteens, circa 1750–1870. (25) 13" diameter; painted red, with interlocking wooden hoops. (26) A double compartmented variation having three wooden straps; 9¼" long. (27) Triangular in cross section, 9" in length; it includes a handle. CAPS (see "Headgear.") CAPE (see "Coats.") CARBINES (also see "Belts, Frogs, Scabbards," "Fusils," "Muskets," "Horse, Equipage," "Horseman"): The term "carbine" was used to describe either a short-barreled shoulder firearm, or a musket having a smaller than normal bore diameter. For example, the British used three standard military barrel sizes; .75 cal. (musket); .65 cal. (carbine); and .56 cal. (pistol—which also used .65). The French musket was .69 caliber—their carbine .67 cal. Carbines were carried mostly by horsemen, light infantry, and artillerymen. (1) A cut down British Brown Bess musket (Long Land pattern), c. 1735–1750; marked "NICKSON" (maker) on the lock; barrel 34", 50⅜" overall.

Source: George C. Neumann.

(2) English light dragoon carbine variation, c. 1750–1765; "I LUDLAM" on the lock; 47⅛" total, 31⅜" barrel; brass fittings. (3) Regular British light dragoon model, circa 1756–1760; full length 51" and a .65 cal. bore; stocked to the muzzle; note the side bar with a ring for the shoulder strap hook (see "Belts, Frogs, Scabbards.") (4) French cavalry carbine Model 1733 "mousequeton de cavalerie"; stocked to the muzzle with a pinned barrel; 45" long, barrel 30¾"; weight 6 lbs, .67 cal. (5) French Model 1766; its brass furniture includes a double strap center band; 45" overall, 31" barrel. (6) Dutch-German carbine, circa 1770–1780; it has known American use; totals 52", 37¾" barrel; .76 cal., brass mountings. (7) English heavy dragoon carbine; 42" barrel with Long Land furniture; used from the 1740s to about 1770; 57¾" in length, .75 cal. bore. (8) British light infantry carbine, by "VERNON," dated 1757; 42" barrel, .65 cal.; 7.1 lbs. (9) French heavy dragoon carbine, Model 1766; brass furniture plus an iron double strap center band; length, 57¼". **CARTRIDGES** (see "Ammunition.") **CARTRIDGE BOXES** (or "Cartouche boxes," "Cartridge pouches"; also see "Ammunition," "Horns," "Hunting Bags," "Pouches, Bullet"): (10) 1776 receipt for leather used by a tradesman making cartridge boxes. (cont.)

Sources: 1–9—George C. Neumann; 10—Frank J. Kravic.

CARTRIDGE BOXES (cont.) The 18th century regular soldier employed a cylindrical paper-wrapped cartridge. It was normally kept in a "box" carried just behind the right hip (held by a shoulder strap), or in the front on a waist belt. The cartridge box was simply a block of wood (beech, maple, walnut were common) with vertical holes to hold the cartridges, and covered by leather which provided one or two flaps. In some cases just a single flap was nailed along the rear upper edge of the block. The number of holes varied from 9 to 36 despite periodic specifications. Tin cannisters were also used to relieve a shortage of leather, and American horsemen were assigned waist boxes holding 12 tin pipes. Loading with loose powder from a horn, and bullets or shot from a bag-like pouch remained popular among most riflemen and militia. The surviving American cartridge boxes are often difficult to date between the late 18th and early 19th centuries as many of them were made locally and continued to follow established patterns. (1) American box flap with a red cloth heart sewn to the face. (2) A box opened with its block removed to show the common bottom wooden tray (often tin) for supplies and tools.

Sources: 1, 2—George C. Neumann; 3, 4—West Point Museum; 5—Newport (R.I.) Historical Museum; 6—Edward Charol; 7—Brigade of the American Revolution, photo by Michael Cleary.

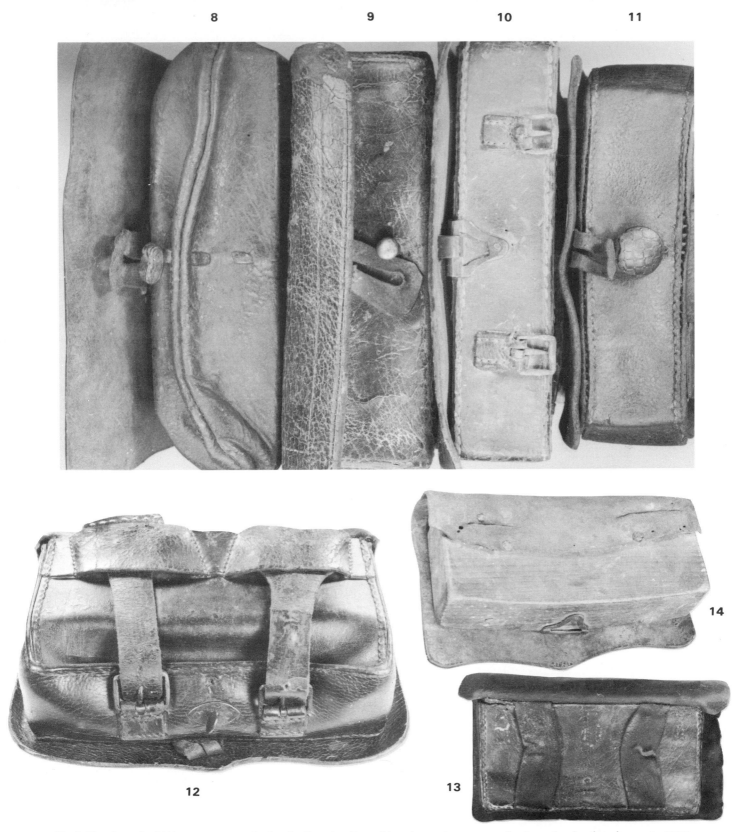

(3, 4) The Board of War recommended a tin (i.e. tin dipped iron) cannister as a substitute for leather boxes in 1778; the measurements were 6½″ x 3¼″ x 2⅞″; it carried 36 cartridges in layers of 4 across. (5) The body of a waist box with 10 tin pipes worn by Col. Henry Sherburne of the Continental Army. (6) An American waist "belly" box with a brass plate, "No 75, RALEIGH." (7) Colonists wearing the leather cartridge box and a tin cannister. (8–12) Methods of securing flaps, i.e. (8) a knotted leather ball, (9) oval brass stud, (10) brass hook and open triangular catch, (11) civilian coat button. (12) A pointed brass base plus a turnable flat stud. (13) American box having waist belt loops sewn at the rear. (14) A worn specimen recreated from an old reused flap nailed to the rear of a wooden block; note the slits for a missing shoulder strap which had its ends nailed to the bottom of the block. (cont.)

Source: 12—Don Troiani; 8–11, 13–14—George C. Neumann.

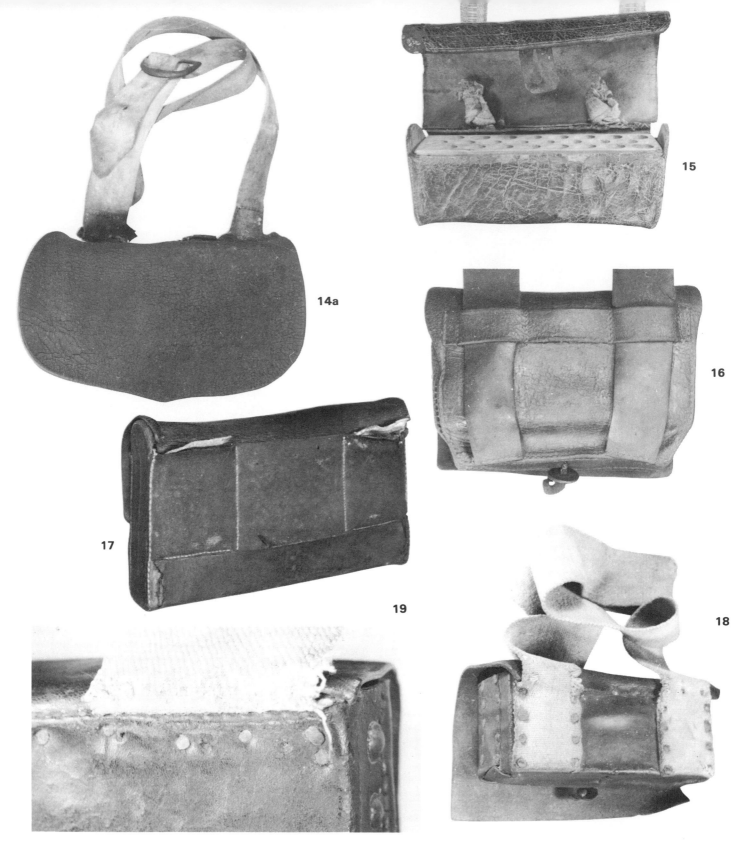

CARTRIDGE BOXES (cont.) (14a) American, with a pointed flap and a buff leather shoulder strap. (19) The typical attachment of linen shoulder straps, i.e. by sewing the two ends into the rear flap seam and then using nails through the leather to hold them to the block. (15) Straps held by knotting the ends inside the leather flap seam. (16) Leather cross-straps sewn to the leather at the bottom seam after passing under a cross-support binder. (17) Remains of the shoulder strap sewn to the rear of a box. (18) Nails hold this linen strap in place.

Sources: 14a, 15, 16, 19–George C. Neumann; 17–Robert Nittolo; 18–J. Craig Nannos

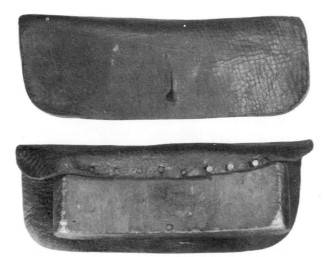

20. BRITISH WAIST BOX: Gold "GR 3" and crown embossed on flap—nailed to rear of block; belt loops on front to hold it against stomach; 18 holes; block: 8⁵/₁₆″ x 2″ x 2⅞″ high. (George C. Neumann)

21. BRITISH SHOULDER BOX: Same block as #20, but support binders and buckles on the rear are for a light shoulder strap; curved block: 8⅝″ x 2″ x 3¼″ high; note leather tie-knob. (George C. Neumann)

22. AMERICAN WAIST BOX: Like #20 with front belt loops, but a larger nailed-on flap; block has 17 holes (9, 8), measures 8¾″ x 2⅛″ x 2⅞″ high. (George C. Neumann)

23. AMERICAN WAIST BOX: Red cloth visible through a cut-out heart shape; the lower front flap pulls down to open a bottom pocket; its buff leather belt has a red linen covering; 24 hole block (9, 8, 7) is 8½" x 2⅜" high. (Wm. H. Guthman)

24. AMERICAN WAIST BOX: A crude militia box having all leather nailed to the block instead of sewn around it; the waist belt is also nailed to the rear; block: 25 holes (8, 9, 9). (George C. Neumann)

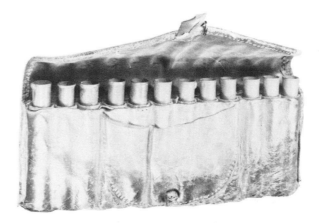

25. AMERICAN DRAGOON WAIST BOX: c. 1775–1810. In 1778 Congress recommended a waist box with 12 tin pipes for horsemen. This unique version has each tin removable and divided in the center to form 2 compartments, i.e. allowing 24 cartridges; 11¼" x 5¼" x 4¼" high. (George C. Neumann)

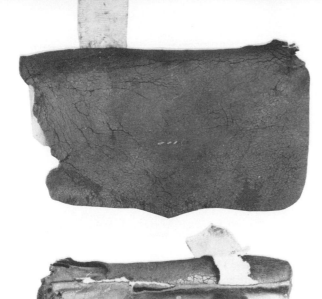

26. **AMERICAN BOX:** c. 1755–1763; This long straight block with 23 holes (12, 11) is identical to one recovered from the site of the Jersey Blues ambush at Sabbath Day Point on July 21, 1757 (Don Troiani Collection). Note the double flap, long overhang, pocket under the block, and 2¼" wide linen strap; block: 11¾" x 2" x 2¾" h. (George C. Neumann)

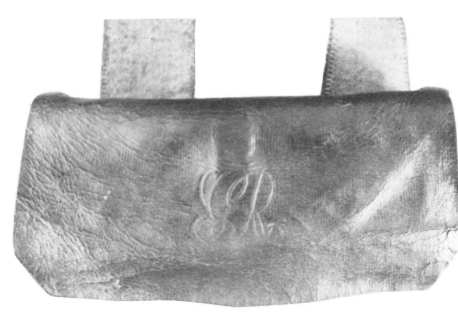

27. **SHOULDER STRAP BOX:** Although of typical American styling, this box has a "GR" cypher embossed on the flap; its provenience is unknown . . . loyalist?; block, 8¾" x 3½" h. x 2" across; 26 holes (9, 8, 9). (Edward Vebell)

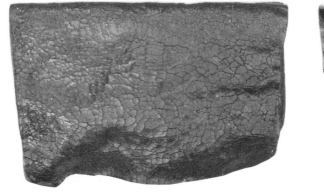

28. AMERICAN MILITIA WAIST BOX: C. 1775–1820; all of the leather is tightly nailed to the block with brass brads, and the rear belt loops by iron nails (which would not hold long in the field); body is 9⅜" x 3¼" h. x 3" deep; 24 holes (8, 8, 8). (George C. Neumann)

29. AMERICAN SHOULDER BOX: The addition of a second inside flap by nailing a piece of leather to the inside rear top of the block reflects requests for double flaps like the British to retard rain penetration; block: 24 holes (8, 8, 8), 7¼" x 3" h., 2¾" deep. (George C. Neumann)

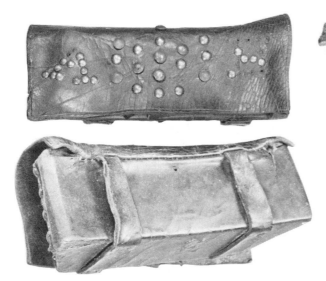

30. AMERICAN MILITIA WAIST BOX: C. 1775–1820; all leather is nailed to the block; brass brads were also used to create initials and a design on the flap; its tapered block has 24 holes (9, 8, 7). (George C. Neumann)

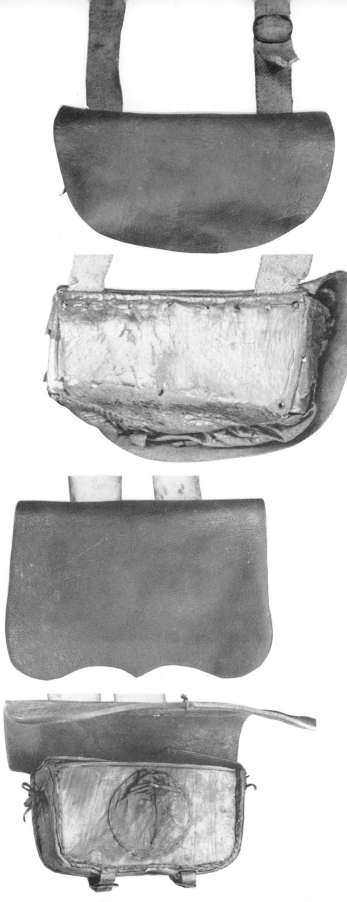

31. AMERICAN: A popular type with a sagging pouch left in the leather beneath the block for storage or easier fitting when making; note its double flaps and sewn seams, plus 1 5/8" linen strap; the block has 17 holes (9, 8)—measures 9¾" x 2" deep x 3¼" h. (George C. Neumann)

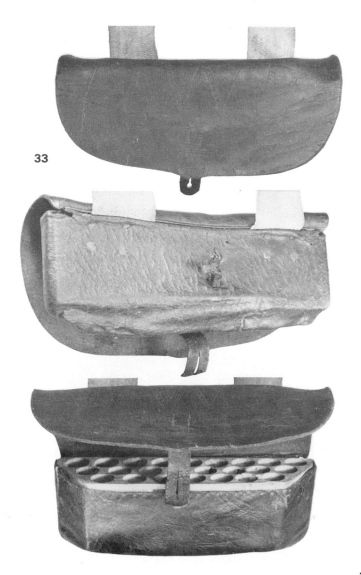

32. (above) AMERICAN: Large pointed flap; 3" buff leather cross-belt; tool and flint "tie" pockets on ends and face plus "carry straps" underneath. (Right) **33. AMERICAN:** c. 1775–1810; pouch pattern; 2" linen shoulder straps sewn and nailed at rear seam; block tapers forward, 24 holes (9, 8, 7). (George C. Neumann)

34. AMERICAN SHOULDER BOX: The flap's embossed panel shows a light infantryman holding his musket in front of two tents and a cannon:—plus "THIS IS FAIR / LIBERTY" (tents and cannon were painted); an additional block adds 7 holes to the original's 17; leather straps 1⅝" wide; body, 9½" x 4⅛" h. x 3 1/16" deep. (Ft. Ticonderoga Museum)

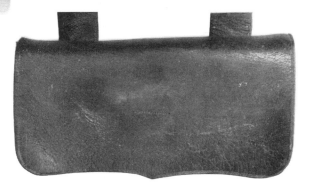

35. AMERICAN: Loose "pouch" pattern; pointed flap, 1½" dark leather shoulder strap; block, 18 holes (9, 9), 9" x 1¾" x 2¾" h. (George C. Neumann)

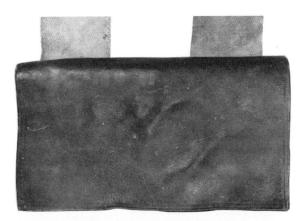

36. AMERICAN: Pouch styling having a squared flap; leather sewn and nailed to the block; linen strap 2¾" wide; 27 holes (10, 9, 8). (George C. Neumann)

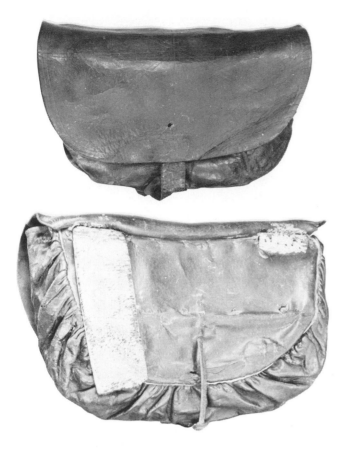

37. **AMERICAN:** We know that riflemen were converted to use muskets and this appears to be a hunting bag altered to a cartridge box. The block is loose fitting (not a replacement), held high in the bag by nails plus a heavy thread through both the leather and wood along its upper rear edge; also note an original bag type draw string, and the back's single gathered seam. The 1¾" wide strap is painted with white lead; block has 18 holes (9, 9). (George C. Neumann)

38. **AMERICAN:** This long overhanging leather flap has a thin leather inner liner and a pouch covering two blocks—25 holes (8, plus 8, 9); the 2¼" linen shoulder straps entered the rear flap seam before being nailed in place to the block. Note too the continuous curving profile of the deep flap. (George C. Neumann)

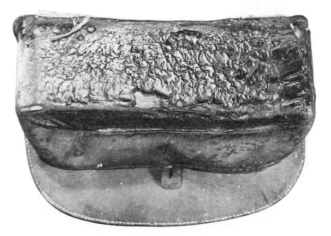

39. AMERICAN SHOULDER BOX: Displays the iron strap buckles found on most camp sites and the cross-binder to secure a 2½″ wide linen strap with leather ends; the block has 25 holes (8, 9, 8); body: 8⅜″ x 2⅝″ deep x 4½″ h. (George C. Neumann)

40. FRENCH GRENADIER BOX: It includes a 2¾″ wide buff leather strap and a front accessory pocket; the unique block holds 6 center holes and 2 wide side openings; body, 8¾″ x 4½″ h. x 2¾″ deep; circa 1770–1800. (George C. Neumann)

41. (above, left) **GERMAN GRENADIER BOX** (19th century reproduction): 4″ wide buff leather straps; brass Prussian oval badge and 4 bomb plates; body, 10″ x 5⅝″ h. x 3⅝″ deep. (George C. Neumann)

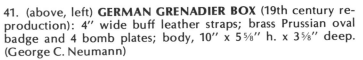

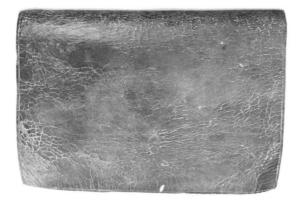

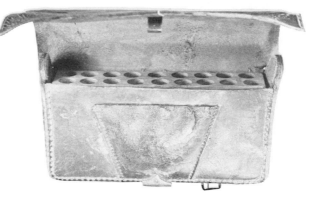

42. AMERICAN: C. 1775–1820; a common pattern with the rear cross-binder and bottom iron buckles for the shoulder straps. Its squared flap attaches with a brass hook to a triangular clasp; the block contains 18 holes (9, 9) and a wooden tray beneath. The body is 9″ x 4⅜″ h. x 2″ deep. Note too the flat accessory pocket. (George C. Neumann)

43. AMERICAN SHOULDER BOX: A squared front flap with a shallow accessory pocket at the front; the original linen shoulder strap had a triple colored vertical line design; its block includes 24 holes (8, 8, 8). The covered body measures 8½″ x 4⅛″ h. x 2¾″ deep. (George C. Neumann)

44. AMERICAN SHOULDER BOX: A simple rectangular style with a shoulder strap-binder and leather buttons to secure the strap ends (1 missing). Of special interest are the remaining paper cartridges in the block; covered body measurements: 8½″ x 4⅛″ h. x 2¾″ deep. (George C. Neumann)

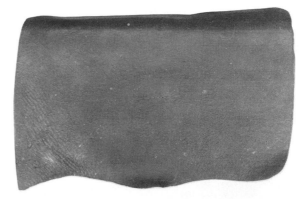

45. AMERICAN: Circa 1780–1815; near the end of the Revolution the Americans began to use boxes with a pull-out flap which gave direct access to a tin implement tray below the block; it culminated in the Model 1808. Note the characteristics of this interim period—the "pull-out," 3-pointed flap, and 26 holes (9, 8, 9). (George C. Neumann)

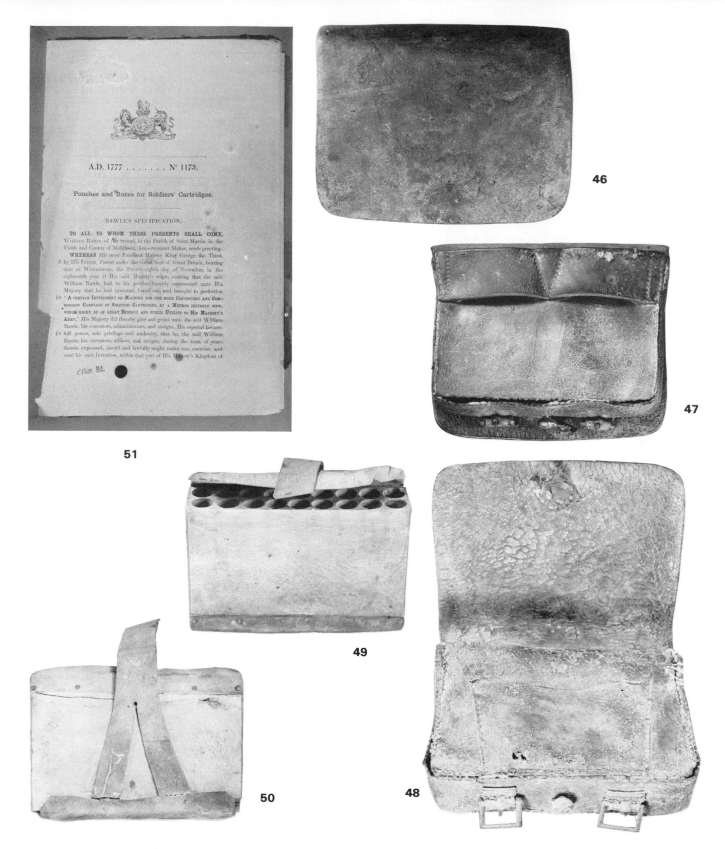

46

47

51

49

50

48

THIS PAGE: British Cartridge Box. The official British cartridge "pouch" is described in writing, but no existing example is known to us. It hung from a 3" wide whitened buff leather shoulder strap and was made of the "stoutest blackened calf skin" having an inside flap lined with thick painted linen—and a block containing 36 holes for cartridges. The unusual box shown on this page is a variation found in Boston with a reported history of use by British forces; it matches a 1777 English patent by William Rawle (51). The block contains 36 holes like the standard pattern, but permits a smaller size because they are arranged with 18 each in the top and bottom (49). A flap and strap cover and hold the 18 underneath (50) and when the first 18 are gone a pull of the upper end of the strap lifts out the block to be reversed in the pouch. The front (46), back (47), and inside (48) resemble many late 18th and early 19th century patterns; covered body, 8³/₈" x 5¹/₂" h. x 2¹/₈" wide. (cont.)

Source: Edward Charol.

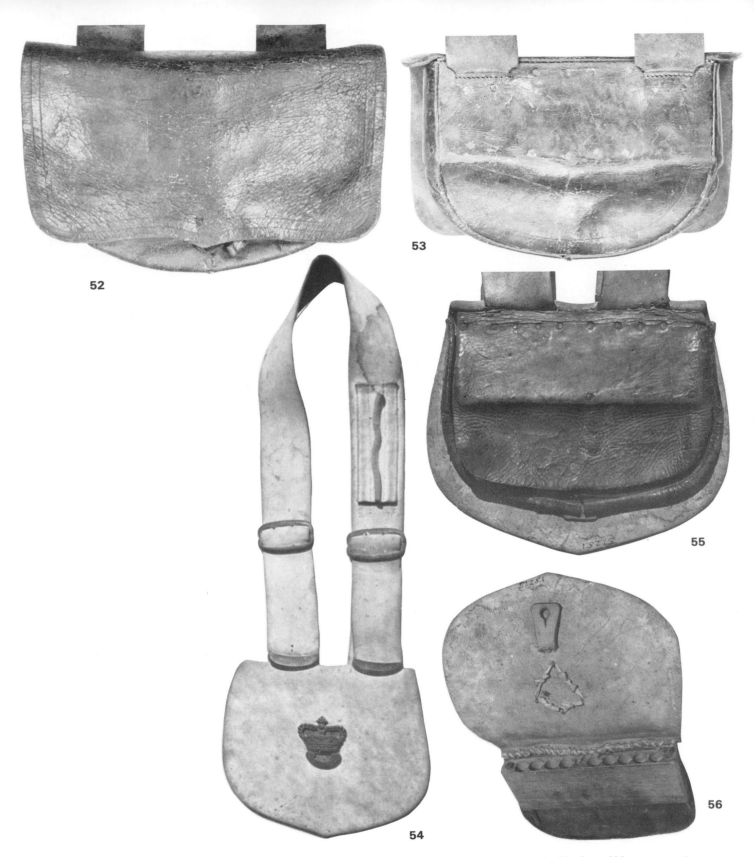

CARTRIDGE BOXES (cont.) (52, 53) American, a deep flat style which retains the pouch under the block (and like most similar pockets, it is not usable because the block is nailed to the leather); its dark leather straps are 2¼″ wide and the curved block holds 21 cartridges (11, 10); full pouch, 7″ x 10″ wide. (54-56) British Royal Artillery Pouch (also see "Plates, Uniform"), last quarter of the 18th century. The pouch itself is of tanned leather with a buff flap and cross-belt (which meets fixed extensions from the pouch where the brass buckles are seen (54). Note too the belt's loops for vent picks. The narrow block's 9 holes (1 row) also have a center hole for a vent pick or gimlet, plus 2 end holes probably containing spikes to "spike" the gun if capture threatened (56).

Sources: 52, 53–Edward Vebell; 54-56 Charleston Museum (S.C.).

CAVALRY (see "Carbines, " "Horse, Equipage," "Headgear," "Horsemen," "Pistols," "Swords.") **CERAMICS** (see "Drinkingware," "Eatingware.") **CHAINS:** Another product of the blacksmith was chain for use in heavy hauling or support when ropes were inadequate. (1) A large link believed part of the great chains which stretched across the Hudson River at West Point to impede hostile ships; 32" long. (2) Excavated links illustrating the variety of shapes employed. **CHARGERS** (see "Measures, Powder.") **CHESTS** (also see "Bottles," "Luggage"): Chests ranged from petite personal boxes (typically of wood with paper lining and outer leather covering) to large storage containers. (3) Small leather-covered document boxes; lengths (l to r), 7", 9", 7¾". (4) An 18th century chest covered by tooled leather; 12" length; a military notation on the bottom includes the date, "1742." (5) A similar tooled leather British document chest with a crown and "GR" (i.e. "Georgius Rex" for King George) design around the handle; 13" long. (6) C. 1770–1820; "hair" chest (most fur gone here) with brass brads securing the deerskin and also forming the owner's initials; 12½" length. (7) Painted wood plus nailed-on leather straps; 11" x 7" x 7". (cont.)

Sources: 1—Morristown National Historical Park; 2, 4, 7—Frank J. Kravic; 3, 6—George C. Neumann; 5—William H. Guthman.

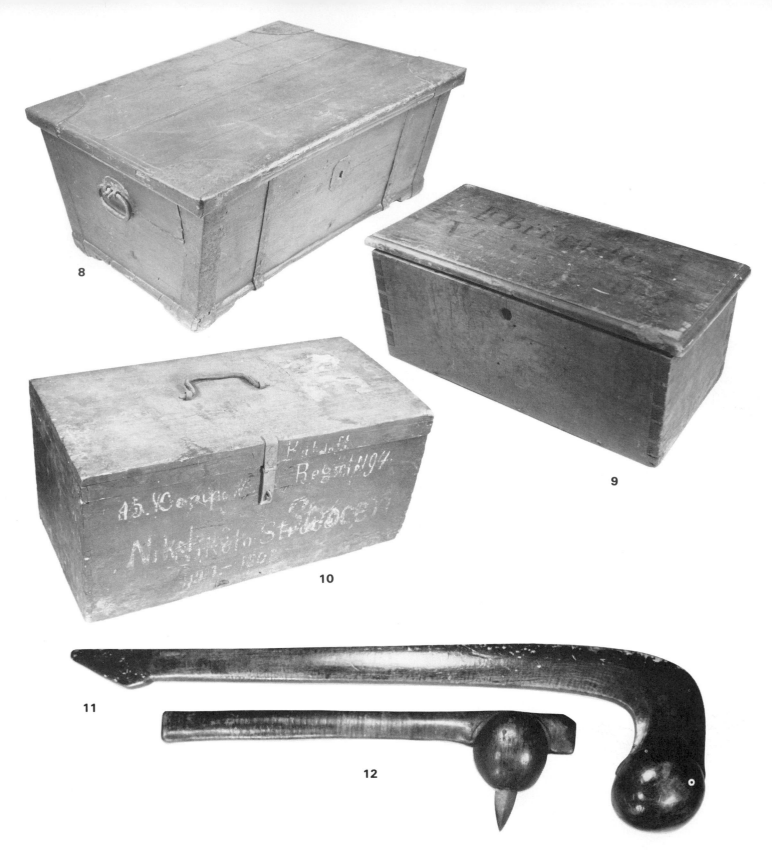

CHESTS (cont.) (8) Map and chart chest, circa 1700–1750; painted dark green , it includes metal bands and corners plus a large lock. (9) American record and document chest with dovetailed corners, simple wire hinges, and the remains of a cover inscription, "II Brigade VI DiviSion." (10) The personal chest believed to have been used by a German officer in America; the corners are of dovetailed construction; its measurements: 23½" x 11" high x 11⅝" deep. **CLOAK** (see "Coats, Cloaks.") **CLOTH** (see "Blankets," "Fabric.") **CLOTHING** (see "Breeches," "Coats," "Footwear," "Headgear," "Horsemen," "Infantry," "Leggings," "Marines," "Sash, Officer," "Seamen," "Stockings," "Stocks, Neck," "Waistcoats.") **CLUBS, INDIAN:** Indian ball-headed wooden clubs were called "tomahawks" by the early 17th century colonists and they continued in use through the War for Independence—persisting with western tribes into the late 1800s. (11) Northeastern Indian war club (or "ball-headed tomahawk"); circa 1700–1725; 24¾" long. (12) Northeast Indian, circa 1750; it is made of curly maple and adds an iron blade to the ball at the point of impact; 15¾" in length.

Sources: 8—Frank J. Kravic; 9—George C. Neumann; 10—Edward Charol; 11, 12—David Currie.

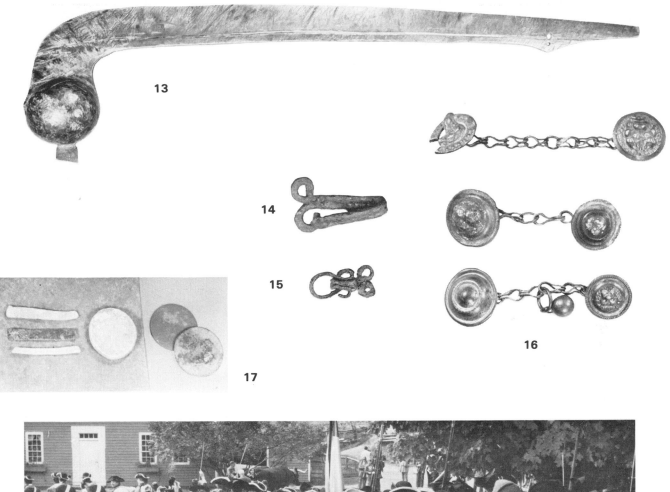

(13) Indian war club circa 1740–1765; an iron blade extension is included in the ball head. **COATS, CLOAKS** (also see "Buttons," "Horsemen," "Infantry," "Marines," "Music," "Seamen," "Shirts"): (14) Excavated coat hook. (15) Fused hook and eye. (16) Cloak "tie chains." (17)Various unearthed "coat weights": (left) lead strips and a round lead disc, (right) reused old coins. (18) American troops in a typical variety of coats and shirts plus an officer wearing a cloak. The formal regimental coat used by both sides functioned as part of the man's dress, protection as his overcoat, and an indication of the regiment itself. Colors on the facings of American military coats usually denoted the unit's state or geographic area—while the pattern and color of lace (around the buttons) plus facing designs were individual to each European regiment. A typical military coat had a flat collar, long and narrow lapels, high set on the shoulders, a snug fit in the chest and shoulders, and full skirts (which were normally hooked or "turned back" in good weather). The British soldier, for example, was fitted by the man kneeling on both knees to have his skirts cut 6" from the ground; the light infantry's was cut at 9" (per Simes, 1776). (cont.)

Sources: 13, 16—Edward Charol; 14, 15, 17—Frank J. Kravic; 18—Brigade of the American Revolution, photo by Michael Cleary.

19

20

22

21

COATS, CLOAKS (cont.) They were mostly of wool. Enlisted men's coats were invariably coarse (about 65 threads per sq. inch) and of cheap plain-woven woolen broadcloth. It was colored with natural dyes, e.g. madder for dark reds, cochineal for bright reds, and indigoes for blues. Contractors usually furnished a few standard sizes with wide seamage for later altering by the regimental tailors. Great numbers of the American forces had to serve with their civilian coats. As a Hessian described colonial troops at Saratoga's surrender, "Not a regiment was properly uniformed, but every man was in the clothes he wore in the field, at church, or at the ale-house." (19) An American officer with spontoon wearing the short light infantry coat. (20) A red velvet civilian coat, c. 1760; reportedly worn by a Col. Marchmants of Pennsylvania during the Revolution. (21) Close-up of the rear shoulder tailoring on a Loyalist officer's coat (Munson Hoyt of Norwalk, Conn.). (1) A common infantry officer or soldier coat pattern (American, British, plus some French and German); c. 1768–1783; note the low collar, tight sleeves, and heart shapes covering the "turnback" hooks and eyes. (2) The short light infantry coat (also see #19) including the "winged lapel" favored in New England.

Sources: 19—Brigade of the American Revolution, photo by Michael Cleary; 20—Edward Charol; 22—The Conn. Historical Society.

(3) A typical civilian design as used by militia and many non-uniformed regulars (see #20, p. 84). (4) A winter "Blanket Coat" (also "Canadian Capote," or "Watch Coat") made from a woolen blanket usually of light color with a stripe as shown. (5) Civilian cloak with an inner cape which could also be worn outside; 50" long, cape 37". **COCKADES** (also see "Headgear."): Practically all military hats and caps bore cockades. Traditionally of cloth, they varied their color by nationality or special units. The British enlisted men wore black, and the French, white. Some Germans, especially the jaegers, displayed green. The colonists adopted England's black but added a white rosette in 1780 to mark the French Alliance. (22) Various cockade patterns (opposite page); they were usually held by a button or colored cord and formed of silk, silklike ribbon, linen, mohair, or dimity. Militia and non-uniformed troops often put pine sprigs, paper, or similar temporary markings in their hats to achieve mutual identification. Among the officers, various colored cockades helped to identify rank—e.g. at the Battle of Long Island the field officers wore red, the captains used white, and the subalterns green (per Joseph Plumb Martin). **COFFEE MILL** (see page 88.)

Source: 5—Edward Charol.

COLORS ("Flags"): Flags of the Revolution fall into three basic groupings; first, those used at sea; second, garrison flags flown over forts and public buildings; third, military colors. The first two categories were generally made of bunting and included a canvas sleeve pierced for attachment to a halyard. The use of silk with a simple gold fringe and designs painted on each side was popular for military colors—although geometric designs were often made by sewing pieces of colored cloth together. Most regimental flags attached to 8–10 foot staffs by sleeves, while the Germans used four rows of brass tacks (about 1" apart). A comissioned officer (the "Ensign") normally carried the flag over his shoulder (as slings were not used) except during the observance of honors or when fully displayed in battle. These colors represented the regiment and its honor; their location marked the unit's official position in combat and to lose them to an enemy was a lasting disgrace.

Three official types of military flags were employed in the American Army. The national colors (e.g. the Grand Union and later the stars and stripes) have no evidence of ever being carried into battle by a unit of the Continental Army. The two types used by line regiments were the "Grand Division" (1776) or "Standard of the United States" (1779)—their designs are not known—plus the individual regimental flags.

The latter were assigned background colors by regimental number in 1775, and then adopted fields of their facing color in 1779. Following the European preference for two flags per regiment, the English Warrant of 1768 specified the "First Color" (King's Color) as the Union Flag, and the "Second Color" or regimental flag in the facing color of the regiment. It also specified regimental flag size as 6' 6" long by 6' high, but there is little uniformity in the surviving specimens of all forces. (1) Second Connecticut Regimental Flag (red silk field). (2) Colors of Col. John Proctor's Independent Battalion of Westmoreland County Militia, 1775 (red silk, 70" x 76"). (3) King's Colors of the British 9th Regt. of Foot. (4) French Saintonage Regimental Flag (a white Greek cross; each canton is blue, yellow, green, and red). (5) Regimental Colors of the Queens Rangers (light blue field). (6) Polaski's Legion Cavalry Guidon (red field, gold fringe). (7) American Grand Union, 1776 (red and white stripes) (8) A British Union Flag ("King's Color") with the crosses of St. George and St. Andrew. (9) Flag of France; gold design on a white field. (10) German Anspach Beyreuth Colors; design embroidered of a white damask field. (11) British Regimental Camp Color, i.e. 9th Regt on a field matching its facing color; 18" x 18". (12) Naval Flag flown on *Serapis* by John Paul Jones (1779); red, white, and blue stripes; blue field with white stars. (cont.)

COLORS (cont.) (1, 2) Excavated American iron flag staff tips (Champlain Valley). (3) Recreated regimental flag in battle. **COFFEE MILL:** In the 17th century, coffee beans were commonly ground in a mortar and pestle. By the time of the American Revolution—spurred by the great acceptance of coffee houses—portable brass coffee mills such as this were in use, and are still popular in some eastern Mediterranean countries. (4) Shown open and closed, with its removable folding handle; 10½″ long.

Sources: 1, 2—Frank J. Kravic; 3—Brigade of the American Revolution, photo by Richard Gerding; 4—George C. Neumann.

COMBS (also see "Wigs"): Generally rectangular in shape, head combs of the period were both single and double-edged. They were made of horn, bone, ivory, tortoiseshell, brass, pewter, and close-grained wood. Wig combs usually had widely spaced teeth which were rounded instead of rectangular in cross-section. (1) Wooden comb of a style usually found in pairs. (2) A double-edged brass example. COMPASSES, POCKET (also see "Naval," "Surveying," "Timekeeping"): The wide stretches of forest and uninhabited land in the colonies made the pocket compass a necessary accessory for most travelers. It utilized a rotating iron needle on a brass pivot and often added a folding sundial. (3) Germanic type compass and sundial, early 1700s. (4) A larger wooden cased compass with flat hinged cover and a glass enclosed needle; 4¼'' x 1''. (5) British brass type having a screw-on cap and folding sundial, c. 1750–1765; 2¼'' x ⅝''. (6) A turned wooden case using a glass covering over the hand painted face, circa 1750. (7) Wooden French compass and sundial (not folding) with a friction-fitted cover and small card mounted on the compass needle; circa 1760; the face is open and hand colored; 2½'' x 1⅝''.

COOKINGWARE (Also see "Eatingware," "Drinkingware"): Much of the cooking and domestic chores of the army were done by wives and women who accompanied their men. The British, for example, officially allowed six per company during the 1776–1777 campaign, and General Burgoyne sanctioned three per company; children, too, were fed and clothed from public stores. Probably the most commonly found piece of cookingware in camp sites is the iron pot. Most had both precast angular handle lugs set into the body mold before casting the rest of the pot. A rounded sprue mark in the center of the bottom occurs more often than the raised thin sprue line (which became more popular in the 1800s). Crude mold seams also often appear on both sides extending halfway down. Those illustrated here have been matched to excavated fragments. Brass and copper pots with iron supports for the handle were also widespread. Moreover, fragments indicate that copper and brass-made vessels were normally cut apart for other purposes once the original was damaged. (1) Large cast-iron camp kettle; 20" maximum diameter. (2, 3) Two smaller kettles; one is marked "Glasscow ½"; maximum diameters, 8", 7". Such types were issued to every 6 or 7 men (often with linen covers) and usually carried in the hand.

Source: Frank J. Kravic.

(4) Another cooking kettle pattern found in military sites. The mold mark on this base is a straight ridge along the bottom; maximum diameter, 12''. (5) Cast-iron teakettle having three short legs; mid-1770s. (6) A dipper hammered into its crude shape from a piece of sheet iron; excavated from a Pennsylvania soldier's hut circa 1775–1776. (7) Long handled iron frying pan; 46'' total length. (8) Wafer iron: in the 18th century thin wafers bearing the design cut into the face of the iron were rolled into a cone and filled with various sweet creams and syrups. The iron was first heated and then the batter put on the iron to be cooked by the retained heat. Similar irons with religious designs were employed for making communion wafers. (9, 10) Three-legged skillets which were placed over the coals; #10 was originally recovered from the American gondola, *Philadelphia*, 1776. (11) Iron trivet with a riveted handle. (12) Large copper pail includes iron bales and handle holders. (cont.)

Sources: 7, 8, 12—Frank J. Kravic; 9—Morristown National Historical park; 10—William Osborne; 11—Robert Nittolo.

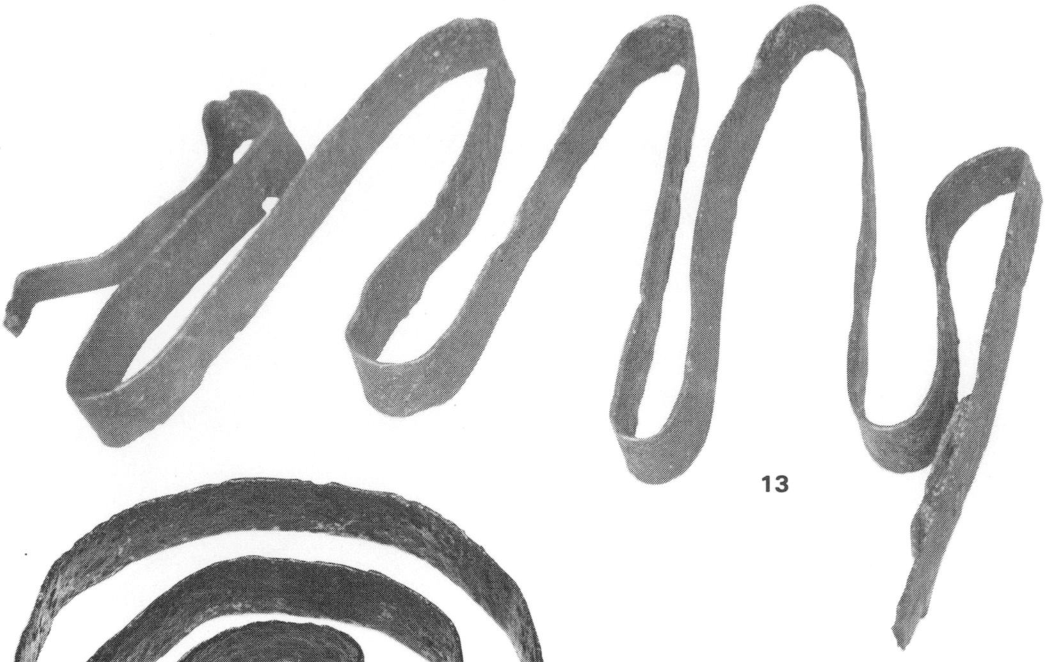

COOKING WARE (cont.) (13, 14) Iron barrel hoops were often cut and reshaped into broilers as shown here. (15) Pot hooks made using available material such as barrel hoops and bar iron; from military sites circa 1755–1778. (16) Pot hook with alternate heights. (17) Hook made from an old bayonet (American camp, 1775–1776). (18) The hastily collected American Army besieging Boston in 1775 needed supplies to maintain itself and Joseph Trumbull of Connecticut was appointed Commissary General. Here he records the beef supplied to various Boston camps by one of his assistant commissaries from Nov. 25 to Dec. 4, 1775.

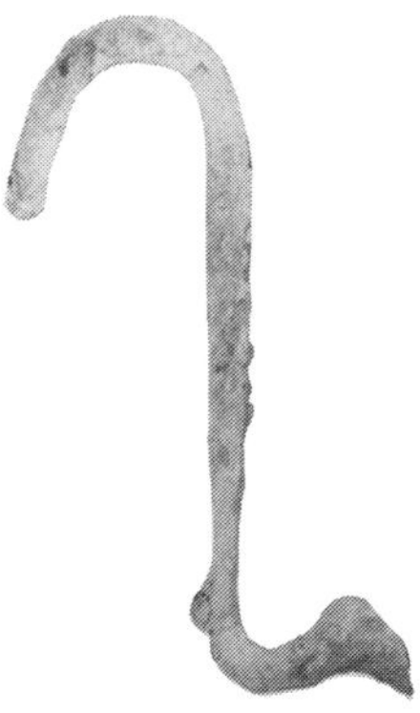

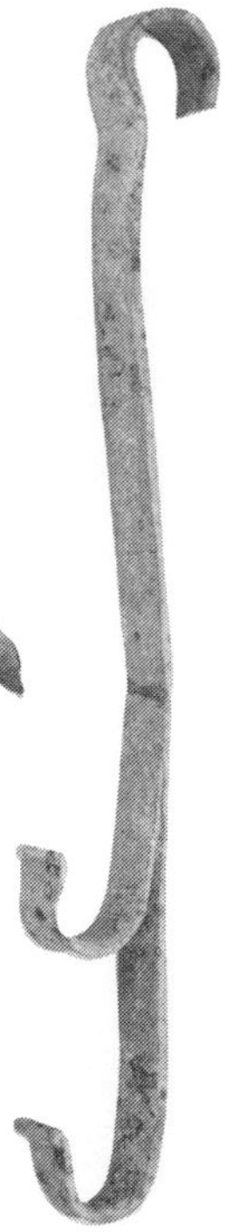

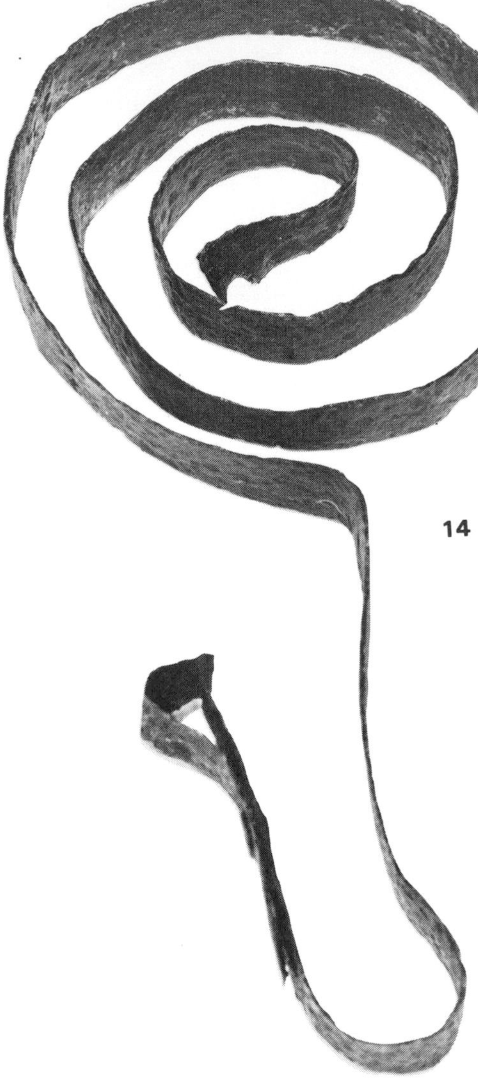

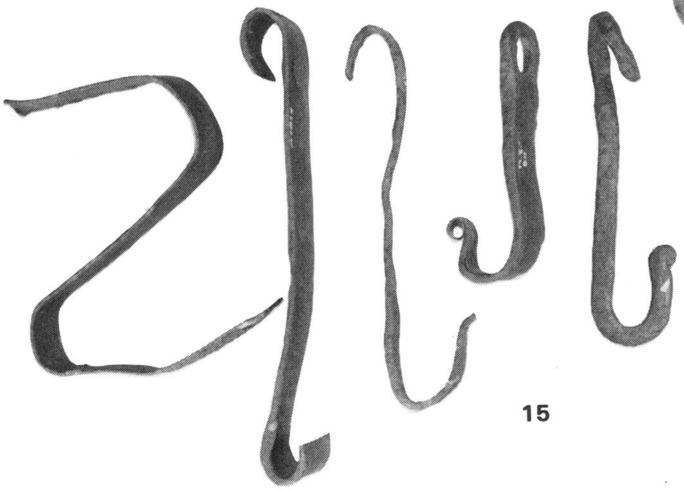

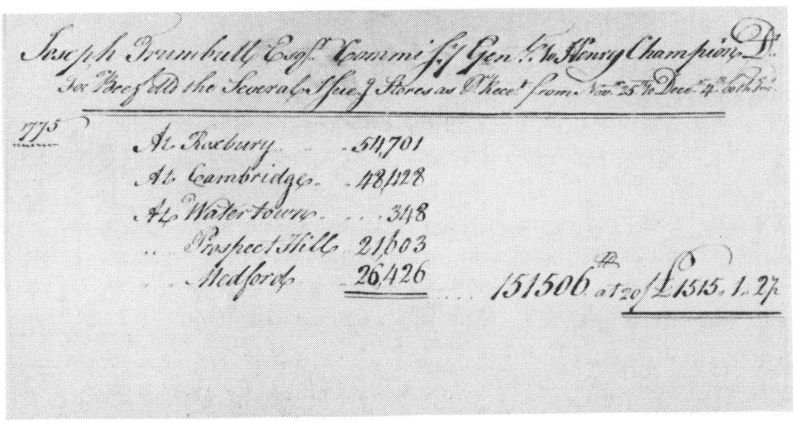

Sources: 13—Morristown National Historical Park; 14—New-York Historical Society; 15–18—Frank J. Kravic.

(20, 21) Two gridirons for broiling; from camps circa 1776–1780. (22) Rotating gridiron; (23) Skewer, circa 1776–1780 site. (24) A typical toaster used in front of the fire; the handle flips over to turn the toast. (cont.)

Sources: 19—Brigade of the American Revolution, photo by Michael Cleary; 20, 24—Frank J. Kravic; 21, 23—George C. Neumann; 22—Webb, Deane, Stevens Museum, N.S.C.D.A.

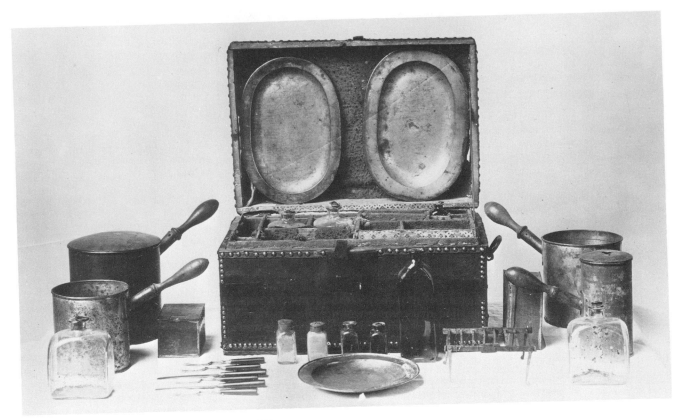

25

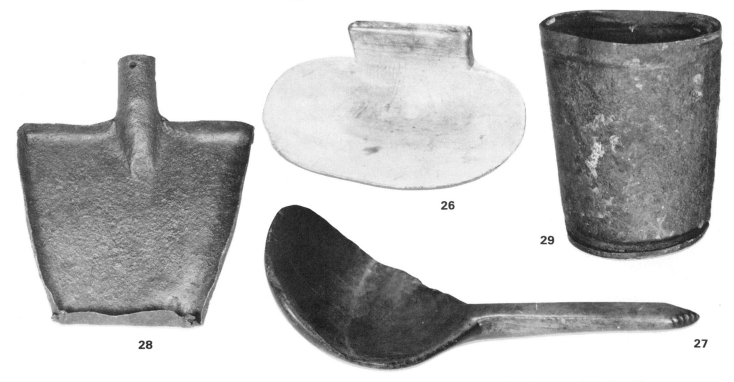

26

28

27

29

COOKINGWARE (cont.) (25) George Washington's mess kit; leather covers a wooden frame and it is lined by green wool. The interior divides into 14 compartments, and a removable tray adds 9 more. Equipment includes 6 tin plates, 3 tin platters, 4 tin pots having detachable handles (wood), 2 knives, 4 forks (black handles), a gridiron with folding legs, 2 tinder boxes, 2 glass bottles for holding salt and pepper (pewter tops), plus 8 glass bottles using cork stoppers. (26) Wooden scoop. (27) A cherry spoon for mixing, dipping, or eating. (28) An 18th century shovel converted into a cooking pan. (29) Tin container excavated from a military camp c. 1760–1780; while tinned iron deteriorates rapidly in soil, many fragments are found, indicating a wide and varied use of this material.

Sources: 25—Smithsonian Institution; 26—Diana M. Neumann; 27, 29—Frank J. Kravic; 28—Morristown National Historical Park.

(30) Wooden container style, circa 1750–1850, used variously to hold herbs, cheese, sugar, meal, spices, butter, and jewelry; it was usually fastened by handwrought nails or wooden pegs. (30a) A staved holder for dry material. (31, 32) Portable iron braziers which held coals in the bottom for a variety of uses, e.g. heating wig curling irons, cooking, or just adding heat to a room or hut. (33) Copper pan brazier with iron legs and points. (34) Earthenware baking pots; this type is often found on French-American sites. Crudely glazed in yellow or red with distinctive handles, such vessels date from the 18th century until about 1840. (35) Redware baking pots; redware fragments are found in Revolutionary War trash heaps although its greatest popularity was reached in the early 1800s. These three glazed pots were favored for baking foods such as beans and rice pudding; circa 1770–1840. (cont.)

Sources: 30, 31, 34, 35—Frank J. Kravic; 30a, 32, 33—George C. Neumann.

COOKINGWARE (cont.) (36) Corn and other grains were ground in large mortars and pestles made from partially hollowed tree trunks when mills were not available; 21″ high. **CORKSCREWS** (also see "Bottles"): The long corks in bottles could most easily be removed by a corkscrew. Some even had a small brush in the wooden handle to wipe away the dirt and dust before opening. Note that the iron spirals in these examples are round in cross-section vs. the latter flattened shape. **CROSS-STRAPS** (see "Belts, Frogs, Scabbards.") **CROSSES, CRUCIFIXES** (also see "Trade Ornaments, Indian"): A common trade item to the Indians, especially from the Catholic French, were crosses made of silver, brass or other metals. They vary greatly in size and workmanship with many of the silver ones hallmarked in Europe or Canada. (5) A thin silver cross 9¾″ long; attributed to Robert Cruickshank of Montreal, c. 1770–1780. (6) Crucifix. (7) A brass Cross of Lorraine, c. 1750; 3¾″ tall. (8) A smaller similar cross of silver; 1¾″ high. (9) Large thin silver example that is 7¼″ in length; c. 1775–1800. **CUFF LINKS:** Cuff links are often found bearing hearts, cupids, and symbols of love—as if given to a soldier by his dear ones. (10) The eyelets of this cast pair are linked with a single looped metal wire.

96   *Sources: 36, 1-4, 9, 10–Frank J. Kravic; 5, 7, 8–Edward Charol; 6–George Juno.*

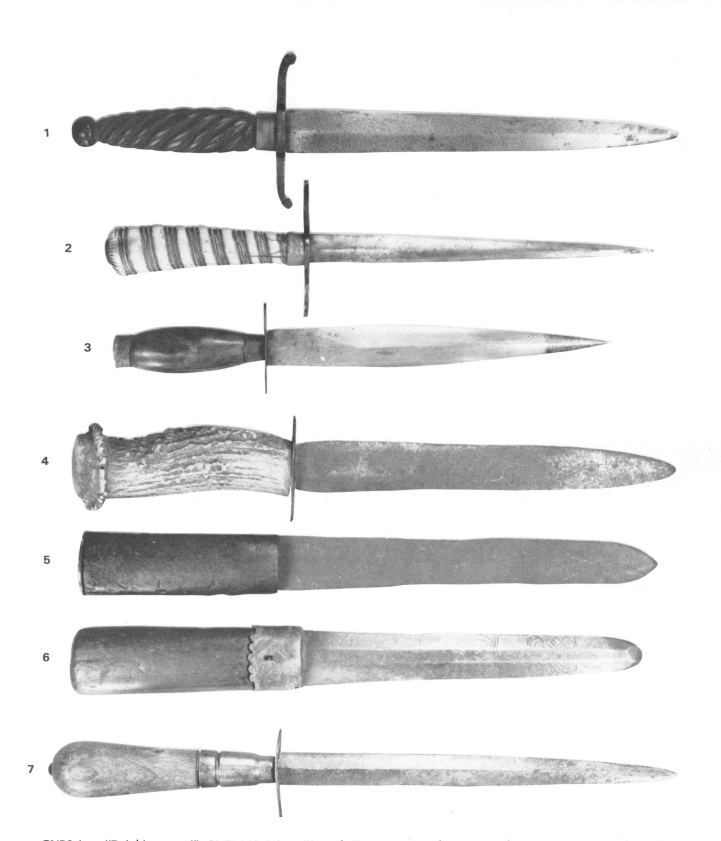

CUPS (see "Drinkingware.") **CUTLASSES** (see "Swords.") **DAGGERS** (also see "Dirks," "Knives"): Developed for fighting, daggers traditionally had a straight symmetrical double-edged blade designed for thrusting and stabbing. Although "unofficial" weapons in the Revolution, many were carried as personal arms—especially by the frontiersmen and militia who often lacked bayonets for close infighting: (1) A belt dagger with down-turned iron guard and carved horn grip; circa 1770–1800; 15" length. (2) European; ivory grip and a horizontally curved "S" guard; c. 1750–1790; 13⅝" long. (3) American, mounting a cherry wood grip, and elliptical iron guard; c. 1720–1800; 12¼" overall. (4) American, circa 1750–1850; antler grip plus a blade shaped from an old file; 13¼" length. (5) A simple cylindrical wooden hilt; 12¼" long; probably 1700–1800. (6) The wooden grip has a pewter base and secures a faceted blade fashioned from an old sword; circa 1750–1800. (7) American dagger having an iron guard and ferrule; 12½" overall; c. 1750–1820.

Source: George C. Neumann.

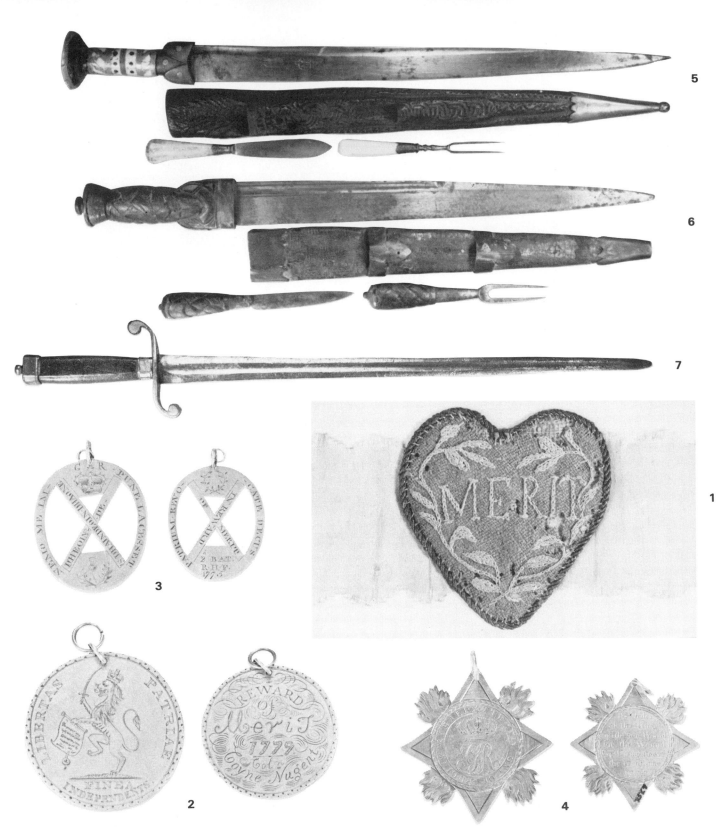

DECORATIONS, MERIT: Military decorations were rare in the War for Independence. Those which were awarded covered length of service, good conduct, and bravery in action. On August 17, 1782 the "Honorary Badge of Distinction" was created for American noncoms and privates having honorably served more than three years. They were permitted to attach a narrow white cloth "in angular form" on the left arm of the uniform coat. Two were granted for six years. (The color was shortly changed to match the coat facings.) Also in August 1782 Washington created the "Badge of Military Merit" for unusual gallantry and meritorious actions. It was the first decoration ever awarded American enlisted men for bravery and consisted of a purple heart of silk or cloth edged with lace or binding, and worn over the facings on the left breast. (1) The Badge of Military Merit awarded to Sgt. Elijah Churchill, Second Continental Dragoons, on May 1, 1783 at New Windsor, N.Y. Other awards were made by localities to their heros; the British also issued special decorations—but traditionally within the regiment. (2) Probably American; a "Reward of Merit" marked "1779," "Col. Coyne Nugent;" it is flat, silver, 2" in diameter, and may have been an award to a member of his regiment. (3) A silver British decoration inscribed "In Reward of Merit, 2d Bat. RHF 1775."

Sources: 1—New Windsor Cantonment; 2, 3, 4—Edward Charol; 5, 6, 7—George C. Neumann.

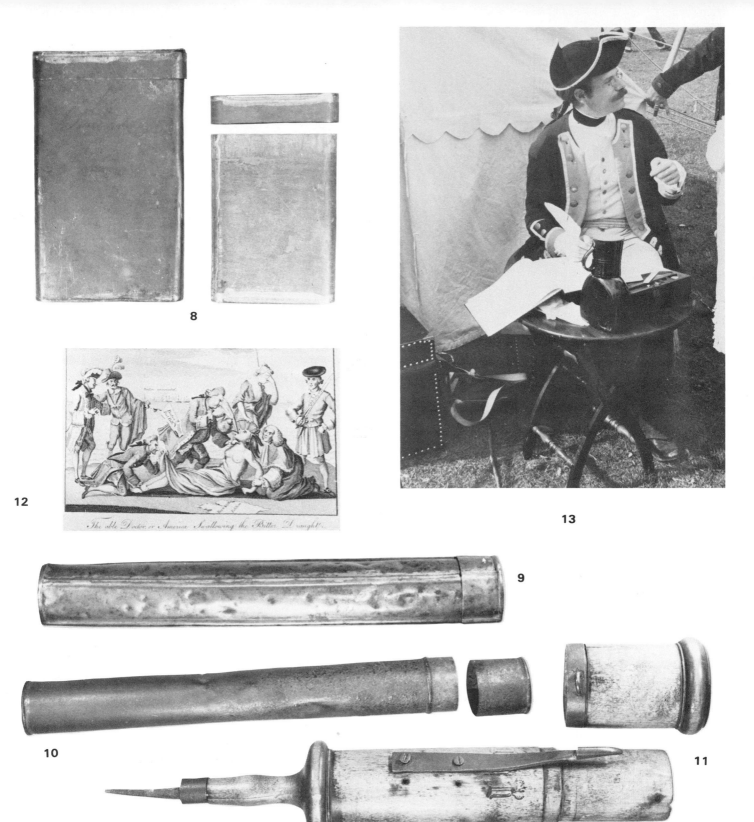

(4) British silver decoration, "A Testimony of Public Regard," "By Order of the King with 300 Pound for the wound Capt. Ewing Reev^d the 17 of June 1775." Lt. Peter Ewing of the 1st Marine Battalion lost an arm at Bunker Hill on this date; he became a Captain in 1781 and died during 1794. **DIRKS** (also see "Daggers," "Knives."): The dirk was originally a dagger type weapon with an even tapered blade of which only one edge was sharpened. By the end of the Revolution it had also come to designate a naval side arm with either a knife or dagger blade. (5) Scotch dirk, c. 1675–1700; ivory and horn hilt with pewter bands; German marked blade; its early sheath is typically not metal bound and holds the knife and fork in side pockets; 19⅞" length. (6) Scotch, c. 1725–1750; carved wooden grip with a flat brass cap; by this date the sheath is brass bound; 19⅛" overall. (7) English naval dirk, c. 1780–1820; the rectangular wooden grip was originally bound with twisted brass ropes; 19½" length. **DOCUMENTS** (also see "Books," "Periodicals," "Tactics, Battle"): (8) Personal document holders of tinned iron; c. 1750–1850; 7" and 4¾" long. (9, 10) Metal document and dispatch holders; 12" and 12¼" lengths (11) Wooden message container with a spike to thrust into a tree or post for couriers; c. 1720. (12) English anti-Tory cartoon, 1774–1775. (13) A junior German officer. (cont.)

Sources: *8, 9, 10—George C. Neumann; 11—Edward Charol; 12—Frank J. Kravic; 13—Brigade of the American Revolution, photo by Michael Cleary.*

99

JONATHAN TRUMBULL, Esquire,

Governor and Commander in Chief, of his Majesty's Colony of CONNECTICUT in NEW-ENGLAND.

To *Samuel Chapman Esqr* GREETING.

WHEREAS you are appointed by the General Assembly of said Colony to be *Colonel* of the *twenty second* Regiment of Horse and Foot in said Colony. Reposing special Trust and Confidence in your Loyalty, Courage, Care, and good Conduct, I DO, by these Presents, constitute and appoint you to be *Colonel* of said Regiment. You are therefore to take the said Regiment into your Care and Charge as their *Colonel* and carefully and diligently to discharge that Care and Trust in ordering and exercising of them, both Officers and Soldiers in Arms, according to the Rules and Discipline of War: keeping them in good Order and Government, and commanding them to obey you as their *Colonel* for his Majesty's Service, and they are commanded to obey you accordingly. And you are to conduct and lead forth the said Regiment, or such Part of them as you shall from Time to Time receive Orders from me, or from the Governor of this Colony for the Time being, to encounter, repel, pursue and destroy, by Force of Arms, and by all fitting Ways and Means, all his Majesty's Enemies, who shall at any Time hereafter in a hostile Manner, attempt or enterprize the Invasion, Detriment, or Annoyance of this Colony. And you are to observe and obey such Orders and Instructions as from Time to Time you shall receive from me, or other your Superior Officers, pursuant to the Trust hereby reposed in you, and the Laws of this Colony.

GIVEN under my Hand, and the Seal of this Colony, in *Hartford* the *30th* Day of *May* in the *15* Year of the Reign of our Sovereign Lord GEORGE the Third, King of Great-Britain, &c. Annoque Domini, 1775.

By His Honor's Command,

George Wyllys Secretary

Jon. Trumbull

1

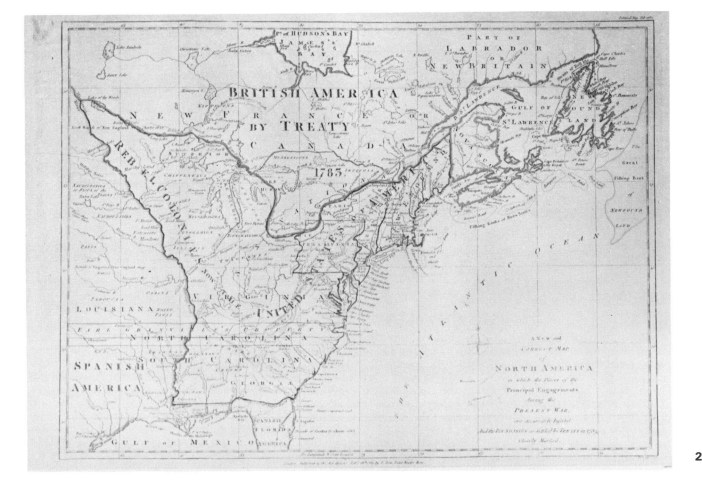

2

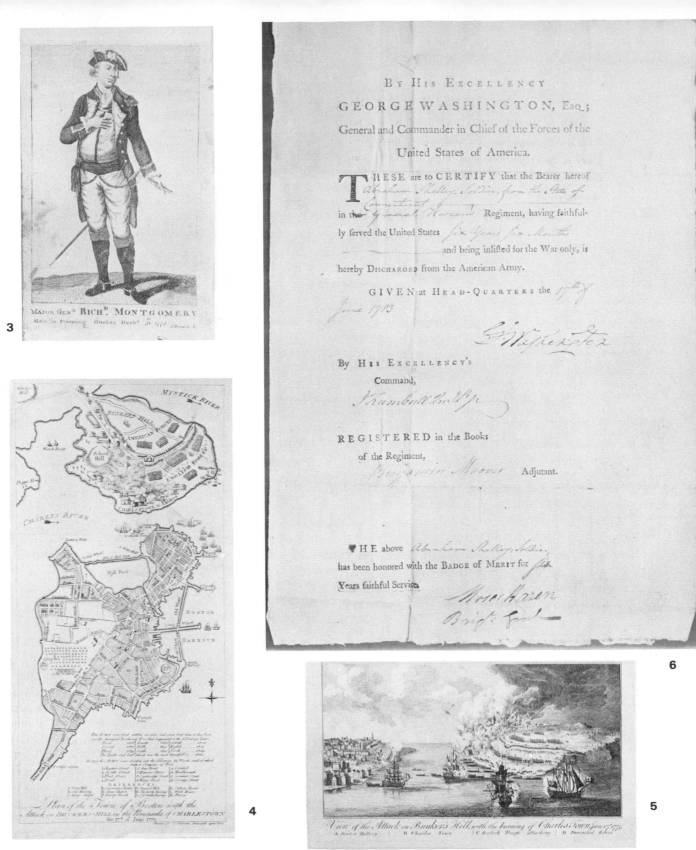

DOCUMENTS (cont.) Paper in the 18th century was made of linen that had been pulled apart to make a thick slurry when suspended in liquid. This was then poured onto a fine screen which retained the linen and dried as a sheet of paper. The lasting quality of such acid-free stock is attested to by the fine condition of the many documents, books, newspapers, and prints which have survived from this period. (1) An early commission in the fledgling colonial army for a Connecticut officer, signed by Jonathan Trumbull, Governor, on May 15, 1775. Note that at this time, prior to the Declaration of Independence, the man was being appointed to deal with "His Majesty's Enemies," i.e. the British Army opposing them was considered the Ministerial Army of Parliament and they were the King's troops upholding the rights of Englishmen and the King. (2) A map from an English political magazine dated Feb. 28, 1783 and titled, "Rebel Colonies now the United States of America." (3) An American print of General Montgomery, 1776; 4" x 6⅜" without borders. (4) English map print, 1775, "Plan of the Town of Boston with the Attack on Bunkers-Hill in the Peninsula of Charlestown the 17th of June 1775." (5) An American print of the Battle of Bunker Hill, 1775; 7¾" x 4¾" print size. (6) In 1783, when the soldiers of the Continental Army were sent home, General Washington personally signed thousands of these honorable discharges. (cont.)

Source: Frank J. Kravic.

1

2

3

4

DOCUMENTS (cont.) (1) A discharge from the Loyalist Regiment of the famed New York Tory leader, Lt. Col. Oliver DeLancey. (2) A mezzotint of George III done in 1761 just after he assumed the throne; a typical print that would have been displayed in public buildings and the homes of staunch loyalists; 9⅞″ x 14″. (3) English, c. 1690; there was such great interest in the early colonies by Europeans that many enterprising printers issued fanciful illustrations of the wild new world; this represents upstate New York. (4) An English map of the battle areas in the Philadelphia region; from the London Magazine, 1777; 9¾″ x 7½″.

Sources: 1—Edward Charol; 2, 3, 4—Frank J. Kravic.

DRAGOONS (see "Horsemen.") **DRINKINGWARE** (also see "Bottles," "Canteens," "Cookingware," "Eatingware"): There was a wide range of drinking containers in the military camps. Liquor chests of the officers (see "Bottles") carried fine goblets, and the soldiers drank from whatever was available. Camps also had traveling taverns that settled on their outskirts, as well as the regular army sutler shops which provided drinking vessels. (2) Horn cups. (3) Crude wooden cup. (4) A handle cup fashioned from a burl. (5, 6) Popular tinned iron cups; #6 is from a Hessian site in New York City. (7) A small portable copper still; apparently the mash was added and slung on the back or carried in a wagon where the motion during the day hastened its fermentation. In the evening the stopper was removed and a wooden plug with a hole inserted. A copper coil was then entered into the hole and the whole unit placed in a fire. As the distillation began a cup would catch the daily yield of beverage. (cont.)

Sources: 1—Brigade of the American Revolution, photo by Richard Gerding; 2, 3, 5—George C. Neumann; 4—Diana M. Neumann; 6—New-York Historical Society; 7—Gerard L. Gruber.

3

1   2

DRINKINGWARE (cont.) (1, 2) Following the barrelmaking skills of the cooper, wooden tankards were often constructed of slats, a fitted bottom, and wooden retaining bands. Carved handles and lids completed a very serviceable drinking container. (1) Tankard used in the War for Independence by Major Benjamin Throop of Bozrah, Ct.; 7½″ high. (2) An example from Pennsylvania with typical designs of that area; 4⅝″ in height.

Sources: 1—The Connecticut Historical Society; 2—Mercer Museum, Bucks County Historical Society; 3—Brigade of the American Revolution, photo by Michael Cleary.

(1, 2, 3) Pewter drinking mugs typical of the second half of the 18th century in shape and styling. This heavy alloy metal contains lead in varying amounts and was considered more fit for common people. The makers often impressed their identity marks in the base or on the sides, which aids in determining dates and origins. (4) A thin sheet iron quart mug. Crude drinking vessels such as this found their way into the many taverns and inns on both sides of the Atlantic at that time; they were rugged, durable, and inexpensive to make. (5) Stoneware drinking mug with scratch blue incised squares, c. 1750. (6) A flip glass with a wooden toddy stick for mixing. Flip was a mixture of beer, spirits, and sugar; it was commonly made by warming and spicing ale, to which brandy and eggs were added. The mixture was poured from one mug to another until it frothed and creamed, then returned to the original mixing vessel where it was reheated by a hot loggerhead thrust into the liquid. (7) Drinkingware ranging from simple tavern glasses to fine air and ribbon twist stemware; many of the officers' liquor chests contained these items; c. 1750–1780; (l to r): (1st and 2nd) bar glasses, (3rd) a stem glass, (4th–7th) ribbon twist goblets, (8th) air twist stemware. (cont.)

Sources: 1—Mercer Museum; 2, 6, 7—Frank J. Kravic; 3—William H. Guthman; 4—George C. Neumann; 5—Fortress Louisbourg.

8

9

10

11

12

DRINKINGWARE (cont.) (8) Renish stoneware with an incised scratch blue design which includes "GR" for King George; 10" high; c. 1760–1800. (9) A large French military pitcher of copper; 16½" tall. (10) Pitcher carved from one piece of wood. (11) A high wooden "noggin" that was usually passed from mouth to mouth. (12) Large stoneware pitcher having an incised scratch blue design; c. 1760–1780; the number "2" refers to its stated capacity.

Sources: 8—William H. Guthman; 9—Edward Charol; 10, 11—George C. Neumann; 12—Frank J. Kravic.

14

15

19

17

16

18

20

21

(13) French faience, mid-18th century; sometimes referred to as niederwiler, this delftware jug with its pewter top is richly decorated in green, yellow, blue, and black; height, 7½". (14) A slipware earthenware jug found in Virginia. (15) A redware jug also from Virginia and much heavier than #14; c. 1770–1820. (16) Decorated redware with its original cork; such a style covers a long period of manufacture in America and Europe (c. 1770–1850), but this shape is typical of the Revolutionary War era. (17) Plain stoneware jug; c. 1750–1820. (18) An early two-handled Germanic pattern found in the Dutch area of Albany, N.Y. (19) While blue decorated gray stoneware is normally associated with the 19th century, this crude specimen in form and shape typifies fragments excavated from Revolutionary sites (Mohawk Valley, N.Y.). (20) Glazed redware jar of red and yellow; c. 1770–1820. (21) (At left) An English teapot, cup and saucer typical of the Dr. Wall Worcester porcelains dating from 1751–1783; (center) An English porcelain sauce boat representative of the underglaze blue decorated porcelains exported to America in the 1700s; c. 1770. (upper right) Leedsware creamer from England handpainted over the glaze; c. 1760–1790; (lower right) A common mustard pot having a feather edge below the rim; English, c. 1760–1820. (cont.)

Source: Frank J. Kravic.

DRINKINGWARE (cont.) Dippers for liquids were created out of a number of materials and changed little in shape through the 1700s and 1800s. Some were quite fragile as those made from dried gourds (2, 3); 15″ and 19″ lengths—while others were fashioned out of wood (1, 4). (5) A dipper manufactured from horn with a whistle in the handle; it was left by Hessians in Long Island, N.Y.; 13″ length. (6, 7) Brass brandy warmers which heated the beverage over a candle during the 18th century. **DRUMS, DRUMMERS** (see "Music.") **EATINGWARE** (also see "Cookingware," "Drinkingware," "Knives," "Molds"): Spoons were also fashioned from a variety of materials during the 1700s; easily melted lead or pewter was poured into molds, as were the three at the left (see "Molds"; these were excavated from American military debris, c. 1760–1780); the center spoon is of silver, c. 1770–1790; (5th from left) one carved out of wood, c. 1750–1850; (6th and 7th) both shaved and carved from horn, c. 1750–1850.

Sources: 1—The Connecticut Historical Society; 2, 3—Mercer Museum, Bucks County Historical Society; 4, 6—George C. Neumann; 5—Nassau County Museum (N.Y.); 7, 8-Frank J. Kravic.

108

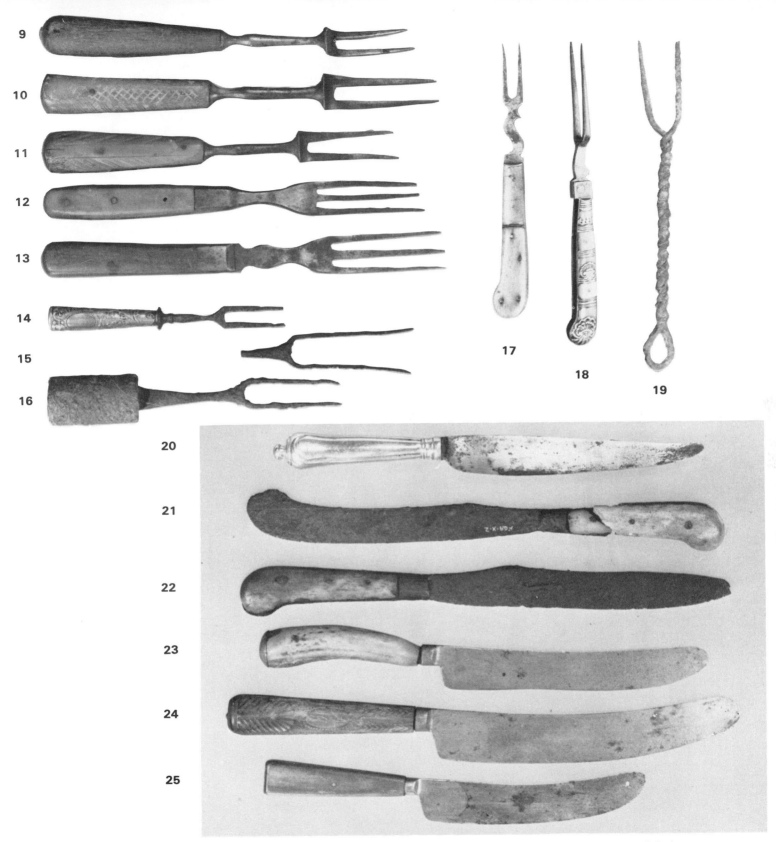

Forks are rarely found in camp debris, whereas spoons and knives are quite common. (9, 10, 11) 2-tined forks, c. 1750–1820. (12, 13) Such 3-tined types have been found in British camps in New York City. (14) A small 2-tined silver-handled specimen; c. 1760. (15, 16) Excavated from circa 1759–1777 camps; #16 had been broken and refitted with a wooden handle and holding sleeve. (17, 18) Personal forks with folding blades. (19) A crude fork of twisted iron; from an American site. Various table knives have been recovered in quantity out of military camps: (20) a silver-handled Dutch example with its iron blade tang extending through the grip to the rear capstan; circa 1700–1730. (21, 22) Table knives found in British camps of 1759–1777; both have bone panels attached by iron pins. (23) Staghorn grip; circa 1760–1840. (24, 25) Horn handles; dated c. 1780–1840. (cont.)

Sources: 9–13, 20, 23–25 George C. Neumann; 14–16, 21, 22—Frank J. Kravic; 17, 18—William H. Guthman; 19—Robert Nittolo.

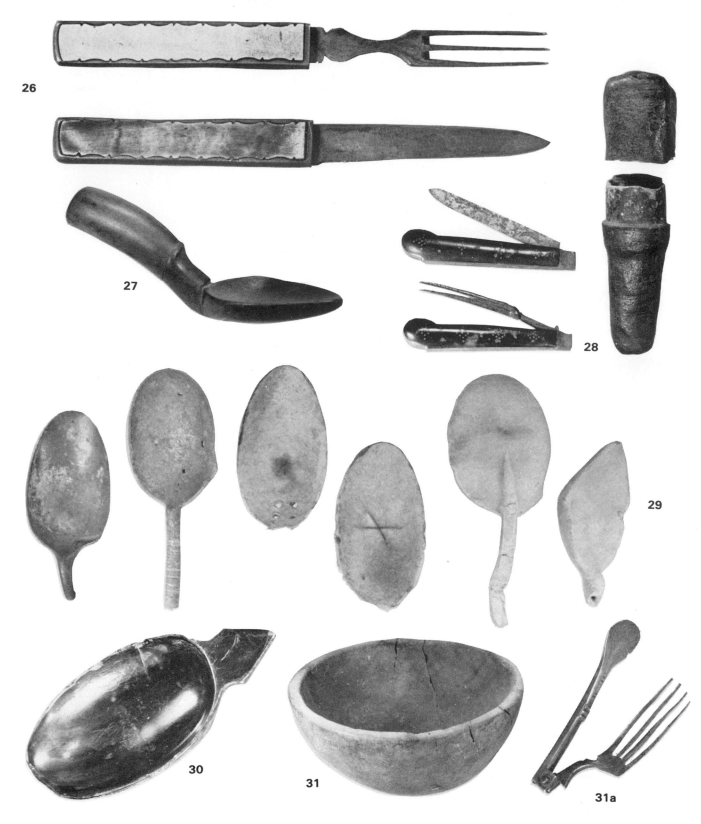

EATINGWARE (cont.) (26) Camp fork and knife set with horn panels presented to Lord Stirling by General Washington. (27) American wooden spoon; circa 1750. (28) A folding knife and fork set with their carrying case of pressed paper; c. 1770–1820. (29) Reused spoon bowls (with their handles broken off) excavated from American camps, c. 1775–1777; the first four are pewter and show various markings, repairs, and decorations. The two at the right are made of lead. (30) A horn spoon with short handle; c. 1760–1850. (31) Wooden bowls for home use were best made from the swirled growth rings of burls which reduced the danger of drying cracks. However, the quantities needed for army use led to much production from regular wood. (31a) A folding fork of brass and iron; dated "1782."

Sources: 26—Mt. Vernon Ladies Assn.; 27, 30, 31a—George C. Neumann; 28—William H. Guthman; 29, 31—Frank J. Kravic.

(32) Common wooden trencher or plate carried by most of the troops. (33, 34) Typical pewter plates; few specimens of pewter are found in camp debris since damaged items were melted down for other uses. (35) English Punch bowl; this type of delft was very popular in the first half of the 18th century and often carried political, patriotic, or military sayings, e.g. the fragment of a similar piece inscribed "Success to Jeffrey Amherst" was excavated at Fort Ticonderoga. A great deal of eatingware was imported from China at this time and fragments are found in many sites. (36) Clobbered Chinese export bowl;, as shipped from China to Europe where additional designs were often added; 6" x 3". (37) Chinese export bowl (Canton type, c. 1780–1830); as the 18th century came to a close the finely executed Chinese export porcelains became much more debased in decoration; details were blended together in crowded underglaze blue designs as seen here in the common house, boat, tree, and bridge motif which continued until about 1830; size, 5¾" x 2¼". (38) English Leedsware bowl, c. 1760–1780; this was a soft paste artificial poreclain of ground glass stiffened with white clay. (39) A redware plate as produced for use in America from 1770–1830. (40) Poor quality delft-like plate with a blue imitation Chinese figure; probably from southern France in the 1770s. (cont.)

Sources: 32—George C. Neumann; 35—William H. Guthman; remainder Frank J. Kravic.

EATINGWARE (cont) (41) Wooden bowl from an Indian source, circa 1760–1840. (42) Such tinned sheet iron bowls were made from about 1750 until at least 1840. The shallow angle of these places them early in that period; partial specimens have been recovered from Revolutionary War camps with the same construction details. Tin does not survive well, but the many fragments excavated indicate popular usage in military sites. (43) Saltglaze plates and platter; by the mid-1700s the British were producing this common tableware in great quantities. More durable than delftware, its fragmented pieces are recovered from the camps in large quantity. Various patterns were made including the "Bread and Reed" (left), "Dot, Diaper, and Basket" (center), and the "Barley" design (lower right). Saltglaze was produced in large amounts until just after the War for Independence.

Sources: 41—David Currie; 42, 43—Frank J. Kravic.

(44) A fine saltglaze plate with piercings and raised design; c. 1760–1780. (45) Chinese export porcelain plate, c. 1780–1820; As the 1700s drew to a close the basic shape of plates began to change as seen here; note that the two rises in the rim are sharply angled and noticeably dished. The griffith figure is probably a family crest as often ordered on sets of such wares. (46) A large continental European faience plate; early 18th century. (47) Whieldon type dinner plate, about 1760–1780; from Staffordshire, England. This creamware in the "Dot, diaper, and basket" pattern has been decorated in various colors to produce a clouded glaze; 9" diameter. (48–50) Chinese export plates, c. 1750–1780. Military campsites yield quantities of various types of dishware, but none is more prevalent than the Chinese export porcelain plates as illustrated here. They formed the basis for a large business in the colonies—being imported first to England and from there to America. The more cluttered scene with the elaborate border and undulating rim (50) dates from the latter part of the period; the simple, clearer designs were earlier; 6½" to 9" diameters. (51) Waterford style salt holder; circa 1750. Such fine molded glass items would have found their way to the officer's table in America. The presence of delicate glassware in colonial military and Revolutionary War sites attests to the elegance enjoyed by the commissioned ranks; size, 2¾" x 3⅝". (cont.)

Source: Frank J. Kravic.

EATINGWARE (cont.) (52) An English delft platter finely done in blue. (53) Faience bowl of the late 18th to early 19th centuries; this is a tin-enamelware product in soft blue (8¾" dia.), and is typical of southern Europe or France. (54) Delftware plate, c. 1760–1770; the British prevention of imports to America of continental European painted earthenware was in force until the War for Independence. Thus, prior to that date we can expect to find few examples in the colonies except from the spurious West Indian trade. With the outbreak of war such merchandise began to be imported; this overglaze hand painted faience or delftware plate is typical of such European exports and often associated with the Roen area of France; 9" diameter. (55) English creamware shakers, c. 1760 (probably from the Leeds factories); they ordinarily held pepper or sugar and provided a fill hole and stopper in the base. **EPAULETTES:** (1) A pair of American officer epaulettes (two sides; 9" as shown) illustrating the inner linen crinoline lining and large bullion over the smaller strands.

Sources: 56—Brigade of the American Revolution, photo by Wayne M. Daniels; 1—William H. Guthman; remainder, Frank J. Kravic.

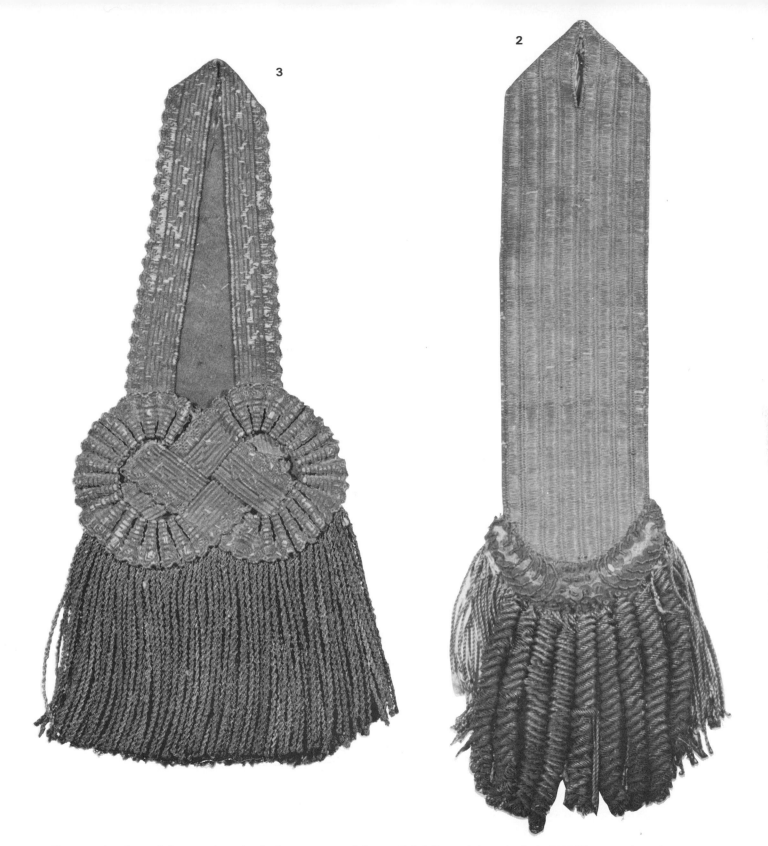

The French adopted the epaulette in the late 1750s, and the English followed them in their 1768 Warrant. Americans also wore epaulettes throughout the Revolution. In the British Army, light infantry and grenadier company officers had two; all other officers were limited to one (right shoulder for infantry; left for cavalry). Their sergeants normally wore sashes, but corporals carried a silk epaulette or cord or the right shoulder. America's Army in 1775 ordered sergeants to wear a red epaulette or strip of red cloth on the right shoulder; corporals used the same in green. By 1779 sergeants and corporals of infantry had white worsted epaulettes, the artillery employed yellow, and dragoon noncoms, farriers, plus saddlers used blue (on both shoulders for sergeants; on the right for corporals). American commissioned officers finally adopted a system in 1780: generals to majors wore two, all others used one (on the right for captains; left among subalterns; silver designated infantry or cavalry, gold represented artillery). The French favored the embroidered "looped" or double rosette style, while most Germans retained the earlier shoulder knots, yet portraits indicate a wide latitude in actual use. (2) Popular American pattern with a strip of lace and metal sequins over the juncture with its heavy and light boullion; 8¾" long. (3) Early embroidered type having two rosettes of lace at the juncture of crescent and boullion; presented by Lafayette to Capt. Samuel Craig, 1st Pa. Rgt., 1777; 8¾" length.

Sources: 2, 3-New-York Historical Society.

115

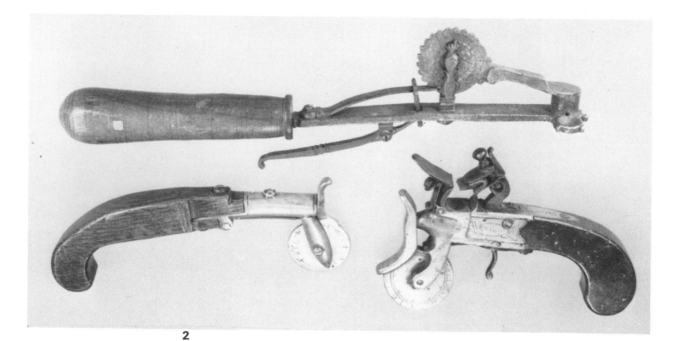

1

3

2

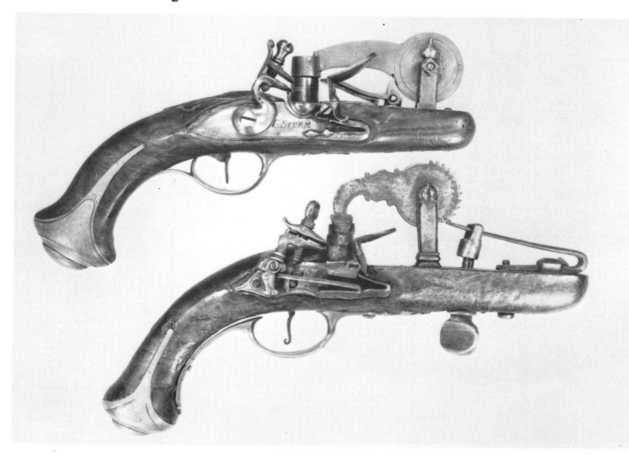

4

5

EPROUVETTES ("Powder Testers"; also see "Gunpowder," "Flintlock, Action"): Since gunpowder varied greatly due to the impurity of ingredients, its tendency to absorb moisture, and outright adulteration—i.e. the adding of coal dust, soot, or even dirt—it was necessary for most users to test the strength of each lot. This was usually done by an eprouvette. Its method was to ignite a measured amount of powder in a short barrel or chamber; this ignition, in turn, pushed up a rotating wheel with numbers on its face to register the powder's force. (1) European, dated 1703; an iron match ignition pattern probably fired by a hot wire, coal, or slow match held outside the touch hole at the far right; the wheel ratchets operated against the curved spring; 11" long. (2) English "match" or "Queen Anne" type with a brass body and walnut pistol grip. The smooth wheel rotated against a steel spring under the barrel; early 18th century. (3) British flintlock "box lock" ignition, c. 1775–1810; brass plus a wooden handle. (4) German pistol type, c. 1740; it fired the powder in a short vertical iron barrel by the action of the pistol size flintlock; the smooth brass wheel rubbed against a friction spring (numbers on the reverse side); marked "C STURM, Suhl," 10" long. (5) Spanish eprouvette with a miguelet lock; c. 1750-60.

116   *Source: George C. Neumann.*

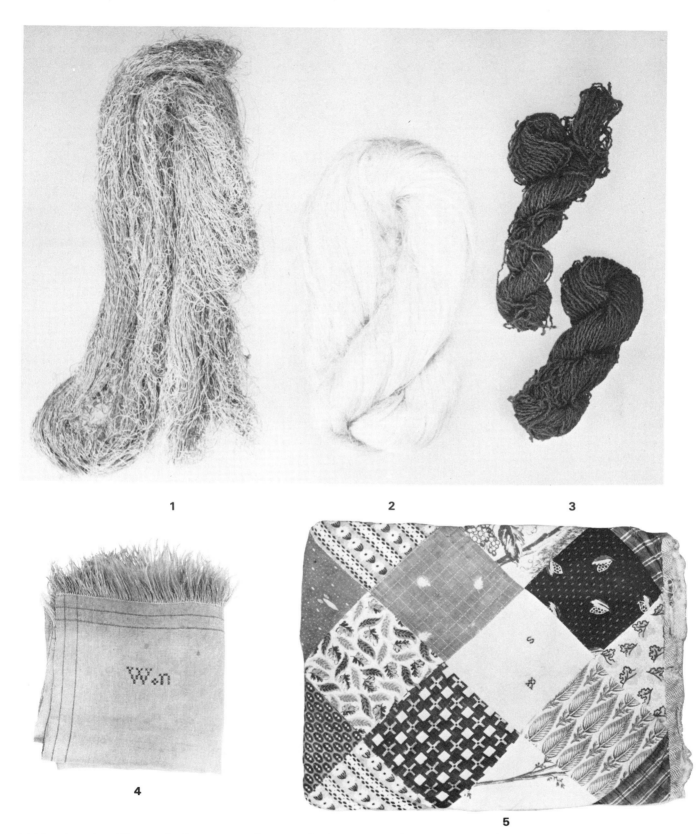

1   2   3

4

5

EYEGLASSES (see "Spectacles.") **FABRIC** (also see "Blankets," "Breeches," "Coats," "Shirts," "Waistcoats"): Americans at this time raised most of their own flax for linen and sheep for wool—the two primary fabrics. (1) Heavy tow linen used for sacks, mattresses, tents, and other needs requiring strength. (2) More finely hetcheled linen for making cloth and clothing. (3) Dyed 2-ply wool as employed in homespun blankets, etc. (4) A linen towel used by General Washington. (5) Import prints; these are squares of representative cotton and linen prints which were available to the American colonists from England.

Sources: 1, 2, 3—Elaine Salls; 4—Mt. Vernon Ladies Assn.; 5—Frank J. Kravic.

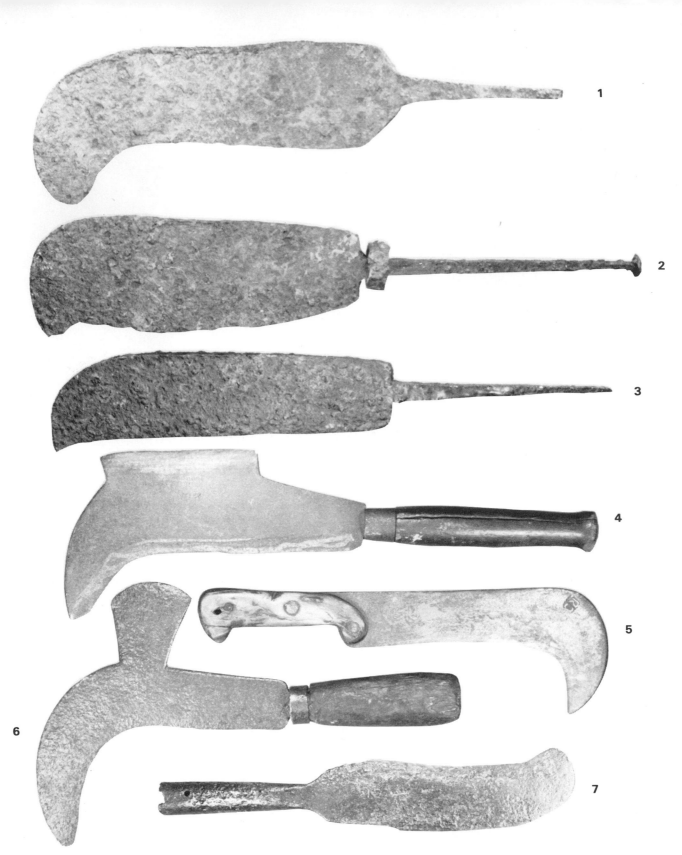

FASCINE KNIVES ("Bill Hooks"): These were cutting tools used in clearing brush and light growth. They were officially issued to the troops for engineering purposes, but because of the large numbers recovered from military sites, must have been a common camp implement. (1) An excavated blade showing the tang which pierced a cylindrical wooden handle; its cutting edge is inside the curve; 15″ long. (2) From an American camp; the iron ferrule and flattened end of a tang which secured the missing wooden handle have survived; 17½″ overall. (3) A similar American blade; 16″ length. (4) Variation with an axe-like blade added to the back for heavy cutting; 16″ total length; circa 1750–1820. (5) A sharp hook style with horn handle panels riveted to each side of the flat iron tang; 12¼″ long. (6) Another pattern including an extended axe-type addition; 13½″ length. (7) European, having a socket for mounting its handle; 16″ total. **FASCINES** (see "Fortifications, Field.") **FIELD FORTIFICATIONS** (see "Fortifications, Field.") **FIFE** (see "Music.")

Sources: 1, 2, 3—Frank J. Kravic; 4, 5, 6—George C. Neumann; 7—Fort Ticonderoga Museum.

FIREBACKS: Typical cast-iron firebacks as found in many of the homes and semi-permanent military establishments. (1) An early 18th century design having two raised figures in double panels under a scrolled profile. (2) Marked "Colebrook Dale Furnace 1763"; 35" high. **FIREARMS** (see "Artillery," "Blunderbusses," "Carbines," "Flintlock, Action," "Fowling Pieces," "Fusils," "Muskets," "Pistols," "Rifles," "Wall Guns.") **FISHING:** When located near water, fishing by the troops was one of their prime sources of food. (3) Iron fishhooks excavated from campsites, circa 1760–1780. Note the absence of loops for the line; it was usually tied to the straight shank. (4) A fish or eel spear of the style popular at that time and well into the 1800s. (5) Lead line and net sinkers taken from a c. 1775–1776 American camp. (6) An iron hand mold for making lead net weights (with a center hole).

Sources: 1—Joan and Edward Friedland; 2—Mercer Museum, Bucks County Historical Society; 3, 5—Frank J. Kravic; 4—George C. Neumann; 6—Edward Charol.

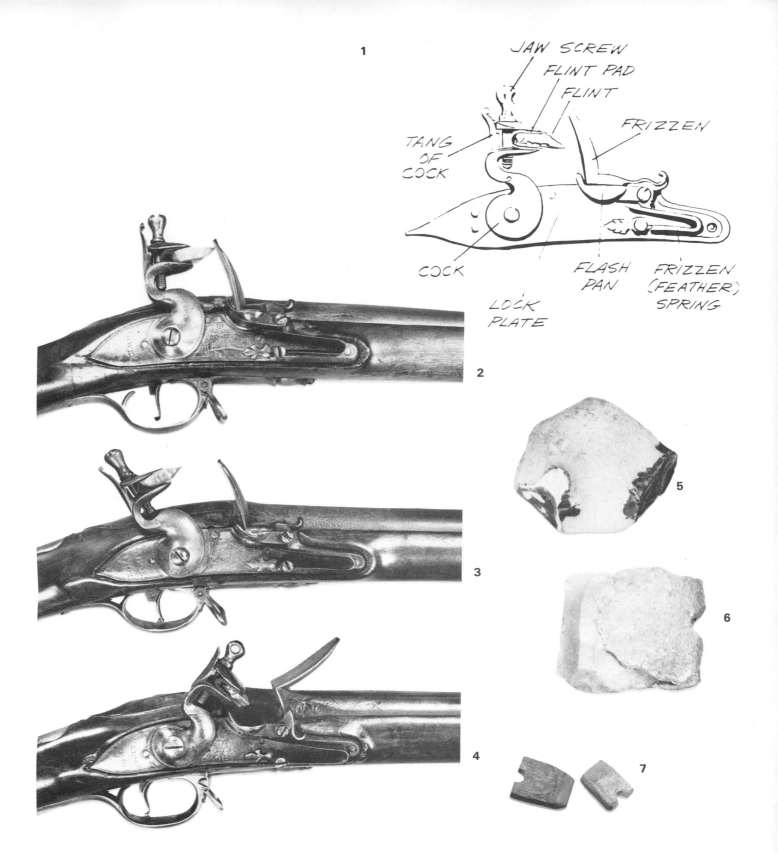

FLAGS (see "Colors.") **FLATIRON** (see "Irons, Pressing.") **FLINTLOCK ACTION** (also see "Firearms," "Flints, Gun"): (1, 2) A typical 18th century lock for igniting the flintlock firearm. The "cock" (or "hammer") holds a rectangular piece of flint in its upper jaws. For firing, the cock is rotated back against a spring to position #3. When the trigger is pulled, it snaps forward hitting the face of the hardened steel "frizzen" (or "battery"). This flint-on-steel action creates sparks that fall into the curved "flash pan" (which becomes uncovered as the frizzen pivots upward—see #4). A small amount of black powder has already been poured into the pan during the loading process. It now flashes and sends flame through a small touch hole in the side of the barrel to ignite the main charge of loose black powder inside. (13) Firing at night; the center flash is from the lock's "flash in the pan." Despite the mechanism's involved operation it functioned surprisingly well in good weather and reigned as the basic ignition method from about 1700 until the 1840s. **FLINTS, GUN** (also see "Flintlock, Action"): Since the striking of flint on steel was the ignition method for 18th century firearms, the availability of gun flints was critical to an army, and they are one of the most common discoveries on military sites of the period.

Source: George C. Neumann.

8

9

10

11

12

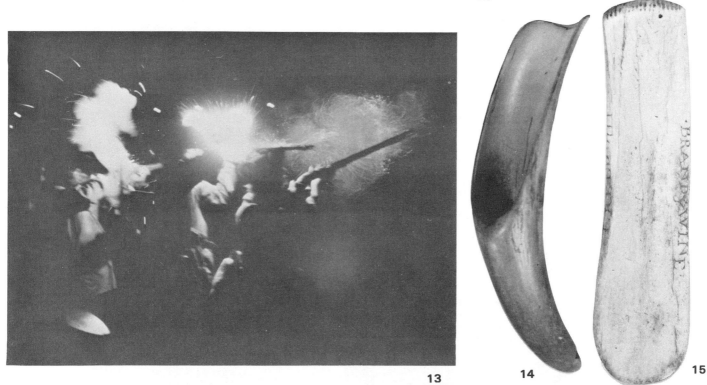

13   14   15

The gun flint normally came from an irregular "nodule" (5) before "knapping" or striking with a sharpened hammerlike tool into a long rectangular-shaped "flake." The "knapper" then held the flake with its end overhanging a thin-edged anvil and used continuous light vibrating taps with his knapping hammer to fracture across the flake a succession of thin gun flints. An expert could average 5,000 to 7,000 per day (Woodward). Almost half of the gun flints on French and Indian War sites are wedge-shaped Dutch "spall" types (many are Indian-made). Almost all of those recovered from British and American Revolutionary War camps are the honey-colored French prismatic style (considered superior to the dark gray English flints). By the War of 1812, about half of those found are French, half are English. A flint might function for from one to over forty shots depending on its structure and edge. Since the flint was harder than the frizzen it struck, the sparks were pieces of burning steel—requiring the frizzen to be re-hardened periodically and even refaced after long service. (6) A musket flint in the common lead sheath used to hold it between the hammer's jaw; Brandywine Battlefield; for other sheaths, see #12. (7) Wooden "flints" found in unfired weapons and for use in drill. (8–11) Typical variety of excavated gun flints varying from large musket to small pistol types. (8, 9) Spall shape. (10, 11) Prismatic form. **FOOTWEAR:** (14, 15) Shoe horns made from horn and bone. (cont.)

121

Sources: 8–12 Frank J. Kravic; 13—Brigade of the American Revolution, photo by Michael Cleary; 14—George C. Neumann; 15—Edward Charol.

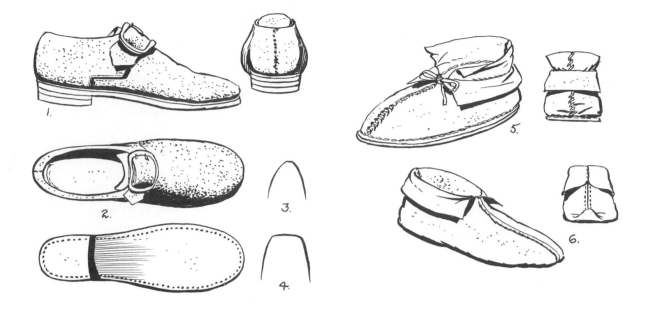

7

FOOTWEAR (cont.) Most shoes were of the buckle style, although laced ones have also been found (see p. 123 #9). The majority were made identical and needed to be broken in for the right or left foot. Their construction was normally of three pieces above the sole, i.e., a "vamp" or "front end" with a large tongue, and two rear "quarters" which curved around the heel and provided the two straps for the buckle (1, 2). The toe shapes were rounded (#2 most popular), pointed (3), or semi-squared (4). Boots were worn mostly by mounted troops and officers. Deer or elkskin moccasins were common among woodsmen and Indians. Two of the most popular styles were (5) those having a separate sole sewn to the upper sections (usually by leather thongs), and (6) "self-soled," i.e. having the sole a continuation of the sides.

Source: 7—Brigade of the American Revolution, photo by Richard Gerding.

(8) An excavated round toe shoe which has lost the buckle straps. (9) An unearthed pointed toe pattern still holding its linen tie. (10) Heavy jackboots of very stiff boiled leather worn by horsemen in rough country during the 17th and 18th centuries. They were seldom used for walking, although it is claimed that some dismounted Hessian horsemen wore these in the Burgoyne campaign. (11) Overshoes like the early "start-ups" or "buskins" were worn by civilians over regular footwear in inclement weather or muddy conditions (these used by Thomas Jefferson). (12) A bootjack improvised from a tree branch. (cont.)

Sources: 8, 9, 12—George C. Neumann; 10—Edward Charol; 11—Thomas Jefferson Memorial Foundation.

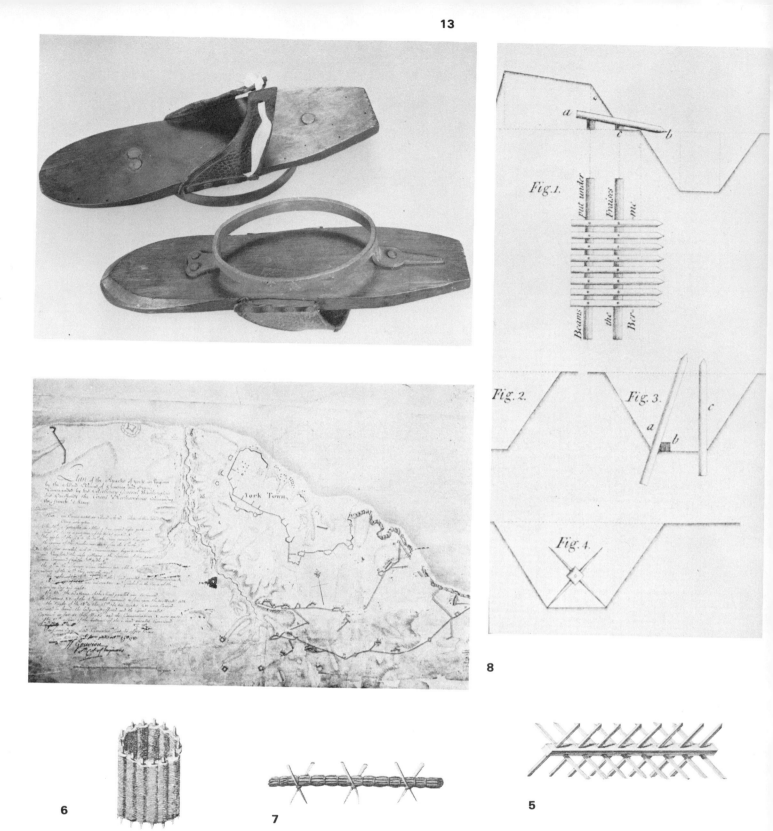

Fig. 1.

put under Fraises

Beams the Bier

Fig. 2.   Fig. 3.

Fig. 4.

York Town

8

6

7

5

FOOTWEAR (cont.) (13) Pattens or "mud shoes" having a raised iron base for attaching under the regular shoe when walking in mud (17 and 18th centuries); usually associated with women, an identical iron base was excavated from a campsite of General Burgoyne (for a woman or officer ?). **FORTIFICATIONS, FIELD** (also see "Tools, Hand"): The most common methods of preparing breastworks included the use of: (1) Fraises: sharpened stakes (usually 7–8 feet long) prepared as shown to protrude from a fortification's wall of earth. (2, 3) The planting of sharpened "pickets" in the outer ditch ("fosse") of an entrenched position. (6) Gabions (pronounced "gab-beans" per Joseph Plumb Martin)—open-ended baskets (usually two or more feet in diameter) of woven brush filled with dirt. They were made by inserting vertical sticks into the ground and weaving pliable branches around them horizontally; finally they were filled with dirt as a stable base for earthworks. (7) Fascines ("fa-sheens"): bundles of sticks tied together firmly in lengths of from five to more that ten feet, with the ends trimmed evenly (held in by long stakes or mortar to secure the facings of earthworks). (4, 5) Cheveaux de Frize: large beams holding sharpened or iron-tipped spears (used to oppose infantry, horsemen, or underwater against ships). Abatis (not illustrated) were small branches and treetops with sharpened tips placed in front of breastworks (like barbed wire). (8) A field map of fortifications at Yorktown.

Sources: 13—George C. Neumann; 1–7 "An Essay on Field Fortifications" by J. C. Pleydell, London 1767; 8—National Archives.

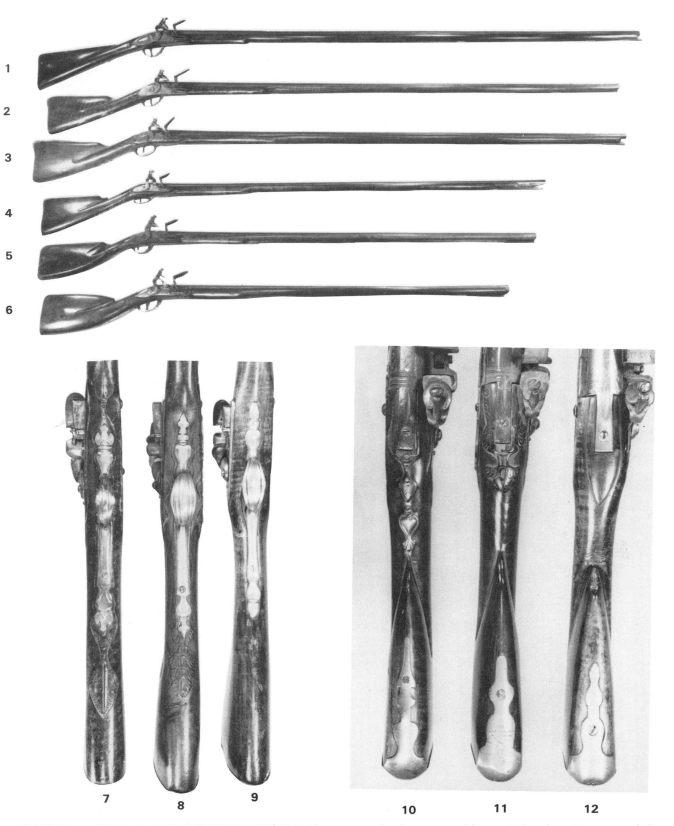

FORKS (see "Eatingware.") **FOWLERS, FIREARM:** These were the long smoothbore civilian hunting guns of the 1700s. Although normally too long to serve as regular military firearms and stocked to the muzzle (i.e. not allowing an exposed section of the barrel to accommodate a socket bayonet), they did see considerable service with short term American units. Walnut, cherry, or striped maple were usually employed in the stock, while bore size varied from about .65 to .80 caliber. (1) American fowler, circa 1750; 82½" long. (2–4) American "Hudson Valley" types with Dutch style furniture and raised carving; circa 1720–1760; their lengths 76", 75", 69¾". (5, 6) Examples of the club butt pattern popular in New England, c. 1740–1750; 66¼" and 59½" long. (7–12) Typical raised carving and Dutch type brass furniture found on American "Hudson Valley" fowlers; circa 1720–1760. (cont.)

Source: George C. Neumann.

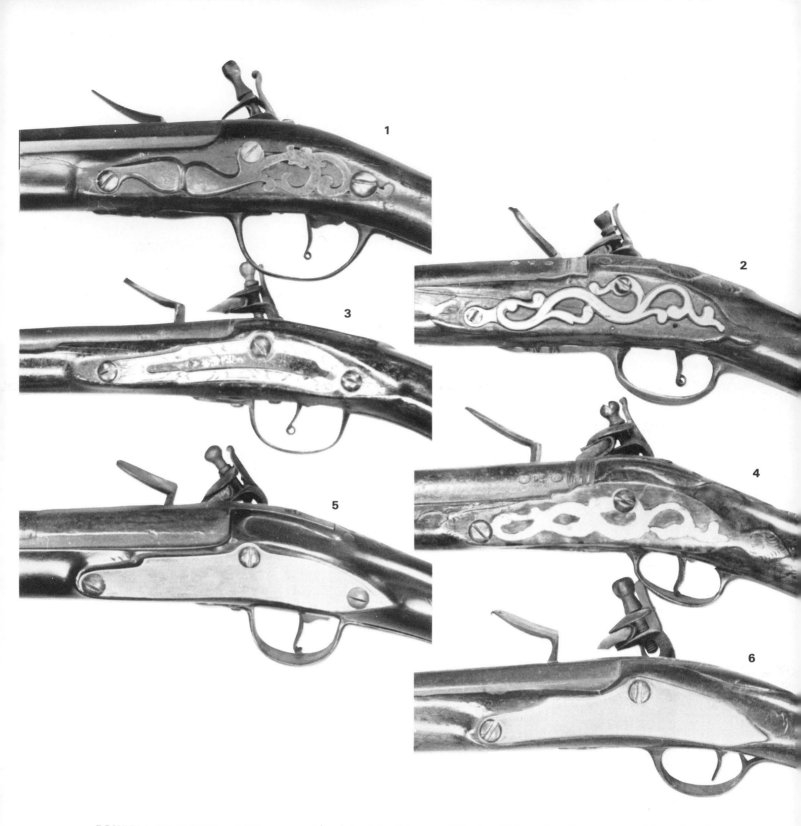

FOWLERS, FIREARM (cont.) Common side plate styles (also see "Muskets") found on European and American long fowlers: (1) Germanic, circa 1690; this pattern combines the open and closed designs. Note too that its early long lock requires 3 screws through the side plate to secure it. (2) An English open brass pattern popular circa 1680–1700. (3) Open 3-screw European/American type; c. 1710–1730. (4) American improvisation; a design was occasionally cut into the stock, filled with molten pewter and filed level with the surface. (5) An American triangular design for a 3-screw lock; early 18th century. (6) A later triangular shape made to hold only 2 screws (the number which prevailed for most of the 1700s); circa 1740–1760.

Source: George C. Neumann.

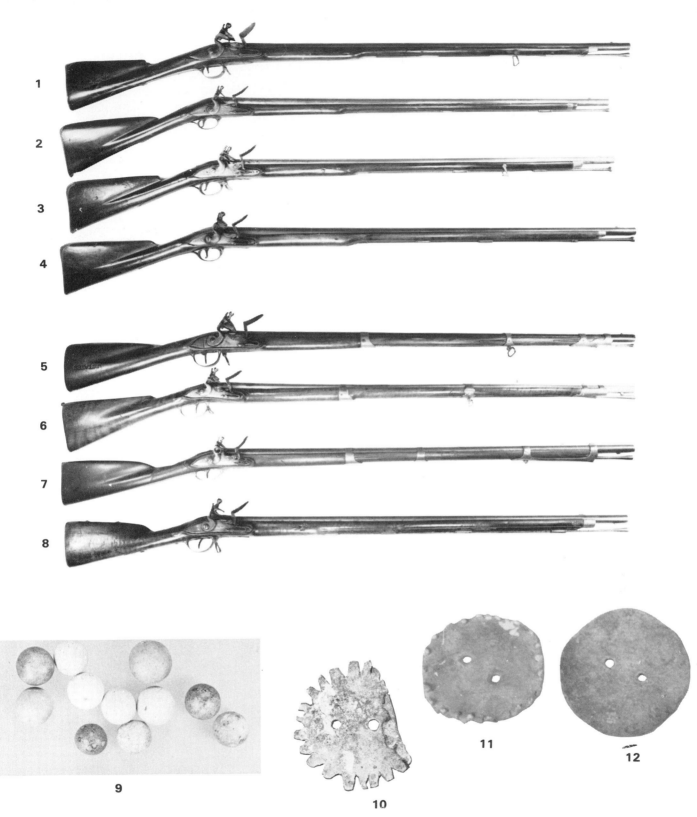

1

2

3

4

5

6

7

8

9

10

11

12

FROCKS (see "Coats," "Shirts.") **FUSILS** (or "Fusees"; also see "Carbines," "Firearms"): A light musket, shorter and usually of smaller caliber than the regular soldier's firearm. It served primarily as a commissioned or noncom officer's weapon, and was often purchased privately by him. The weight averaged 6½ to 8 lbs. (1) American, using a British pattern with a cherry stock; circa 1775–1783, 54⅝" long; .69 cal. (2) English, c. 1744–1758; "I LUDLAM" on the lock (maker); length 52⅝", .68 cal. bore. (3) English light dragoon carbine converted to a fusil, i.e. the stock is cut back for a bayonet, swivels are added, and its side bar removed; lock markings, "EDGE 1762"; 51¾" overall, .68 cal. (4) British; the lock is engraved "GALTON 1762"; .68 bore, 54¼" long. (5) French fusil, surcharged "U STATES"; the stock has been shortened (i.e. 3 bands not equidistant); 8.3 lbs., 55" length, .72 cal. (6) French, with engraved brass furniture; 54¾" overall; .72 cal., circa 1760. (7) Dutch, by Thone of Amsterdam; c. 1775–1780; 53⅞" long, .67 caliber. (8) German fusil, 53" length, .73 cal. **GABIONS** (See "Fortifications, Field.") **GAITERS** (see "Leggings.") **GAMES:** (9) Clay marbles. (10–12) "Buzzers" made by pounding a musket ball flat; wound on string through the holes, it spun when released. (cont.)

Sources: 1–8—George C. Neumann; 9, 11, 12—Frank J. Kravic; 10—Fortress Louisbourg, Dept. Indian and Northern Affairs, Parks, Canada.

GAMES (cont.) Soldiers had long periods of inactivity during which they turned to various forms of amusements. (1) An excavated chess pawn (Fortress Louisbourg). (2) A jackstraw. (3) Game or point counter. (4) Checkerboard painted on wood with checkers made from cross-sections of corn husks. (5) Mahogany gaming table, c. 1760; the top is 30'' x 30'', height 29¾''.

Sources: 1, 2, 3—Fortress Louisbourg, Dept. of Indian and Northern Affairs, Parks, Canada; 4—Frank J. Kravic; 5—Webb, Deane, Stevens Museum, N.S.C.D.A.

(6) French playing cards, 1720–1760; fanciful portrayals of America extended from plates in books to such common graphic items as playing cards. The South Sea land speculations and collapse of the companies about 1720 gave new interest to America and its native inhabitants, the Indians. These were to have been pasted to stiffer cardboard. They are labeled: "Afrique Cheval," "Amerique Roy," "Amerique Dame," "Amerique Valet," "Amerique Cheval"; each measures 2¼" x 3¾". (7) Lacquered boxes and counters for the popular Chinese game of "Loo," c. 1740. (8) Board for "Fox and Geese," a solitaire game of the period that survives today; a checkerboard is painted on the reverse side. (9) A pressed paper shaker with dice having British crown markings; c. 1770–1810. (10) Excavated lead dice formed from musket balls. (11) Bone dice.

Sources: 6, 8—Frank J. Kravic; 7—Webb, Deane, Stevens Museum, N.S.C.D.A. 9—George C. Neumann; 10—Don Troiani; 11— Fortress Louisbourg.

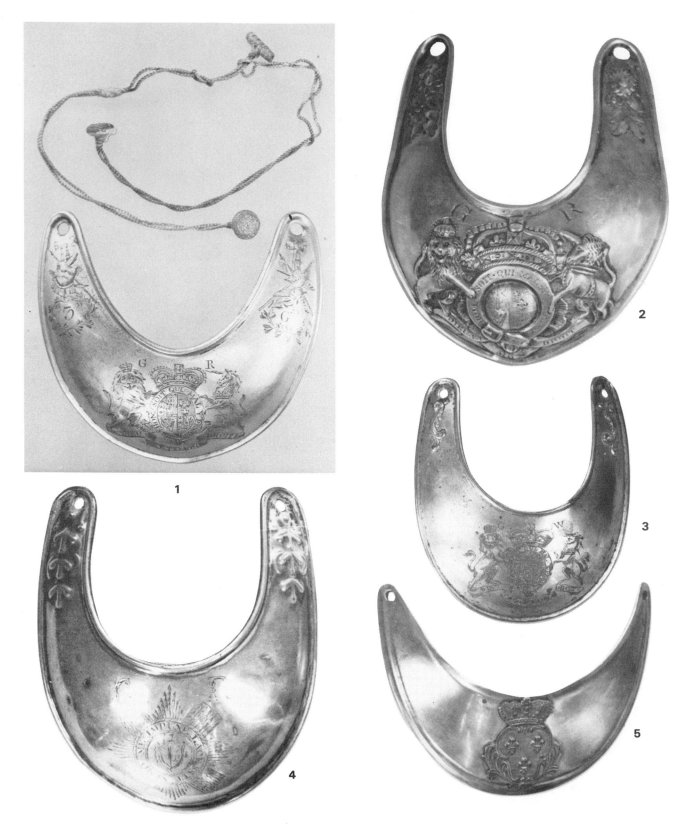

GLASSWARE (See "Bottles," "Drinkingware.") **GORGETS:** This halfmoon-shaped metal insignia technically represented the last vestige of armor, and was worn in the 18th century around the neck from a ribbon or cord as an indication of rank by commissioned officers. It was losing favor during the Revolution, but still saw considerable service on both sides. The British Warrant of 1768 specified that gorgets be engraved with the "Kings Arms" and the regimental number; they could be gilt or silver—according to the color of the regiment's uniform buttons. French officers usually had gorgets of gilded copper or brass with the Royal Arms affixed in the center, while the Germans typically included the principality's or regiment's insignia in enamel. Silver gorgets were also a common gift to Indian leaders who often wore several in series. (1) British gorget (gilded) bearing the Royal Coat of Arms and "GR" (for "Georgius Rex," i.e. King George), plus "3ᵈ Gᴰˢ" (the 3rd Guards); note also the gold neck cord; circa 1775–1783. (2) Embossed silver; English, c. 1770–1780; 4½" wide x 5¼" high. (3) A brass gorget believed worn by American General Anthony Wayne; it bears typical British markings except for the change from "GR" to "GW" (presumably to designate Washington); 4½" x 5½" high.

130   *Sources: 1—George C. Neumann; 2—E. Norman Flayderman; 3—William H. Guthman; 4, 5—Valley Forge Historical Society.*

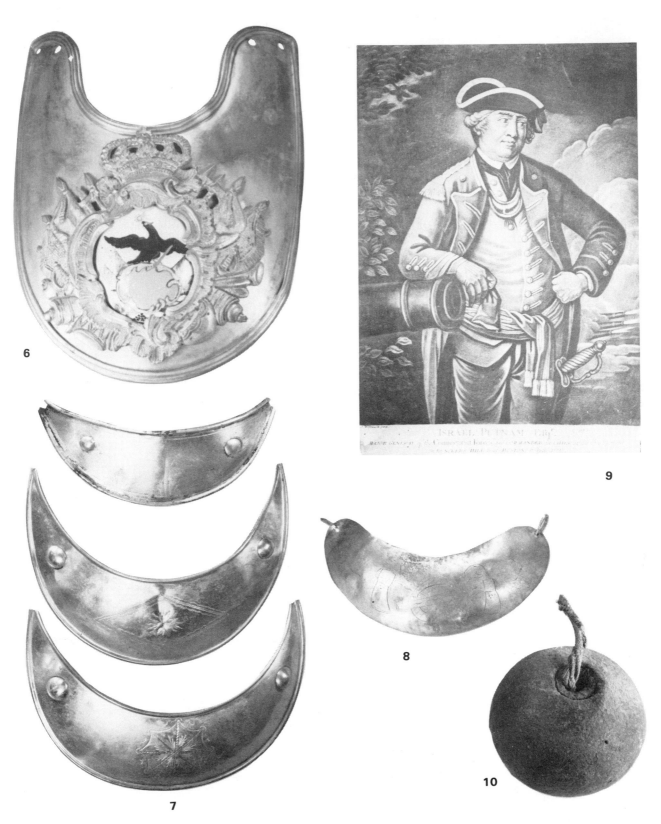

(4) A brass gorget engraved with "GR" and the regimental device of the Scots Guards; circa 1760, 4½" wide x 5½" high. (5) French, bearing a raised Royal device in silver on a brass base; circa 1775–1790. (6) German gorget includes an enamel regimental design; its base is brass covered with silver; circa 1760–1790; 6¾" high. (7) Silver Indian trade gorgets commonly worn in series as shown. (8) A single Indian silver trade example; its engraving shows a serpent and two axes; made by Joseph Mailloux of Quebec, 1708–1826 (family); 4½" length. (9) English mezzotint (1775) of the American General Israel Putnam wearing a gorget, sash, and gloves. **GRENADES:** (also see "Ammunition," "Artillery"): A small hollow iron ball 2½"–3" in diameter filled with gunpowder. The tapered wooden plug (beech preferred) was hollowed to admit a fuse which projected down into the center. The grenade was lighted and thrown by hand, or at times by a small mortar. Small cannon shells were customarily used for this purpose. (10) A typical hand grenade; 2⅝" diameter. **GRENADIERS** (see "Infantry.") **GROUND IRONS** (see "Butt Cone.")

Sources: 6, 8—Edward Charol; 7—William H. Guthman; 9—George C. Neumann; 10—Fort Ticonderoga Museum.

6

7

GWOODBRIDGE

GUNPOWDER (also see "Ammunition," "Barrels," "Eprouvettes"): All but about 10% of the powder used by the Americans came from abroad (mostly France)—either as the finished product or the vital ingredient, saltpeter. Its formula approximated: saltpeter 75%, charcoal 15% (willow, hazel, birch, beech or alder preferred), and sulphur 10%. Gunpowder easily absorbed moisture, which altered its shooting characteristics; more importantly, when ignited more than half remained as a residual fouling which accumulated inside the barrel. This forced the use of undersized bullets (which, in turn, made the musket grossly inaccurate at distances beyond 50–80 yards). (6) Modern black powder depicting the various grain sizes for cannon, musket, priming, etc. (8) Clouds of blue gray powder smoke typically covered the battlefield, often obscuring the enemy until the last moment. **GUNSMITHING** (see "Blacksmithing," "Rifles.") **HACKLE** (see "Headwear.") **HAIR** (also see 'Combs," "Headgear," "Wigs"): Care of the hair was rigidly enforced among the regiments on both sides. Most men kept it unpowdered and clubbed. Among many officers, or for soldiers on formal occasions the hair was powdered by soaking it with oil, fat, or pomatum and sprinkling with flour or other white powder. The soldier was also required to be clean shaven.

Source: 7—George C. Neumann.

8

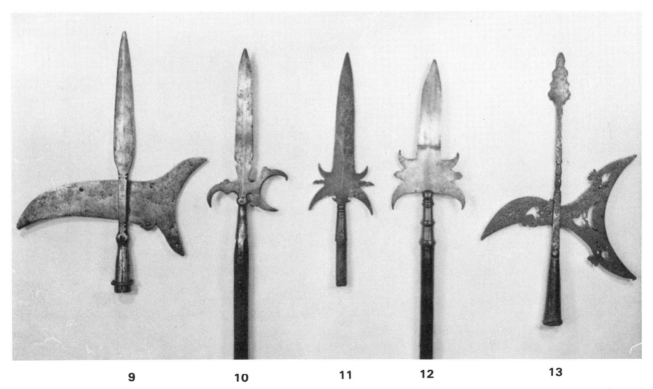

    9   **10**   **11**   **12**   **13**

(#1; previous page) The typical officer and infantry soldier hair style having the top cut short, one or two side curls, and the queue double looped with no ends showing—bound by a ribbon or tape. (2) A traditional practice among select troops, e.g. British grenadiers and dragoons, was to "plait and braid up" under the cap; note too the string behind the ear to help hold the tall grenadier cap in place. (3) A less formal version of the style in #1. (4) The German military pattern with its long pigtail bound in leather or linen tape (and sometimes employing false hair). (5) An informal cut and tie favored by many American riflemen, militia, and some light infantry. **HALBERDS** (also see "Butt Cones," "Halberd Tomahawks"): These were pole arms carried by noncommissioned officers. They were rapidly being replaced by fusils and other firearms in the field during the Revolution, but still saw considerable service. (7) American, with a man-in-the-moon profile, c. 1740–1750. (9) American, c. 1730–1760. (10) American, c. 1750; from Connecticut. (11) French, c. 1720–1758. (12) German, c. 1760–1780; 74½" long. (13) Spanish, c. 1740. (cont.)

Sources: 8—Brigade of the American Revolution, photo by Michael Cleary; 9–13—George C. Neumann.

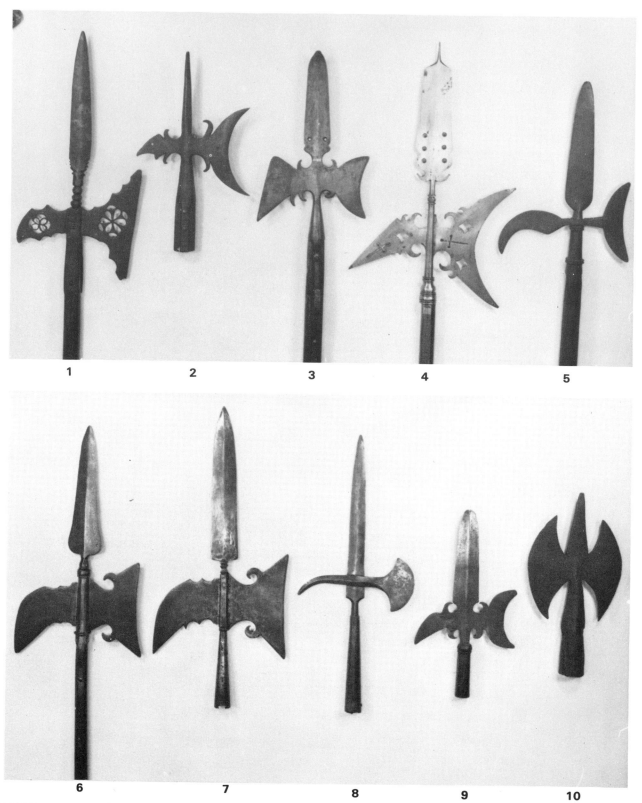

HALBERDS (cont.) They served primarily as a symbol of rank, a control staff to straighten lines of men, and to form a structure to which men were tied while being flogged. The heads were usually mounted on poles of ash, hickory, or walnut in heights of 76″ to 80″. This form was also used by local civilian officials as indications of authority during the 17th and 18th centuries. (1–5) American examples: (1) c. 1700–1720, from Pennsylvania; (2) c. 1720–1740, New York; (3) c. 1720–1750; (4) c. 1750–1760; 87″ total length; (5) c. 1720–1750, 83¼″ long. (6) British, c. 1740–1780 (the typical English pattern). (7) An American copy of the British style; from Pennsylvania; c. 1760–1780. (8) American with the crosspiece split to admit the spear point, c. 1775–1780, New England. (9) American, c. 1750–1770. (10) American, the double-bladed pattern, c. 1720–1750.

Source: George C. Neumann.

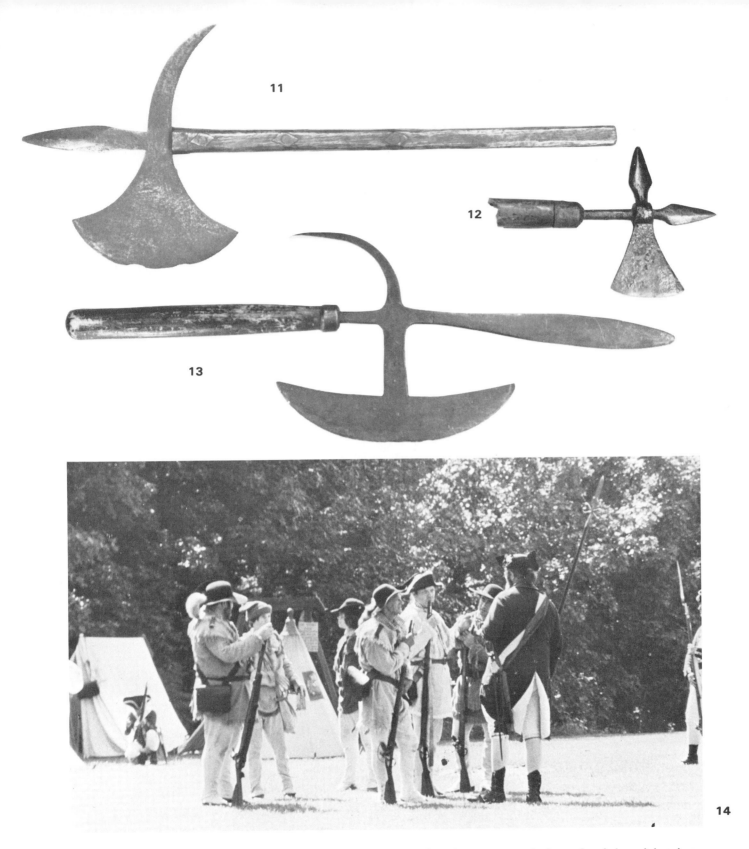

HALBERD TOMAHAWKS (also see "Axes," "Halberds"): Many Indian dignitaries carried tomahawk-length hatchets with heads resembling the halberd. They served mainly as indications of rank, but were already losing much of their popularity by the time of the American War for Independence. (11) Iron headed example, circa 1700–1750; 22½" long. (12) A surviving iron head found in Connecticut, c. 1730–1780. (13) Crude flat head attached by driving its nail-like spike into the end of the wooden handle; the head measures 12⅞". **HANDCUFFS** (see "Irons, Imprisonment.") **HANDGUNS** (see "Pistols.") **HANGERS** (see "Swords.") **HATCHETS** (see "Axes.") **HATS** (see "Headgear.") **HAVER-SACKS** (see "Knapsacks.") **HEADGEAR** (also see "Cockades," "Horsemen," "Infantry," "Marines," "Riflemen," "Seamen"): The traditional military hat of the period was the cocked pattern having a cockade or rosette on its left side. However, a wide range of headgear was employed ranging from fur specimens to knitted caps and hard leather helmets. It was also popular to add feathers, animal tails, green sprigs, or plumes ("hackles") by individuals, units, and officers. (14) Typical variety of headgear found among American forces. (cont.)

Sources: 11—Harold L. Peterson; 12, 13—George C. Neumann; 14—Brigade of the American Revolution, photo by Richard Gerding.

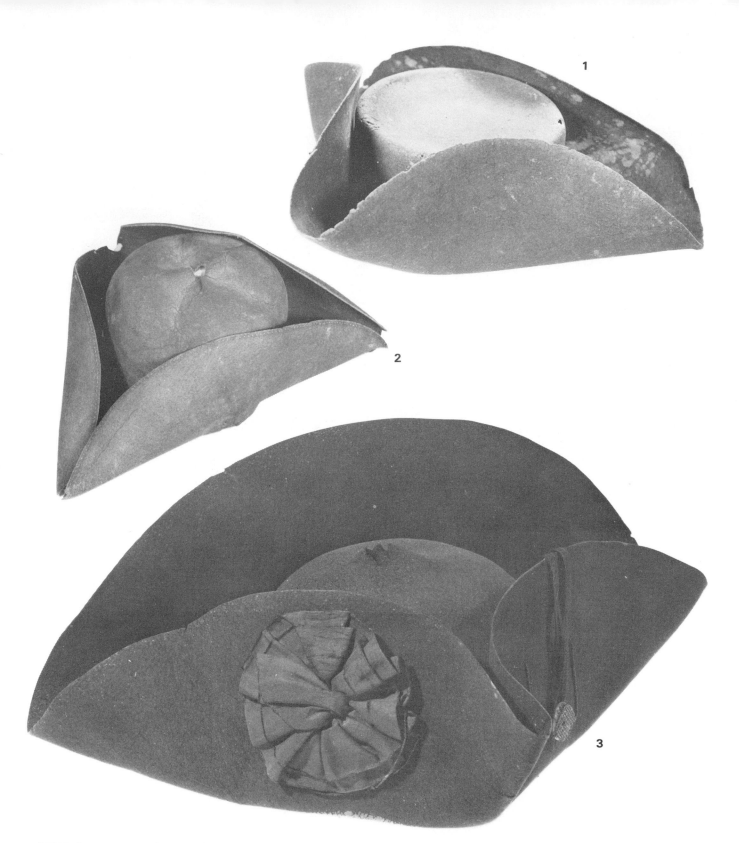

HEADGEAR (cont.) The popular military cocked hat (or "tricorn") was normally made from black wool felt, had a crown of about 4", and a brim (or "leaves") specified for the British at 4½". But the Americans often exaggerated the brim size—alternately leaving it flat, cocked only in the rear (a "fantail" hat), or only on one side ("round hat"). Its cloth binding (i.e. along the edges of its brim) averaged 1–1¼" wide and was of linen tape, worsted, mohair, or silk tape (typically white or black for infantry; yellow for artillery), and gold or silver lace among officers). (1) An American civilian cocked hat (Massachusetts) of black felt with a 4" high square-sided crown; 5" rear cock; the sides are sewn to the crown (no cockade). (2) The low civilian cocked hat pattern popular in the 1750s–1760s, and still worn by many American militia and civilians during the Revolution; 4" crown, side leaves 14" long (rear 12½"). (3) American military cocked hat (tricorn) worn by Capt. John Shethar of the 2nd Continental Lt. Dragoons; the cockade was originally fixed under the tie on the opposite side.

Sources: 1—Edward Charol; 2—E. Norman Flayderman; 3—New-York Historical Society.

(4) A recreated American infantryman typically wearing his cocked hat turned with the forward crease above the left eye to minimize its projection over the left shoulder while carrying the musket. In the 1750s the forward crease was almost horizontal; by the Revolution it had moved up closer to a bicorn. Most had a linen or cotton lining with a drawstring. (5) Round hat worn by Capt. Phineas Meigs of Connecticut who was killed on May 19, 1782; 12½'' front to rear, 4'' crown, side leaf 4¼'' high. (6) The round hat recreated. (7) American Light infantry leather cap with a cloth turban around the crown's base, plus a side plume (hackle). (8) A common workman's cloth cap. (cont.)

Sources: 4, 6, 7, 8—Brigade of the American Revolution, photos by Richard Gerding; 5—The Connecticut Historical Society.

9

10

11

12

HEADGEAR (cont.) (9) The practical flat-brimmed hat favored by many American troops. (10) A knitted cap excavated from the New York waterfront; probably naval, it was originally tarred over the knitting. The more popular style of knitted cap was longer and flopped over to one side. (11) The European soldier's fatigue or forage cap is worn by this German Grenadier. (12) The "Canadian Cap" used by both sides was usually a red wool cap trimmed with fox or raccoon fur, and occasionally a tail at the rear.

Sources: 9, 11, 12—Brigade of the American Revolution, photos by Richard Gerding; 10—Don Troiani.

14

13

15

16

(13) Two recreated black bearskin caps worn by members of a British grenadier company plus a shorter fusilier hat at the right. Painted linen covers were often used on the march to help preserve them. (14) The British grenadier cap plate of black japanned metal bearing the motto, "NEC ASPERA TERRENT." (15, 16) An original English grenadier cap per the Warrant of 1768; the cords and tassels were added in most regiments by 1778. (cont.)

Sources: 13—Brigade of the American Revolution, photo by Michael Cleary; 14—E. Normal Flayderman; 15, 16—Edward Charol.

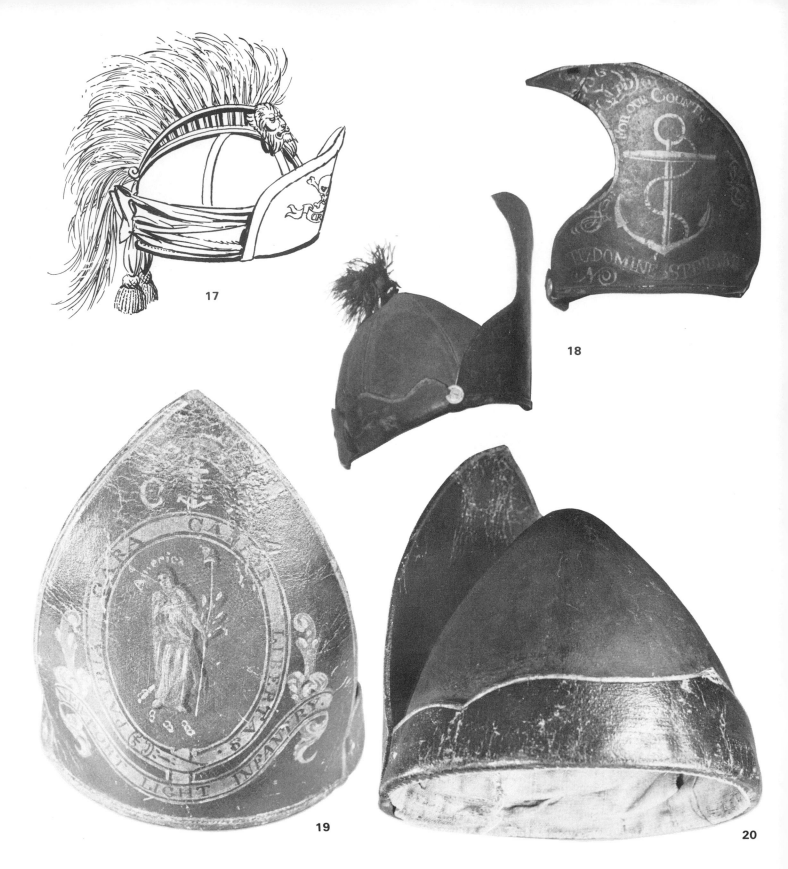

HEADGEAR (cont.) (17) British 17th Light Dragoon helmet of jack leather reinforced by brass decorations and straps; also present are a horsehair crest, colored cloth turban, and woolen worsted tassels. (18) American cap worn by Captain-Lieut. Benajah Carpenter of the Rhode Island train of Artillery, killed at the Battle of Long Island in 1776; the motto, "INTE DOMINE SPEVAMUS." (19, 20) An early cap of the Newport, Rhode Island Light Infantry (1774) with a leather front (10" high) painted to depict a maiden (America) breaking the chains of bondage. Its pointed crown is of hard leather lined with buckskin.

Sources: 18—Varnum Museum, East Greenwich, R. I.; 19, 20—Edward Charol.

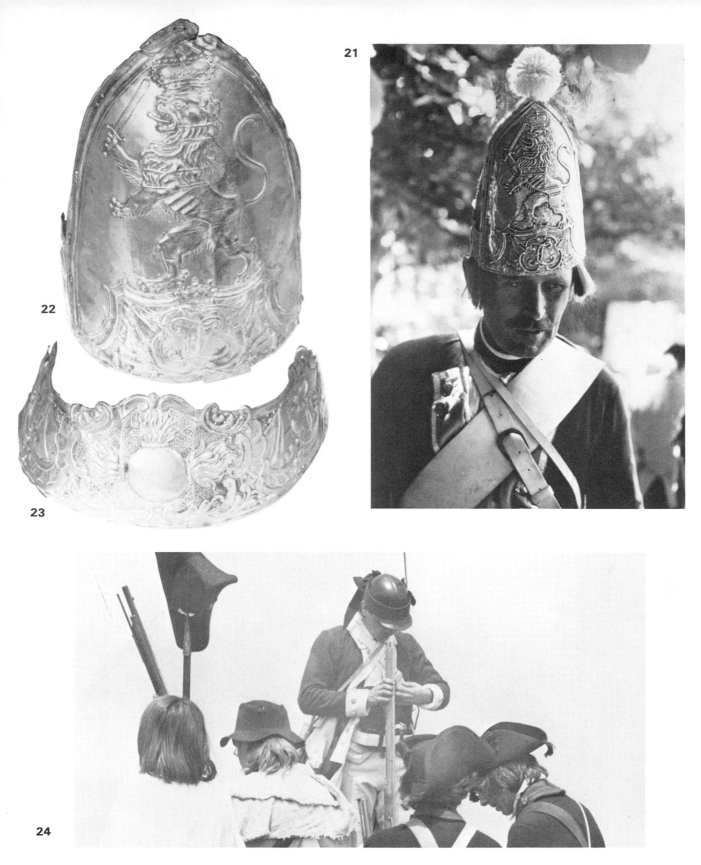

(22, 23) The front and rear metal facings from a German grenadier cap of Hesse Cassel. (21) A recreation of the German grenadier. (24) A variety of American headgear including a leather dragoon cap in the upper center. (cont.)

Sources: 22, 23—Valley Forge Historical Society; 21, 24—Brigade of the American Revolution. Photos; (21) by Richard Gerding, (24) by Michael Cleary.

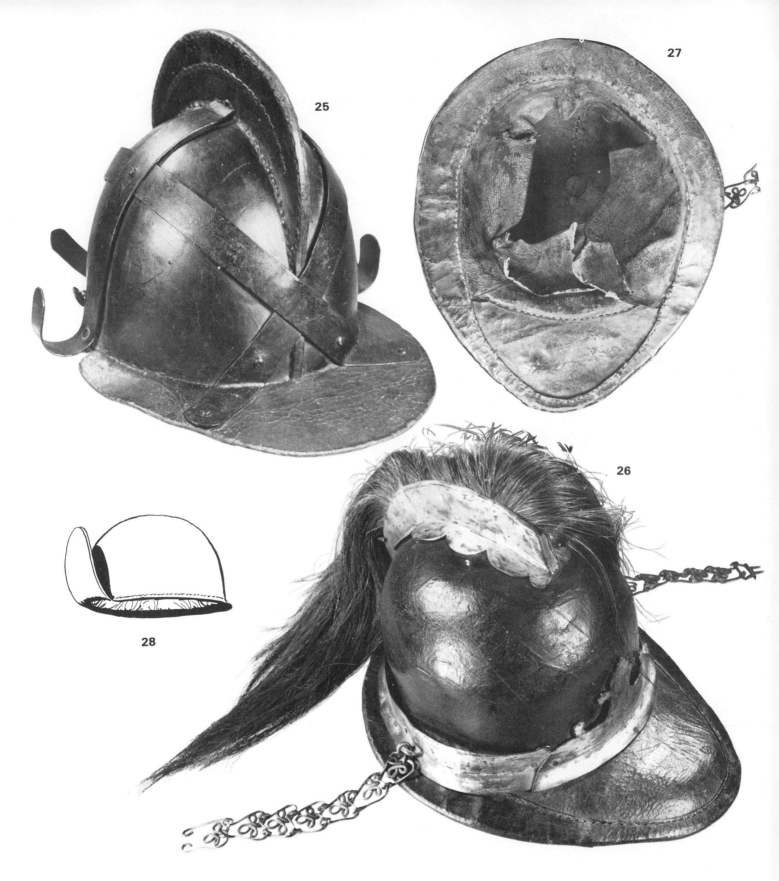

HEADGEAR (cont.) (25) An American helmet of jacked leather having three iron straps and four looped ends to protect against sword strokes; probably for mounted troops, provenance unknown; 8″ high; the interior includes a 1½″ leather sweat band having a 2″ linen top with a draw string; circa 1778. (26, 27) A jockey type American dragoon helmet, circa 1778–1790. It mounts a brass comb, base band and ornamental chin strap, as well as a horsehair plume originally dyed green; the inside (#27) includes a 3″ high leather sweat band. (28) A cap style which became popular in the French and Indian War and continued into the Revolution among both Americans and British; it was made by cutting down and altering a common cocked hat.

Sources: 25—Edward Vebell; 26, 27—William H. Guthman.

142

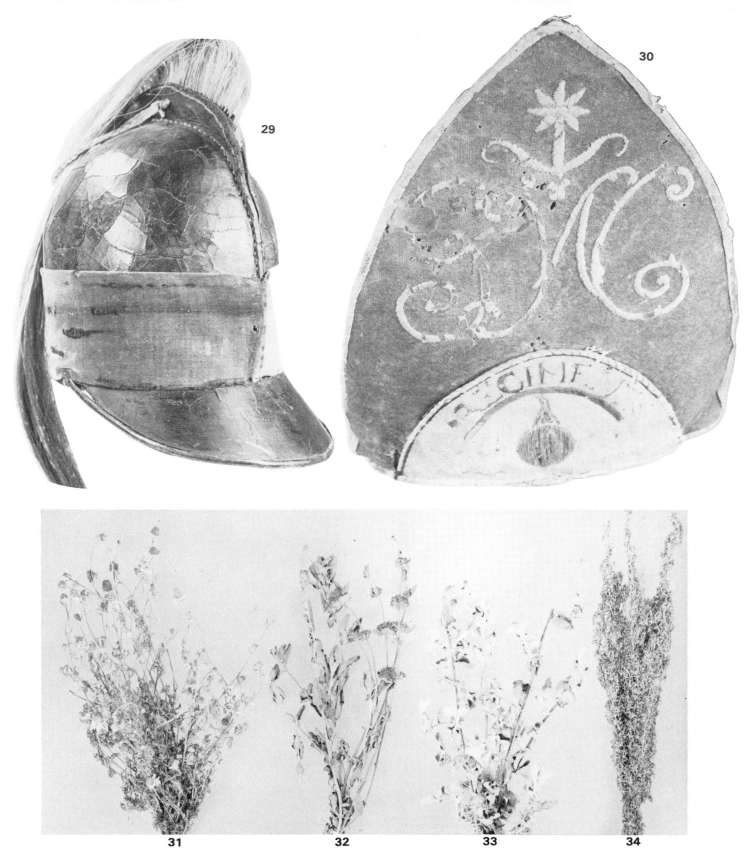

(29) American light dragoon jockey style helmet, c. 1780–1800; note the upper loop to contain the horsehair, and its red velvet turban. (30) A 12½" cap worn by the George Washington Regiment of Grenadiers from Gloucester, Mass.; the stiffener inside the red wool front was pasteboard impregnated with beeswax. The American Continental Line included light infantry companies like the British, but not grenadiers—except for local militia units such as this. **HERBS** (also see "Medical Equipment"): While the army had a medical staff to help soldiers' ailments, the 18th century was a time when native plant materials and home remedies were better trusted by country people. A soldier might well pack a number of herbs that worked best on the ailments he normally experienced or would help him in an army with few supplies. Some of the more common herbs were: (31) Chamomile, which could be made into a tea that helped cure headaches and an upset stomach. (32) Mint—used for a tea to ease indigestion and toothaches. (33) Licorice; often taken as a laxative or for colds. (34)Yarrow, a useful herb to heal wounds and help stop the flow of blood. (cont.)

Sources: 29—Edward Vebell; 30—Edward Charol; 31—34 Elaine Salls.

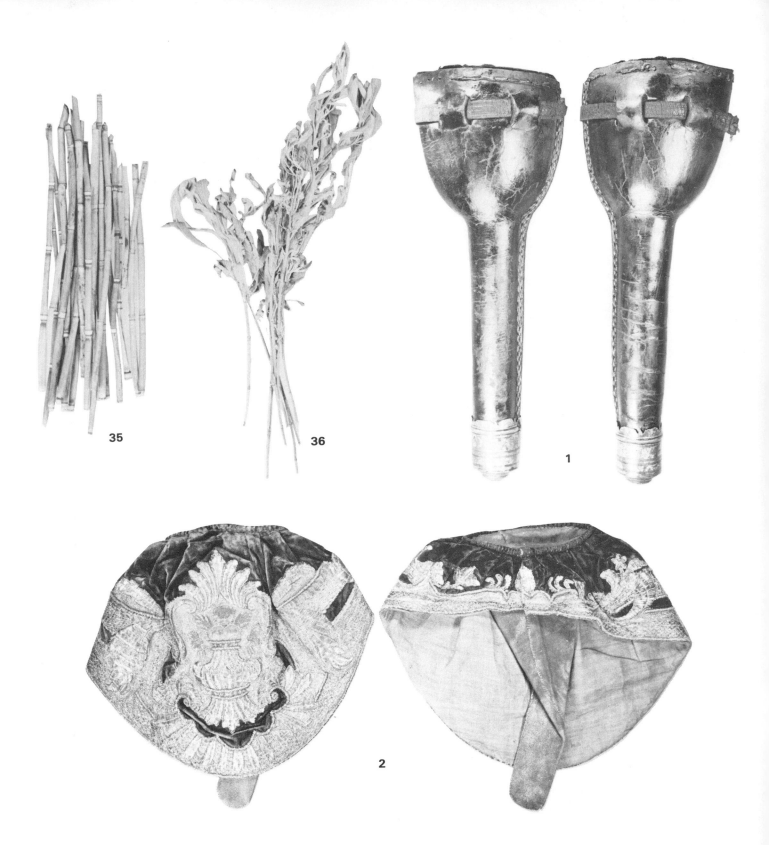

HERBS (cont.) (35) Horsetail was helpful in stopping bleeding and relieving irritation from scratches. (36) Sage; it soothes and reduces itching. **HESSIANS** (see "Infantry.") **HOES** (see "Tools, Hand.") **HOLSTERS, PISTOL** (also "Horse, Equipage," "Pistols"): Pistol holsters were standard equipment for most mounted officers and cavalry. Fastened at the front end of the saddle as a pair, or singly, their pistol butts normally pointed forward. The holster was constructed of heavy leather and usually included a protective top flap of cloth, fur, or leather. (1) British dragoon holsters (for the long 12" barrel pistols) mounting brass tips with a silver wash, and lacking their covers; 17⅝" full length; c. 1750. (2) A pair as used by high ranking officers; the elaborate covers are velvet embroidered by gold and silver thread plus linen backing; European, c. 1730–1760; 14½" high.

Sources: 35, 36—Elaine Salls; 1—Robert Nittolo; 2—Edward Charol.

144

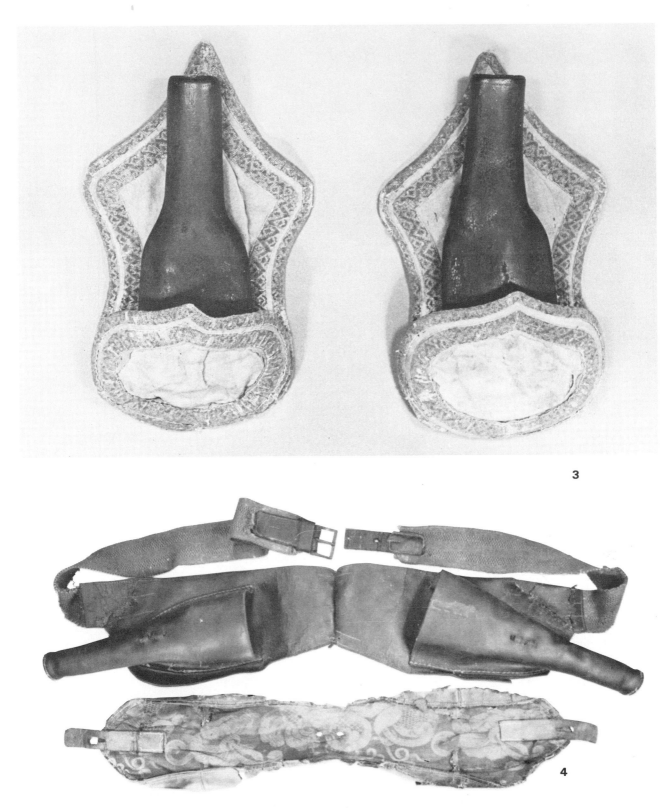

(3) The pair of holsters carried by General Washington. Construction is of black leather for the bodies plus fabric covers and housings trimmed in red braid. (4) American holsters with the leather bodies sewed to a base which also holds a heavy linen body strap; the covers are of cloth and leather; circa 1775–1800. (cont.)

Sources: 3—Mt. Vernon Ladies Association; 4—George C. Neumann.

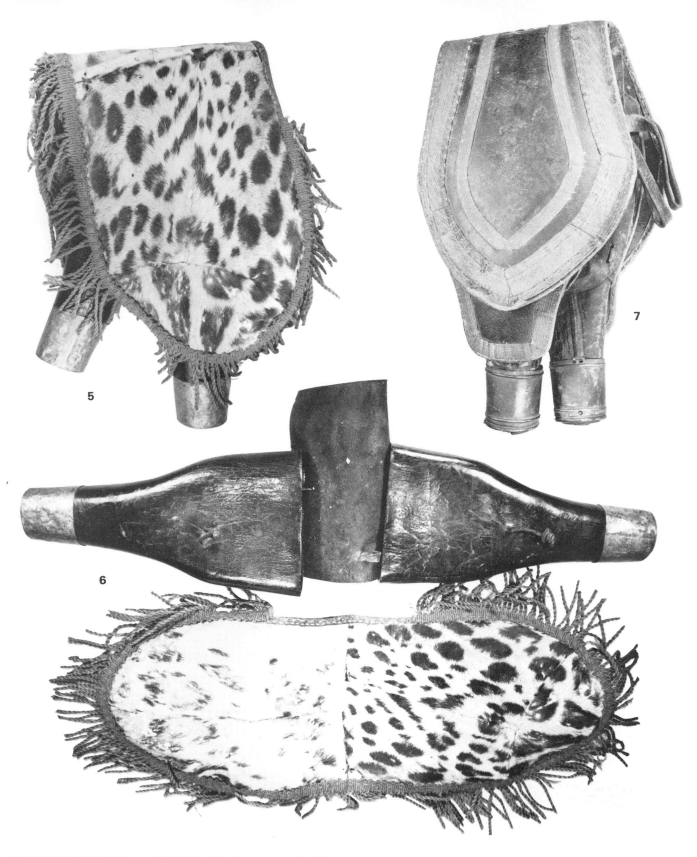

HOLSTERS, PISTOL (cont.) (5, 6) A pair of American leather holsters with an underpad (#10 next page) and covers of leopard skin edged by a red fringe. The tips are silver-plated brass; circa 1775–1810. (7, 8) Believed to have been used by General Herkimer (N.Y.). Decorative braid is included on both the inner skirts and leather covers; the tips are of thin brass.

Source: George C. Neumann.

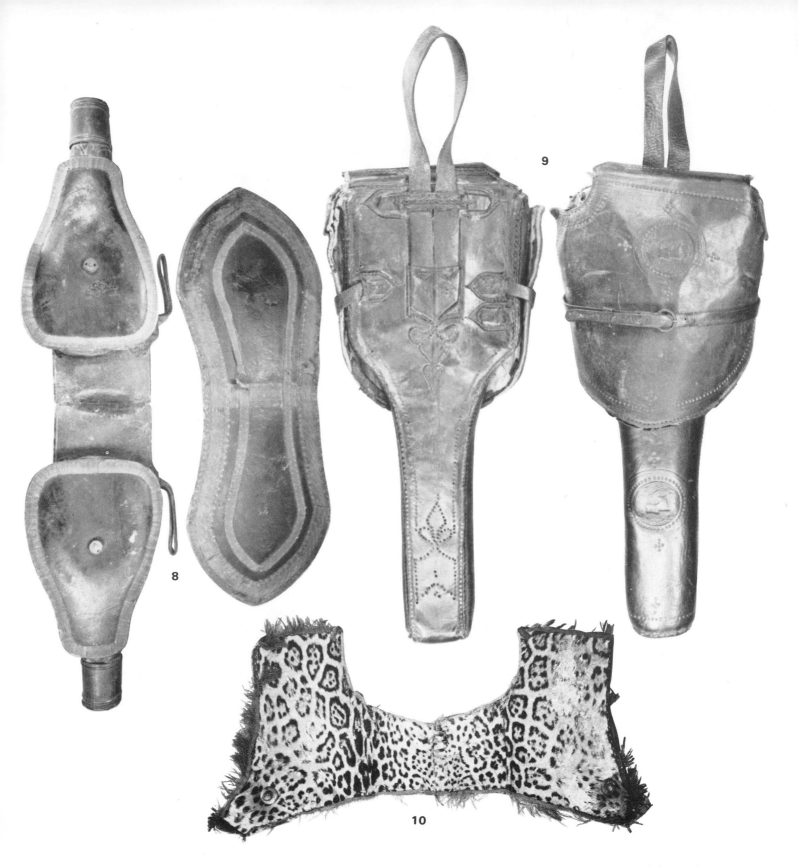

(9) A single holster (front and back shown) believed to be French. Note the interesting embossing and decorative sewing; a narrow strap helps to secure the cover; it measures 15″ overall without the saddle loop; circa 1750–1780. (cont.)

Source: George C. Neumann.

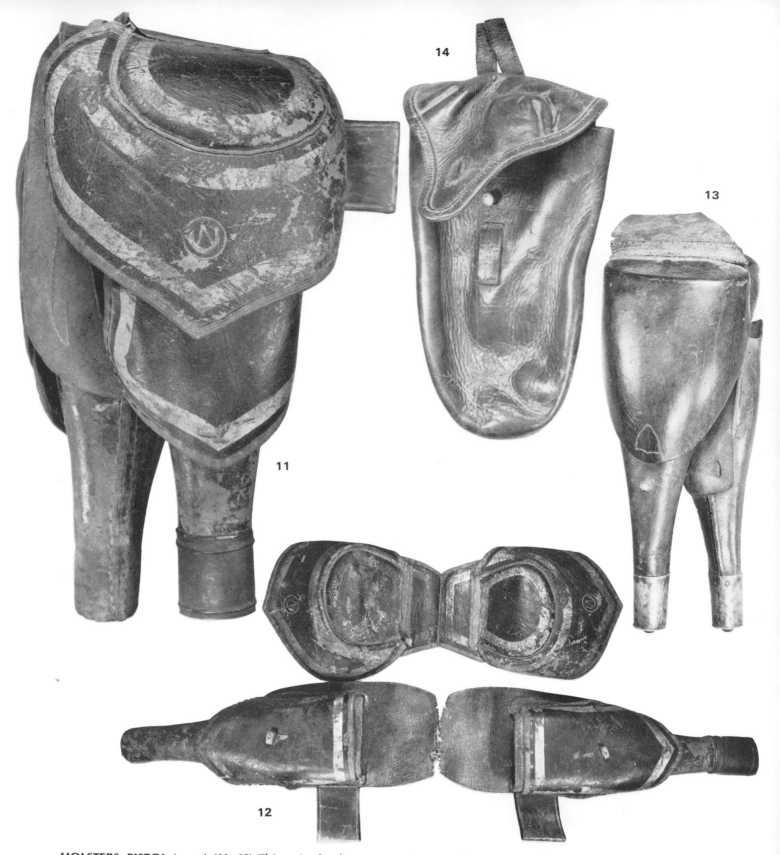

HOLSTERS, PISTOL (cont.) (11, 12) This pair also has an association with General Herkimer (see #7, p. 146). The leather inner skirt and cover are both edged in gold lace and decorated with bands of gold paint plus the rendering of a hunting horn. One brass tip is missing. Its leather loop at the side is for attachment to the surcingle (belt securing the saddle to the horse). (13) An elementary American pattern having brass tips and shaped leather covers; circa 1775–1820. (14) British civilian pocket type holster for small personal pistols; 12½" high. **HORNS** (also see "Ammunition," "Drinkingware," "Eatingware," "Hunting Bag"): Despite the official use of military cartridge boxes the familiar powder horn remained very popular among militia and reflemen. Easily obtainable from slaughtered cattle, the horn was light, strong, watertight, impervious to mold or decay, and would not build up static electricity or strike a spark against metal. First, the inner material was boiled out in water, then the surface was scraped (often thin enough to see the powder level inside), and a wooden stopper inserted in the wide end (after softening in hot water). Plugs were often caulked with beeswax, tallow, or hemp.

Source: George C. Neumann.

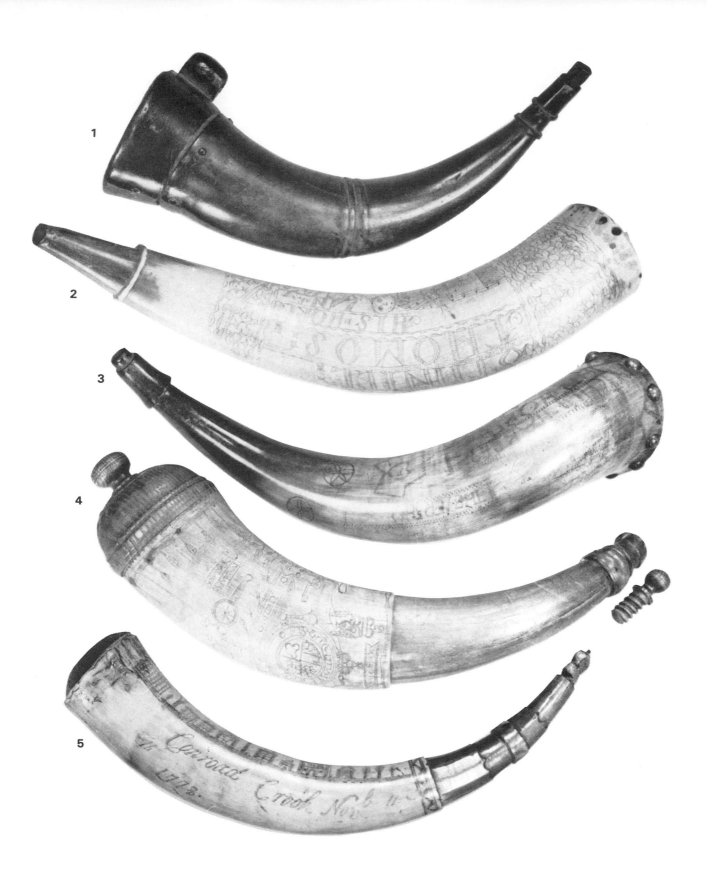

It was also popular to cut, scribe, or punch designs, illustrations, and names into the horns. Many were inscribed by professionals in Europe and shipped here; these better horns were often given a bath of orange dye to achieve an amber hue, and then had their surface rubbed with a dark color to fill the engraved lines before being polished with emery and oil. (1) A 17th century horn with a loop carved in the wooden base for the shoulder strap; 12½" long. (2) Note the short recessed neck of this 1750 period; it is signed by Nathaniel Thomas, "Jan ry ye 1752"; 15¼" overall. (3) A pattern without the popular narrowed neck profile; carved, "John Harris / His Horn / New York / The Jershis / 1776"; 13" length. (4) Inscribed, "New York Annu 1756" as well as the Royal Coat of Arms; note also the screw threaded stopper, rounded plug, and long recessed end; 13¾" long. (5) A uniquely carved neck with round and faceted surfaces; the inscription reads, "Conrad Crook / Nov 11th 1778" under a row of buildings and trees; 12⅛" length; he is listed with the 4th Rgt. Ulster County Militia (N.Y.). (cont.)

Source: George C. Neumann.

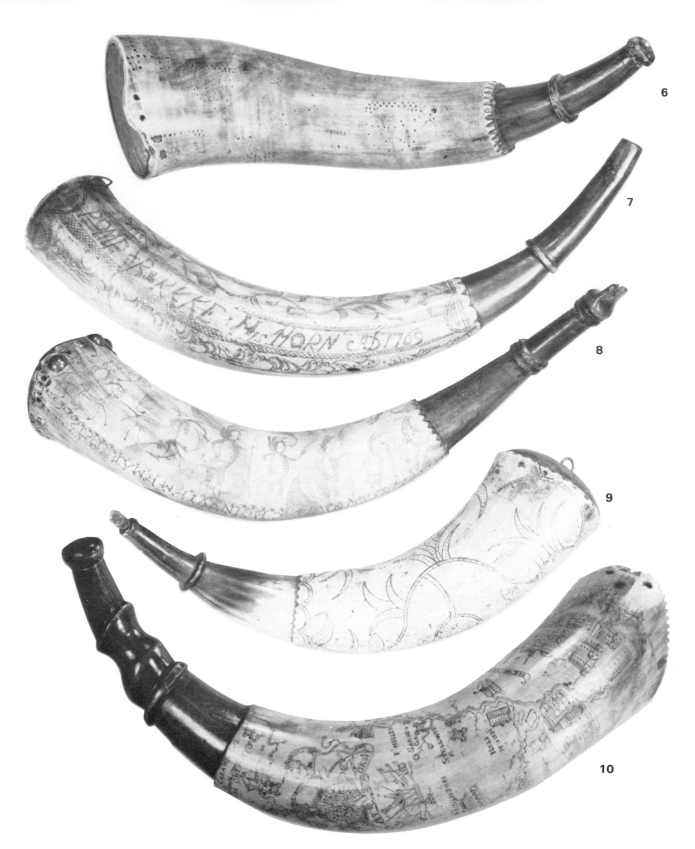

HORNS (cont.) (6) The inscription on this example is "Jonah Gross / His Horn / Made at RIGH March the 1 1777," as well as scribed and punched illustrations; 13" long. Note here the typical recessed neck patterns which were so common at the time of the American Revolution. (7) An unusually long neck style; the carved date is "1769"; 14½" overall. (8) Brass brads secure the wooden end of this horn (usually small wooden pegs were used); its engraving includes a line of marching soldiers. (9) Geometric designs cut with a compass were common and Indian horns are also found with this type of surface design; 11½" length. (10) A professional map horn showing New York and the Hudson Valley extending into Canada; it was probably made in England and measures 11" overall. (11) A rifleman type horn with an Indian style shoulder strap of moosehair and white edging beads (1¾" wide). Its carving displays a unique raised heart design; 12" long, c. 1755–1760. (12) A map horn of the Hudson River Valley including the British Royal Coat of Arms; circa 1750. The beaded strap measures 2" across; note too the adjustable powder measure and charger attached by a small chain. (cont.)

Sources: 6–9—George C. Neumann; 10—Fort Ticonderoga Museum; 11—William H. Guthman; 12—Edward Charol.

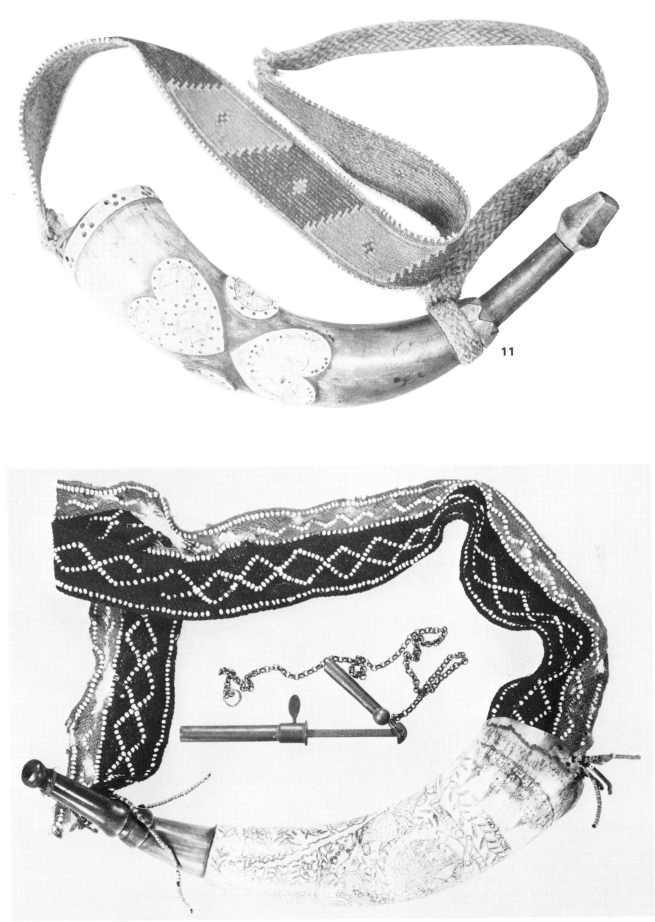

11

12

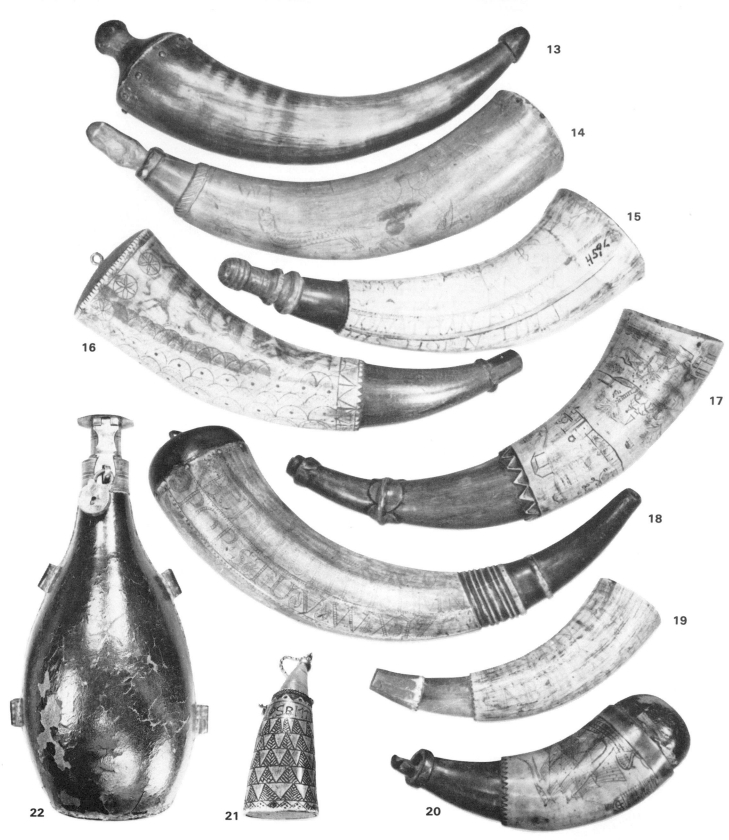

HORNS (cont.) (13–17) A variety of the shorter powder horns 7″ to 10″ in length especially favored by riflemen, who fired smaller charges and carried them in conjunction with their hunting bags. (18) The alphabet is included in this inscription; note too the rounded end plug profile and unusual multi-channeled neck design; 11″ long. (19, 20) Two small pocket horns of the type used with pistols or for fine priming powder; both measure 6¾″ in length; the lower one bears a ship engraving. (21) A priming horn having a silver spout; it is believed to be Indian and has markings, "JOS B 1771"; 6½″ long. (22) An English sporting powder canteen of leather with side loops for a shoulder cord and a small padlock to secure the latch; 11″ tall; circa 1770.

Sources: 21—Edward Charol; 13-20, 22—George C. Neumann.

(23) (top) A raised panel carving, 15" long; (middle) an artillery type priming horn used by both Americans and British; the wooden terminal unscrews to admit powder for filling; a brass charger at the other end has a spring lever; c. 1770–1810; 15½" length; (lower left) a flattened horn reshaped after softening in hot water; (lower right) a "pocket horn" scraped thin to show the powder level; its screw-top also serves as a powder measure; 7½" overall, circa 1770–1840. (24) The common practice of extending part of the edge beyond the base plug and piercing it to secure a shoulder strap. (25, 26) Pocket type horns, circa 1780–1820. (27) Use of a ram's horn. (28) Priming horn inlaid with a pistol escutcheon plate engraved to the British 17th Light Dragoons. (cont.)

Source: George C. Neumann.

HORNS (cont.) (29) A man firing with a horn of priming powder to supplement his box of paper-wrapped cartridges. (30) Tin powder holder having a wooden threaded stopper (probably carried in a hunting bag). (31–37) Typical American horn engraving styles: (31) The facade of a small town ("1778"). (32) Crude fort including a center building, plus a deer. (33) Various animals and birds. (34) The Royal Coat of Arms ("1756").

Sources: 29—Brigade of the American Revolution, photo by Richard Gerding; remainder George C. Neumann.

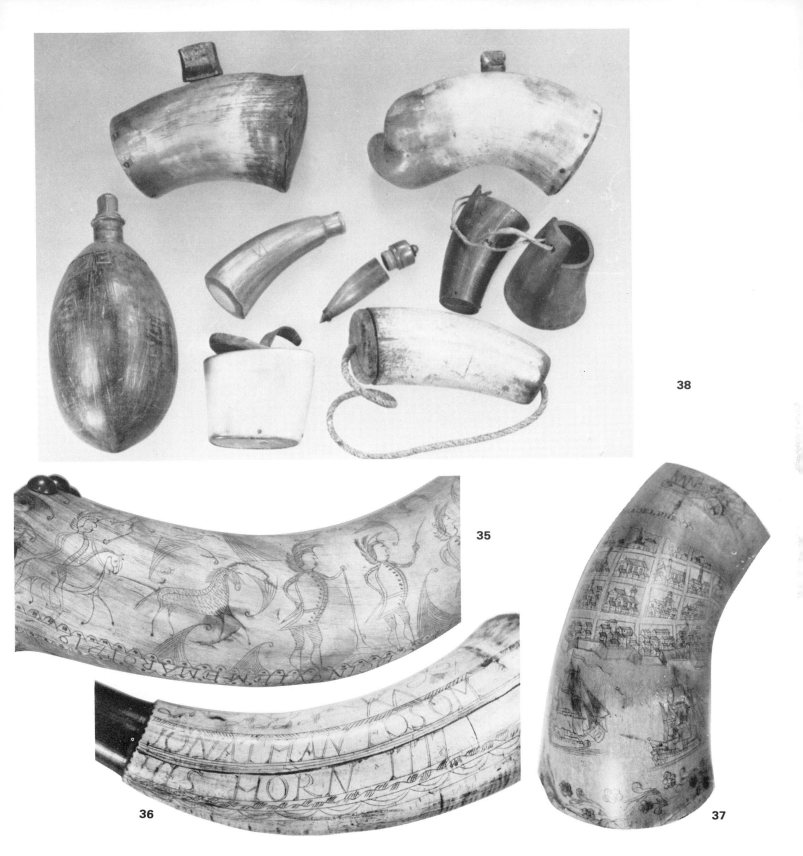

(35) Engraving of a mounted officer and men in light infantry uniforms ("1779"). (36) Typical lettering (dated "1777"); many of these horns were used by succeeding generations who often added their own names and dates to the original inscription. (37) The City of Philadelphia with ships in the harbor. (38) Common horn and related personal containers as used for gunpowder, salt, tobacco, snuff, etc., e.g. (top) two center-hole horn carriers; (lower left) a coconut as often employed to hold gunpowder, or as a canteen; its spout is made of pewter; (center) two small salt holders (needed to preserve meat). The availability of horns led to numerous other uses—not only as containers, but, after boiling and roasting over a flame, they could be separated into layers for use in sword grips, combs, snuffboxes, window panes, spoons, etc.

Sources: 37—E. Norman Flayderman; 35, 36, 38—George C. Neumann.

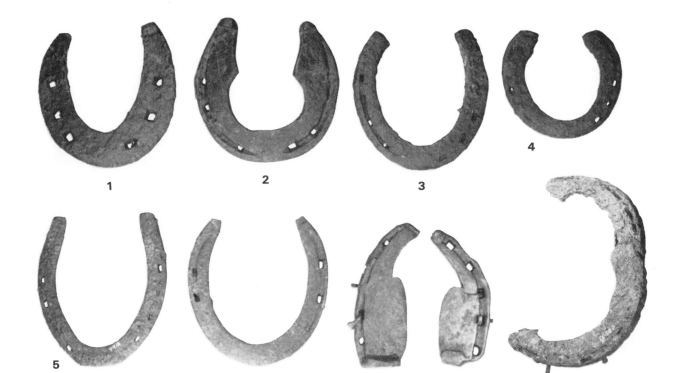

HORSE EQUIPAGE (also see "Buckles," "Horsemen"): Since horses were critical to the movement of an army and its sustenance, the remains of their shoes and metal fittings are found in most campsites. (1–6) Horseshoes, all excavated from military debris, circa 1760–1780. They tend to be broader than most modern specimens. (7) Ox shoes (i.e. requiring double branches for their split hoof); oxen were commonly employed to pull large wagons, heavy artillery, and sledges. (8) A broken and repaired but greatly expanded horseshoe (American camp 1776–1777). (9) An early 18th century colonial stirrup employing a pivoting swivel and double bars in the base. (10) Heavy German officer stirrups, circa 1770–1810.

Sources: 1–8—Frank J. Kravic; 9, 10—George C. Neumann.

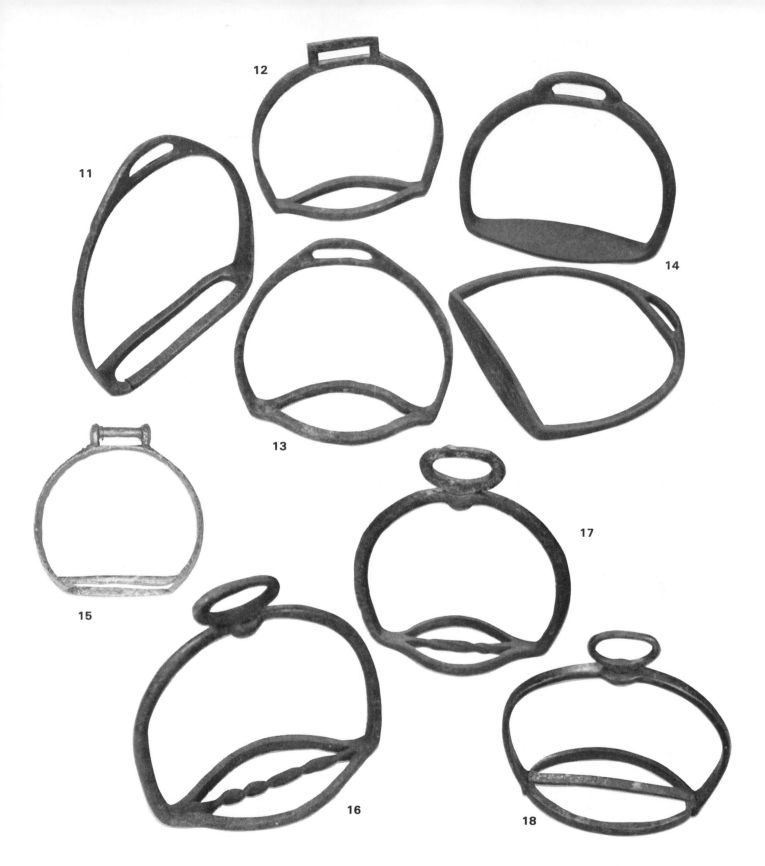

Excavated stirrups are mostly of functional wrought iron with either an oval swivel (9, 16–18) or a fixed loop at the top (10–15). These typical variations show both open and solid platform designs. (cont.)

Sources: 15—Morristown National Historical Park; remainder, George C. Neumann.

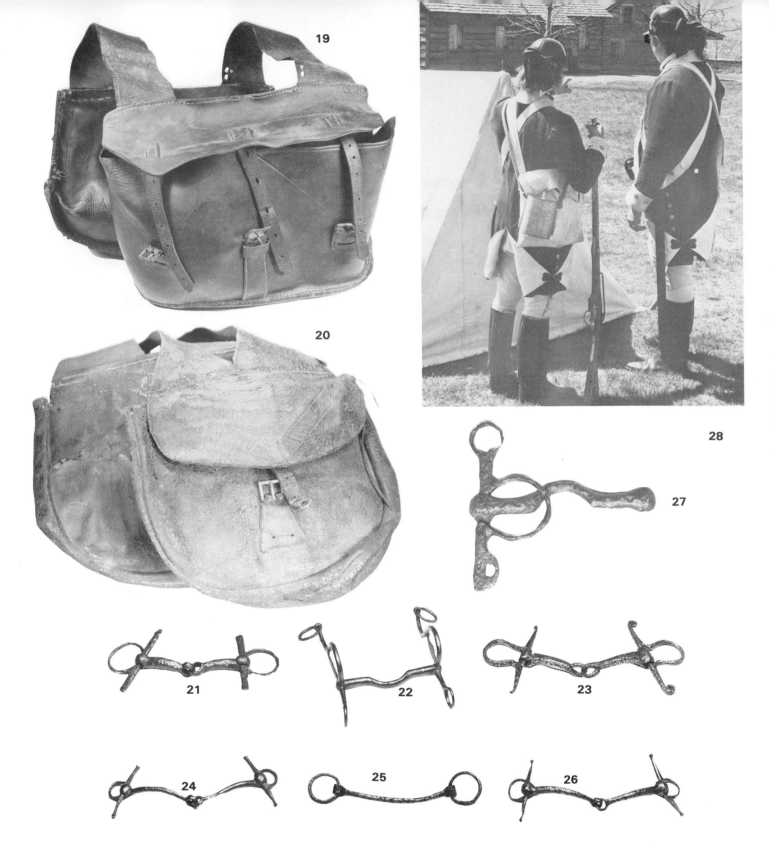

HORSE EQUIPAGE (cont.) Most horsemen carried a blanket roll or portmanteau (holding personal gear plus items for care of the horse, i.e. hoof pick, combs, nose bag, etc. Saddle bags were larger and also used when available; normally made of leather, they included both single and double suspension straps. (19) Saddle bags with two suspensions, as well as three tie belts for each flap. (20) A pair from New Hampshire lined with heavy linen. (21–26) Horse bits excavated from New York City camps. There were three principal types at this time: first, the "snaffle" (or "watering" bit) which favored a straight cheekpiece with a central rein loop and, in most cases, a jointed bit (see 21, 23, 24, 26); second, the "curb" bit having elongated cheekpieces linked with a lip strap and a chain passing under the chin (see 22); (25) A check snaffle bit which omits the cheekpieces; third, the Pelham bit that combined the curb and snaffle, #27 is a part of one of them. (29) An English officer saddle. (30) The common British and American riding saddle. (31) A French cavalry pattern with the carbine and pistol secured in position.

Sources: 19—George C. Neumann; 20—Frank J. Kravic; 21–26—New-York Historical Society; 27—Morristown National Historical Park; 28—Brigade of the American Revolution, photo by Michael Cleary.

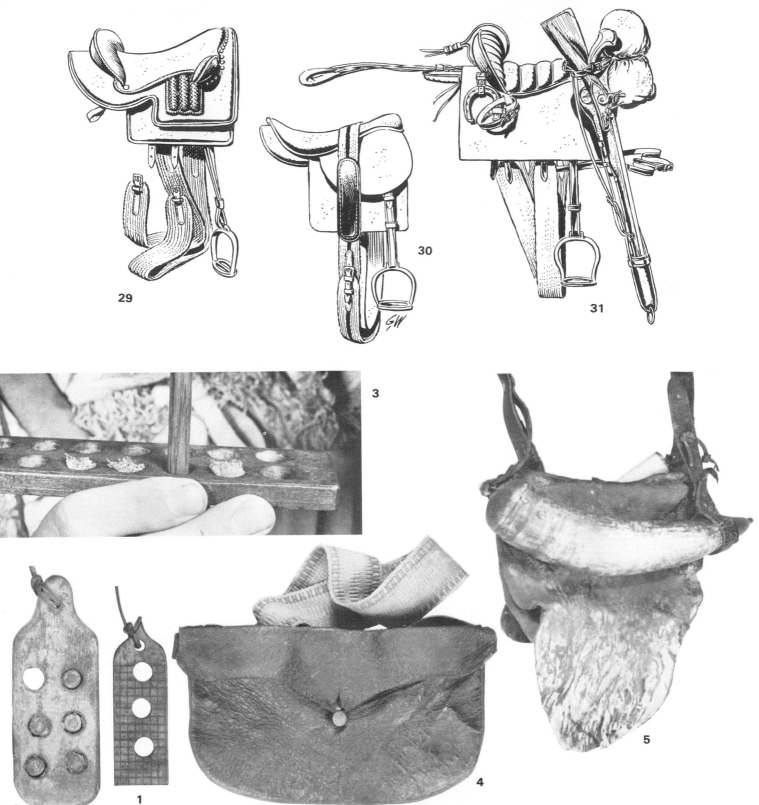

29   30   31

3

2   1   4   5

HORSEMEN (also see "Belts, Frogs, Scabbards," "Carbines," "Cartridge Boxes," "Coats," "Headgear," "Horse Equipage," "Holsters, Pistol," "Pistols," "Spurs," "Swords"): The formal cavalry (light dragoons) provided mobility and were expected to spy on enemy movements as well as to fight from horseback with the pistol, carbine, and sword (their primary weapon). Specific duties included harassing the enemy in small parties, patrolling the approaches to camp, preceding the army on the march, and attacking in battle at propitious moments. There were four regiments of Continental Dragoons created initially (under Sheldon, Baylor, Bland, and Moylan), plus numerous militia and supplementary mounted units. The English utilized two regiments, i.e. the 16th and 17th Lt. Dragoons, plus Loyalist commands. By 1780 both sides had also combined cavalry with light infantry to form mobile "legions" (which usually used a ratio of two mounted to one on foot). France contributed Lauzun's Legion (part of Rochambeau's naval force); the Hessians included some heavily equipped dragoons but, lacking horses, most served on foot. (28) American light dragoons wearing hard leather helmets, sabers, carbines, and boots. **HOSE** (see "Stockings.") **HUNTING SHIRT** (see "Shirts.") **HUNTING BAGS** (also see "Horns," "Infantry," "Rifles"): (See next page.)

Sources: 1, 2, 5—George C. Neumann; 3—Richard Gerding photo; 4—Robert Nittolo.

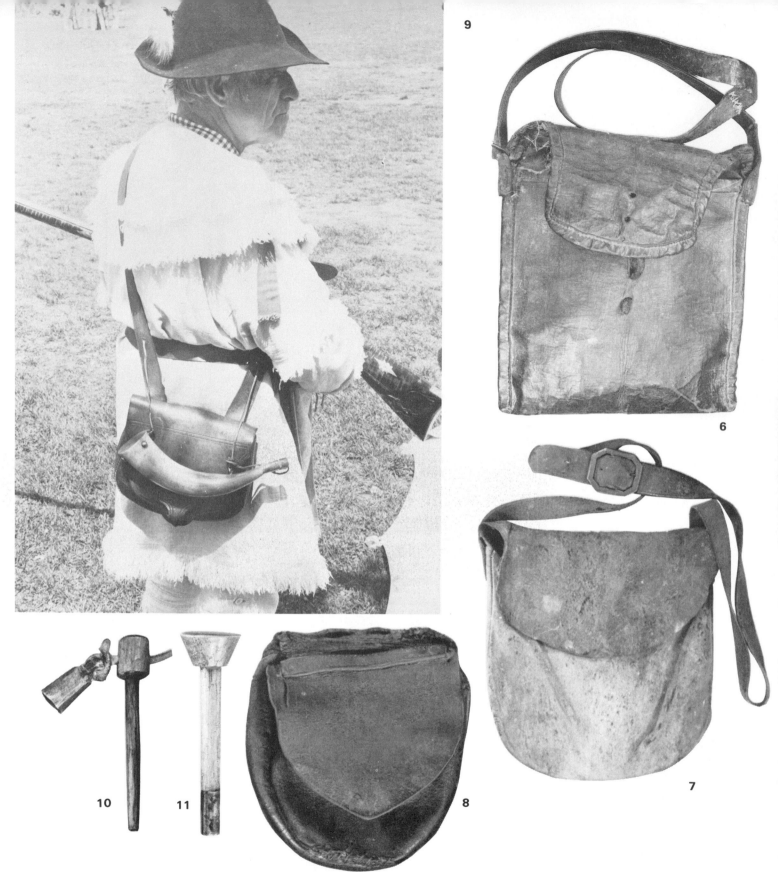

HUNTING BAGS (cont.; refer to page 159 for numbers 1–5) These leather bags usually held shooting supplies for the American woodsman and were suspended on the right side from a shoulder strap. They are difficult to date because similar designs were used by hunters into the late 1800s. The powder horn was normally carried outside of the bag suspended on its own strap or by extensions from the bag's shoulder belt. (1–3) Wooden loading blocks used in speed firing. Their holes contain the round bullets already patched and greased for the rifle. When loading, the block was held over the muzzle and one of the balls was pushed down the bore by the rammer (see #3). (4) A simple bag (10½″ wide) with a divided pocket and a linen cross-belt. (5) A single pocket style having an overhanging flap; note that some deer hair is still present and the top of a patch cutting-utility knife sheathed to the rear; its powder horn attaches to the cross-strap. (6) A square single pocket bag painted red and used with an unattached horn. (7) A pocket pattern having an inside partition; it originally included hair on the outside. (8) An oval-shaped example with a later strip of patch leather across the top. (9) A typical rifleman wearing his hunting bag and powder horn.

Sources: 6, 7, 8, 10—George C. Neumann; 9—Brigade of the American Revolution; photo by Michael Cleary; 11—Valley Forge Historical Society.

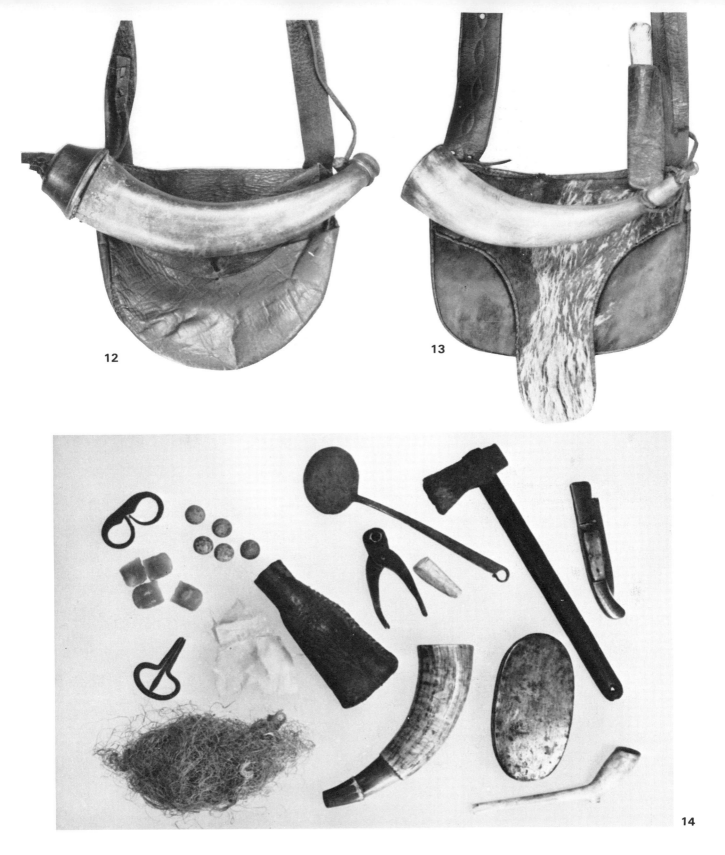

(10, 11) Wooden bullet "starters" to help seat the patched ball in the rifle bore; #10 includes an attached powder measure. (12) A shallow double pocket design, i.e. it divides vertically like saddle bags; its horn is suspended from the bag's shoulder strap. (13) A single pocket type with the patch cutting knife in a sheath sewn to the cross-belt; note the surviving fur on the flap. (14) Typical material found in old hunting bags: a steel striker, flints, cloth patches, a Jew's harp, tow (for cleaning, wadding or tinder), a leather bullet bag, a piece of trade lead, ladle, bullet mold, priming powder horn, a small animal butchering hatchet (9½" long), a folding knife, an oval tobacco container, and a clay pipe.

Source: George C. Neumann.

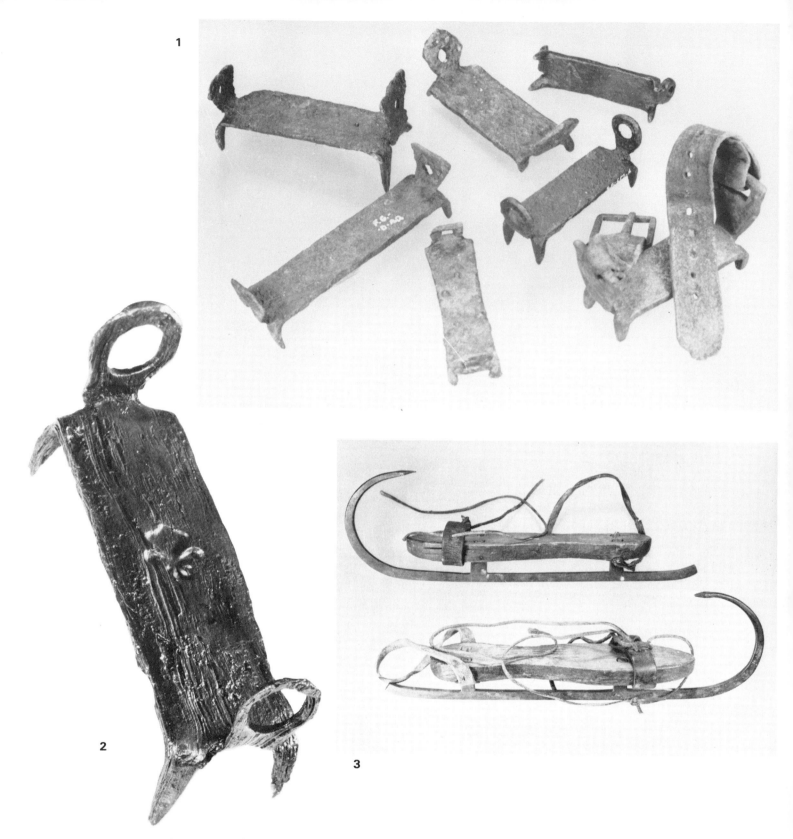

ICE CREEPERS (also see "Ice Skates"): Because of the rough country in America, waterways were a much used means of travel. This also included the winter when ice creepers were commonly worn—held to each instep by a leather strap. They were normally cut from a flat piece of iron to provide four pointed legs and two belt loops. (1) One ice creeper retains its strap and buckle; the others are from military sites, circa 1760–1777; note the British broad arrow (i.e. to mark government property) at the upper right. (2) A midcentury example stamped with the French fleur de lis (Fortress Louisbourg). (3) **ICE SKATES** (also see "Ice Creepers"): Just as snowshoes served on snow-covered surfaces, skates were a means of traversing the iced waterways both for travel and recreation. References mention their use and it is known that Roger's Rangers employed them regularly in raids during the French and Indian War. (3) Ice skates having iron runners and supports plus wooden platforms with leather tie-straps, and nail points protruding at the heel to anchor the shoe.

Sources: 1, 3—Frank J. Kravic; 2—Fortress Louisbourg, Dept. of Indian and Northern Affairs, Parks, Canada.

1

2

INDIANS (also see "Arrowheads," "Axes," "Beads, Trade," "Breeches," "Clubs, Indian," "Gorgets," "Halberd Tomahawks," "Medals," "Pouches, Indian," "Trade Ornaments, Indian"): During the Revolution the majority of Indian tribes sided with the British. The most important ones included the Creek, Seminole and Cherokee in the southeast, plus the Delaware, Chippewa, Miami, Peqequot, Sauk, Fox, and Shawnee—as well as the powerful Iroquois, or "Six Nations" (i.e. Cayugas, Mohawks, Oneidas, Onondagas, Senecas, and Tuscaroras). Apart from frontier raiding and acting as scouts they lacked the discipline for 18th century warfare and usually proved unreliable in a stand-up fight in the open. Their numbers, too, are far less than most realize; the total arms-bearing warriors available from the mighty Iroquois, for example, totaled only about 1600 during the Revolution (Hewett, *Handbook of the American Indians*). (1) The cartouche from a map published in the Pennsylvania Magazine during 1775 showing an Indian and frontiersman in accurate dress of the period. **INFANTRY** (also see "Breeches," "Coats," "Hair," "Headgear," "Leggings," "Recruiting," "Shirts," "Tactics, Battle"): (2) A company of American riflemen in their popular flat-brimmed hats and long linen hunting shirts. (cont.)

Sources: 1—Frank J. Kravic; 2—Brigade of the American Revolution, photo by Richard Gerding.

163

INFANTRY (cont.) Infantry was divided into light and regular troops; to them were added short term local militia and irregulars. The American Continental Line ("regulars") varied in size from under 4,000 to as many as 35,000. Militia was also mustered when needed, so the total colonists who participated in the war approached 250,000 (entire pop.: 2,500,000). The King maintained a force here approximating 50,000—averaging about 50% British, 35% German, and 15% Loyalist. An English regiment consisted of 10 companies—8 of which were the regular "battalion companies," and the others the elite light infantry and grenadiers (the two "flank companies"). Most American regiments numbered nine companies—omitting the grenadiers. Regimental size in the field varied from under 100 to in excess of 1,000. (3) The British regular soldier ("battalion companies"). (4) The 42nd Regiment of Foot, Royal Highland Regiment ("Black Watch") in their dress uniform. (5) British grenadiers (usually massed with other grenadiers); note their tall bearskin caps (see "Headgear") and shoulder "wings" (worn also by most light infantry). (6) British leather-helmeted light infantryman (right), not wearing the usual shoulder wings. (7) Typical officer's uniform as worn by General Peter Gansevoort, Jr. of the 3rd Regt., Continental Line. (cont.)

Sources: 3, 4, 5, 6—Brigade of the American Revolution, photos by (3, 6) Richard Gerding, (4, 5) Michael Cleary; 7—Smithsonian Institution.

5

7

6

8

9

166

10

11

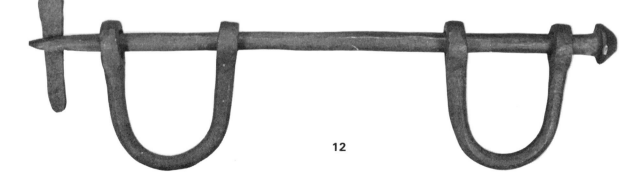

12

INFANTRY (cont.) (8) Local militia practicing the manual of arms. American forces consisted of the Continental Line (regular army), local militia who lacked the required discipline for sustained battle but mustered when danger threatened in their area, and state regiments ("levies") which served for specified periods especially early in the war. (9) Continental line troops wearing the regimental coat whose facing color usually designated their state or geographic area, and the shirt-like frock used in camp fatigue work or as a normal uniform. (10) American light infantry, the elite soldiers of the Continental Army. They were formed as one company in each regiment and usually served grouped with other light companies. Note the hard leather caps and short coats. (11) German grenadiers with their mustaches, tall caps, pigtails, short swords, fur covered haversacks, and high canvas gaiters. **INK STANDS** (see "Writing Implements.") **IRONS, IMPRISONMENT** (also see "Punishment"): Heavy shackles were employed on prisoners both in transit and during confinement. (12) Iron shackles as used for either ankles or wrists; both loops slide along the retaining bar; the wedge at the end splits at its base like a cotter pin. (cont.)

Sources: 8, 9, 10, 11—Brigade of the American Revolution, photos by Michael Cleary; 12—George C. Neumann.

1

2

IRONS, IMPRISONMENT (cont.) (1) Leg shackle with an iron ball on the end of a short chain, and pivoting handcuffs fashioned to clip tightly over the wrists. **IRONS, PRESSING:** These four pressing irons were excavated from hut and camp sites circa 1760–1777. Preheated in front of a fire, they would be used to press the linen and wool uniforms of the officers. (2) upper left, An iron formed of one piece with the handle shaped and hammered hot onto the pressing base. The other three were made of two pieces (the handle being separate and attached by means of riveted screws driven into the hot malleable iron). **JACKKNIVES** (see "Knives.") **JAEGERS** (weapons, see "Rifles.")

Sources: 1—Fort Ticonderoga Museum; 2—Frank J. Kravic.

168

4

5

JEW'S HARP (also see "Hunting Bag"): These were very popular as trade items and personal possessions in this period. A substantial number have been excavated in a wide range of sizes. (1, 2) Common patterns; #2 has lost its vibrator. KEYS (also see "Locks," "Luggage"): Keys were needed for the variety of locks used in camp to secure buildings, storage areas, ammunition, liquor, chests, trunks etc. (3) These were excavated from military camps. KETTLES (see "Cookingware.") KNAPSACKS, HAVERSACKS (also see "Hunting Bags," "Infantry," "Pouches, Indian"): A wide range of equipment and improvised techniques were utilized by the troops to carry their personal possessions in the field. Most popular were the knapsack (on the back) for clothing, blankets, and related items, plus the linen haversack (under the left arm) holding food and small properties. (4) The British Warrant of 1768 specified square infantry knapsacks of white goatskin hung over the shoulders by white leather straps (and joined across the chest). They were to hold shoes, a black ball, and brushes—as well as linen. On service the soldier also carried his coarse linen haversack on the left side. Note too the black cartridge box and tin canteen. (5) Americans with the single strap "combined knapsack and haversack" design. Made of canvas it was often painted with regimental identification. (cont.)

Sources: 1, 2—George C. Neumann; 3—Frank J. Kravic; 4, 5—Brigade of the American Revolution, photos by (4) Michael Cleary and (5) Wayne M. Daniels.

KNAPSACKS (cont.) (1) The common double shoulder strap knapsack worn by both Americans and Crown troops (who did not all use the official goatskin construction—see #4 on p. 169). It was usually of canvas and often painted on the outer flap. Clothing was kept in the side pocket and the black ball in the center panel; straps were mostly buff leather. (2) The combined "knapsack and haversack" pattern with a single cross-shoulder belt (see #5, p. 169). Made of canvas and often painted for waterproofing, it was a favorite among the colonists and also used by some of the King's forces. Blankets were usually folded down the center. (3) A typical linen canvas haversack (unpainted) for food and personal items which hung under the left arm from its cross-belt. (4) The tumpline, a common conveyance for both Indians and woodsmen. A blanket formed the cover and the single coarse webbing or leather strap held it against the back by passing across the forehead or chest.

KNIVES (also see "Daggers," "Dirks," "Eatingware," "Hunting Bag"): The knife is usually defined as having a single-edged blade—thus qualifying for a variety of uses ranging from fighting to daily chores. It was a necessity on the frontier and also accompanied most regular soldiers as a belt or pocketknife. One of the frustrations for modern collectors is that the simple knife and dagger patterns of the period continued in use until the mid-1800s. Those shown here were excavated from camp sites or matched to known patterns or incomplete artifacts. (1, 2, 3) American "butcher style" belt knives with common single-edged blades having their tangs inserted into plain wooden handles which add an iron ferrule to retard splitting. Total lengths: 12½", 10¾", 9½"; blades: 8¼", 6¼", 5". (4) Butcher style, with flat horn panels riveted to the tang for a handle; 13" length; blade 9". (5) Excavated example (Hudson Highlands) bearing an unsharpened clipped point and bone grip; 11⅛" overall, 6¾" blade. (6) A short knife made from a cut-down silver mounted hunting sword; 11¹³/₁₆" long, 6⅜" blade. (7) Antler grip; 10¼" length, blade 5¾". (8) An early "trousse," circa 1650–1700; these sets were carried in cases by hunters. This one includes a bone paneled knife, fork, and skewer; the knife is 8⅝" long. (cont.)

Source: George C. Neumann.

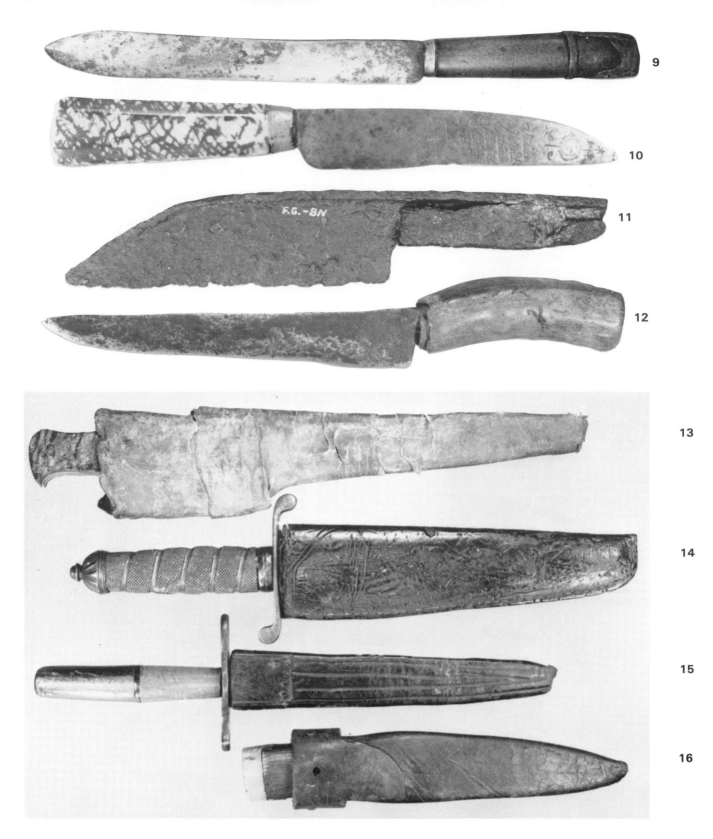

KNIVES (cont.) (9) A long knife (13½'') which includes a pewter inlay at the end of its wooden grip; 8⅝'' blade. (10) An octagonal dyed bone handle holding a cut-down sword blade having a "sheeps foot" point and dated 1763; 9¼'' overall. (11) A complete knife fashioned from an old scythe blade; 9¼'' length. (12) A crude specimen with its tang piercing a section of antler for the grip; 11⅛'' long, 7'' blade. (13–16) Types of sheaths (most were simply thrust through the waist belt): (13) Hardened buckskin wrapped around the knife and providing a small area for a whetstone behind the hilt; c. 1750–1800. (14) A single piece of leather folded on one side and stitched along the other; English, circa 1780–1800. (15) A one-piece sheath folded twice and stitched up the center of the reverse side; c. 1750–1850. (16) A short workman's knife in a sheath having an outboard tab to slip over his waist belt.

Sources: 9, 12, 13, 14, 15, 16—George C. Neumann; 10—Edward Charol; 11—Frank J. Kravic.

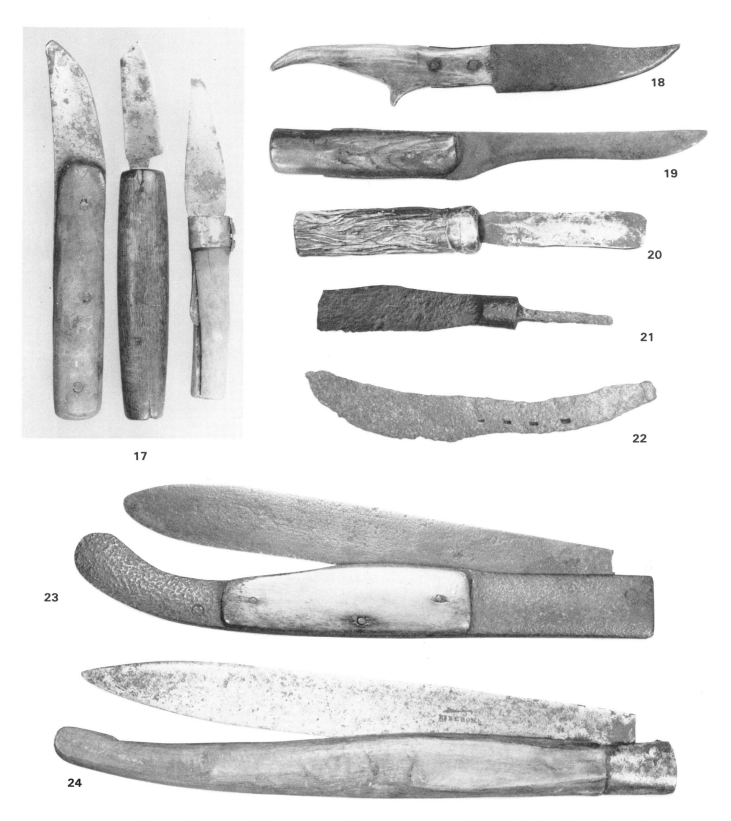

(17–20) Small utility or rifleman patch knives; 5″ to 7″ long. (21) A common knife blade from Champlain Valley excavations (handle missing). (22) A crude specimen created from an old horse shoe. (23) A large version of the folding knife pattern found in many sites, i.e. with two long bolsters and a center panel of bone; circa 1750–1840; 14½″ open. (24) Another long pocket version having a simple horn body and single bolster; open length, 15⅝″. (cont.)

Sources: 17, 21—Frank J. Kravic; 18—Madison Grant; 19, 20, 23, 24—George C. Neumann; 22—Morristown National Historical Park.

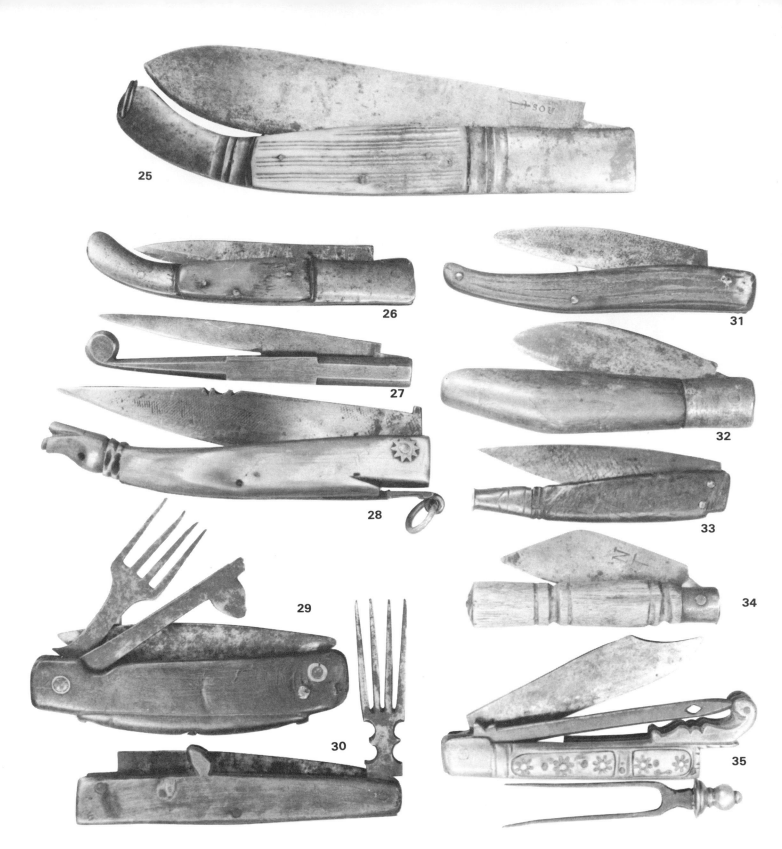

KNIVES (cont.) (25) A large folding knife of the popular double bolster pattern and a channeled bone grip; 13¾″ open. (26) The normal size double bolster pattern found on French and Indian and Revolutionary War sites (especially British); circa 1750–1840; 8″ open length. (27) The cut-steel type; c. 1740–1790; 8¾″ open. (28) A Mediterranean French-Spanish style; a slot in the protruding spring catches the small blade stud to lock it in open position; horn handle; c. 1760–1850; 8¾″ open. (29) There were few multi-blades in the 1700s; this one includes a fork and lancet ("bleeder"); it has a horn body and dates 1730–1790; 8″ open without the fork. (30) Fork and blade combination in a flat horn handle; c. 1740–1780; 8¼″ with blade open. (31) Channeled horn grips; circa 1750–1800; 7¼″ open. (32) A simple wooden handle with a slot for the blade; c. 1750–1850; no spring was used; 7⁵/₁₆″ open. (33) A pipe tamper is included at the end; c. 1750–1820; 6⅝″ with blade open. (34) European "penny knife" pattern; it uses a turned wooden handle without a spring; 6″ open; circa 1760–1900. (35) Dutch sailor's knife with a large needle, bone panels, and a removable fork; c. 1740–1780; 7⅝″ open.

Sources: 25—Joseph E. Fritzinger; remainder—George C. Neumann.

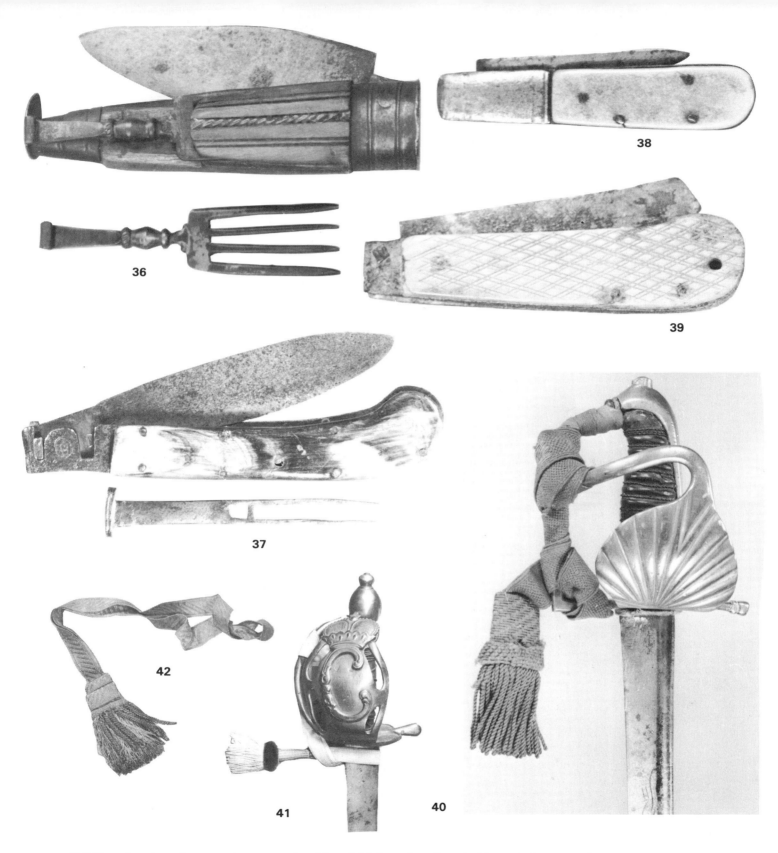

(36) Openings have been cut into opposite sides of this horn handle to hold two forks (second one shown removed from opposite side); 6⅞″ open. (37) The thin fork fits into a side panel of this pocketknife; 6½″ long when closed. (38) An early Barlow with its characteristic long bolster and bone panels; 5½″ open; c. 1780–1820. (39) The popular cross-hatch pattern cut into a bone grip; note the short bolster and clipped blade; 7″ open; circa 1770–1840. **KNOT, SWORD:** It was a popular practice in the 18th century to attach a loop with a tassle to the hilt of a military sword. This "sword knot" was normally carried wrapped around the knucklebow, and had the hand slipped through it to prevent loss during combat. Its colors usually reflected the facing color or lace of the regiment and in that manner also served as part of the uniform. (40) Typical red sword knot on a Germanic infantry hanger, c. 1750–1765. (41) Brunswick dragoon broadsword, circa 1777. (42) The embroidered knot from General Washington's small sword.

Sources: 36, 38, 39, 40—George C. Neumann; 37—Edward Charol; 41—New-York Historical Society; 42—Mount Vernon Ladies Association.

LEG IRONS (see "Irons, Imprisonment.") **LEGGINGS** (or "gaiters"; also see "Breeches," "Infantry"): To help protect the men's legs in cold weather and rough country, leggings were common. Reflecting the European practice, the British Warrant of 1768 specified black linen gaiters having black buttons, small stiff tops (often leather), plus black garters with buckles. Wool was often substituted in winter. They reached approximately 4" above the knee; about 1770 many began to be replaced with "half gaiters" or "spatterdashes." These were usually of stiffened black linen and reached up only to the swell of the calf with a small tip at the back seam (not worn with overalls or trousers). (1) The light infantry officer at left is wearing spatterdashes or "half gaiters;" the German has the long canvas "full gaiters" plus leather garters just below the knee. **LIGHT DRAGOON** (see "Horsemen.") **LIGHT INFANTRY** (see "Coats," "Headgear," "Infantry.") **LIGHTING** (also see "Tinder Lighters"): Illumination in the 18th century was woefully inadequate and did little beyond dispelling darkness from a room or unfamiliar path. Candles melted quickly and were not always available; greases and oils burned with more smoke than light; and rushes were so quickly consumed that they needed continuous replacement.

Sources: 1—Brigade of the American Revolution, photo by Michael Cleary; 2, 4, 5—Frank J. Kravic; 3—Mercer Museum, Bucks County Historical Society; 6—George C. Neumann.

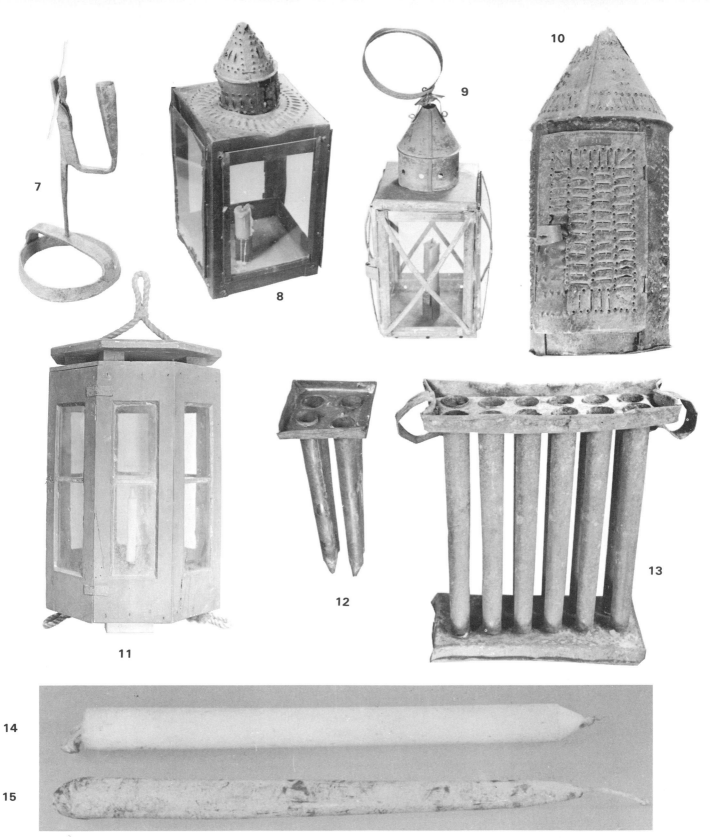

(2) The least light and the most smoke was given off by grease lamps (called "betty lamps" in the 19th century). Wicks were inserted into grease or oil and when lit served at best to outline objects in a room or tent. The left specimen was excavated from a military camp in the Champlain Valley, N.Y., c. 1755–1778. The other has a chain and spike to drive into wood for hanging. (3) A cresset; since softwood knots burned brightly and more slowly that regular wood these iron containers were fashioned to hold them (often soaked in oil) for burning both outdoors and inside; 13" high. (4–6) Simple sockets to hold a candle with a spike to drive into wood. (4) One made from a bayonet socket (military hut source, c. 1760–1780). (5) A double spike to insert into a wall, table, or block of wood; its site dates 1760–1780. (7) A combination rush light and candle holder; 17th–18th centuries. Inexpensive quick burning rushes were used when candles were unavailable; the outer bark of common rushes was stripped away leaving the pith bare; this was dipped in tallow and grease and let harden for use. (8, 9) These lantern patterns were more common than the so-called "Paul Revere" pierced type (i.e. #10) which was more prevalent in the 1800s; #8 has lost its handle (see #9). (11) A ship's lantern of wood, circa 1750. (cont.)

Sources: 11—Peabody Museum of Salem; remainder—Frank J. Kravic.

LIGHTING (cont.) (12, 13; previous page) Candles could be molded or dipped, and the tinned iron molds remained with few changes during the 1700s and 1800s; (12) A four tube mold with an 18th century history; it has lost the tube separator (see #13). Tallow, beeswax, grease, and bayberries were all used in candlemaking. (14) An original molded candle. (15) One formed by successive dippings. (16) An elementary 3-prong holder for rushes or candles; driven into a block of wood, it was easily moved. (17) Such capstan bases with a center drip pan were quite common in the late 1600s and early 1700s; brass construction. (18, 19) Iron spirals were often used to insure the complete burning of the candle, i.e. a platform with a knob could be slid along the spiral forcing upward the steadily shortening candle; early 18th century. (20) This iron candle snuffer—as well as more elaborate brass and silvered varieties (often kept on small trays)—would extinguish a flame without lingering smoke and help to trim the wick. (21–23) Fine brass candlesticks of the mid-18th century. (24) The lines of elegant candlesticks were often copied in lesser metals, including pewter, as shown here; mid-1700s.

Sources: 16—Fort Ticonderoga Museum; 17, 20—Frank J. Kravic; 18, 24—George C. Neumann; 19, 21, 22, 23—William H. Guthman.

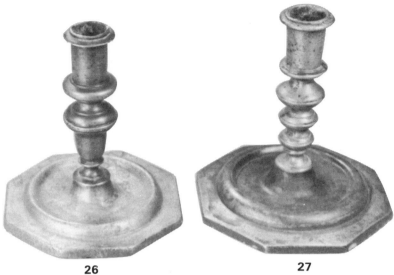

25

26

27

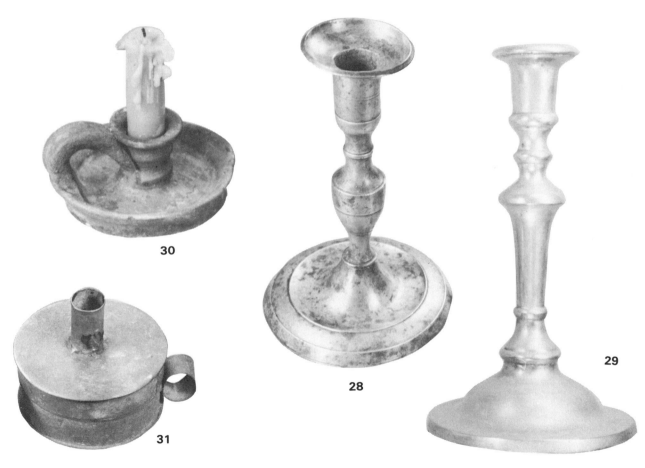

30

31

28

29

(25–28) Brass examples having cast stems and cast or spun bases with the two parts screwed together; they typify the more common types of the period; circa 1760–1800. (29) A heavy bronze candlestick from a two-piece mold; circa 1760–1800. (30) An earthenware holder crudely and cheaply made from local clay; it dates c. 1775–1820. (31) A tinned iron candle holder that contained in its base dry tinder, a striker, and flint for ignition; circa 1750–1850 (also see "Tinder Lighters").

Sources: 25, 28, 31—George C. Neumann; 26, 27, 29, 30—Frank J. Kravic.

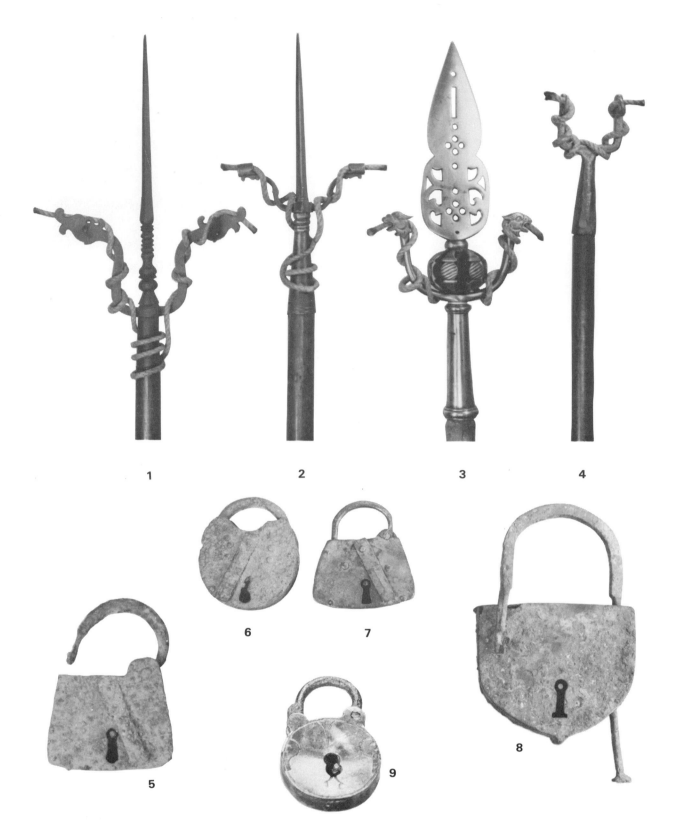

1   2   3   4

6   7

5   9   8

LIQUOR CHESTS (see "Bottles.") **LINSTOCKS** (also see "Artillery"): This artilleryman's pole arm was intended primarily as a holder for the smoldering "match rope" used to ignite cannon by touching it to the primed touchhole. Most of them also included a central spear point to help defend the gun, but by the Revolution, many linstocks omitted the spear and were shortened in height from 6–8 feet to as little as 2 feet (as the portfire gained more acceptance). (1) European, using screw-type fasteners; circa 1680–1730. (2) European, with open slotted arms; c. 1670–1720. (3) German; circa 1740–1760; it mounts a wide pierced blade. (4) American, which omits the fighting blade; circa 1775–1783. **LOCKS** (also see "Keys," "Luggage"): Padlocks such as these have been found in most campsite excavations. The hasp was normally hinged on one side and often the keyhole was protected from ice and water by a pivoting or hinged cover. (5) From a 1750–78 military camp. (6–8) Excavated from Fort Ticonderoga; circa 1750–1780; (9) A small brass type (⅞" across) used for small chests and personal containers. **LOCKS, FIREARM** (see "Flintlock, Action," "Muskets," "Wall Guns.")

Sources: 1–4, 9—George C. Neumann; 5—Frank J. Kravic; 6, 7, 8—Fort Ticonderoga Museum.

LUGGAGE (also see "Chests"): Well-to-do civilians and officers of the period used heavy luggage which usually consisted of a substantial wooden frame covered with leather and patterns of brass tacks. Many were "hair" trunks which preserved the animal fur on the outside. Old newspapers, wallpaper, and documents were often used to line the interior. (1) A hair trunk with brass tacks forming the owner's initials, "BS," and the date, "1733;" 24½" long. (2) Leather-covered with an expandable storage pocket in the lid which was accessible through a small trap door inside; 22" in length; c. 1770–1820. (3) A small leather pack case used by General Washington; the center frame was of light wood and the front pocket is collapsible; 15" wide, 13" high, and 7½" deep. (cont.)

Sources: 1, 2—George C. Neumann; 3—Mount Vernon Ladies Assn.

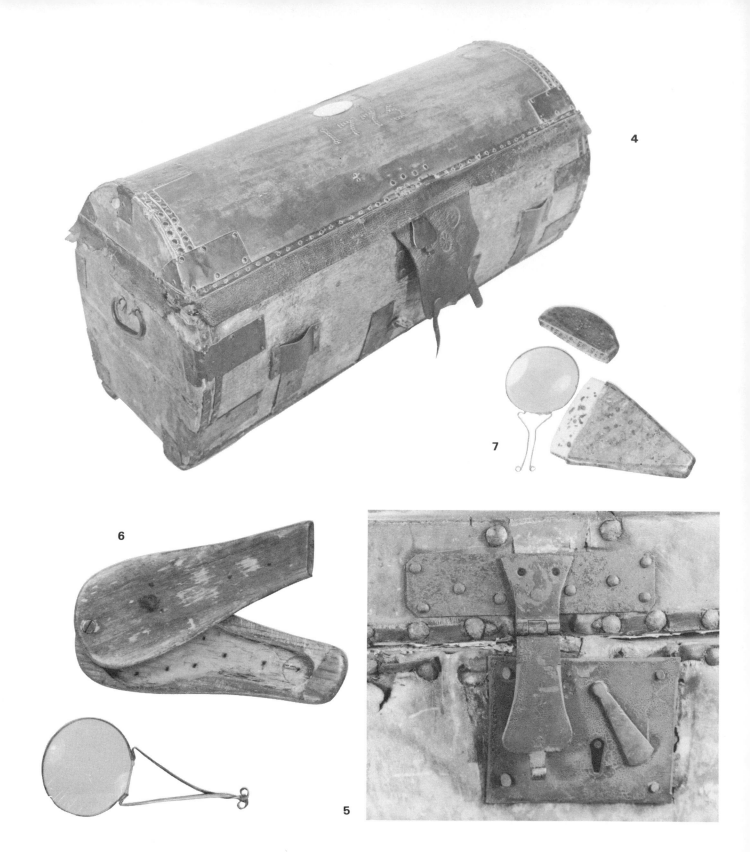

LUGGAGE (cont.) (4) A long rounded hair trunk covered by deerskin secured with iron fittings and brass tacks; it was used during the War for Independence by General Washington and is dated 1775; the length is 36″, depth and height are 15″. (5) A typical trunk lock showing the pivoting cover over its keyhole. **MAGNIFYING GLASS:** Apparently weak eyesight and lighting made magnifying glasses quite common. (6) A brass frame in a wooden box with a pivoting cover; circa 1750–1800. (7) A similar construction in a divided leather case. **MANUALS, MILITARY** (see "Books," "Tactics, Battle.")

Sources: 4—Mount Vernon Ladies Assn.; 5, 6—George C. Neumann; 7—The Connecticut Historical Society.

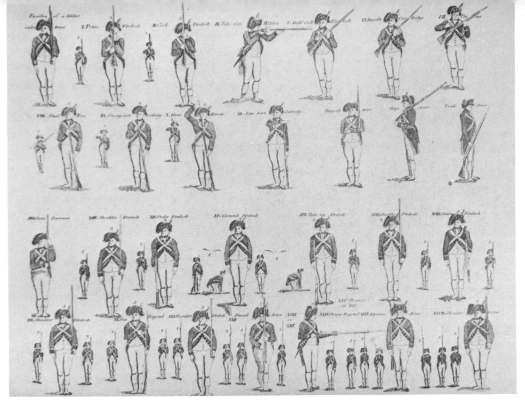

1

2

MANUAL OF ARMS (also see "Books," "Tactics, Battle"): Battle tactics of the Revolution demanded discipline, strict control, and a uniformity of drill. The British were still following their army manual of 1764, but the Americans initially used a number of sources until von Steuben unified them under a system simplified from contemporary English, French, and German practices during the winter of 1777–1778 at Valley Forge. (1) A graphic presentation of the basic von Steuben Manual drill. **MAPS, CHARTS** (see "Documents," "Naval.") **MARINES:** On November 10, 1775 the American Congress approved the raising of two battalions of Continental Marines. They were already in existence in several state navies and participated in practically every battle involving sizable privateers, state fleets, and the Continental Navy. Like their established British counterparts, the marines were intended primarily for boarding, landing parties, firing from the rigging during close engagements, and the maintenance of order aboard ship. (2) Recreated Marine musicians; note the tinned fife case on the man at the left.

Sources: 2—Brigade of the American Revolution, photo by Michael Cleary.

MARKINGS: Among the more common markings found on weapons and equipment are: (1) Continental Army stamps burned into gun stocks, and other property, i.e. "US," "U STATES," "UNITED STATES" ("IP" is an Inspector). (2) A Brown Bess musket escutcheon plate bearing the popular British "fraction"–the unit designation is above and the weapon's individual number below. (3) "The Gun Role" for Capt. Edmund Wells Company in May 1757 (American) listing the "British fractions" on weapons just received. The wide diversion of numbers indicates an odd assortment of old arms shipped to the provincials. (4) The English initial "viewing" and final "gunmaker's" proof stamps found on barrels (at the breech) of muskets from the Royal Armory. (5) London firearm proofs: "V" for the first "viewing" and "GP" signifying the gunmaker's final approval. (6) Broad arrow and crown; the English government's mark of ownership. (7) A British "viewer's" or inspector's stamp (the number denotes the inspector). (8) The Amsterdam control mark. (9) "SVL" is the German manufacturing city of Suhl which also used the hen for its County of Henneberg. (10) The running wolf used by Passau and Solingen, Germany, and widely counterfeited. (11) The English running fox; its center initials are the maker, Samuel Harvey.

Sources: 1, 2—George C. Neumann; 3—Edward Charol.

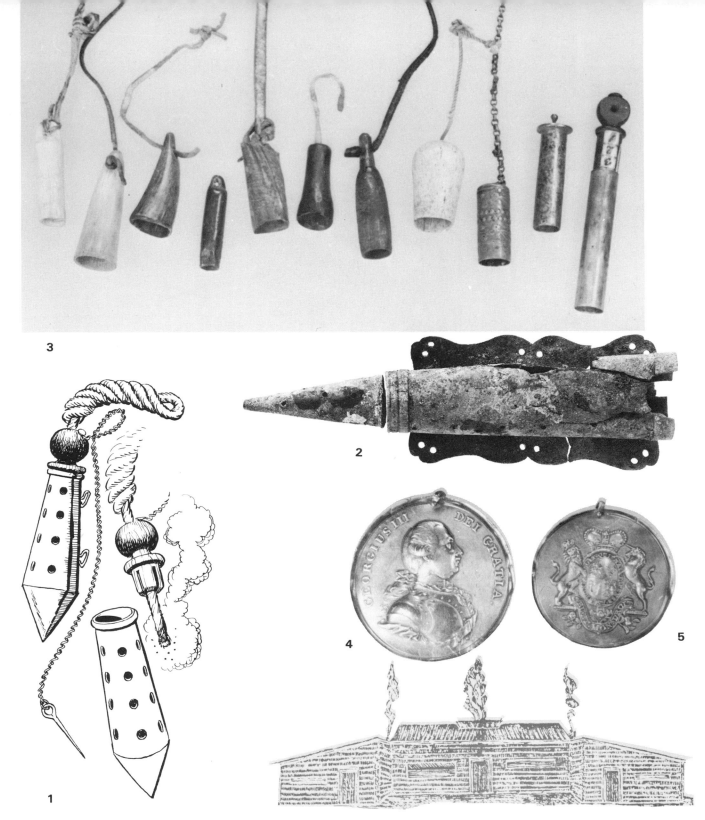

MARQUEE (see "Tents.") MATCHCASE, GRENADIER: Originally worn on the grenadier's cross-belt to light grenades for throwing, it remained in position after they were converted back to full duties with the musket as a mark of tradition and recognition. The usual matchcase (1) was made of perforated sheet brass or white metal having soldered seams. The removable wooden handle held a smoldering match rope which had its reserve length passing through a center hole; note also the brass chain and iron pick. (2) Remains of one found at Fort Stanwix, N.Y., c. 1758–1781; it is mounted on a rectangular base and measures 7" as shown (handle missing). MEASURES, POWDER (also see "Ammunition," "Gunpowder," "Horns," "Hunting Bags," "Tools, Hand"): For those who loaded with loose powder various small measures or "chargers" were used. They usually hung from a cross-belt. (3) These typical examples are made from bone, horn, pewter, tinned iron, wood, brass, iron, and brass-wood. MEDALS (also see "Decorations," "Trade Ornaments, Indian"): It was a common practice to issue commemorative medals for special events or achievements during the 18th century. Most relating to the Revolution were issued after the war, but others, such as this King George silver medal (4, 5) were in wide use at the time—especially among Indians who received them as gifts and wore them around their necks; MEDICAL EQUIPMENT (also see "Bottles"): (6) American regimental hospital (Dr. Joseph Tilton). (cont.)

Sources: 2—Fort Stanwix National Historic Site; 3—George C. Neumann; 4, 5—William H. Guthman.

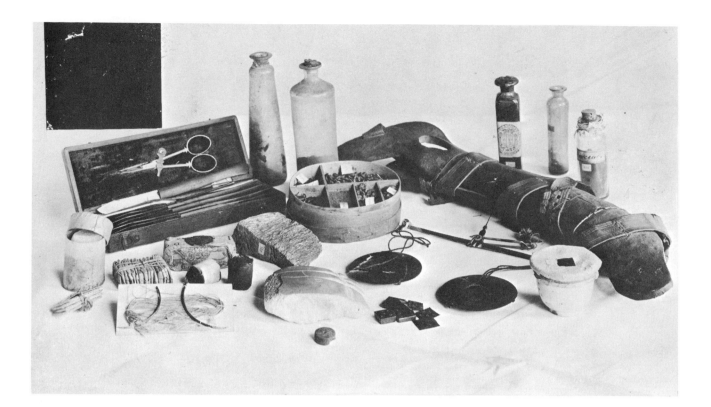

3

1

2

3a

3b

MEDICAL EQUIPMENT (cont.) (also see "Bottles.") Probably the best indication of the medical capabilities available to the American soldier is the estimate (Dr. James Thacher's diary and pension records per David Sabine article) that in eight years of war about 4,400 were killed in battle, 6,200 suffered non-fatal wounds, and some 60,000 died from disease or malnutrition. This tragic record stems from a number of causes: the army's early medical organization was plagued with politics, medicines were scarce, and little was known about basic sanitation in camp. Moreover, of some 3500 "doctors" in the colonies in 1775, only about 200 had medical degrees (most were apprenticed to practicing physicians), and, like the British, few regimental surgeons were required to pass examinations. The men, already weakened by improper nutrition, and often near starvation, were easily susceptible to the ever present typhoid, typhus, dysentery, diphtheria, malaria, measles, mumps, pleurisy, pneumonia, and tuberculosis. When a limb was hit in battle the large diameter bullets usually did sufficient damage to require amputation—which was compounded by unsterilized instruments and dirty dressings. Normal treatment for illness favored both botanicals and chemicals. The most common included sulfur, tartar emetic, calomel, mercury, opium, ipecac, castor oil, epsom salts, rattlesnake root, ginseng (mandrake root), and Jesuit's bark (which contained quinine).

186   *Sources: 1, 2—Frank J. Kravic; 3—Armed Forces Institute of Pathology; 3a—West Point Museum; 3b—The Crown Point Foundation.*

(1, 2) When drugs or liquor were not available to dull pain the man was often given a lead musket ball to bite, e.g. the deep teeth marks in the two excavated bullets at the left. The superficial surface teeth marks on #2 are typical of several found and may indicate the practice of rolling one in the mouth during hot weather (not being aware of lead poisoning). (3) Medical kit used by Dr. Solomon Drowne of the Continental Army. Included are leg splints, raw and processed drugs, a mortar, scales and weights, scalpels, curved needles, and sutures. (3a) An 18th century medicine chest displays scales, drug bottles, and packets. (3b) English brass apothecary measures which nest in the large unit having the hinged cover (excavated at Crown Point, N.Y.). (4) Two multiple lancets or fleams used in the common practice of bleeding patients by cutting a vein; the one at left also includes a scalpel and carrying case; each measures 3″ closed. (5) Horn handled fleam or lancet used by Dr. Hinakins of Montclair, N.J. (1770s); 3½″ closed. (6, 7) Mortars and pestles—one of brass, the other of wood. (8) Automatic fleams which made the vein incision with a rapid spring activated stroke. (9) Typical tinned container for medical supplies. (cont.)

Sources: 4 (left)—George C. Neumann; 4 (right), 6–9—Frank J. Kravic; 5—Robert Nittolo.

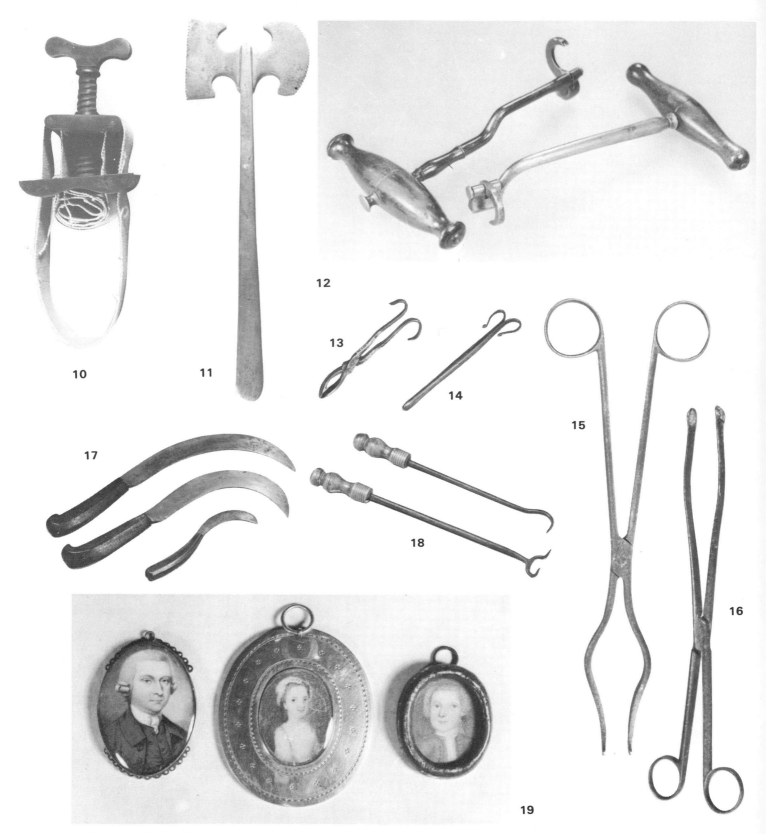

MEDICAL EQUIPMENT (cont.) (10) Mechanical tourniquet. (11) A saw for cranial surgery. (12) Two tooth extractors. (13, 15) Forceps. (14, 16) Bullet Extractors. (17) Three amputation knives. (18) Surgical hooks or retractors. **MILITIA** (see "Infantry.") **MINIATURES:** (19) These small oval paintings, often on ivory, were executed for various members of well-to-do families. Many soldiers carried them as reminders of their wives or sweethearts. In addition, celebrities of the day, especially kings, were commercially reproduced in this manner and sold to the public. Since many family miniatures were painted by itinerant artists in America, quality varies greatly. **MIRRORS** (see "Shaving.")

Sources: 10, 11—Morristown National Historic Park; 12—the authors; 13, 14, 17, 18—Armed Forces Institute of Pathology; 15—Edward Charol; 16—Robert Nittolo; 19—John Ivan.

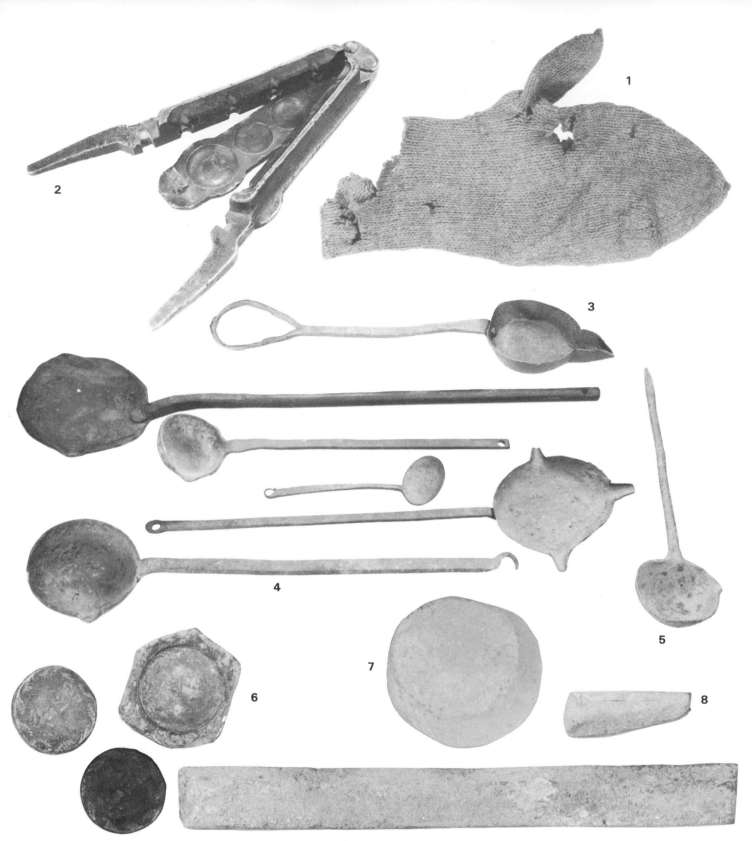

MITTENS (also see #9, p. 131): Both mittens and gloves were used in cold weather. (1) A light brown knit wool mitten recovered from a clay bog next to buttons of the 23rd, 27th, and 40th British regiments; 12″ long. **MOCCASINS** (see "Footwear.") **MOLDS** (also see "Fishing"): Molding was an important craft in the colonies. The pewterer, for example, cast in brass molds, occasionally soapstone, or even plaster of Paris. This included "sadware" (one-piece objects cast in two-part molds), e.g. plates, dishes, buttons, spoons, and sundials, as well as "hollowware" (mugs, tankards, teapots) made of several individually cast parts. Conversely, the brazier in molding brass had to prepare a new wooden or lead pattern for each casting to make the needed impression in a flask of sand (into which the molten brass was poured). Both metals were finished on a lathe by skimming and burnishing, or for irregular shapes by hand scraping and filing. The individual soldier and woodsman also molded—"running lead" to cast round bullets in his brass, iron, or soapstone mold. (2) A 3-piece brass button mold which incorporates the pierced shanks. (3) A dipper for melting lead made from an old grease lamp; 11½″ long. (4, 5) Typical ladles of the period; 7½″ to 25″ long. (6) The dies for an officer's button (shown) of the British 21st Rgt. (cont.)

Sources: 1, 6—Don Troiani; 2, 4, 8, 9—George C. Neumann; 3—Valley Forge Historical Society, Wm. Richard Gordon Collection; 5, 7—Frank J. Kravic.

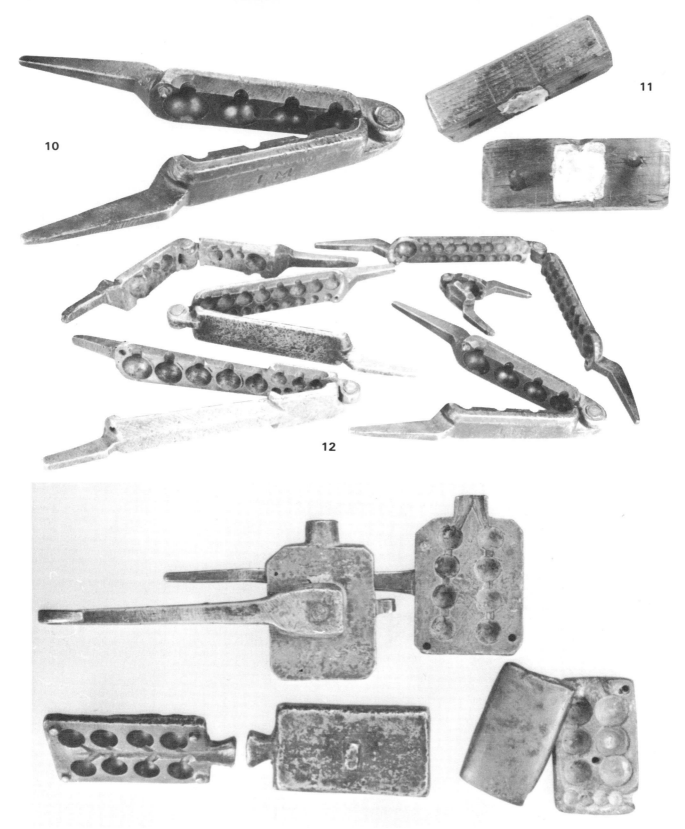

MOLDS (cont.) (7-9 on previous page) (7) An oval piece of lead either the remainder from a ladle or a round pig (Champlain Valley site). (9) A "pig" of trade lead as sold for remelting; 7⅞" x ⅞" x ½"; from an upper N.Y. State excavation. (8) Part of a lead pig (Indian grave in N.Y.). (10) A 4-cavity "V" type mold popular among the troops; its wooden handles are gone; the "IM" marking is believed to be the maker, Josiah Miller (i.e. "J" was written as an "I"); 5¾" long. The use of loose fitting bullets (see "Gunpowder") meant that such a mold with four sizes could satisfy the variety of musket bore diameters in most units. (11) A ball mold set into a pair of wooden blocks to conserve metal and lighten its weight. (12) "V" pattern bullet molds containing a wide variety of ball and buck cavities; the handles are gone. (13) Multiple cavity flat brass molds with and without handles, i.e. some were simply set up between rocks or in the ground.

Sources: 11—Valley Forge Historical Society, Wm. Richard Gordon Collection; remainder George C. Neumann.

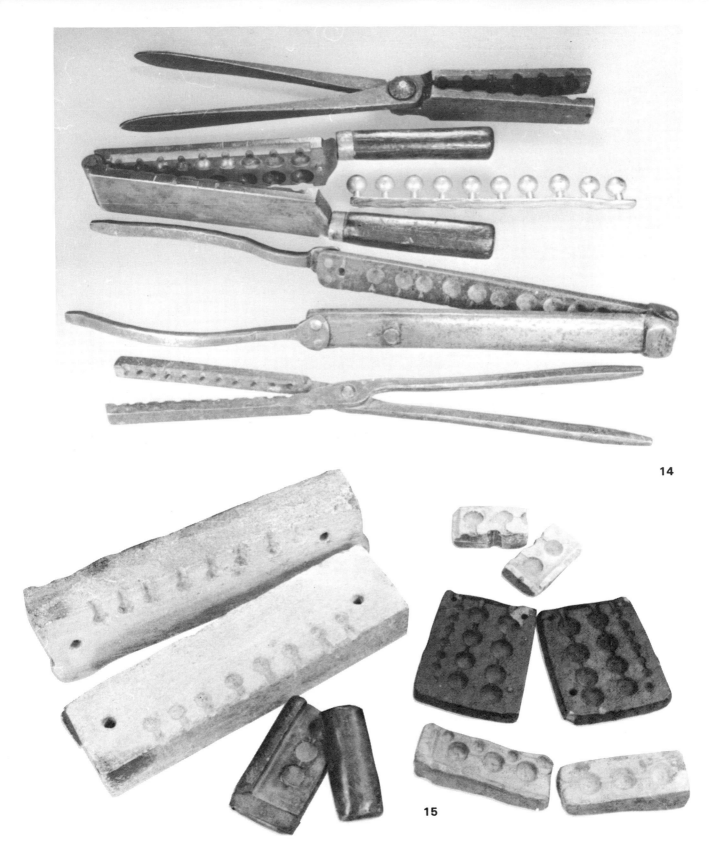

14

15

(14) Large scissor type and "V" molds of brass and iron; 12¾" to 17¾" in length; note the line of cast balls and their sprue. (15) Crude bullet molds cut into soft soapstone and brownstone—a practice also followed in southern Europe and northern Africa. Because the bullet was undersized to offset the buildup of powder fouling in the bore, the uneven balls cast in these molds were a practical improvisation when formal molds were scarce. (cont.)

Source: George C. Neumann.

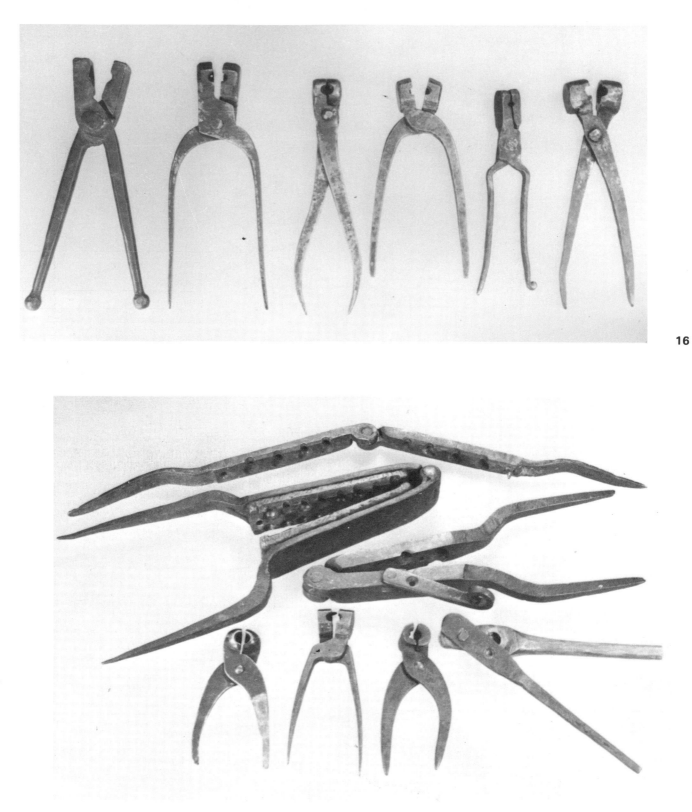

16

17

MOLDS (cont.) (16) Various single ball scissors type iron molds. (17) The right center example includes a pivoting sprue cut-off; left of center is a brass mold held by an outer iron form which provides the tangs for the missing wooden handles; (lower center) three rifle molds—usually individually made for each weapon to achieve an optimum bore fit; at lower right is a wooden base having a crude metal mold form inserted into it, plus a pivoting iron sprue cutter.

Source: George C. Neumann.

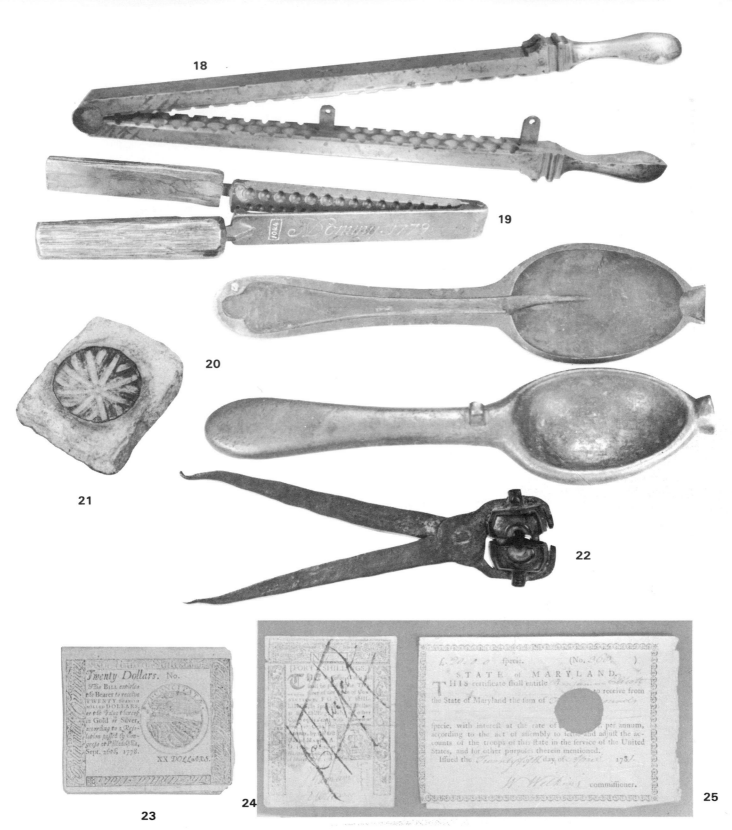

(18) A large British brass mold holding 40 musket size cavities; 24″ in length, it is marked by its maker, "WILSON"; circa 1750. (19) A brass shot mold made and marked "N Dominy 1779" by Nathaniel Dominy IV of East Hampton, Long Island, N.Y. (20) An English brass two-piece spoon mold for pewter casting; c. 1740–1750. (21) A single-piece lead mold probably for pressing out thin button shells; from the American Fishkill, N.Y. camp. (22) Bullet mold with a brass cavity secured in an iron frame; 6¼″ long; a type discovered at Fort Washington, N.Y. **MONEY** (also see "Sutler"): "Not worth a Continental" was more fact than phrase as the Revolution progressed. With the receding of patriotic fervor following 1776 many people looked only to hard money for security. The paper currencies of the various rebelling colonies and their national government depreciated rapidly until many states refused to honor neighboring state issues, and counterfeiting the crudely printed notes became widespread. (23) An unsigned note on blue paper produced as a reference to detect counterfeit versions of that issue. (24) Most bogus currency was burned, but this Connecticut note survives with "counterfeit" written across its face. (25) States issued special notes to cover legislative appropriations. This one dated 1781 from Maryland was authorized to pay state Continental troops; the hole is a form of cancellation. (cont.)

Sources: 18—Edward Charol; 19—Robert Nittolo; 20, 21—George C. Neumann; 22—Don Troiani; 23, 24, 25—Frank J. Kravic.

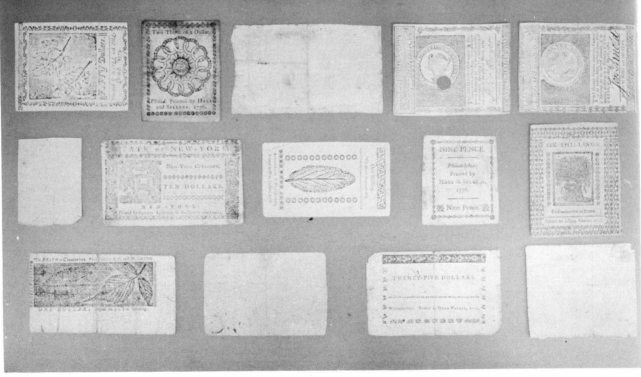

MONEY (cont.) (26) Representative Continental and state bills: (1st row, l to r) Continental, $50, 1779; Continental ⅔ of a dollar, 1776; New Hampshire, 30 shillings, 1775; Massachusetts, $8, 1780; Rhode Island, $5, 1780. (2nd row) Connecticut, 4 pence, 1777; New York, $10, 1776; New Jersey, 1 shilling, 1776; Pennsylvania, 9 pence, 1776; Delaware, 6 shillings, 1776. (3rd row): Maryland, $1, 1779; Virginia, $10, 1776; North Carolina, $25, 1779; Georgia, for a filled-in amount, 1777. (27) The reverse face of the same notes in #26.

Source: The authors' collections.

Many coins of Europe circulated in America prior to and during the Revolution. The fine quality of Spanish silver from Central and South America frequently caused the Americans to back their currency in Spanish milled dollars. Few coins are found in camp debris and even these are often badly worn. Soldiers would carry script more readily or maintain their balance on the paymaster's books. (28, 29) Two English pennies (dated 1782, 1758); the most common coin excavated. (30, 31) British half-pennies (1749, 1746). (32, 33) English 3 pence (1763, 1762). (34) Silver shilling of George II, dated 1723. (35) "Voce Populi"; tokens minted for use in Ireland, but many are discovered here. (36, 37) French sou marques (1740, 1755), issued to pay France's troops for service in America. (38) Two reals of Spain picturing Charles II; Madrid mint. (39) Two brass discs; because of the coin scarcity tavern owners and sutlers issued these brass discs which passed as readily as specie. (40–44) Spanish silver "cobs" (cut from a bar); all are out of British and American camps. (45) Spanish silver milled pillar dollar, "1769." (46) Spanish milled dollar, "1772." (47) 2 real Spanish silver, Charles III. (48) French silver ecu, "1756." (49) George I silver shilling, "1723." (50, 51) Hibernia far-things, 1766. (52) Rosa Americana penny, "1722." (53) Virginia half-penny minted in England, "1773." (54) A Wm. Pitt token. (55) Reverse of a New Jersey one shilling note, 1776. (56) Front of a 3 dollar Continental note, 1777.

Sources: 46—Ed Bradley; 47–49, 52, 55, 56—George C. Neumann; remainder Frank J. Kravic.

MUG (see "Drinkingware.") **MUSIC** (also see "Jew's Harp"): The most important military muscial instrument of the 18th century was the snare drum. It not only provided cadence, but also transmitted the basic orders to troops in camp and on the battlefield with specific beatings which the soldier was trained to recognize. The drums were fashioned from wood (occasionally with a sheet brass shell) plus skin heads, catgut snares, and ropes for tension (that required leather pull-down "lugs" to help tighten the heads). Their shells were generally kept within a 2" difference in depth and diameter dimensions. When marching, the common step was "about seventy-five in a minute," the quick step "about one hundred and twenty" (von Steuben). In addition to use of the drum for signaling infantry, the trumpet was employed by many cavalry units and the bugle horn ("hunting horn") for some cavalry and light infantry. The principal music source for the military was fife and drums. Many European and some American regiments also had bands which were supported privately. They used oboes, clarionets, flutes, horns, bassons, trumpets, and tympani at the start of the Revolution, and by its late years had added Turkish type instruments for percussion, e.g. bass drums, cymbals ("clash pans"), tambourines, and "Jingling Johnnies" (mounting many small bells).

Sources: 1—Brigade of the American Revolution, photo by Michael Cleary; 2, 5—Edward Charol; 3—West Point Museum; 4—George C. Neumann.

196

(1) Following the British tradition, musicians in many American units wore coats in reverse colors from the facing and body colors of their regiment as shown here; note also that most musicians wore swords. (2) A low American drum with reinforcing pewter bands on the shell; circa 1740–1760. (3) Tympani of the British 9th of Foot captured at Saratoga; it includes a permanent stand. (4) Crude American drumsticks; most were well turned; the British preferred ebony or brazilwood. (5) French buff leather drum shoulder sling; included are three flaming bomb insignia, a brass plate with two stick holders. (6) A typical snare drum with leather lugs to tighten the rope and heads; note the use of brass or iron tacks to create designs on the shell; 16⅝″ x 15½″. (7) A French snare ("side") drum as used by them in America, 1779–1783; the jack and hook for its snares are also illustrated; as with the British, the two "counterhoops" were usually painted; shell, 16.9″ x 13.4″; hoops are 1.6″ wide. (8) British regimental drummer; his buff leather shoulder strap includes loops for drum sticks (a narrower sling around the neck was also used); the two bottom straps on the drum are shoulder belts for carrying the drum on the back during long marches. (cont.)

Sources: 6—The Connecticut Historical Society; 8—Brigade of the American Revolution, photo by Michael Cleary.

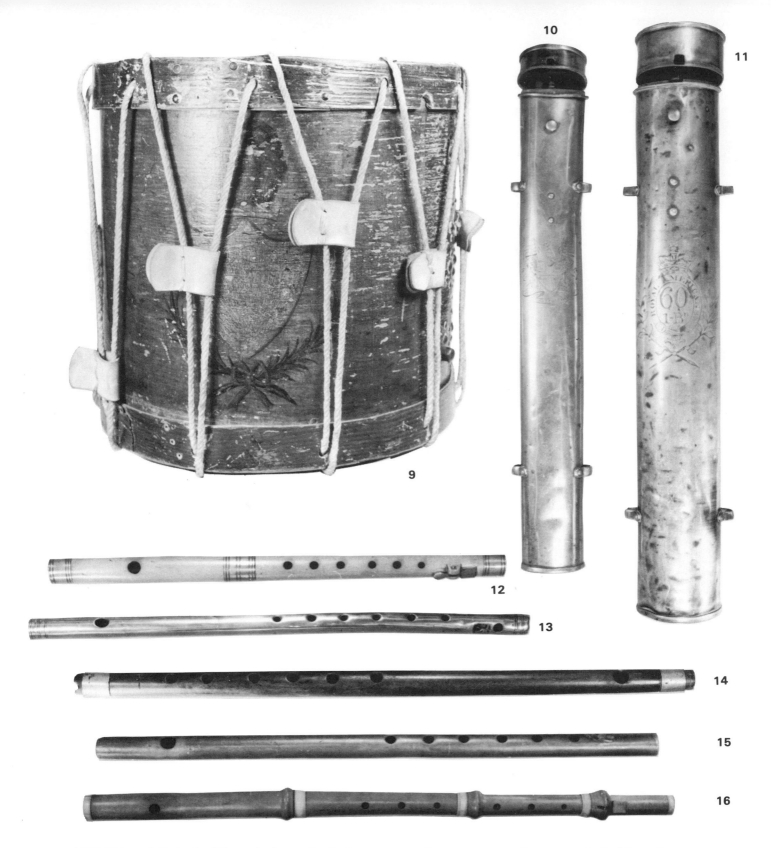

MUSIC (cont.) (9) An English made drum; the shell measures 16″ x 14½″, counterhoops are 2½″ wide; its lugs were reattached inverted. (10) A brass English drumstick case which includes side loops for a shoulder cord and an engraved heraldic device on the face; 15¾″ x 2⅛″ x 1½″; oval in cross-section. (11) Brass fife case marked for the British 60th Royal American Regiment; its cover is hinged and the side loops are riveted; 17¼″ x 2¾″ (round); American musicians favored similar cases of tinned iron (see "Marines"). (12–15) Fifes believed to be representative of the 18th century: (12, 14) Wood with brass fittings. (13) Brass. (15) Pewter. (16) A wood flute with one key; 23½″ in length.

Sources: 9–13 Edward Charol; 14—William H. Guthman; 15, 16—George C. Neumann.

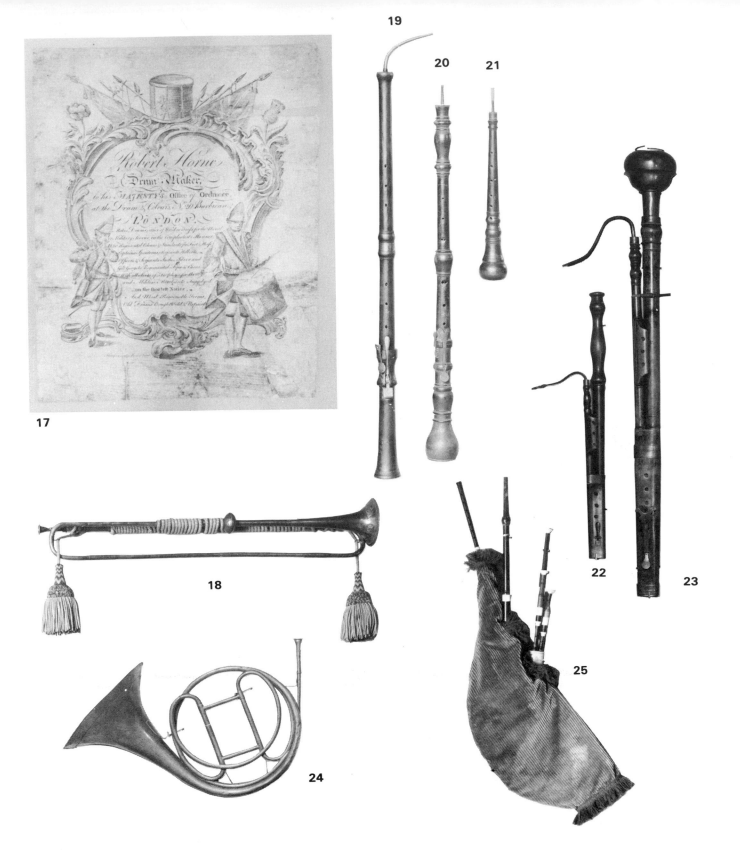

(17) A typical English drummaker's label (found inside the shell). (18) A representative 18th century trumpet by Dampier of Paris; as used by dragoons for signaling. (19) English bass oboe with two keys; oboes used a double reed which vibrated when blown. (20) A German 2-key oboe, circa 1725. (21) A late version of the earlier shawm. (22) An octave bassoon with 3 keys; French. (23) A large 3-key Swiss bassoon. (24) French horn. (25) 18th century Northumbrian bagpipe (British border area) having 3 drone pipes. (cont.)

Sources: 17—George C. Neumann; remainder, Metropolitan Museum of Art (New York).

26

1

27

Norwich march 11th 1777

*These may certify to the Committee of Pay Table for the State of Connecticut that Mr Elisha Edgerton of D Norwich in the year AD 1775 Did Voluntarily Lend a Gun to D State which was carried in the Army Cagainst the Enemy at Boston: D Gun was Detained there and hath never been Returned. & there can be no account found of the Price of D Gun. but we the Subscribers by the best account we can Get about D Gun are of opinion that he the D Edgerton ought to Receive for D Gun and the use thereof at Least four Pounds Squd

Joshua Perkins
Elijah Brewster
John Huntington*

MUSIC (cont.) (26) A bugle horn (or hunting horn) used by George Washington at Mount Vernon; this type of instrument was also employed to transmit orders among some dragoon and light infantry units. (27) British bass drum; it was usually played with a stick or stick and brush. **SLINGS** (see "Belts, Frogs, Scabbards.") **MUSKETOONS** (see "Blunderbusses.") **MUSKETS** (also see "Firearms," "Flintlock, Action," "Gunpowder," "Tactics, Battlefield"): The foot soldier's standard fighting arm was the smoothbore musket. It fired a round lead ball or multiple balls, and loaded from the muzzle with loose black powder (see "Gunpowder" and "Ammunition"), which was ignited by a flint lock (see "Flintlock, Action"). Although the flint ignition contributed its share of misfires, the 18th century firearms' real problem was the black powder. When fired, less than half of it changed into a gas; the rest remained as a clinging black fouling which rapidly accumulated—especially inside the barrel. This build-up prevented the ramming down of a tight fitting ball required for accuracy and led to the use of an undersized bullet (usually .04 to .06 caliber smaller than the bore). While such a solution permitted rapid loading, when the musket fired much of the powder's force leaked around the ball—which then moved toward the muzzle deflecting against opposing sides of the bore; thus its last contact greatly affected the final trajectory.

Sources: 26—Mount Vernon Ladies Assn.; 27—George C. Neumann; 1—Frank J. Kravic.

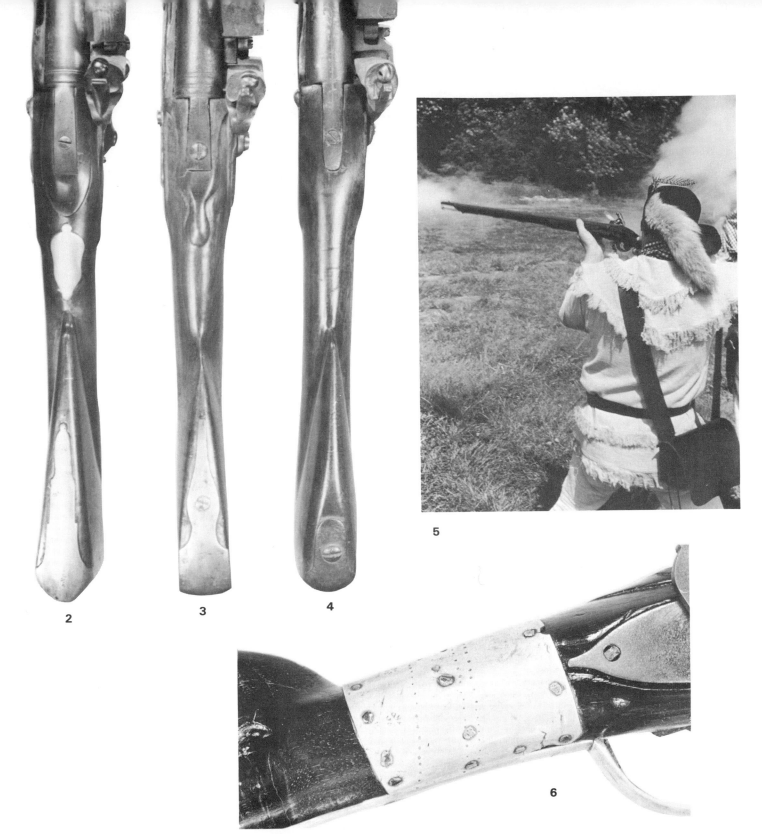

2   **3**   **4**

5

6

Muskets generally lost all accuracy against a man-sized target beyond 50 to 80 yards and led to a concentration on speed loading by the troops, which averaged about four rounds per minute (also see "Rifles" and "Tactics, Battle"). The standard English musket ("Brown Bess") had a .75 caliber bore, brass fittings, and a 46" or 42" pinned barrel; most French models favored a .69 cal. banded barrel, and iron furniture. The American, German, and Dutch muskets employed a mixture of the above patterns. (1) A request for compensation from a citizen in 1777 who had loaned a gun to the troops marching toward Boston in 1775; it had not been returned. (2–4) *Characteristic butt patterns:* (2) The British Long Land Brown Bess (46" barrel) with its stepped brass butt tang (note, no top screw visible), shield-like escutcheon plate, and lobe-shaped raised carving around the barrel tang. (3) A Dutch-German long brass butt tang (1 or 2 screws on top), an optional escutcheon, and the usual raised teardrop carving surrounding the breech. (4) The French musket of the 1760s and later mounts an iron-lobed butt tang with one top screw, but omits an escutcheon plate, raised carving, and rings on the barrel breech. (6) A typical brass repair for the all too common break in the narrow wrist of the stock. (cont.)

Sources: 2, 3, 4, 6—George C. Neumann; 5—Brigade of the American Revolution, photo by Richard Gerding.

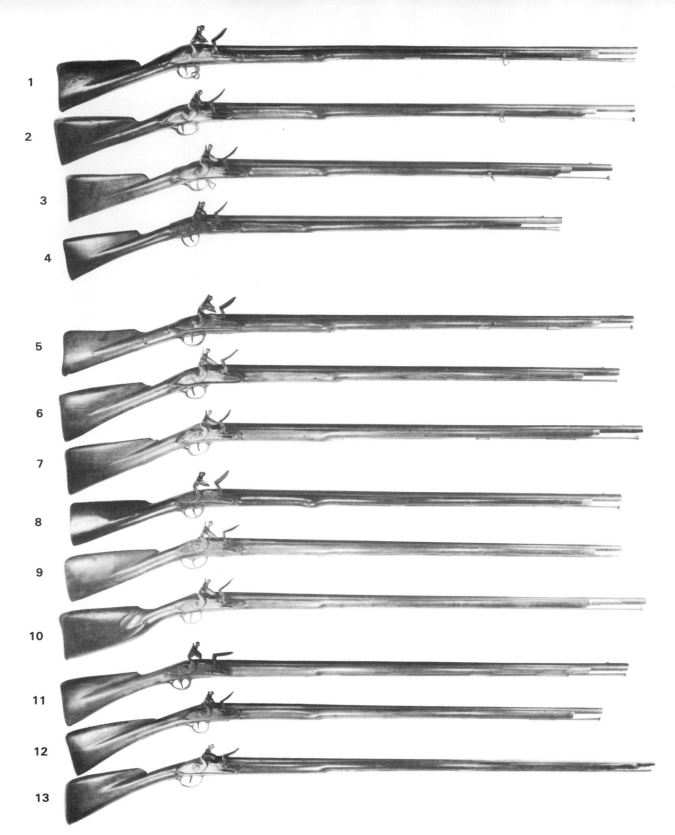

MUSKETS (cont.) (1–4) *British:* (1) Long Land pattern Brown Bess; c. 1728; pinned 46″ barrel of .75 cal.; 61¾″ overall; early banana-shaped lock and wooden rammer; marked "Royal Welsh"; maker, "Wilson." (2) Long Land design by midcentury; "1761 Vernon"; has a straight lock, iron rammer and long flared upper ramrod pipe; still a 46″ barrel; weight 10.8 lbs.; normal walnut stock. (3) Short Land model (adopted in 1760s) that shortened barrel to 42″ (.75 cal.) and modified brass furniture; 58″ length; 10.0 lbs. (4) Royal Navy musket; "EDGE 1759"; flat lock and reinforced hammer; .75 cal.; 38⅞″ pinned barrel; 54½″ long. (5–13) *American:* (5) Copy of Long Land Brown Bess; barrel, 43⅞″, .71 cal.; old British lock; c. 1775–1776. (6) Copy of Short Land model; chestnut stock; Dutch lock and barrel; 42″ pinned barrel; from Mass., c. 1775–1780. (7) British brass furniture copied; German type lock; 44″ barrel marked "SP" (New Jersey). (8) Crude, follows British styling; most furniture of sheet brass; c. 1750–1760. (9) Lock and iron furniture remounted from an early French musket; 8.6 lbs., c. 1760–1776. (10) Club butt stock popular in New England; 62⅞″ length; 8.9 lbs.; c. 1770–1783. (11) Mixes French lock and British furniture; c. 1760–1778; usual walnut stock. (12) Roman nose stock of cherry; English trade lock; from Mass. (13) Uses French, Dutch, and American components; barrel 47½″, .78 cal.

Source: George C. Neumann.

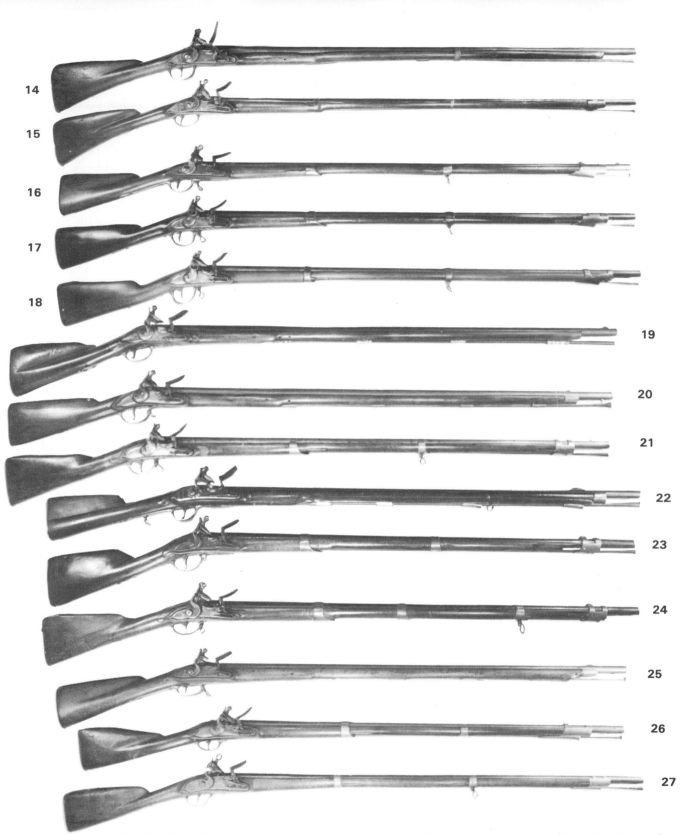

14

15

16

17

18

19

20

21

22

23

24

25

26

27

(14–18) *French:* (14) Model 1717, the first standardized pattern in Europe; iron furniture; pinned barrel with a single band; 46¾″ barrel; 62¾″ length. (15) Model 1746, 46½″ barrel held by 3 iron bands; sling swivels on side; walnut stock; 62¼″ long. (16) 1763 Series with flat lock and reinforced hammer; lower swivels; shorter 44¾″ barrel; .69 cal.; 8.4 lbs., 60″ overall. (17) Model 1772; like the 1763 Series, but rounded lock, lower profile, shorter trigger guard. (18) Model 1777; an innovative design adding a brass flash pan (previously iron), recessed cheek rest, shorter trigger guard; .69 cal.; 59⅞″ length; 8.8 lbs. (19–26) *German-Dutch:* (19) Early Dutch musket, c. 1710–1730; brass furniture, wooden rammer; 45½″ pinned barrel; .75 cal.; 60″ long. (20) Iron mounted German musket; c. 1710–30; wooden rammer; 59½″ length. (21) Dutch, c. 1770–1780; simplified brass fittings (wartime production); 3 bands, rounded lock; marked, "GENERALITETT" (Dutch Govt. property). (22) German, Potzdam-made model favored by Prussians; "POTZDAM MAGAZ" marking; high comb and heavy brass; 41″, .75 cal. barrel. 10.9 lbs.; c. 1750–1782. (23) Dutch, c. 1750–1770; high butt profile. (24) German-Dutch type; .75 cal., 40½″ barrel. (25) German-Dutch, c. 1770–1780; 59½″ length. (26) Dutch contract, "N. TOMSON/A. ROTTERDAM; brass furniture like British; c. 1775–1780. (27) Spanish, Model 1752 (used in America in Revolution); 43½″, .72 cal. barrel; brass furniture; 59⅝″ overall. (cont.)

Source: George C. Neumann.

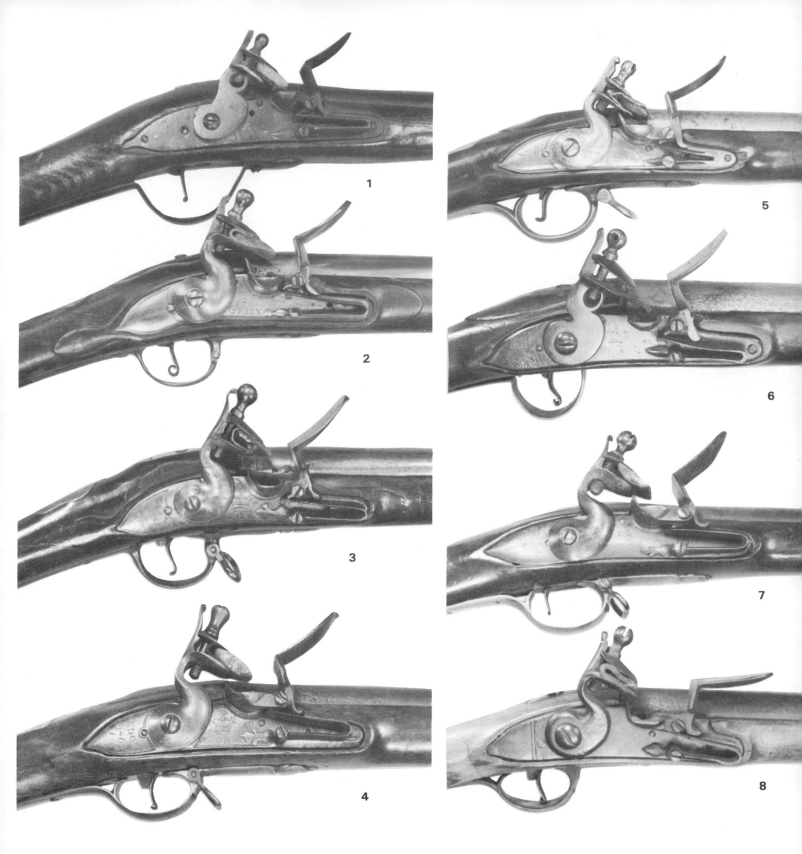

MUSKETS (cont.) (1–6) *British musket lock evolution:* (1) c. 1700–1710; flat lock and reinforced hammer; it requires 3 side screws. (2) c. 1710–1720; rounded lock with curving profile (banana shape) surrounded by heavy raised carving; narrow post on hammer; no supporting bridle from flash pan to frizzen screw; early curled trigger; lock by "T GREEN." (3) c. 1728; early Long Land pattern of the Brown Bess which evolved in the 1720s; flat back on hammer; lock marked "TOWER 1728" (i.e. the Royal Arsenal in the Tower of London). (4) c. 1750–1780 styling for later Long Land (46" barrel) and Short Land (42" barrel); the lock's lower edge is now straight; flash pan-frizzen bridle added; less carving; rear trigger bow post now split. (5) c. 1760–1770 light dragoon carbine lock, "EDGE 1762"; note return of the narrow hammer post (re #2). (6) Royal Navy musket, "EDGE 1759"; typical flat lock, reinforced hammer, squared frizzen top. (7) American copy of midcentury British lock (see #4). (8) American copy of the French c. 1728–1754 lock (see #11), but still keeping the English style trigger guard; note too the colonists' tendency not to drill the trigger guard loop for a sling swivel.

Source: George C. Neumann.

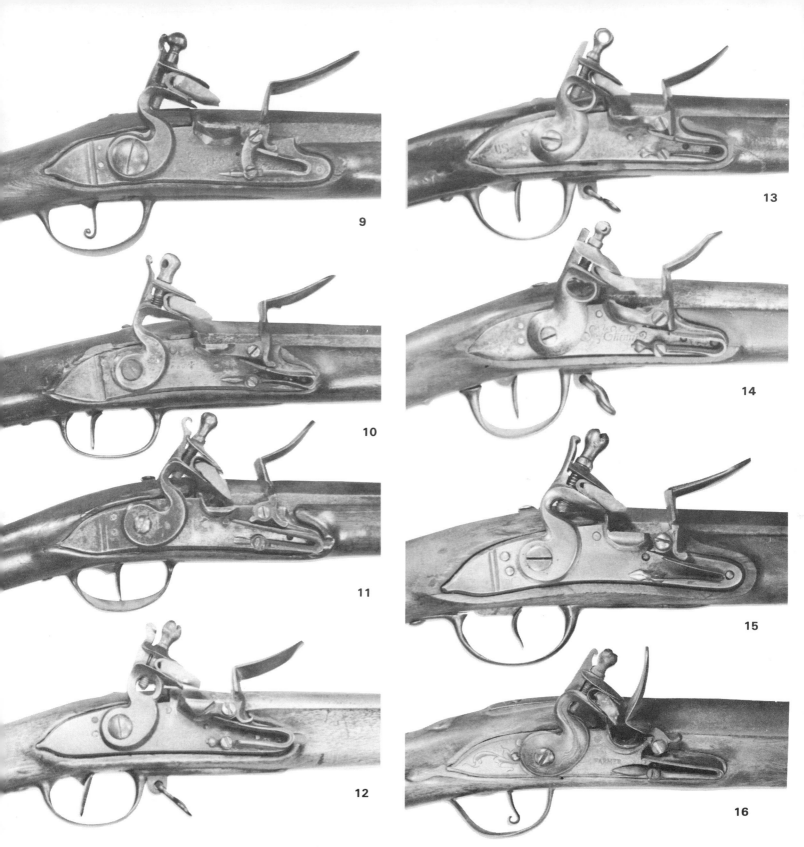

(9–14) French musket locks: (9) Model 1717 having its distinctive vertical bridle on the frizzen spring; note the minimal raised carving by the French; 6½" long. (10) Model 1728; the earlier vertical bridle is now horizontal from flash pan to frizzen. (11) Model 1746; the bridle has been omitted: 6½" length. (12) Model 1763 Series; a shorter (6¼") flat beveled lock was introduced including a reinforced hammer and the return to a horizontal bridle; (13) Model 1772; a rounded lock, pan, and hammer appear vs. the flat styling of the 1760s (see #12). (14) Model 1777; a slanted brass pan was added in place of the iron one (to reduce corrosion). (15) Liege-Low Country popular trade lock style; circa 1740–1760. (16) English trade lock; marked by its maker, "FARMER", and incised designs; c. 1760–1770. (cont.)

Source: George C. Neumann.

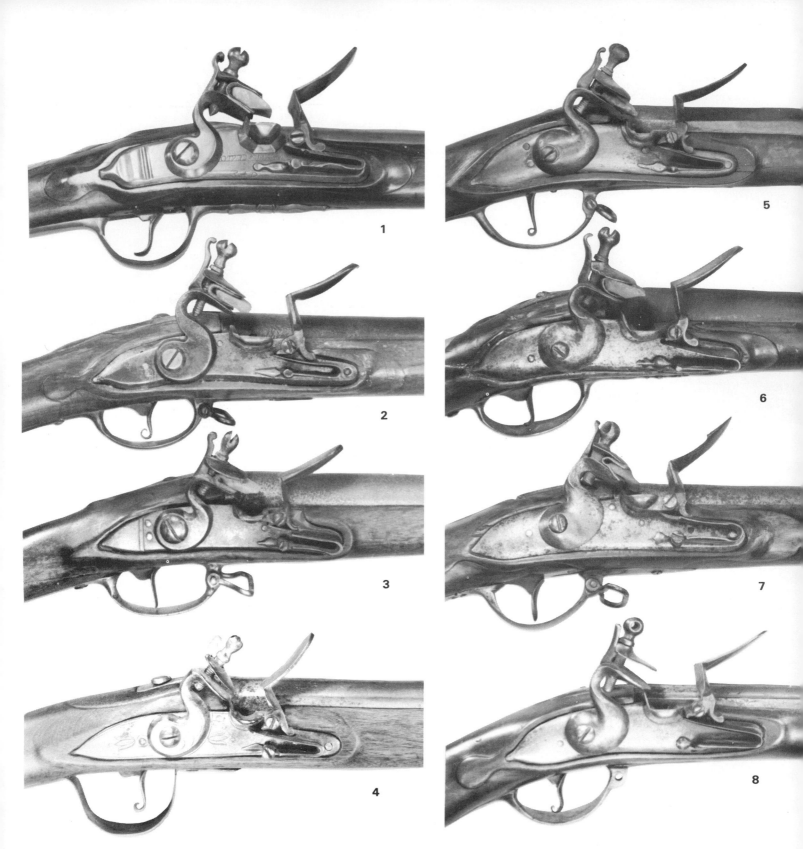

MUSKETS (cont.) (1–3, 5–7) *German-Dutch musket locks:* (1) Potzdam lock pattern with an unbridled, faceted flash pan; single neck; square edged hammer; undulating tail surface; heavy raised stock carving; c. 1720–1782; marked "POTSDAM MAGAZ", "S&D" (for Splittgerber and Daun who operated the arsenal from 1723 to 1775; "DSE" markings would mean David Splittgerber Erben, from 1775–1795). (2) Beveled flat lock-hammer styling, circa 1740–1770; it usually omitted the horizontal bridle; 6⅝" long. (3) A smaller and later flat lock, c. 1770–1780 (now with a bridle), which resembles the pre-1763 French models; 6⅛" length. (4) A common British flat trade lock engraved with the popular tulip design. (5) Rounded German "banana" shape of c. 1710–1730 which includes the early curve on the hammer post; 6⅝" overall. (6) Circa 1710–1730 Dutch rounded lock with an early bottom line curving profile; 6¾" long. (7) Dutch, c. 1770–1780; like the British pattern, the curved lock assumed a straighter form after midcentury; note too the retention of raised carving and the addition of a horizontal bridle; 6⅞" length. (8) American copy of an early Dutch lock (see #6); c. 1770–1785.

Sources: 4—Frank J. Kravic; remainder—George C. Neumann.

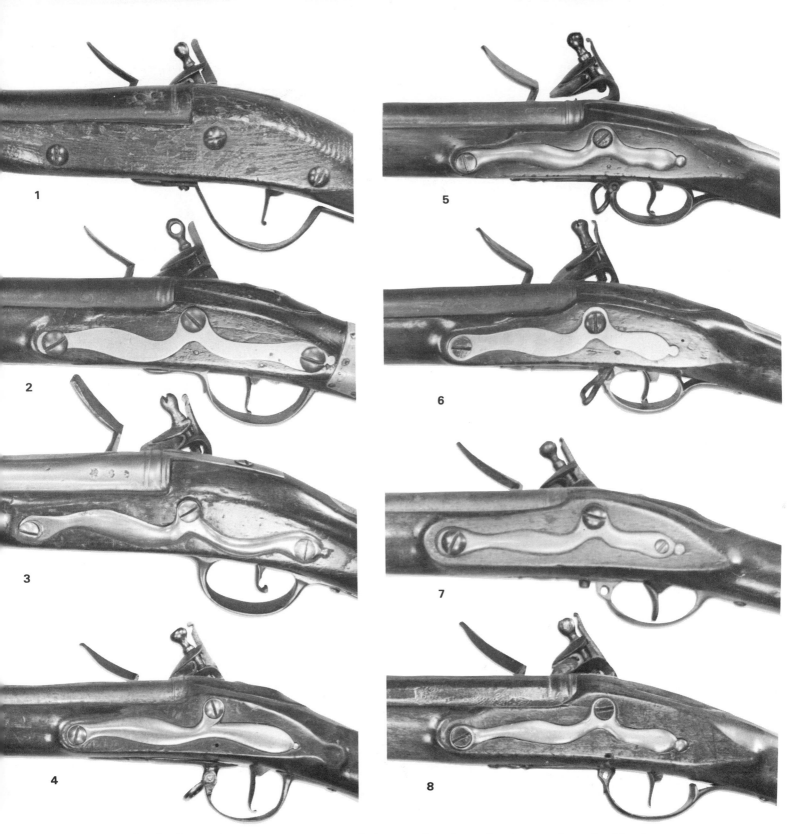

(1-6) **British side plate evolution:** (1) C. 1770-1710; the large early lock requires 3 screws from the side plate to secure it. (2) c. 1710-1720; an almost symmetrical side plate (flat) with two lobes from the center lock screw. (3) c. 1710-1720; a rounded iron design with the rear lobe slightly shorter than the other. (4) c. 1720; still iron and rounded, but the rear lock screw has been discarded. (5) c. 1725-1760; the Long Land Brown Bess pattern emerges in its rounded brass form. (6) c. 1755-1790; beginning with select models in the late 1750s, this flat brass version finally gained standard acceptance in 1768 on the new Short Land musket. (7) Dutch contract musket copies the English Long Land styling (see #5), but adds a short rear wood screw; c. 1775-1780. (8) An American imitation of the rounded brass British Long Land design (i.e. #5); c. 1775-1776. (cont.)

Source: George C. Neumann.

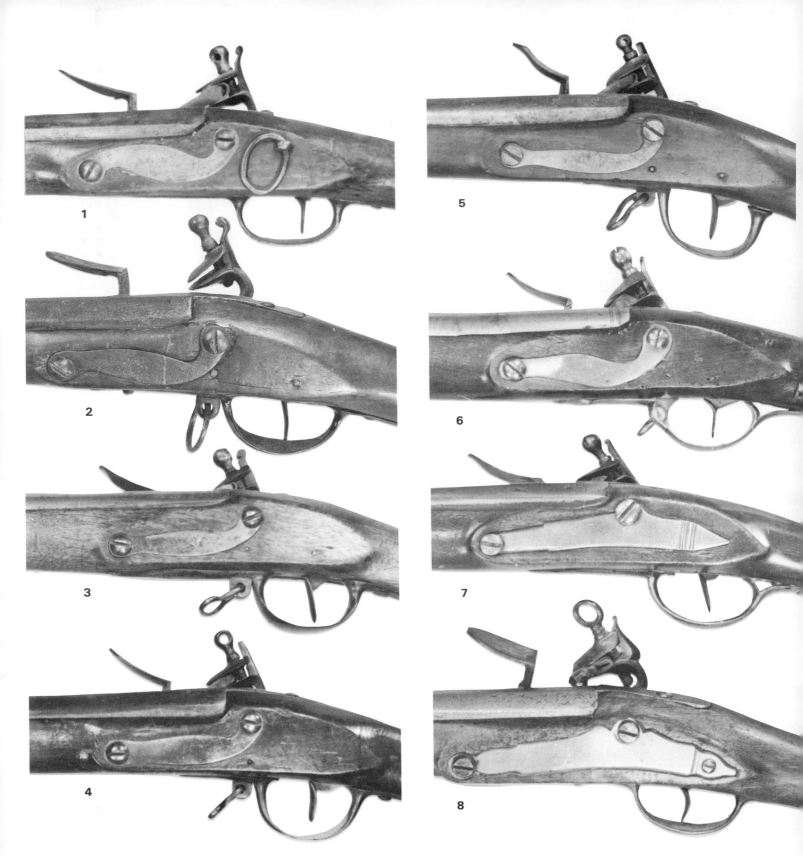

MUSKETS (cont.) (1–5) *French musket side plates:* (1) Model 1728; a typical French 2-screw "S" shaped flat iron pattern; its oval ring is the side sling swivel used until the 1750s. (2) Model 1754; the side plate continues wide but is flattening its curve; the sling swivel is now round and hangs just forward of the trigger loop. (3) 1763 Series; the familiar "S" contour is narrower and the sling swivel flattened. (4) Model 1772; the side plate continues to straighten. (5) Model 1777; its thinner form is now almost straight across the lower edge. (6) An American brass copy of the traditional iron French side plate—plus a British type trigger guard. (7) American triangular brass style including decorative channels. (8) Spanish, Model 1752; a triangular form with a short wood screw added to secure the rear point.

Source: George C. Neumann.

208

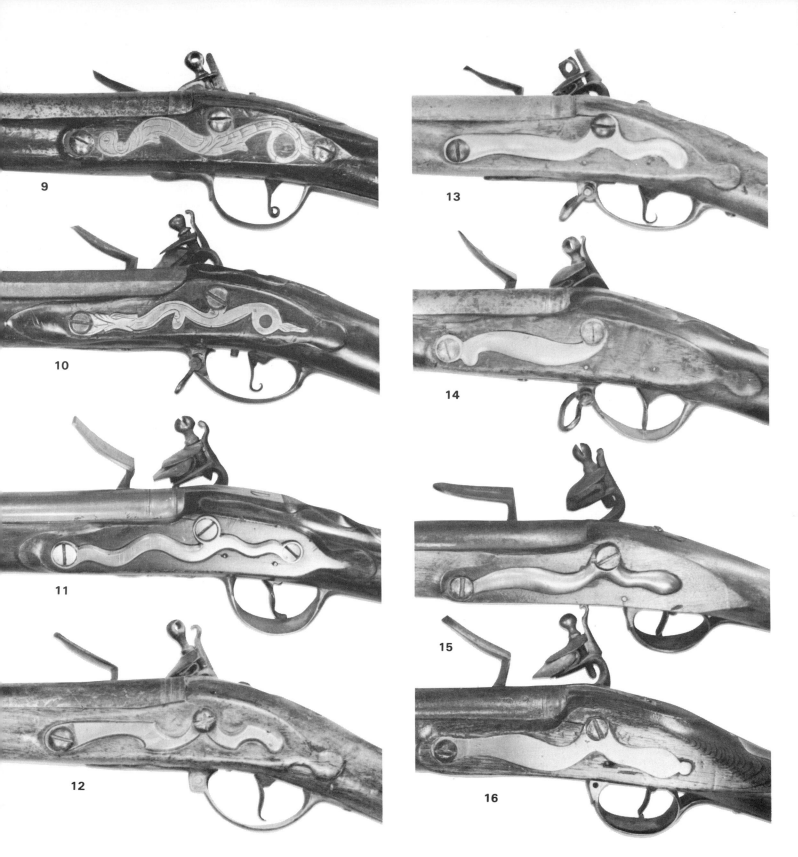

(9–14) **German-Dutch musket side plates:** (9) An English/German 3-screw brass dragon side plate; circa 1700–1715. (10) German dragon type but with less detail than #9 and only 2 screws; c. 1710. (11) The German "Potzdam Magaz" pattern; c. 1720–1782; it retains the dragon outline with a flat surface and adds a short third (wood) screw. (12) German-Dutch, c. 1750–1770; the flat beveled shape is shortening at the tail. (13) German-Dutch; circa 1760–1780; the outline continues to simplify, but the surface is rounded (see British style #5, p. 207). (14) Dutch, c. 1770–1780; under wartime pressures the tail is now omitted (as the English did with their India pattern). (15) An American rounded side plate, circa 1760–1778, which copies the British Long Land style (#5, p. 207), as well as the Dutch (#13 this page). (16) American brass copy of the flat English Short Land Brown Bess design (i.e. #6, p. 207). (cont.)

Source: George C. Neumann.

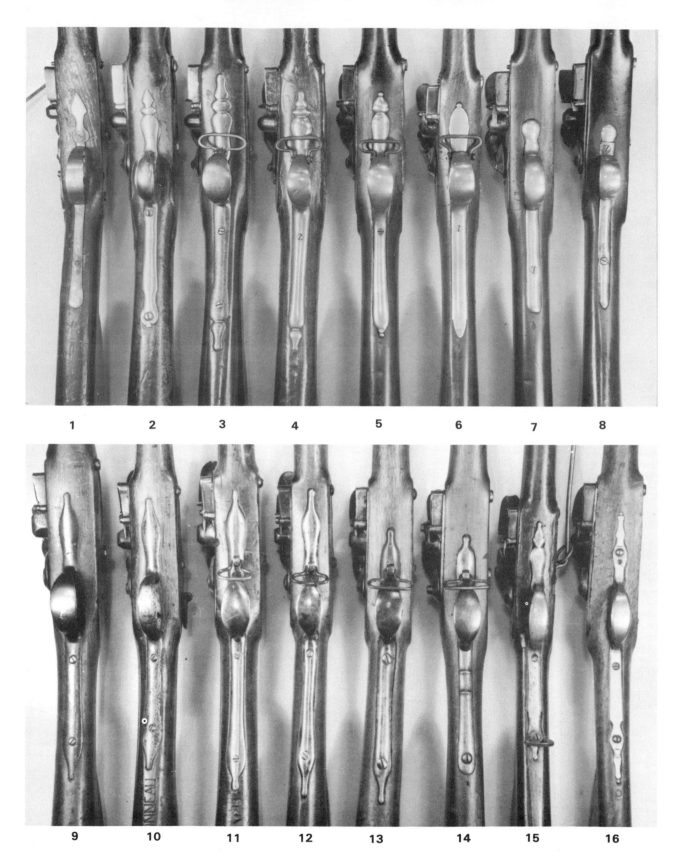

1   2   3   4   5   6   7   8

9   10   11   12   13   14   15   16

MUSKETS (cont.) (1–8) ***British musket trigger guards:*** (1) c. 1700, brass. (2) c. 1710, iron. (3) c. 1720, iron. (4) c. 1720–1730, brass; early Long Land Brown Bess. (5) c. 1720s to 1790; brass, typical Long Land and Short Land Brown Bess. (6) c. 1757, brass; light infantry type carbine. (7) Naval-utility pattern, c. 1755–1790. (8) Royal Navy musket; c. 1755–1790. (9–15) ***French musket trigger guards;*** note the steady shortening of their length and the practice of using two rear screws; regular infantry muskets were mounted in iron. (9) Model 1717. (10) Model 1728. (11) c. 1750s; the sling swivel now moves from the side of the stock to a stud just forward of the trigger bow. (12) 1763 Series; the swivel is flattened in shape. (13) Model 1774. (14) Model 1777; at this point the rear tip becomes rounded, only one screw remains visible, and finger ridges are added. (15) The Model 1733 cavalry carbine (in brass). (16) Spanish, Model 1752.

Source: George C. Neumann.

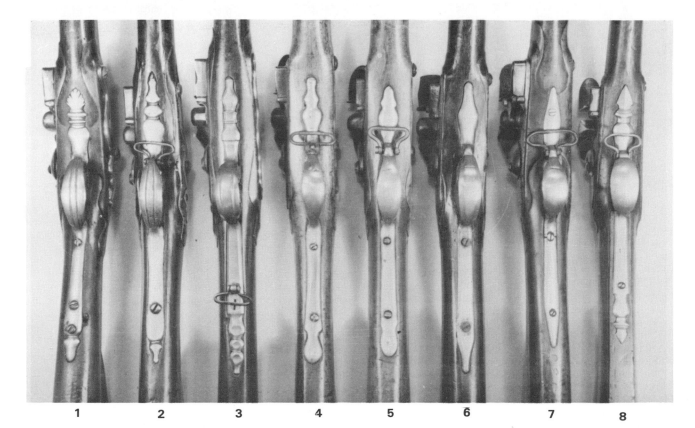

1 2 3 4 5 6 7 8

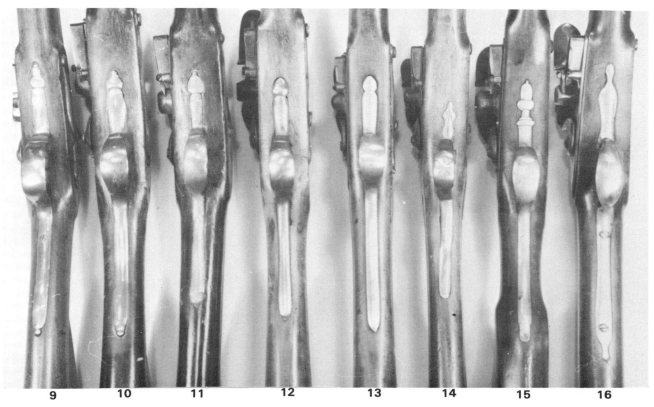

9 10 11 12 13 14 15 16

(1–8) *German-Dutch trigger guards;* these were mostly of brass with two screws visible at the rear and often two channels in the trigger loop. (1) Dutch, c. 1710–1720. (2) German, c. 1710–1730. (3) German; the "Potzdam Magaz" pattern, c. 1720–1780. (4) German-Dutch, c. 1750–1770. (5) German-Dutch, c. 1760–1780. (6) German-Dutch, c. 1765–1780; note the continuing simplification of design. (7) Dutch, c. 1770–1780; an elementary wartime pattern. (8) German, c. 1740–1780; the popular arrowpoint styling. (9–16) *American musket trigger guards:* (9–13) Various simplified versions of the British Brown Bess design (see #5, p. 210); most Americans omitted the lower screw that the English used to pierce the stock wrist and secure the escutcheon plate—which the colonials often did not include or held with a short screw from the top; all brass; c. 1750–1783. (14) Uneven and engraved brass; c. 1760–1770. (15) A copy of the popular British civilian acorn shape; c. 1770–1783. (16) A brass version of the French pattern; c. 1760–1770. (cont.)

Source: George C. Neumann.

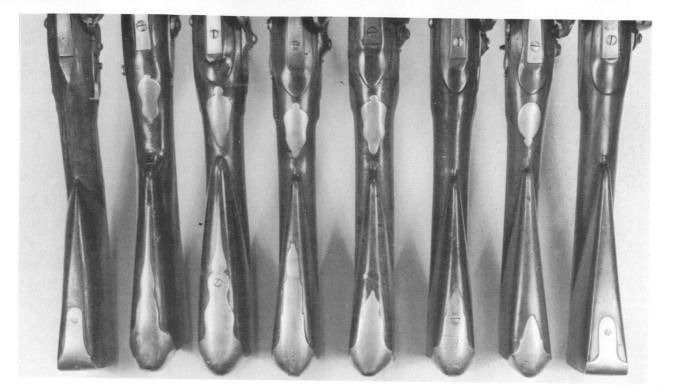

1   2   3   4   5   6   7   8

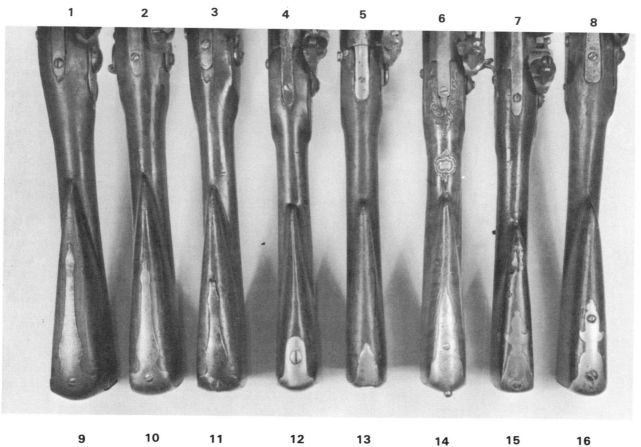

9   10   11   12   13   14   15   16

MUSKETS (cont.) (1–8) *British musket butt styling;* (1) c. 1700, brass. (2) c. 1710–1720, iron. (3) c. 1720, iron. (4) c. 1725–1790; Long Land Brown Bess; brass. (5) c. 1760–1790; Short Land Brown Bess, brass. (6) c. 1755–1765; the Militia and Marine Model; like #5 but with a screwhead showing; brass. (7) Light infantry carbine style; c. 1757; brass. (8) Naval-utility brass type; c. 1755–1790 (note similarity to earlier #1). (9–15) *French butt styling:* (9) Model 1717, iron. (10) Model 1728, iron. (11) Model 1746, iron. (12) Models 1763–1777, iron. Note the continual butt-tang shortening. (13) Fusil, c. 1750–1760; brass. (14) Fusil, c. 1760; engraved brass. (15) Carbine Model 1733, brass. (16) Spanish musket, Model 1752; notice the two screws and the influence of the French re. #15; brass.

Source: George C. Neumann.

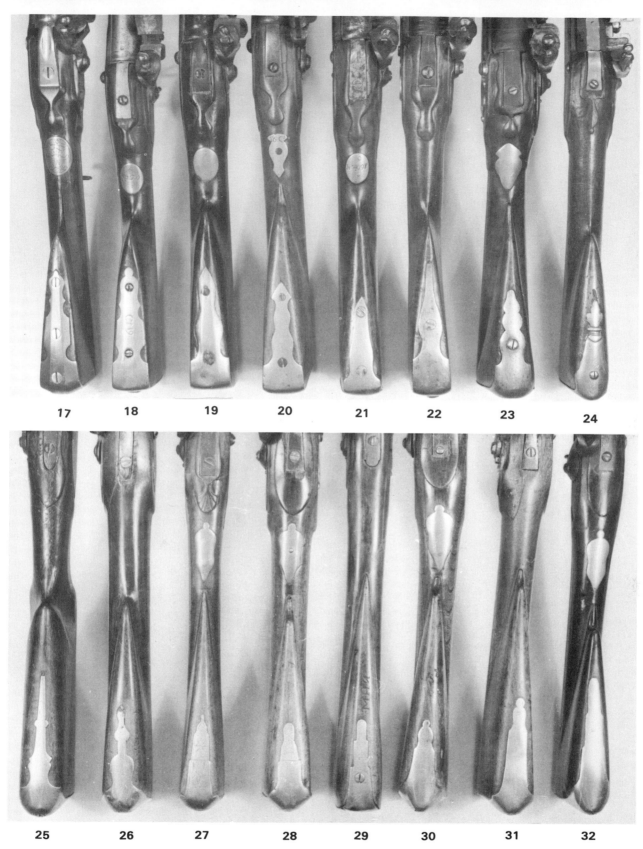

(17–24) **German-Dutch butt styling;** all of these fittings are brass: (17) German "Potzdam Magaz" type; c. 1720–1782; note the 3 screws visible. (18) German-Dutch, c. 1740–1760. (19) German-Dutch, c. 1750–1770. (20) German-Dutch, c. 1760–1780. (21) Dutch, c. 1770–1780. (22) Dutch, c. 1750–1770. (23) Dutch, 1710–1720. (24) German-Dutch, 1740–1780. (25–32) **American butt variations:** (25, 26) Early Dutch/English influence; see page 212, #2, #3 and this page, #22, #23. (27–32) Variations taken from British patterns; see page 212, #4–#6.

Source: George C. Neumann.

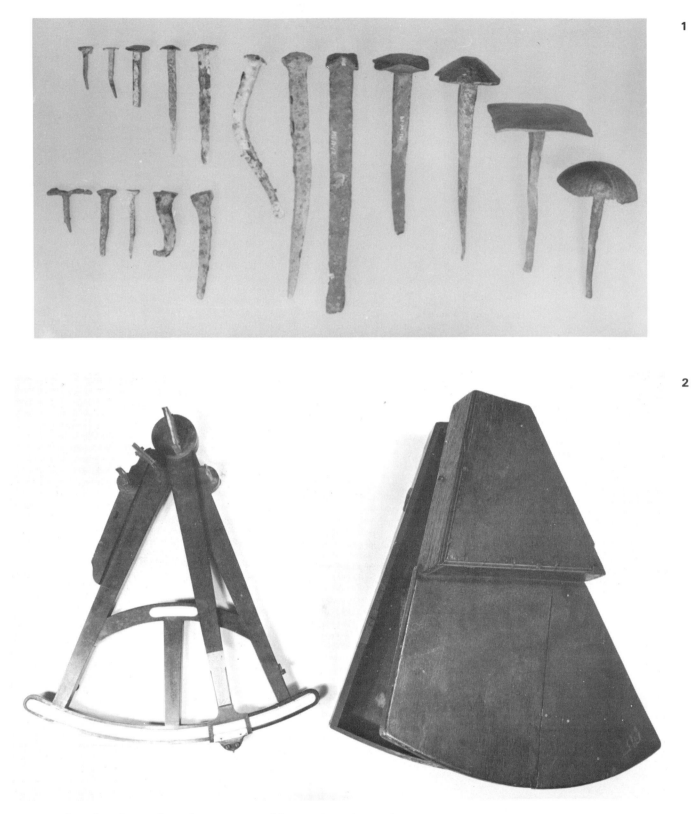

NAILS: These handwrought nails are excavated from military hut and camp sites, circa 1760–1780. Cut nails with hammered heads appeared after the Revolution and are identified by the evenness and uniformity of the shank. 18th century nails came in a variety of forms developed for specific uses. The heads of many spikes were hammered on an angle five times to produce the "rosehead" pattern, and one strike on the shank's tip produced a spatula point that helped hold the nail after penetrating the wood. (#1; the first 8 nails, top row from the left) Various sizes with typical "roseheads." (last 4, top row) Such large-headed spikes were used to stud doors, hold large strap hinges to thick wood, or attach iron wheel shoes. (far left, lower row) a clabboard nail. (2nd and 3rd from left, lower row) To attach trim and flooring was the common use of these "L" headed nails. (last 2, lower row) A screw used as a nail and an odd tapered example. **NAVAL** (also see "Armor," "Breeches," "Dirks," "Headgear," "Lighting," "Muskets," "Pikes," "Pistols," "Seamen," "Swords," "Telescopes") (2) An ebony sextant with ivory panels by "Gregory and Son, London" with its wooden case; an attached brass panel reads "Seth Wheaton, Providence 1779"; height, 17."

Sources: 1—Frank J. Kravic; 2—William H. Guthman.

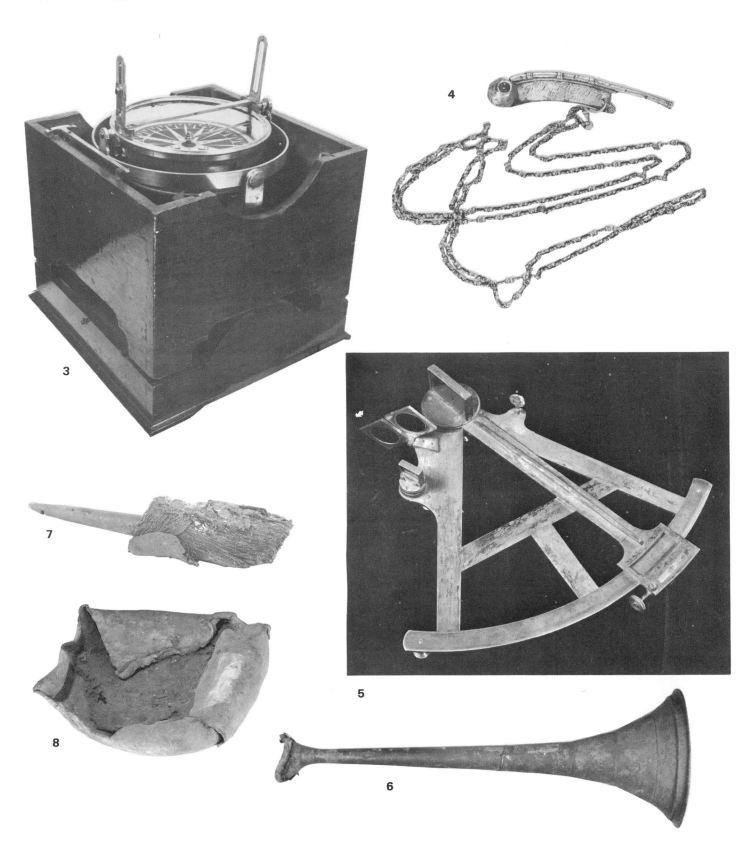

The American effort against Britain on the seas was conducted mostly by individually owned privateers sailing under letters of marque. Estimates vary from 1,100 to 2,500 privateers operating during the war and they are credited with taking about 600 enemy vessels. Congress and the states also commissioned fleets totaling less than 100 official warships, of which 53 were in the Continental Navy (and none bigger than frigates). Only two Continental ships were still in action by 1783—although the American navy accounted for almost 200 British warships from 1775–1783. During this time the English fleet grew from 270 to 468 ships. The French quietly furnished ships for raiding and participated with their fleet at Newport, Savannah, and, most importantly, at Yorktown. (3) A ship's compass; it was usually a dry compass with a light paper card on top of the needle to indicate direction. (4) Bosun's pipe and chain. (5) A quadrant believed used by John Paul Jones. (6) A tinned iron captain's speaking trumpet; circa 1780–1810; 26'' length. (7, 8) Tar brush and pot from the American gondola, *Philadelphia* (1776). (cont.)

Sources: 3—National Maritime Museum, Greenwich, England; 4—Edward Charol; 5—U.S. Naval Academy Museum; 6—John Ivan; 7, 8—Smithsonian Institution, Dr. Philip K. Lundeberg Collection.

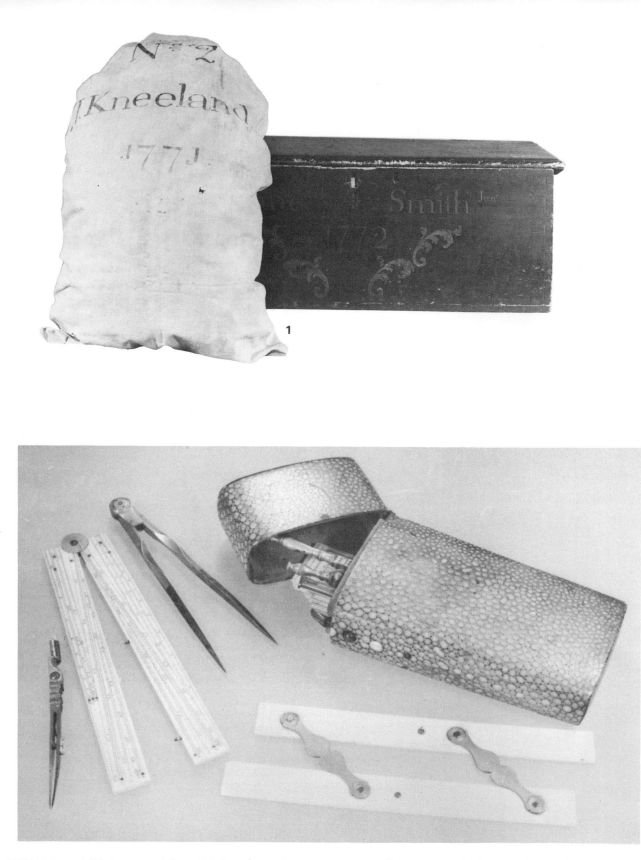

NAVAL (cont.) (1) A seaman's bag (1771) and sea chest (1772). (2) Small navigation-drafting set having brass-iron and ivory instruments in a green shagreen case; c. 1770–1820; 6¾" long. (3) An iron boat hook. (4) Dividers for use in navigation. **NEWSPAPERS** (see "Periodicals.") **OFFICERS** (see "Epaulettes," "Headgear," "Infantry," "Sashes, officer.") **OVERALLS** (see "Breeches.") **OXEN** (see "Horses, Equipage.") **PADLOCKS** (see "Locks.") **PAILS** (see "Buckets.") **PAPER** (see "Documents" and final chapter.) **PATTENS** (see "Footwear.") **PENCILS** (see "Writing.")

Sources: 1—Peabody Museum of Salem; 2—George C. Neumann.

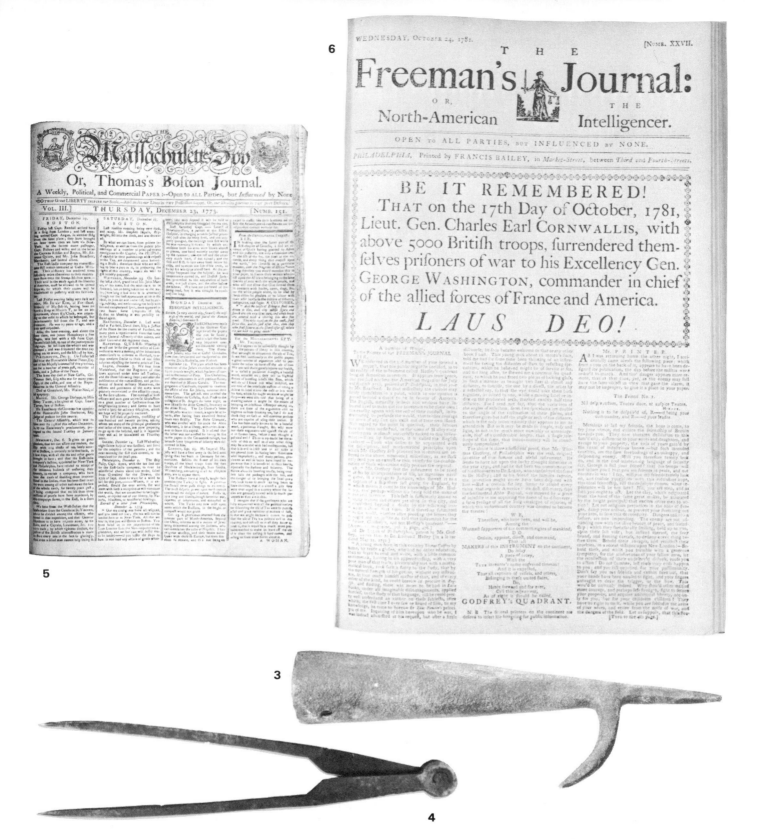

6

WEDNESDAY, OCTOBER 24, 1781.   [NUMB. XXVII.

THE Freeman's Journal:
OR,
North-American   THE Intelligencer.

OPEN to ALL PARTIES, but INFLUENCED by NONE.

PHILADELPHIA, Printed by FRANCIS BAILEY, in *Market-Street*, between *Third* and *Fourth-Streets*.

BE IT REMEMBERED!
THAT on the 17th Day of October, 1781, Lieut. Gen. Charles Earl CORNWALLIS, with above 5000 British troops, surrendered themselves prisoners of war to his Excellency Gen. GEORGE WASHINGTON, commander in chief of the allied forces of France and America.

LAUS DEO!

5

PERIODICALS (also see "Books," "Documents"): Weekly newspapers and monthly magazines disseminated most of the news—supplemented by books and pamphlets. There were many newspapers printed during the war and the publishers often placed ads for clean linen rags which were turned into paper. Shortages of undyed rags often forced the use of colored cloth that, in turn, also colored the paper. (5) Prior to the outbreak of fighting in April 1775 newspapers were filled with news of colonial unrest. Boston was the center of this agitation and much of it was reported in this very pro-American *Massachusetts Spy* by Isaiah Thomas. Its masthead was engraved by Paul Revere. Of interest in this Dec. 23, 1773 issue is that the first news of the Boston Tea Party (Dec. 16) appears on the third page and is limited to four column inches—while the meeting that led to the Tea Party is on page 2 and consumes about thirty column inches. This reflects their propaganda interest in justification of the deed rather than the actual act. (6) The most important news was often not on the first page but reported rather matter of factly on the inside. An exception is shown here with the bold headlines proclaiming the victory at Yorktown, Virginia (The *Freeman's Journal*, Philadelphia, Oct. 24, 1781). (cont.)

Sources: 3, 4—George C. Neumann; 5, 6—Frank J. Kravic.

PERIODICALS (cont.) (1) The Royal Coat of Arms graces the masthead of this loyalist newspaper printed by James Rivington in New York City during its British occupation. This issue, dated just after the Treaty of Peace (July 2, 1783), carries news and ads concerned with the impending evacuation by both English troops and large numbers of Loyalists. (2) While England had a number of monthly magazines, there was a counterpart in America called the *Pennsylvania Magazine*. It was published by R. Aikin during 1775–1776, the last issue being illustrated here (July 1776). Each copy contained about 50 pages and included a wide variety of topics; this particular issue has the first printing of the Declaration of Independence in a magazine, as well as articles on a ship wreck, the danger of ladies wearing wires in their caps, an ode to independence, and monthly intelligence. **PIKES** (also see "Butt Cones.") The shortage of firearms and bayonets among American forces, especially early in the war, led to the use of long spear-like pikes (or "trench spears.") They were usually manufactured by local blacksmiths and employed primarily in close fighting aboard ship or in defense of fixed positions on land. (4–8, 11) Typical iron heads as used by infantry and naval forces. (9, 10) Pikes with specific naval association; all circa 1775–1780.

Sources: 1, 2—Frank J. Kravic; 3—Brigade of the American Revolution, photo by Michael Cleary.

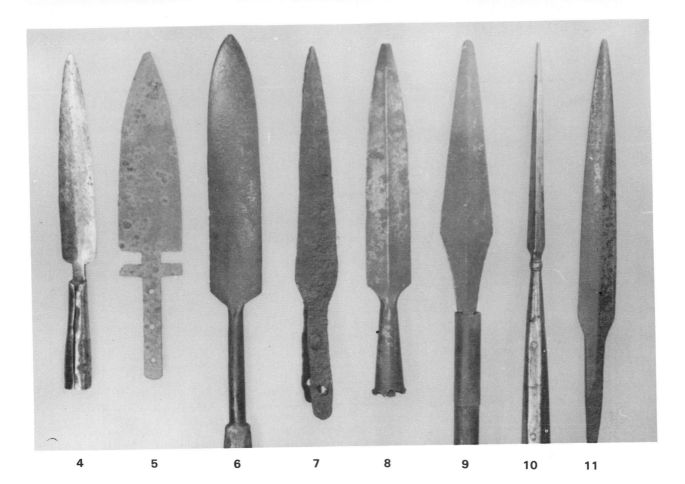

4   5   6   7   8   9   10   11

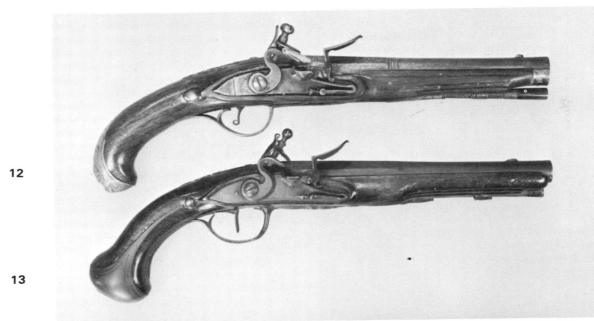

12

13

PIONEERS (also see "Fortifications, Field," "Tools, Hand"): These were the construction units of the regiments on both sides used for clearing and mending roads, working on entrenchments and fortifications, or preparing mines and approaches. (3) Recreated American pioneers with the usual leather aprons, hatchets, saws, spades, and pickaxes. The British Warrant of 1768 required their pioneers to have an axe, saw, apron, and a cap with a leather crown, plus a black bearskin front on which was the King's crest in white on a red ground plus the regiment's number on the back. Much of their official status was overshadowed in the Continental Army by formation of the Corps of Sappers and Miners in 1780. **PIPES, PIPE TAMPERS** (see "Smoking.") **PISTOLS** (also see "Flintlock, Action," "Holsters, Pistol"): The great majority of handguns used here were European-made smoothbores. Like the muskets, they fired a round lead ball by flintlock action after being loaded from the muzzle. Their short barrel compounded the musket's inaccuracy, which left them of little value except at extremely close range. (12, 13) *Two French officer pistols:* (12) Brass mounted, c. 1760, .60 cal. with a raised grotesque face on the butt cap; length, 14¾". (13) Iron furniture; c. 1745–1760 with raised carving around the barrel tang and lock; 14¾" overall. (cont.)

Sources: 5—William McInerney; 7—Frank J. Kravic; remainder—George C. Neumann.

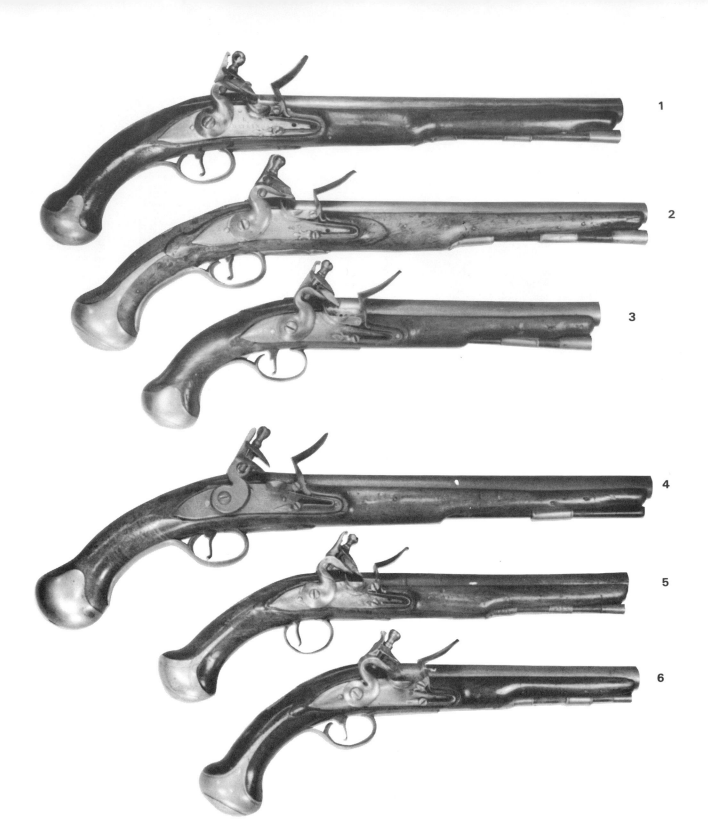

PISTOLS (cont.) Military horseman pistols at the beginning of the 1700s commonly mounted barrels 16″ long; by the Revolution the popular length was about 9″ (and many early long ones are found cut back to that length). They were used by mounted officers or troopers and usually carried as pairs in holsters. (1–6) ***British pistols:*** (1) An early dragoon pistol, c. 1720, with brass furniture and a .65 cal., 12⅜″ barrel; marked on the lock is "R WATKIN" (the maker); 19½″ long. (2) Midcentury brass-mounted dragoon pattern, "SMITH 1743"; 12″ barrel, .56 caliber; 19½″ long. (3) Light dragoon pistol for the light horse troops developed in the 1750s. A 10″ barrel was first used from 1756–1759, when it was shortened to 9″ (shown here); this size persisted through the War for Independence; .65 cal.; 15¼″ long; marked, "GRICE 1760." (4) A naval boarding pistol by "EDGE 1759." Note the usual flat lock and abbreviated brass furniture; it also includes a long hook on the opposite side for slipping over a waist belt; barrel 12″, .56 cal.; 19¼″ overall. (5) English officer's or gentleman's pistol, c. 1730–1750; brass furniture; 9″, caliber .68 barrel; the lock is marked "R FARMER"; 14¾″ length. (6) Circa 1750–1770; signed, "RICHD KING"; brass furniture; barrel measures 7¾″, .62 cal.

Source: George C. Neumann.

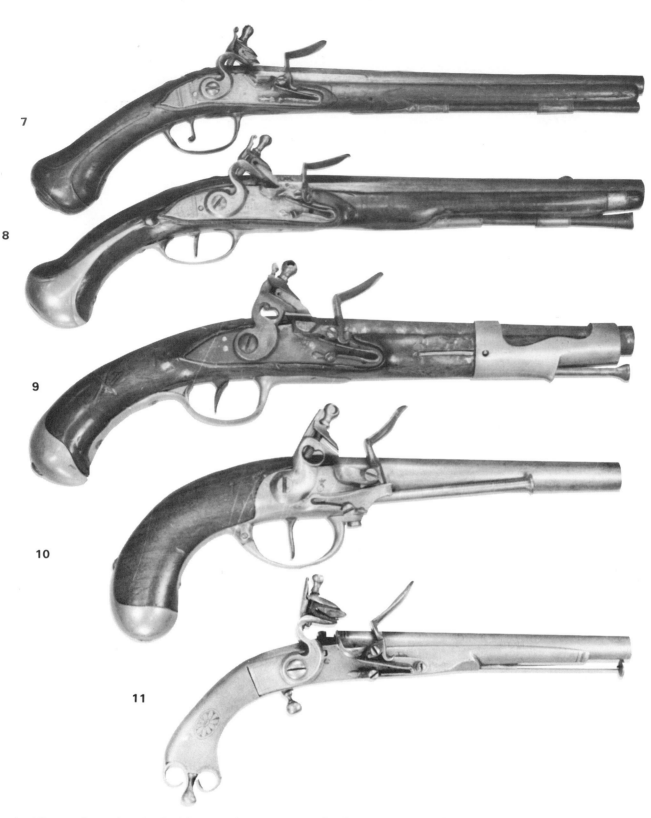

(7–10) *French cavalry pistols:* (7) An early iron-mounted style, c. 1710; 12⅜″ barrel of .56 caliber; 19⅜″ length. (8) Model 1733; brass furniture, 19⅜″ total length; barrel, 12″ and .69 cal.; Saint Etienne manufacture. (Note: Royal arms were made at three manufactories at this time—Charleville, Maubeuge, and Saint Etienne.) (9) Model 1766 with a flat lock and reinforced hammer like the contemporary musket; brass fittings: barrel is 9″, .67 cal.; 16⅛″ total length. (10) Model 1777 with the barrel projecting from a central brass housing; the barrel measures 7½″, .67 cal.; 13½″ long. (11) The all metal Scotch infantry pistol normally had a clip on the reverse side to fit over a cross-strap under the left arm; its barrel is 8″ long and the lock is marked "BISSEL"; 12½″ overall. (cont.)

Sources: 7–10—George C. Neumann; 11—Robert Nittolo.

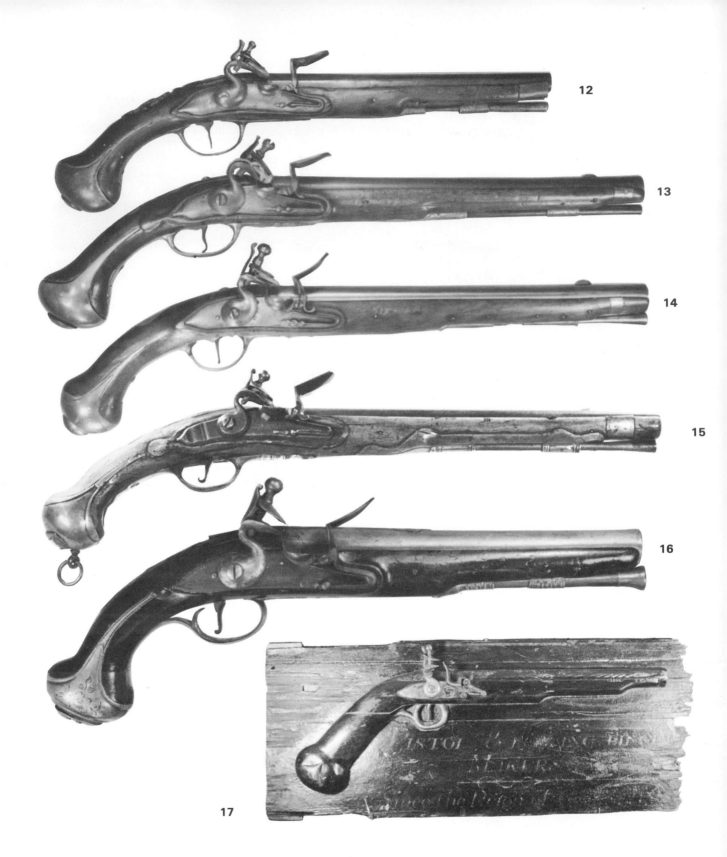

PISTOLS (cont.) (12) A Dutch pistol, c. 1690–1700, with early iron furniture and its barrel cut back to 10⅝" (originally 14" to 16"). (13) German-Dutch cavalry pistol; circa 1710–1720; the barrel measures 14", .71 caliber; brass fittings. (14) German, circa 1750; 13¾" barrel; .72 caliber; brass furniture. (15) "Potzdam Magaz" type Prussian cavalry pistol having a butt ring for a lanyard; 14⅜", .68 cal. barrel; 22⅜" total length. (16) British officer's pistol; brass furniture; by "E NORTH" with a 7¾" barrel and a .67 cal. bore; the wooden rammer had a brass tip; 13¾" length. (17) A carved wooden shop sign for an English gunsmith, "PISTOL & FOWLING PIECE MAKERS / Since the Reign of George II."

Sources: 12, 13, 14—George C. Neumann; 15—West Point Museum; 16—Frank J. Kravic; 17—William J. Jurgensen.

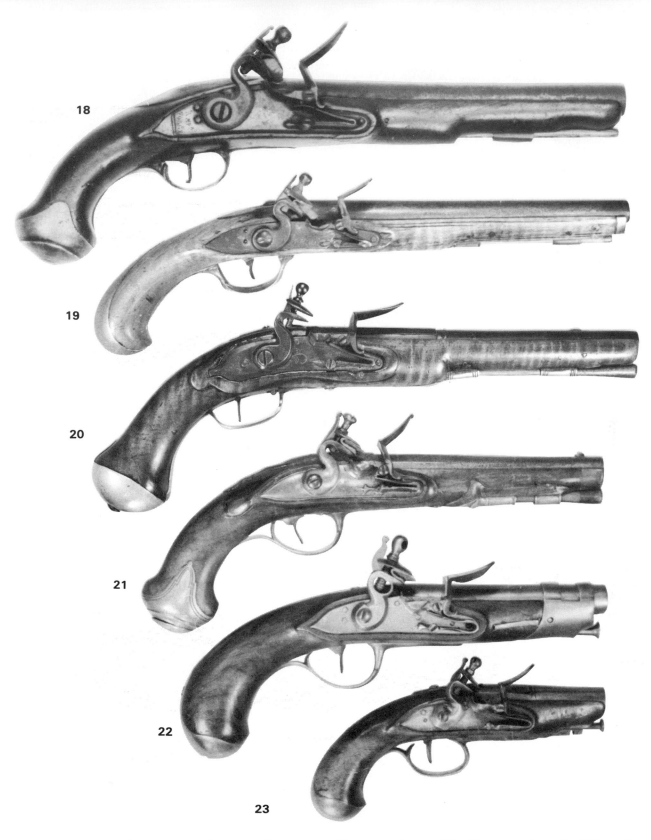

(18) American light dragoon pistol (copied from the British pattern; (see p. 220, #3); its lock is marked "Rapa Forge" for the Rappahannock Forge of Falmouth, Virginia; the barrel measures 9¹/₁₆" and .69 cal.; brass mounted and 15⁵/₁₆" in length. (19) An American "Kentucky" pistol style by "T HILLS": brass furniture; c. 1777–1785; 8¾", .50 cal. barrel; 14⅞" total length. (20) American, made and signed by MATTHEW SADD (Hartford, Conn.); it mounts a home-made lock in a striped maple stock; barrel is 10⅜", .52 cal.; 16½" overall. (21) German silver-mounted pistol; c. 1760–1770; .44 cal. barrel; 11⅜" long. (22) French military pistol used by gendarmes; 1770; 10½" long; barrel measures 5", .61 cal.; (23) A small French civilian pocket pistol; iron-mounted furniture; 3¼" barrel; .50 cal.; 7½" total length. (cont.)

Sources: 18—Edwin W. Bitter; 19—Kindig Collection; 20—Robert Nittolo; 21, 22, 23—George C. Neumann.

PISTOLS (cont.) The most popular civilian type pistol was the "Queen Anne," "Turn off," or "Screw off" pattern. Its stock ended just forward of the lock—beyond which the barrel unscrewed to permit loading at the breech; most carried no rammer. (24) A silver-mounted English example of the early style with its lock at the side; a crude American repair is visible on the hammer; c. 1720; 11" long. (25) English, circa 1770–1780; it includes a brass barrel, silver furniture, and a centered "box lock"; 12½" overall. (26) A French version, c. 1760, employing iron furniture; 10⅛" length. **PLATES, EATING** (see "Eatingware.") **PLATES, UNIFORM** (also see "Belts, Frogs, Scabbards," "Cartridge Boxes"): Most of the cross-belt plates, waist belt buckles and box badges were of brass and included molded or engraved references to the regiment or branch of service. The American soldier had a minimum of these accoutrement plates, but the Europeans were apparently well supplied. (1) American rectangular cross-belt plate. (2) British 4th Regt. of Foot shoulder belt plate; brass with two copper studs and a hook on the reverse side; 2" x 2¾". (3) A brass shoulder belt plate of the 1st Battalion, "Royal Americans" (60th Rgt.); 2⅝" x 2⁵⁄₁₆"; hook and two studs on the back.

Sources: 24, 25, 26—George C. Neumann; 1—Frank J. Kravic; 2—Don Troiani; 3—Fort Ticonderoga Museum; 4, 5—Edward Charol; 6—William H. Guthman.

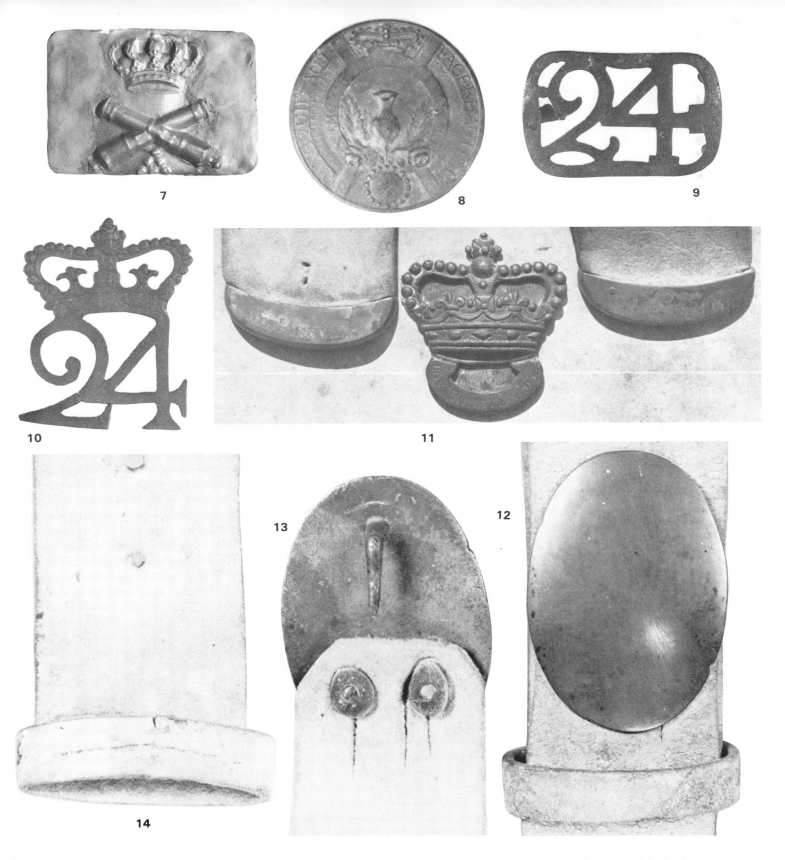

(4) An oval pattern sword belt plate of the 60th Royal American Regiment. (5) American militia sword belt plate marked, "Berks County Light Dragoons"; this was a provost regiment raised in 1775 and disbanded in 1783; 3⅝" x 3". (6) An American militia officer's brass cross-belt plate, Newport, R. I.; circa 1775–1800; 3½" x 2¾". (7) German Anspach Artillery waist belt plate; 3⅜" x 2¼". (8) A brass highlander bonnet badge; 2" diameter. (9) British 24th Regt. of Foot waist belt plate; 1⅞" x 2⅞". (10) 24th of Foot cartridge box plate; brass; 3" high x 2½". (11) A British Royal Artillery brass cartridge box plate and the brass tips on its buff leather cross-belt; engraved "ROY^L ARTILL^Y N° 105" (see #51, p. 80); the badge is backed by dark red leather. (12–14) An American oval sword plate with its buff shoulder belt: (12) From the front, attached; (13) Rear, unhooked; (14) The other belt end with the hook hole and end loop. (cont.)

Sources: 7—New-York Historical Society; 8—Edward Charol; 9, 10—George Juno; 11—Charleston Museum (S.C.); 12–14 George C. Neumann.

PLATES, UNIFORM (cont.) (14a–17, 21) *British brass cartridge box badges:* (14a) The 1st Foot Guards. (15) The Foot Guards. (16) Butler's Rangers. (17) "GR" badge with four mounting studs for a cartridge box; 3⅛" long. (21) 45th Regiment of Foot. (18) A brass sword belt tip worn by Scottish officers (enlisted men's were plain; this has an engraved thistle). (19) Hessian cartridge box plate, Regiment Erbprinz; it bears a crowned lion rampant with the "Grand Hessian Arms" on a star. (20) Hessian box plate of the Regiment Von Bose (Trumbach); included are a crowned lion rampant on a pedestal with the letters "F L Z H" (Friedrich Landgraf Zu Hessen). **PLUME** (see "Headgear.") **POCKET-BOOK** (see "Purses.") **POLEARMS** (see "Butt Cones," "Halberds," "Linstocks," "Pikes," "Spontoons.") **POUCHES, BULLET** (also see "Hunting Bags"): A wide variety of bullet and shot holders were carried by those firing with loose powder from horns or premeasured cartridges which did not include the ball. (22) Various pouches of cloth or leather plus a horn container and hollowed wooden cylinder. (23) Four-hole wooden bullet holder. (24) Wooden box of balls with a sliding cover. **POUCHES, INDIAN:** (25) Indian pouch of moosehide having quillwork designs; 13" high; c. 1750–1800. (26) Iroquois pouch of homespun trade cloth and tiny white beads plus pewter "tinklers" hanging from the bottom; last half of the 1700s; 6¼" x 8¾". (cont.)

Sources: 14a, 22—George C. Neumann; 15—Don Troiani; 16, 25, 26—William H. Guthman; 17, 23—Fort Ticonderoga Museum; 18—Edward Charol; 19, 20—Yorktown National Historical Park; 21—New-York Historical Society; 24—Valley Forge Historical Society.

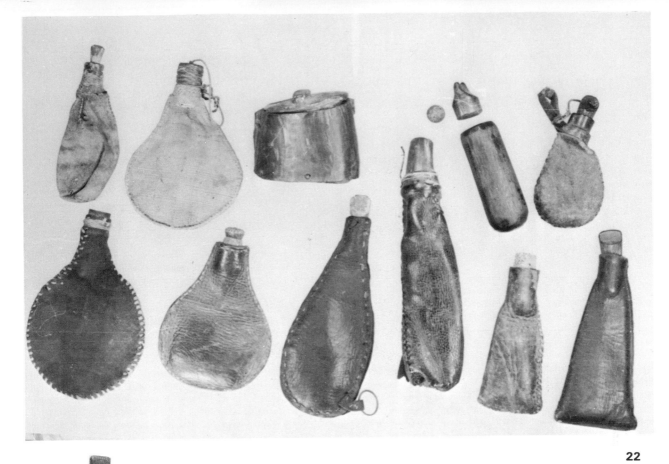

22

23

24

26

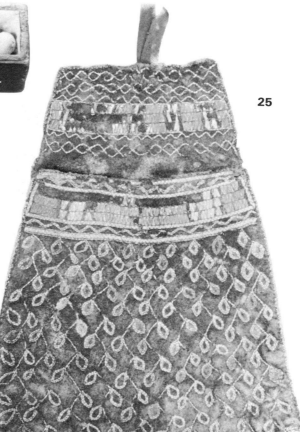

25

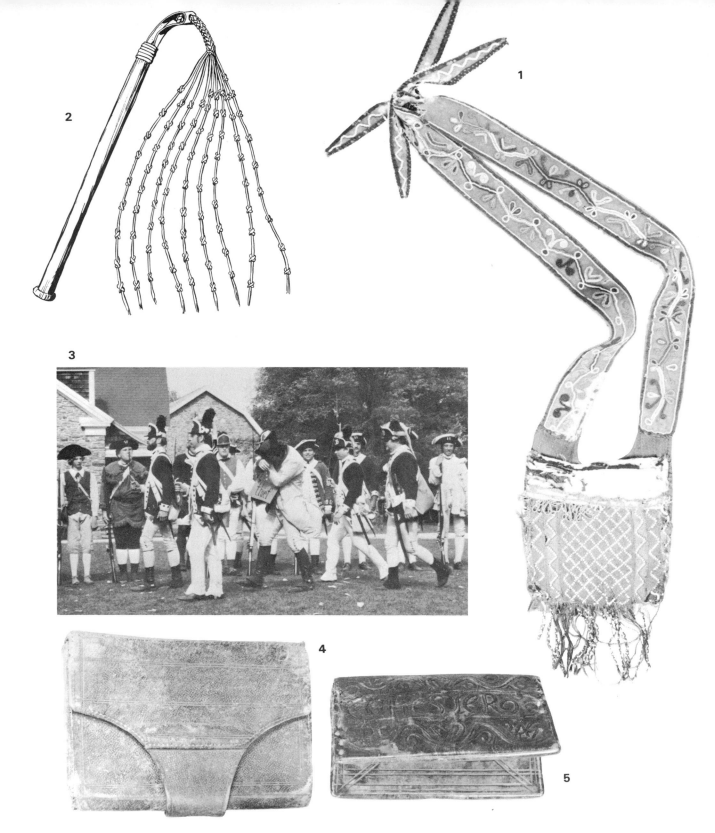

POUCHES, INDIAN (cont.) (1) Iroquois pouch, circa 1760; it includes bead and quill work, as well as its 2″ wide shoulder strap. **POWDER** (see "Gunpowder," "Hair.") **POWDER FLASKS or POWDER HORNS** (see "Horns.") **POWDER KEGS** (see "Barrels.") **POWDER TESTERS** (see "Eprouvettes.") **PROOFS** (see "Markings.") **PUNISHMENT** (also see "Irons, Imprisonment"): Eighteenth century military punishments were incredibly severe and many soldiers and seamen were maimed or died from them. (2) A British regimental (Coldstream Guards) cat-o'-nine-tails used for whipping (usually inflicted by the drummers). It includes nine lashes of whipcord (21″ long) with nine knots in each, plaited at their upper end to pierce and knot inside an open flat leather loop from the 19¼″ handle. (3) A thief being drummed from camp following his court martial with coat reversed and a sign hanging from his neck, "Thief." **PURSES:** The Revolution occurred in a period of transition from the carrying of a small bag for hard money to a flat container for bank notes and letters. The common purse was normally of leather or fabric and folded once or twice in a manner which prevailed through the 19th century. (4) Leather purse with a divided center compartment; inscribed "Lieut. Wilbur June 20, 1779 Royal American Regt"; 6½″ x 4½″ folded.

Sources: 1—Edward Charol; 2—Society for Army Historical Research, Vol. XI, pgs. 54, 55; 3—Brigade of the American Revolution, photo by Michael Cleary; 4, 5—Frank J. Kravic.

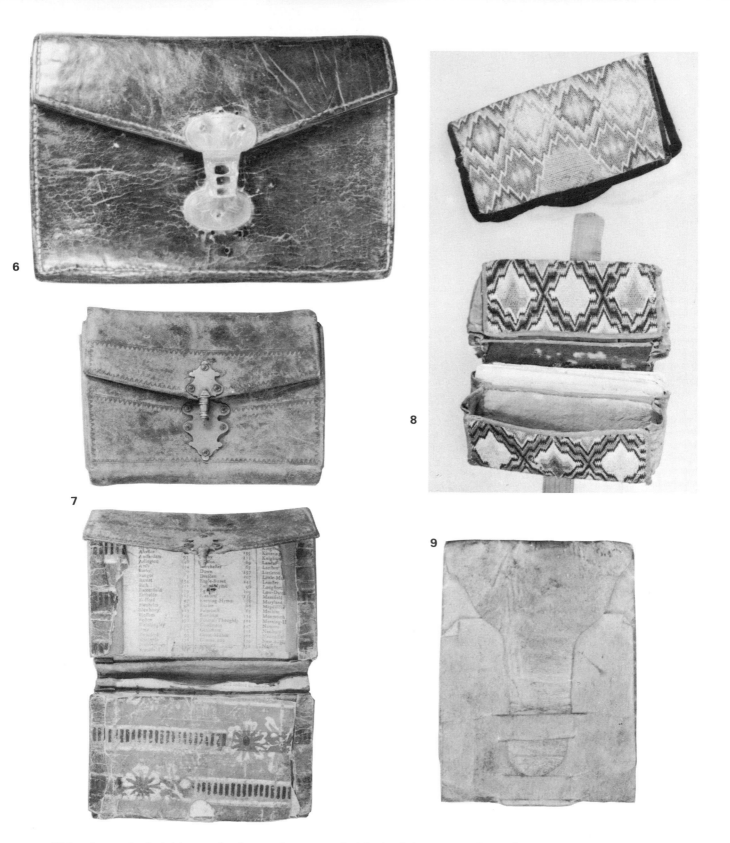

(5) Leather, a single fold purse having pockets on each side; both faces are embossed "Chester"; 5½" x 3¼" folded; c. 1750–1800. (6) One designed with a top flap, brass clasp, and two inner compartments; 7" x 4¾". (7) Lock-flap style; also shown open to illustrate the practice of lining them with wallpaper and old document pages. (8) Two men's folding purses of polychrome crewels in flame stitch; the top one is dated "1776"; the lower example is open. (9) A flat parchment "billfold" folding on all four sides to hold documents or notes: 3⅞" x 5¼". (cont.)

Sources: 6, 7, 9—George C. Neumann; 8—The Connecticut Historical Society.

PURSES (cont.) (10) An embroidered cloth purse (2 views); its closed size is 3¾" x 6½". (11) European; made of red leather with silver thread embroidery, "Doctʳ DAVID MᶜNAIR 1772"; 4" x 7" folded. (12) A British purse of red leather plus silver clasps; inscribed, "JOHN COOPER ROYLE 1776." (13, 14) A common American leather type embossed "David Yeaman 1752." (15) A similar example having an inner date, "1751," plus embossed ship illustrations titled, "Ranger," and "Bilinder." **RAMMERS** (or "Ramrods"; also see "Artillery"): The rammer was necessary to push the bullet down the barrel of a firearm; this was often made difficult by the buildup of powder fouling inside the bore. Yet to fire without seating the ball on the loose powder risked blowing out the breech. The rammer was carried in a channel cut into the underside of the stock and held by tubular metal "pipes." (16) Typical rammer ends bearing permanent cleaning jags or threaded tips for screw-on "worms" to hold cloth or tow when cleaning the bore (see "Tools, Hand"). (17) An assortment of common rammer heads ranging from plain wood or wood with iron or brass tips to a variety of the more popular iron patterns. **READING MATERIAL** (see "Books," "Documents," "Periodicals.")

Sources: 10—George C. Neumann; 11, 12—Edward Charol.

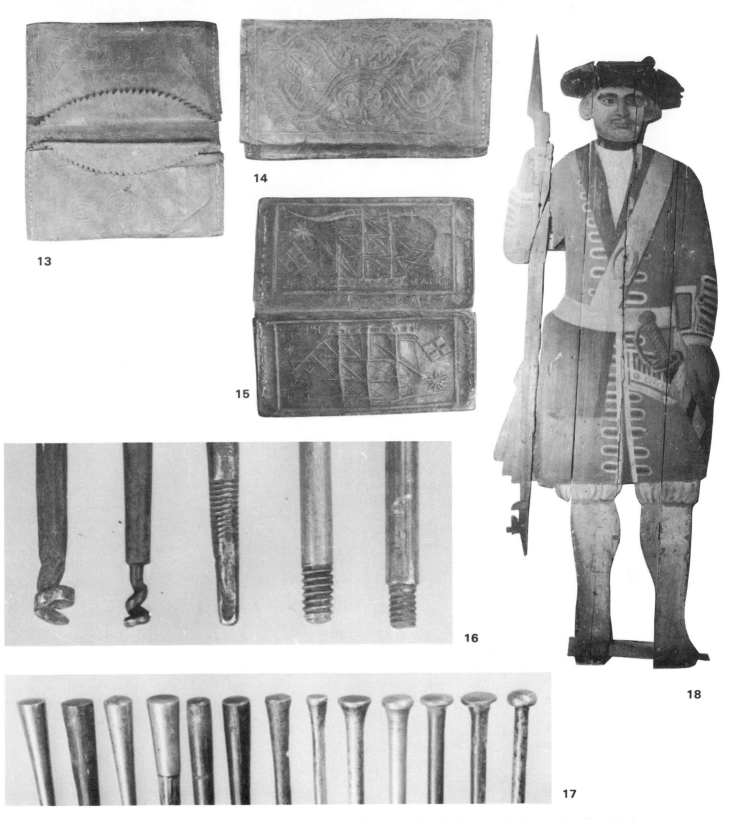

RECRUITING: The American soldiers were mostly enlisted by the individual states which usually offered a bounty, uniform, wages, and grants of land. Provisions were even made to supply substitutes. The specified periods of service varied from a number of weeks to several years or the duration. In England the crown contracted with a distinguished officer or civilian to raise a regiment. He was paid an annual grant to recruit, clothe and equip his men. Many of their enlistments were for life and necessitated the use of bounties, press gangs, released debtors, criminals, and vagrants—as well as the hiring of German mercenaries. (18) A painted wooden outline of a British soldier set up outside an English tavern or public building when a recruiting party was present. **REGIMENTALS** (see "Coats," "Infantry.") **RIFLEMEN** (see "Indians," "Infantry.")

Sources: 13, 14, 16, 17—George C. Neumann; 15, 18—Edward Charol.

RIFLES (also see "Flintlock, Action," "Hunting Bag," "Infantry"): One of the great legends of the Revolution is the deadly accuracy of the Pennsylvania or Kentucky rifle (then called the "rifle" or "American rifle"). Unlike the large caliber smoothbore musket (limited to 50–80 yards in accuracy) these rifled barrels permitted accurate fire to 250–300 yards in skilled hands. The rifled bore had been used in central Europe since the mid-1500s and accompanied the German and Swiss colonists into Pennsylvania about 1710. To meet the new frontier demands their short, large bore "jaeger" style was transformed into a longer, smaller caliber American version by 1760. To help overcome powder fouling and better grip the rifling grooves, their bullets were normally wrapped in a patch of greased cloth or leather. The typical Revolutionary War rifle rarely mounted the elaborate sun, star, moon, and eagle inserts of the later "Golden Age," but did include raised and incised wood carving, as well as simple metal or wood covered patch boxes in the butt (for shooting supplies). It is ironic that despite their amazing accuracy for scouting or sharp-shooting, most Continental Line rifle regiments were eventually changed to musketmen—primarily because of the rifle's expense, weak stock for combat, longer loading time, and inability to mount a bayonet.

Sources: 1—Brigade of the American Revolution, photo by Michael Cleary; 2—George C. Neumann; 3—William H. Guthman.

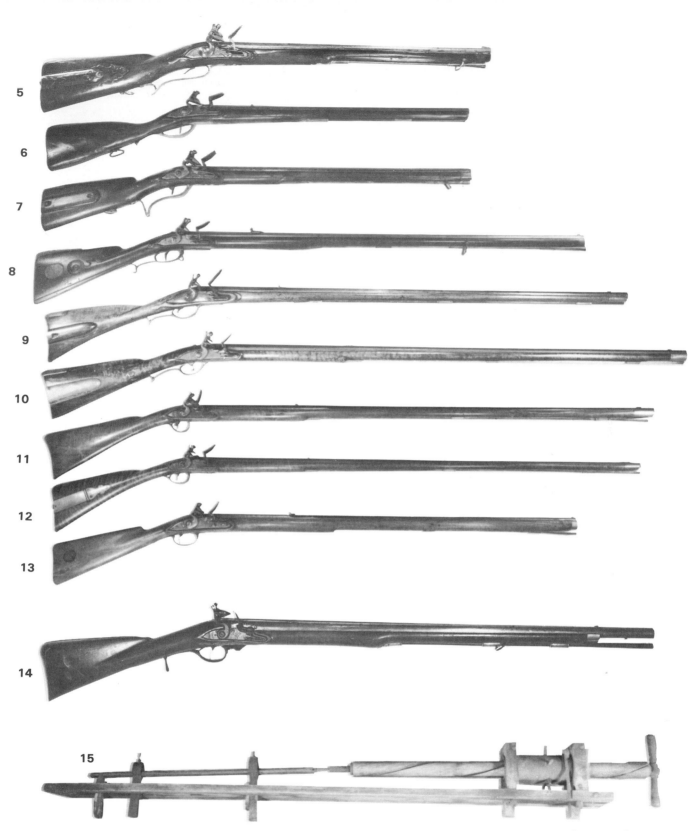

(1) Representative riflemen. (2) Raised carving and cheek rest of a circa 1730–1740 jaeger type rifle; 2⅜'' butt thickness. (3) Incised carving on a slim American ("Bethlehem County") rifle pattern, c. 1775–1800. (4) Breech action of the British Ferguson rifle which lowered a revolving screw as its trigger guard rotated to open the breech top for loading. It saw limited use and was plagued by clogging from powder fouling. (5) German jaeger type, c. 1720; 38¼'' long; 7.8 lbs., cal. .60, 8 grooves. (6) circa 1730–1740; a 29'' barrel; weight 7.4 lbs., 40½'' overall. (7) German military type jaeger with an escutcheon plate and lack of raised carving; barrel 28⅞'', .64 cal., 7 grooves; 7 lbs. (8) A longer jaeger style, c. 1740; 40⅝'' octagonal barrel, caliber .70; 55¼'' length. (9) American, c. 1770–1780; sliding wooden patch box; barrel, 43'', .48 cal.; 58⅜'' overall. (10) American; bottom hinge on brass-covered patch box; c. 1779–1790; 45½'' barrel, .59 cal.; 61⅜'' total. (11) Plain striped maple stock; American, c. 1770–1790; 54½'' length; 8.5 lbs. (12) Simple brass patch box; c. 1770–1785; striped maple; 47'' barrel. (13) Southern mountain style; c. 1760–1770; iron furniture; .66 cal.; 54½'' full length. (14) Ferguson rifle (see #4, p. 232); 49⅜'' long; barrel, 34⅛'', .65 cal., 8 grooves; 6.9 lbs. (15) Rifling machine; pulling the handle rotates the cutting rod moving through the barrel at left. (cont.)

Sources: 5–8, 11, 12, 13, 15—George C. Neumann; 9, 10—Kindig Collection; 14—Morristown National Historical Park.

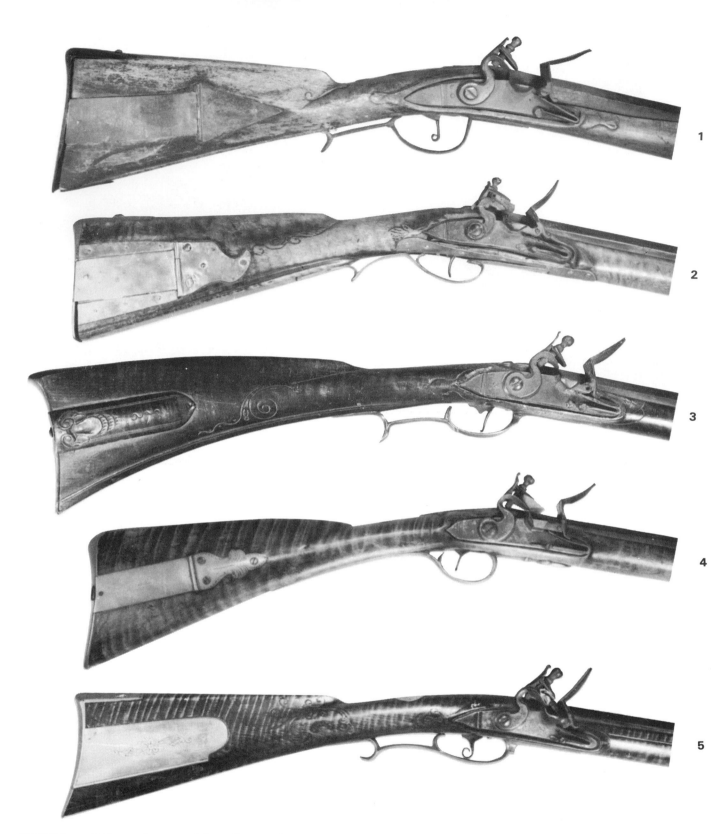

RIFLES (cont.) The real secret of the rifle's performance was the rifleman himself—firing with an open blade sight and holding his point of aim for estimated "Kentucky windage" in all conditions of weather, terrain, and distance, as well as the heat of his barrel. The British had no regular rifle companies (although Ferguson headed a small unit carrying his breech-loading rifle during the Brandywine campaign), but they did employ German riflemen with jaeger arms. There is no record of French troops here with rifles. (1–8) *Representative American rifle stock patterns:* (1) c. 1735–1750 American rifle with an iron patch box and furniture. (2) Crude bird's head brass box in a striped maple stock; circa 1765–1780. (3) A Roman nose style having a sliding wooden cover and incised carving; c. 1775–1800; Bethlehem County pattern. (4) Simple brass patch box design in striped maple; note the plain trigger guard without a rear extension; c. 1770–1785. (5) This brass box cover is hinged at the bottom—a style used by A. Verner of Bucks County, Pa.; c. 1775–1790.

Sources: 1, 2—Kindig Collection; 3—William H. Guthman; 4—George C. Neumann; 5—Harmon C. Leonard.

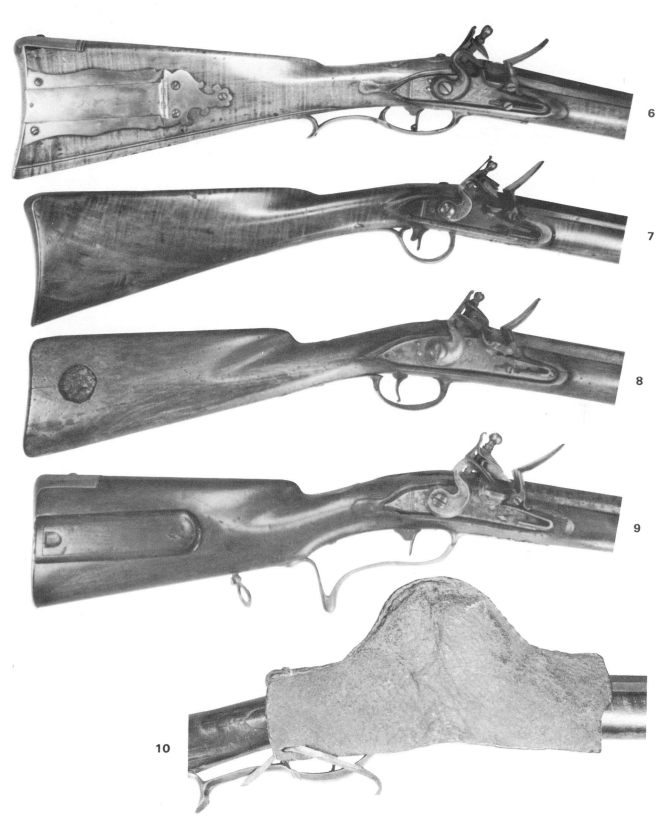

(6) An early version of the brass "daisy-headed" pattern popular in Lancaster County, Pa.; circa 1770–1785. (7) c. 1770–1790; a plain maple stock without a patch box. (8) Southern mountain type rifle; c. 1760–1770; note the open "grease hole" used for grease to lubricate the bullet patches. (9) German military style jaeger; it includes an escutcheon plate and plain sliding wooden patch box cover plus a minimum of carving. (10) A leather "boot" (with bottom ties) to protect the lock in bad weather (also see #1 on next page); many men simply wrapped cloth or a piece of skin around the lock. (cont.)

Sources: 6—Kindig Collection; 7, 8, 9—George C. Neumann; 10—William H. Guthman.

1

2

RIFLES (cont.) (1) Remains of a leather lock and stock cover excavated at Fort Ligonier (c. 1758–1766). **SADDLEBAGS, SADDLES** (see "Horse, Equipage.") **SASH, OFFICER:** Commissioned officers normally wore red silk sashes—over the shoulder during the French and Indian War period, but by the Revolution most were carried around the waist. They were of open mesh with tassels and could expand for use as a stretcher to carry the owner if wounded. Many British sergeants wore red worsted sashes which included a stripe of the regiment's facing color. (2) An officer's silk mesh sash believed used by General Washington; 8 feet long, 28" wide. **SATIRICAL PRINTS** (see "Documents.") **SAWS** (see "Tools, Hand.") **SCABBARDS** (see "Belts, Frogs, Scabbards," "Knives.")

Sources: 1—Fort Ligonier; 2—Mount Vernon Ladies Assn.

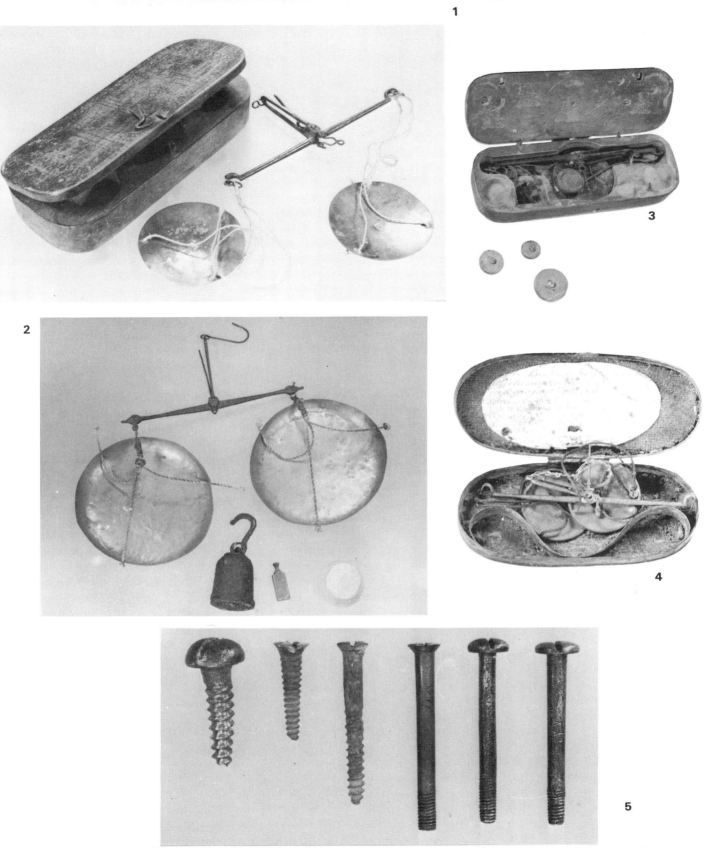

SCALES: Constructed as small boxed sets or large hanging pans, scales were used for weighing medicines, provisions, specie etc. They varied little throughout the century—most often having brass pans with iron scale arms. The weights used were provided in the boxed set or common improvised articles. (1) A small (5½" long) scale by Samuel Casey of Kingston, R.I. in a cherry box; c. 1760. (2) Large example with three excavated weights, i.e. iron with a hook for a single arm scale, a small brass unit, and a circular piece of lead. (3) Boxed apothecary scales with some of the weights displayed. (4) English scales in a tinned iron box lined with linen; the label is dated 1771–1772. **SCISSORS** (see "Sewing.") **SCREWS** (also see "Tools, Hand"): From about 1750 to 1840 wood screw threads were cut by a hand die and had a blunt point. (5) These specimens are typical of those found in the muskets of this period: the three at the left are wood screws for the butt plate (at far left—the domed head favored by Dutch and Germans); the fourth screw uses a tapered head and straight shank to secure the barrel tang (screwed into a metal plate); the two at right are both side plate screws which hold the lock.

Sources: 1, 5—George C. Neumann; 2—Frank J. Kravic; 3—The Connecticut Historical Society; 4—Edward Charol.

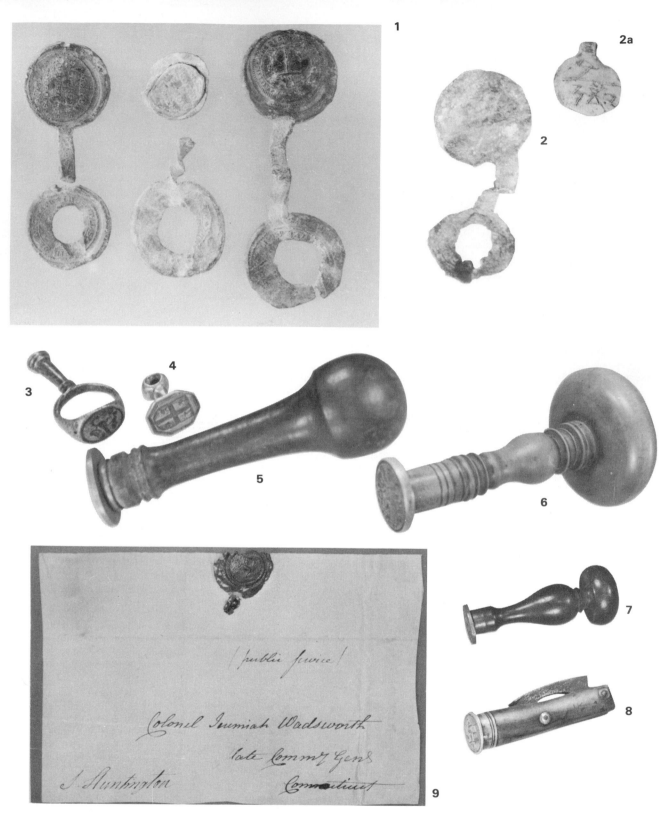

SEALS, BALE: To facilitate the counting of goods shipped in bales as well as to discourage tampering, a lead seal was commonly affixed to the outer binding. Company names, cities, dates, and accounting numbers are found on surviving examples. British merchants often added their own seals before continental European goods were transshipped by them to America. They were attached with pincers that impressed the insignia and information into the lead as the two disks were pressed together (a stud from one side pierced the hole in the other side). (1) Used lead seals from Fort Ticonderoga. (2) Another example (from Michilimackinac), plus a close-up (2a) showing the scratched figures often found on the back, (believed to be the invoice number over the package identification).

SEALS, DOCUMENT: Personal or governmental seals were used to insure that correspondence arrived unopened or to validate a document's authenticity. The soft sealing wax was melted over the folds of the letter or document and the seal pressed into it to leave the impression. (3) A brass ring seal and pipe tamper. (4) A personal seal that hung from a chain, as on a pocket watch. (5–7) Brass seals with turned wooden handles. (8) Originally a clasp knife with a brass seal at the end, it was later converted into a horse's hoof cleaner. (9) A governmental letter from Samuel Huntington, President of Congress, with his seal still attached.

Sources: 1—*Fort Ticonderoga Museum;* 2, 3, 4, 5, 7—*George C. Neumann;* 2a, 6, 8, 9—*Frank J. Kravic.*

SEAMEN (also see "Breeches," "Headgear," "Naval"): The average seaman wore a flat brimmed, knitted, or cocked hat, a coarse jacket, long or short trousers (and, at times, a canvas kilt), plus leather shoes (often remaining barefoot on board ship). (1) A contemporary English print of a sailor on shore. **SEWING:** Linen did not hold up well in everyday use and wool was not much better. Repairs and patches as well as new clothing made sewing an important skill and necessity in the camp life of the Revolution. (2) Excavated brass thimbles, 1760–1778. (3) A long iron needle (from Michilimackinac). (4) Small scissors with the sharp points ground off—perhaps for packing in a knapsack (from site dated 1760–1778). (5) A pair of crude scissors (American camp, 1775–1778). (6, 7) Large shears for cutting cloth etc. These changed little during the century. **SHAVING ARTICLES:** The soldier of the Revolution was required to be clean-shaven. He could shave himself or use the regimental barber and pay him (at least three times per week required). (8) A barber's shaving-bleeding bowl; it fitted under the chin when shaving to catch the extra soap, or against the elbow portion of the arm when being bled (see "Medical Equipment"); 9" diameter; brass. (cont.)

Sources: 1—National Maritime Museum, Greenwich, England; 2, 4, 5, 7—Frank J. Kravic; 3, 6—George C. Neumann; 8—Valley Forge Historical Society.

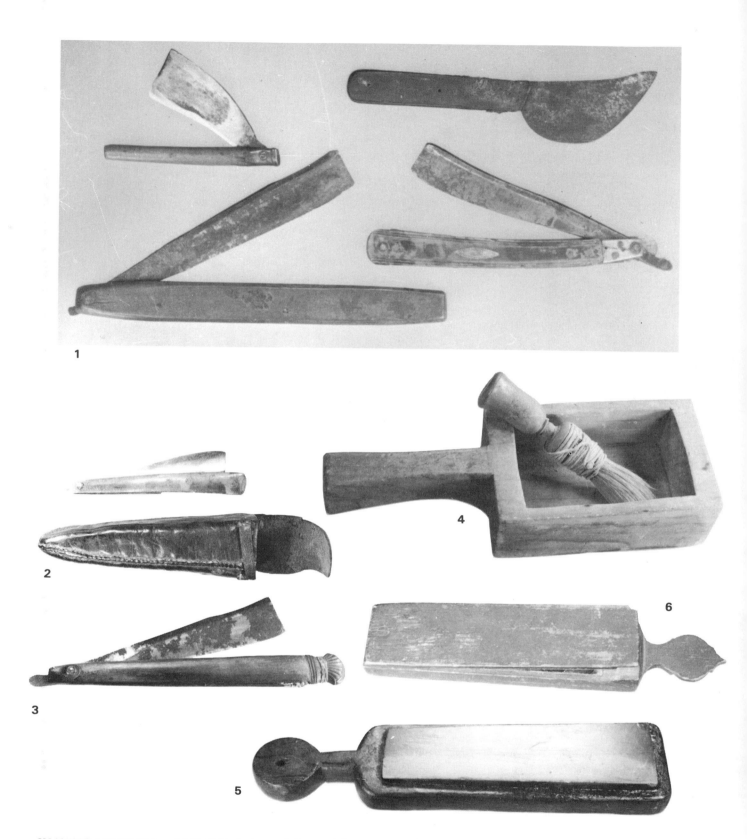

SHAVING ARTICLES (cont.) (1–3) Variations of the straight razors used at this time with horn or wooden handles; the cutting edge was generally continuous, i.e. without the thin neck of the 1800s. Note too, #1 upper left was a type also used by some to cut rifle ball patches; the upper right specimen has a fixed blade. (4) A soap container of wood with a handle and shaving brush. (5, 6) Honing stones in wooden bases having handles (#6 includes a pivoting cover).

Sources: 1—George C. Neumann; 2—Edward Charol; 3, 4—Fort Ticonderoga Museum; 5—Valley Forge Historical Society, Wm. Richard Gordon Collection; 6—Frank J. Kravic.

(7, 8, 9) Small camp size mirrors of the period. **SHEARS** (see "Sewing.") **SHIRTS, FROCKS** (also see "Stocks"): (10) Just as the individual states recruited most of the regiments, they also continued to supply many of their needs in the field. This receipt of July 10, 1778, for example, lists clothing sent from the town of Canaan, Conn. "for use of the officers and soldiers of this State in the Continental Army": 32 pr. men's shoes, 27 pr. stockings, 65 linen shirts, 9 rifle frocks, 2 common frocks, 21 overalls, and 11 trousers. (11) Recreated riflemen in their long linen hunting shirts (see next page).

Sources: 7, 9—George C. Neumann; 8, 10—Frank J. Kravic; 11—Brigade of the American Revolution, photo by Richard Gerding.

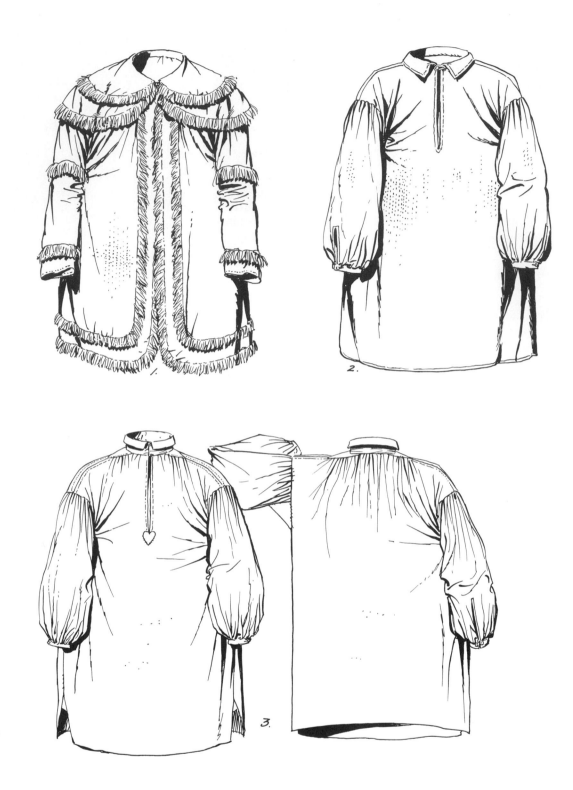

SHIRTS, FROCKS (cont.) Shirts of the period can best be described as those worn either as inner shirts and or as outer garments. The ones worn underneath were mostly a lightweight bleached (or often "checked") linen with texture ranging from a fine 130 thread count per inch to a coarse 90. This front and back rendering (3) typifies the usual civilian and military inner shirt (American and British). Note the arm and neck gussets, and high collar (1 or 2 buttons) to accommodate a neck stock. The two heavier loose fitting outer shirts were: (2) The common frock (also called the "smock," or "wagoner's shirt") which was worn by laborers, farmers, and soldiers (as fatigues by the British regiments and regular clothing or fatigues by many American troops); some officers and well uniformed regiments also used them to protect good clothing against dust and bad weather in the field; (1) The hunting shirt (or "rifle frock") which included fringed shoulder capes. This was the most widely used outer garment of the American Army. Both of these outer shirts were usually made from a coarse linen (about 65 threads per inch) in white, natural, or dyed a variety of reds, browns, blues, greens, etc.

242

(1) An inner shirt with front ruffles as worn by many officers. (2) A linen hunting shirt and its fringed shoulder capes; the fringe was helpful in shedding water during bad weather. (3) Common frocks as used by American troops; most were worn with an outer waist belt. (4) A deerskin shirt reportedly worn by Lemuel Lewis of Barnstable, Mass. **SHOES** (see "Footwear.") **SHOT BAGS** (see "Pouches, Bullet," "Hunting Bags.") **SHOVELS** (see "Tools, Hand.") **SIDE PLATES** (see "Muskets.") **SILVER, INDIAN TRADE** (see "Trade Ornaments, Indian.") **SLINGS** (see "Belts, Frogs, Scabbards.")

Sources: 1—Edward Charol; 2, 3—Brigade of the American Revolution, photos by (2) Michael Cleary and (3) Richard Gerding; 4— First Corps of Cadets Museum, Boston, photo by W. R. Cole.

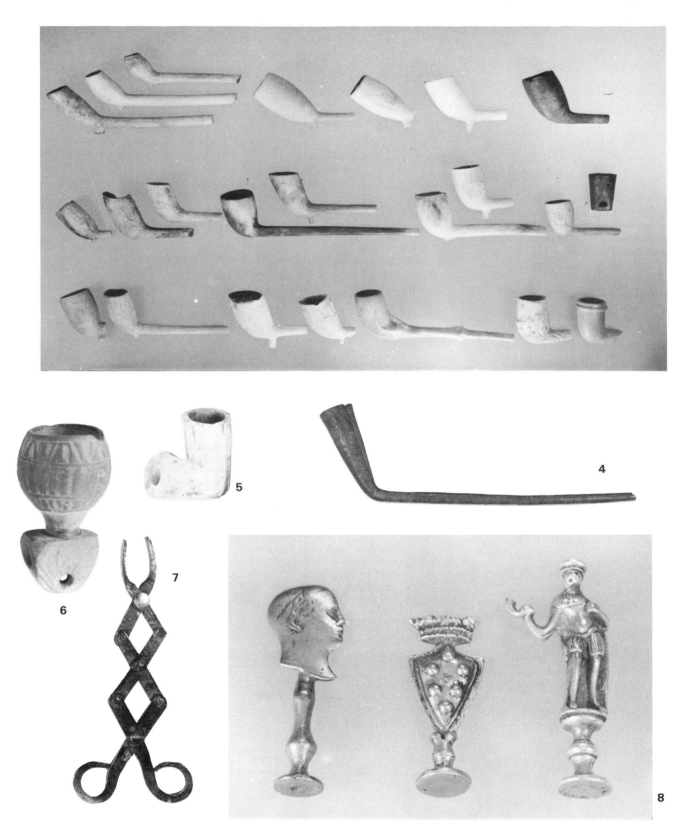

SMOKING: This was done in white clay pipes with long stems. As tars accumulated at the mouth of the stem it was broken off to remove the unpleasant taste. Thus pipes became steadily shorter until they could no longer be used, and the bowl was discarded. Such clay pipes were common in Revolutionary War camps, and improvised ones of pewter, iron, and even stone have also been excavated. The general rule for dating pipes is that with the passage of the 17th and 18th centuries their stem holes became smaller and the bowl gradually turned upward toward a right angle with the stem line. *Row #1,* (first 3) An early flattened heel below a slightly bulbous bowl, c. 1650–1700; (2 in center) These bowls rise only a slight angle from the line of the stem, c. 1680–1700; (2 at right) c. 1750–1790, the angle has now become more pronounced. Clay pipes often were molded with initials, imaginative animals, and other motifs as a trade-mark or to give them an association with the smoker. *Row #2* (l to r): A goblet with a crown above, c. 1730–1760; The British Royal Coat of Arms, 1750–1780; Foliar design, c. 1760–1790; The initials "TD" on its bowl, c. 1770–1800; another "TD," c. 1750–1780; A plain bowl, c. 1780–1810; A sunflower and "TD," c. 1770–1800; An allegorical chimera, with a lion's head, and fish tail, c. 1770–1820; An iron bowl for use with a reed or wooden stem.

Sources: 1, 2, 3, 5, 8—Frank J. Kravic; 4—Robert Nittolo; 6, 7—Fort Ticonderoga Museum.

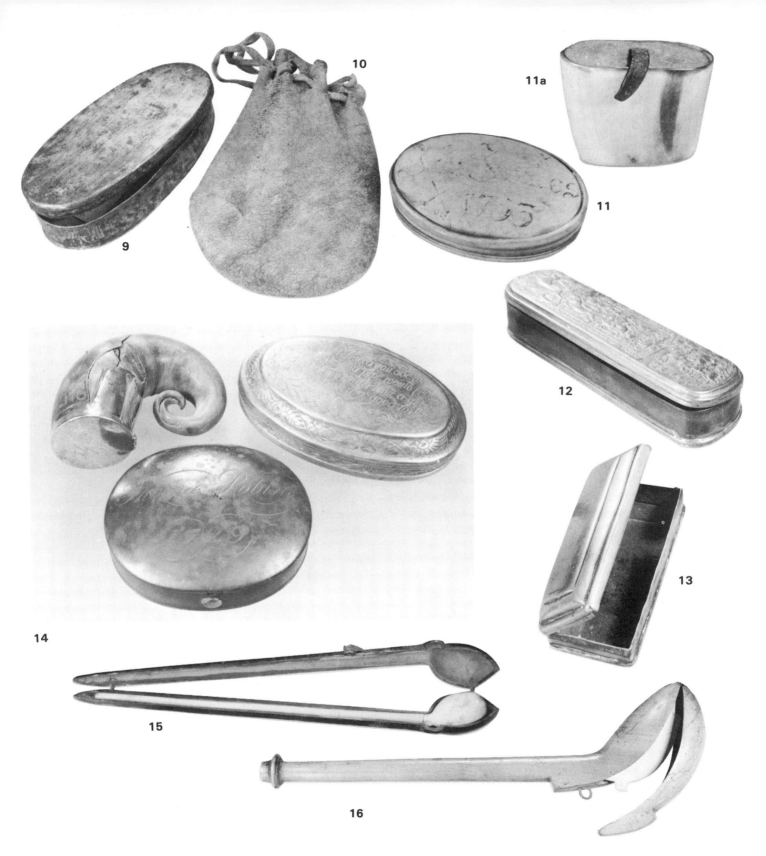

Row #3 (l to r): c. 1770–1800; A winged allegorical animal, c. 1770–1790; A 5-pointed star on the sides, c. 1780–1820; A bird, and 3 plumes (Prince of Wales insignia), 1770–1790; A bird claw stem holds the bowl, c. 1770–1810.; Scottish thistle design, c. 1770–1820; a wide 19th century example for comparison. (4) A sheet iron pipe (Indian site, Connecticut); 6¼"; c. 1725. (5) Reed pipe of the form that began about 1770 and continued into the 1800s. (6) A Micmac pipe usually made of slate, pipestone, or clay that required a wooden or reed stem; c. 1750–1780. (7) Extension tongs used to grasp and hold live coals while lighting a pipe; 8" long as shown. (8) Cast brass pipe tampers. (9–14) *Tobacco containers:* (9) Tinned oval box. (10) A buckskin pouch. (11) Horn box dated 1753. (11a) Horn container with a wooden pull-top. (12) Brass Dutch tobacco box; midcentury. (13) Plain Dutch style. (14) A ram's horn; its silver band is engraved "1778." (center) Iron; the hinged top is marked "1729." (upper rear) Brass and dated "1733"; its hinged cover is inscribed, "Friend if tobacco you doe want/ and here your pipe would fill / First of my master have a grant / And you have my good will." (15) French pipe and wooden carrying case; 10" long; c. 1750. (16) Wooden carrier, c. 1760; 9¼" overall.

Sources: 9–12 George C. Neumann; 13, 16—Robert Nittolo; 14—The Connecticut Historical Society; 15—Edward Charol.

SNUFF BOXES: Taking snuff was a popular habit and many varieties of personal containers were used to carry it. (1) A birch bark holder with a wooden pull top. (2) Pewter box, 3½'' long. (3) An oval lacquered hinged-top case. (4, 5) Rectangular boxes of horn. (6) Excavated tin-plated containers (from Champlain Valley sites). **SOAP** (also see "Shaving"): Large quantities of soap were made around the camps, usually by the women. Soap was mixed in a kettle over a fire requiring wood ashes to create lye which was boiled with fat from the animals, e.g. one formula required 1 barrel of ashes and 12 lbs. of grease of make 40 lbs. of soap. A harder product was possible by prolonging the time over the fire until the mixture thickened. (7) Examples of homemade soap. **SPEARS** (see "Pikes," "Spontoons.")
SPECTACLES: Eyeglasses were normally selected by trying a number of lenses until vision improved. Most lenses were made by grinding ordinary window glass or the more costly rock crystals. Fitting the frames was not difficult as the nose or ears provided little of the support. Spectacles were customarily held to the head by ribbon or cord tied to loops at the ends of the temple bars.

Sources: 1, 2, 3, 8, 9, 10—George C. Neumann; 4, 5, 6,—Frank J. Kravic; 7—Ada Harris.

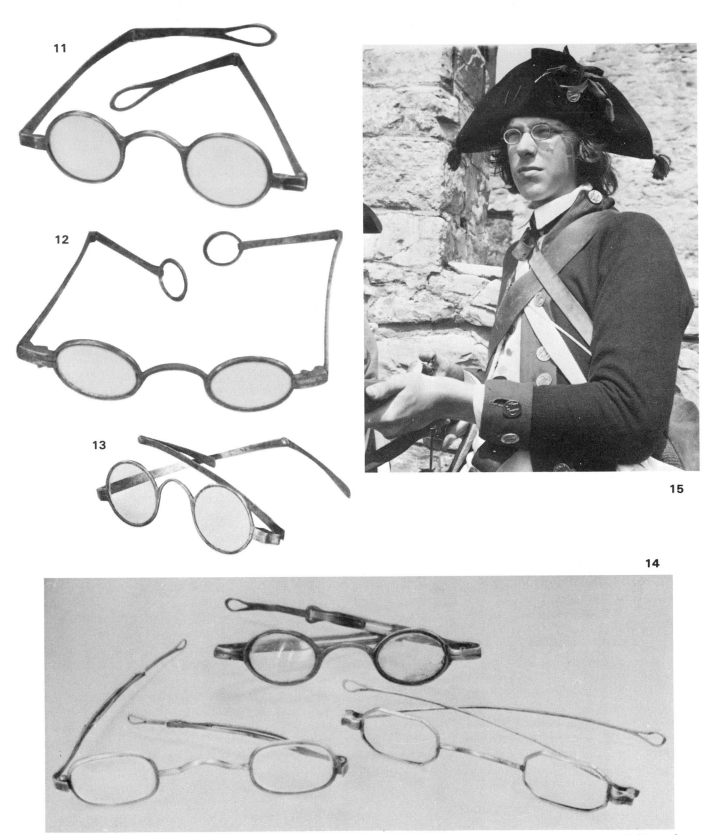

(8) A hinged steel spectacles case marked "1761." (9) Two-part leather holder, c. 1750–1770. (10) A long (6") hinged tinned case, c. 1770–1840. (11–13) Iron and silver frames having oval or round lenses with hinged temple bars (to better fit the head contour and reduce size); c. 1750–1780. (14) Later patterns using narrower oval or near rectangular lenses plus fixed or telescoping side bars (i.e. easier to fit); the frames are of iron, brass, or silver-coated brass; circa 1770–1850.

Sources: 15—Brigade of the American Revolution; remainder—George C. Neumann.

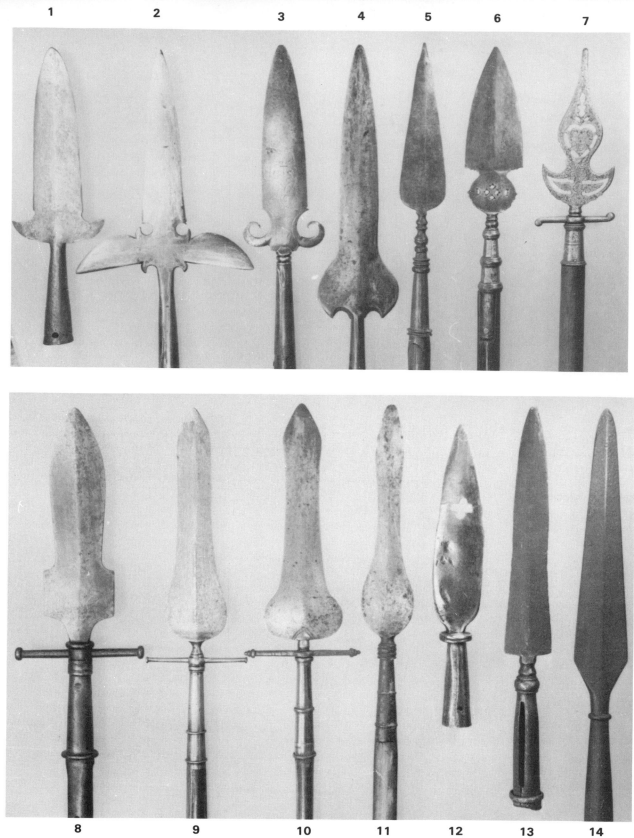

SPIGOTS (see next page.) **SPONTOONS** (also called "Espontoons," "Half Pikes"): Although the infantryman's spear or "pike" was abandoned in Europe by 1700, many commissioned officers on both sides continued to carry spontoons through the War for Independence. Although more and more of them turned to fusils (light muskets) in the field, Washington stressed use of spontoons throughout the conflict—as symbols of rank and to permit more attention toward their men during combat. Specifications at Valley Forge described a staff "six feet and a half, one and one quarter inch thick at largest part" and "an iron point one foot long." (1) c. 1740–1760; Probably American, it follows the 17th century's partizan shape. (2) c. 1755–1780; American. (3) Engraved "GTS 1760"; 14½" total head; source unknown. (4) American, 1740–1780; blade 12⅜". (5) French, c. 1740–1758; 13½" to the base ring. (6) Typical German styling c. 1750–1780. (7) Another German pattern; c. (1710–1750); head 10". (8) English, with a hunting horn engraving, c. 1760–1786. (9) Typical British pattern; c. 1750–1786; 9½" blade unscrews. (10) American copy of British #9; length with staff is 81½". (11) American variation of the English shape omitting the crossbar ("toggle"). (12) Pierced leaf shape; American, c. 1700–1730. (13) From Connecticut; c. 1740–1760; 15½" length. (14) American, c. 1760–1785; note later slope of shoulders.

248

Source: George C. Neumann.

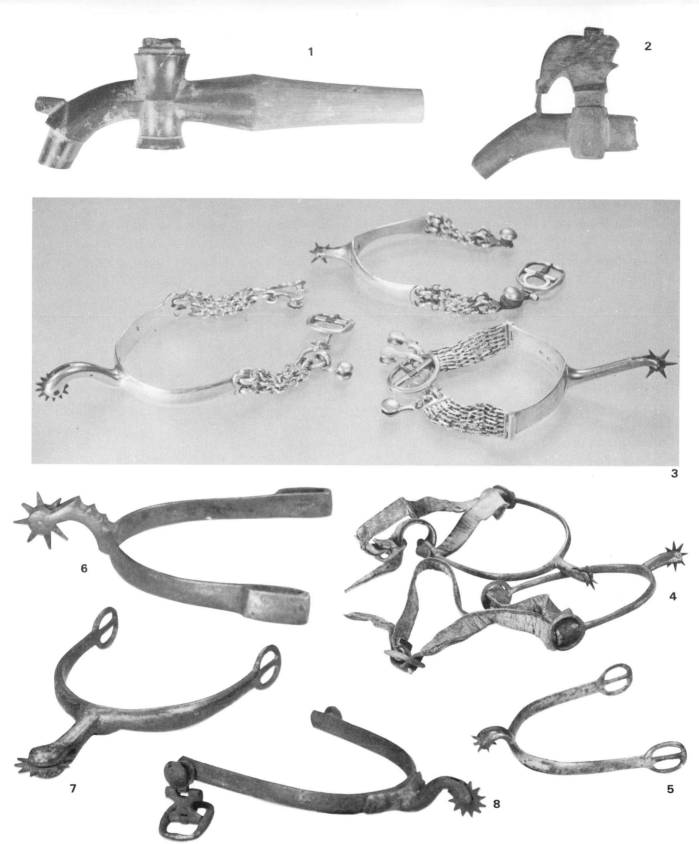

SPIGOTS: These two partial brass spigots show the general form of the type used to dispense beverages from kegs and small casks. (1) Found in a British camp, 1760–1775, this spigot is marked "SPENCER" by the maker and has a stud to support the handle of a tin cup while filling. (2) Taken from an American site, 1775–1780; it retains the handle missing on #1, but has lost the rear extension that penetrates the keg. **SPURS:** Most spurs were of iron, brass, silver, tinned iron, or tinned brass. The great majority ended in figure eight loops or link belts for attachment to the leather straps passing around the boot's instep. (3) English link-belted silver spurs; hallmarked (l to r): 1781, 1775, 1776. (4) An American pair which have retained their leather straps; 1770–1810. (5) Tinned iron pattern having a short raised rowel. (6) An unusual design with a single strap loop reportedly worn by Alexander Hamilton; c. 1775–1804. (7) An example with a horizontal rowel. (8) Stud and buckle type that has its rear projection riveted in position. **STARTER, BULLET** (see "Hunting Bag.") **STILLS** (see "Drinkingware.") **STIRRUPS** (see "Horse, Equipage.")

Sources: 1, 2—Frank J. Kravic; 3—William H. Guthman; 4–8—George C. Neumann.

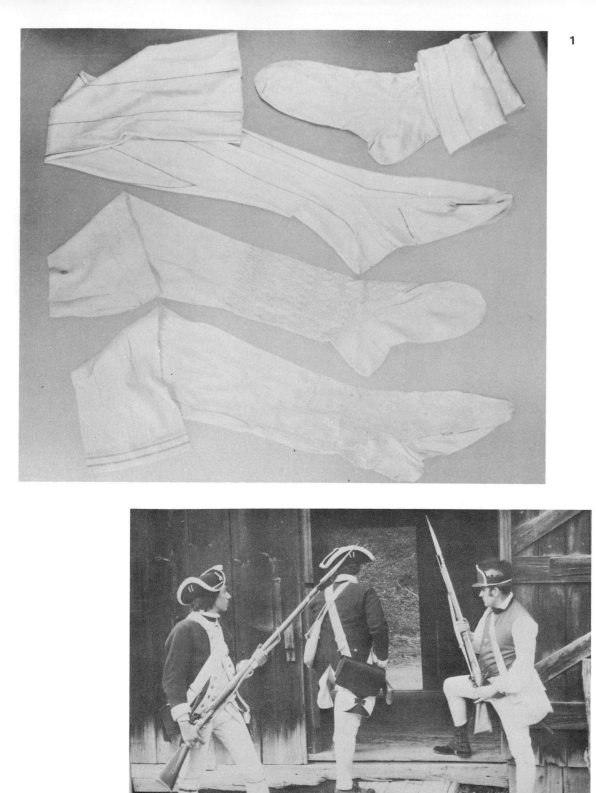

STOCKINGS (or "Hose"): Since men commonly wore knee breeches (and continued them well into the 19th century), stockings were long enough to reach above the knee and were held up by narrow leather garters buckled just below the knee. They were largely of woolen or worsted cloth, cotton or flax. The colors varied little from white or light gray. (1) These stockings belonging to a doctor in the Revolution exhibit the pleats and ribs often added for firmness and style. **STOCKS, NECK** (also see "Buckles," "Shirts," "Infantry"): These neckpieces worn by soldiers varied from light black leather and horsehair to linen, velvet, or velveret. They were either buckled or tied at the rear. (2) Troops wearing neck stocks.

Sources: 1—Edward Charol; 2—Brigade of the American Revolution, photo by Michael Cleary.

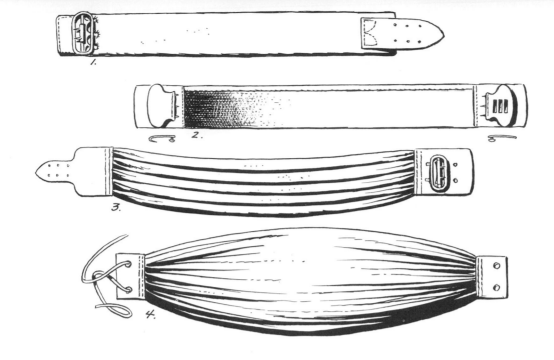

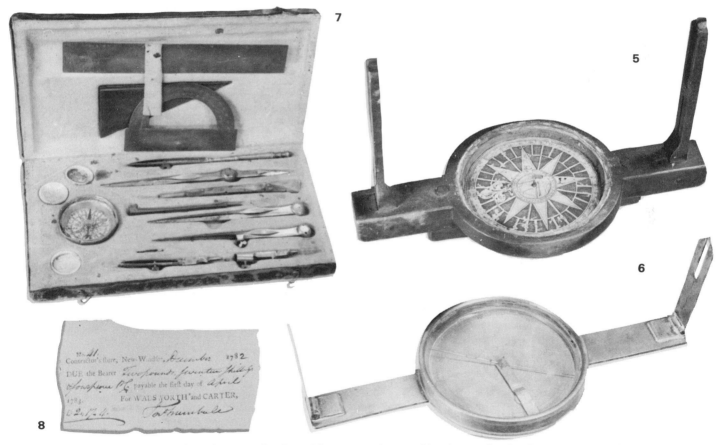

(1–4) *Typical examples of stocks worn by the soldiers:* (1) Fabric and leather with a leather tie strap and buckle. (2) Made of black horsehair and mounting British military brass clasps (see "Buckles"); its cloth binding was often colored. (3, 4) Common fabric patterns having either leather ties, or buckles at the ends. **STOVES** (see "Cooking-ware.") **STRIKERS** (see "Tinder Lighters.") **SUNDIAL** (see "Time Keeping.") **SURVEYING:** Surveying equipment was a critical necessity for the engineers laying out entrenchments, fortifications, or large camps. (5) A wooden compass (which sat on a wooden tripod); circa 1760; 12" long. (6) Brass hinged example by John Avery of Preston, Conn., c. 1787; 13" long. (7) An engineer's drafting set and case; c. 1770. **SUSPENSIONS** (see "Belts, Frogs, Scabbards.") **SUTLERS:** To supply the troops, several reorganizations of the American Commissary and Quartermaster Departments led to the use of contracting agents. Their stores were set up in the camps, and agents would accompany or precede an army on the march for supplies. (8) A printed and filled-in note from the Contractor's Store at New Windsor, N.Y. (1782), the final cantonment of the continental Army. Financing with hard money was a continuous problem that the sutler solved by issuing his own paper promissory notes due at a future date. These allowed him to purchase goods for resale to the soldiers.

Sources: 5, 6—William H. Guthman; 7, 8—Frank J. Kravic.

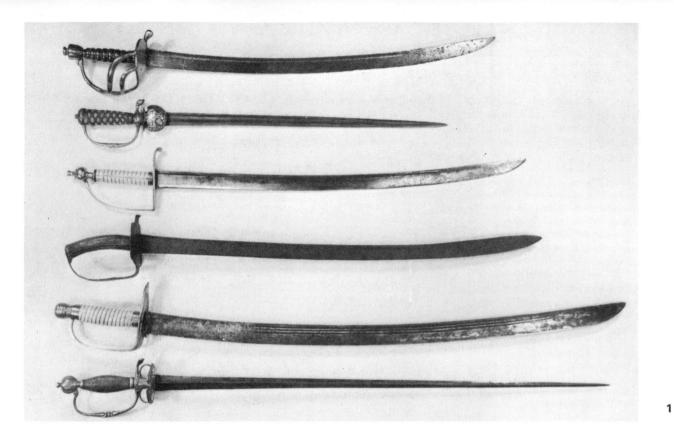

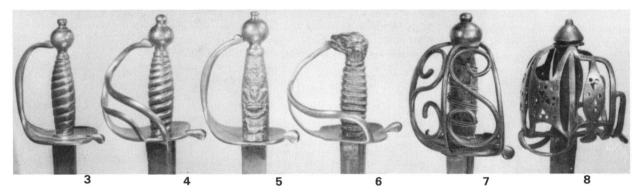

| 3 | 4 | 5 | 6 | 7 | 8 |

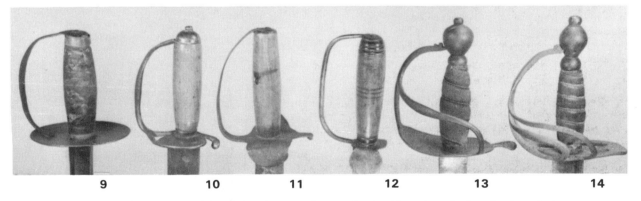

| 9 | 10 | 11 | 12 | 13 | 14 |

SWORDS: (also see "Belts, Frogs, Scabbards"): The sword served a dual function during the Revolutionary War period. First, as an indication of standing and honor—the wealth of its finish reflecting civilian and military levels, as well as employment in duels to defend one's name; second, as a fighting blade, the primary weapon of horsemen and a reliable arm at close quarters by infantry, artillery, and seamen. As the war progressed, its traditional role as the secondary weapon for musketmen gave way to the bayonet, but the sword still retained a major importance on the battlefield. Most blades were made and shipped from large European centers such as Solingen, Germany or France's Klingenthal; the hilts were added locally. (1) *A profile of major sword types* (top to bottom): First, an infantry hanger; blade about 25". Second, a short hunting sword, worn as a symbol of rank by many officers. Third, an officer's short saber; blades 28"–32". Fourth, the naval cutlass. Fifth, a horseman's saber; blades 32"–37". Sixth, the civilian rapier-like small sword worn by most officers. (3–6) *British cast brass-hilted infantry hangers,* c. 1740–1770 (#5 has a cast grip of the 23rd Rgt. of Foot insignia). (7, 8) Iron basket hangers as carried by many British grenadiers. (9–14) *c. 1755–1785: American-made hangers.* (mostly on European blades); grips used wood, cast brass, horn, antler, bone, leather covering, and fishskin wrapping—often supplemented by wire rope.

Source: George C. Neumann.

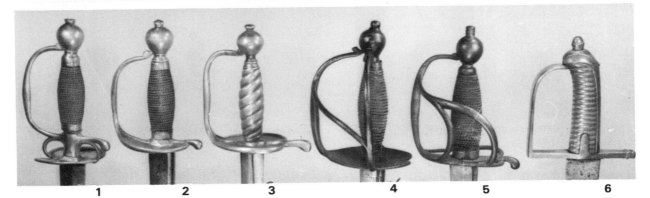

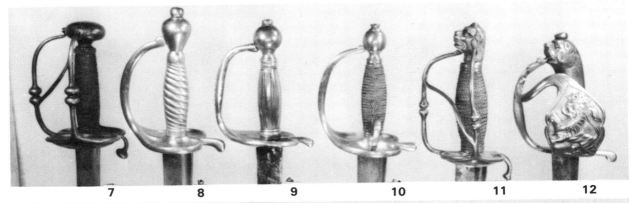

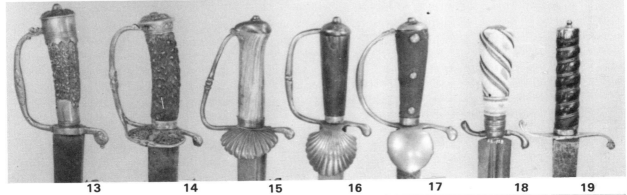

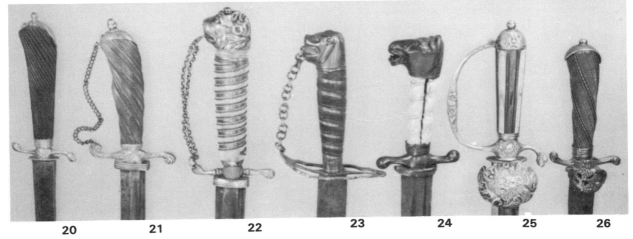

(1–6) French infantry swords: (1) c. 1700–1750; brass-hilted with a wire-wrapped wooden grip. (2) c. 1725–1750; omits the usual inner half of the guard. (3) c. 1740–1760; includes a cast brass grip like the English #3, p. 252. (4, 5) c. 1740–1760; iron mounted. (6) Model 1767 grenadier saber. *(7–12) German infantry swords:* (7) Iron mounted; c. 1650–1700. (8–12) c. 1720–1760; brass hilts; note the popularity of animal head pommels. *(13–17) Civilian hunting sword patterns:* carried socially by many officers: (13, 14) British, brass with antler grips; c. 1700; blades 19″ and 17¼″. (15) Early near horizontal shell guard plus antler grip; c. 1710–1730. (16, 17) Later, almost vertical shell guards; c. 1740–1760; brass hilt; grips of horn, and leather-covered wood. Hunting swords with expensive components are also called *"cuttoes"* *(18–26):* (18) European, c. 1680–1700; an ivory and brass hilt. (19) American, c. 1760–1780 using leather grip wrapping, copper binding. (20) French, silver with an ebony handle, 1767; typical straight blade. (21) English, silver plus a green dyed ivory grip; c. 1765–1780. (22) British; silver and ivory; c. 1765–1780. (23) American; brass-mounted, wooden grip; c. 1770–1780. (24) Brass horse-head pommel; ivory handle; c. 1770–1790. (25) British, hallmarked 1742; horn-paneled grip. (26) Green dyed ivory grip; c. 1750. (cont.)

Sources: 6, 9, 26—Frank J. Kravic; remainder George C. Neumann.

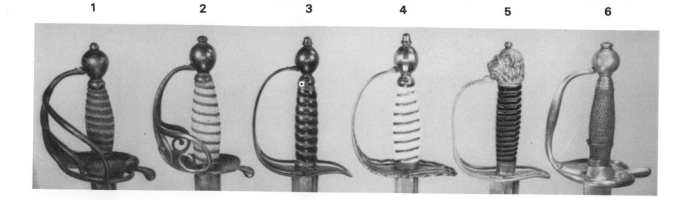

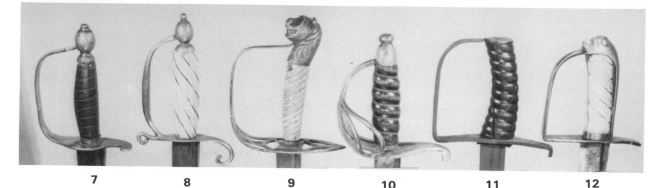

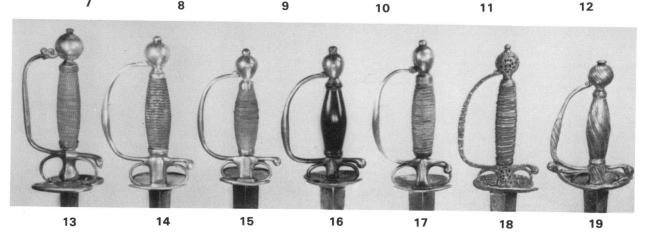

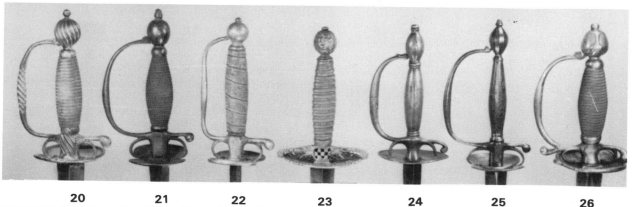

SWORDS (cont.) *(1-5) British officer short sabers:* Iron and brass-bound hilts with grips of shagreen (fishskin) covering wood centers, polished ebony, or bone; their patterns include side branches and slotted counterguards; all blades are single-edged and curved. (6) German, c. 1740–1770; marked with the Prussian eagle; 32½" blade. *(7-12) American short sabers* having brass and iron hilts mounting wooden, bone and ivory handles. *(13-26) The civilian small sword patterns* using long narrow thrusting blades: (13) English, c. 1690–1700; silver wash on brass. (14) Silver-hilted; possibly American, c. 1750. (15) c. 1750 silver-plated design popular among American officers. (16) American, c. 1740–1750; polished wooden grip. (17) Iron-bound with an iron wire-wrapped handle; American, 1750. (18) French, silver-hilted, c. 1745–1750; weight 0.7 lbs. (19) Double quillon boat guard style; cast brass; probably Dutch, c. 1755–1770. (20) Silver, European c. 1750–1760. (21) Blackened English mourning sword (usually an informal town pattern); c. 1740–1750. (22) American; brass plus shagreen grip; c. 1740–1750. (23) French style omitting knuckle bow; c. 1760–1770. (24) Cast brass hilt. (25) French steel pattern; c. 1770–1780. (26) Heavy English brass military version, c. 1760.

Source: George C. Neumann.

1a

(1a) Close-up of an American short saber with a vertically channeled bone grip and brass furniture; the imported single fuller curved blade measures 26½" x 1¼" (a common pattern). *(1–12) Naval Cutlasses:* (1, 2) American/European, c. 1740–1760; iron guards and octagonal bone grips. (3) American and British figure eight type; plain sheet iron-wrapped grip plus an oval spread of the knucklebow at midpoint; c. 1775–1800. (4) Common European and American pattern; a simple iron guard plus a cylindrical wooden grip; c. 1760–1780. (5) American; a wide outboard iron guard and octagonal bone grip; c. 1775–1790. (6) Like #5 with a channeled wooden handle; hilt originally painted black (i.e. preservation in wet conditions). (7) British; wide sheet iron guard; c. 1770–1800. (8) French, it mounts an old saber blade cut down to 22"; c. 1760–1790. (9) European, c. 1760–1790; a decorative brass hilt plus a polished bone grip. (10) American; antler handle and iron guard; c. 1760–1800. (11) Crude American having a bone grip and iron hilt; it mounts a thin small sword blade (cut to 20⅜"). (12) An early version of the French cast brass-hilted cutlass introduced in 1771 and later modified in 1782–1783. (cont.)

Sources: 2a—Brigade of the American Revolution, photo by Michael Cleary; remainder George C. Neumann.

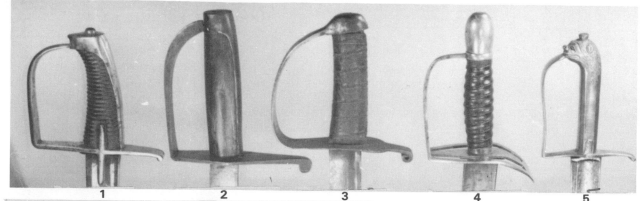

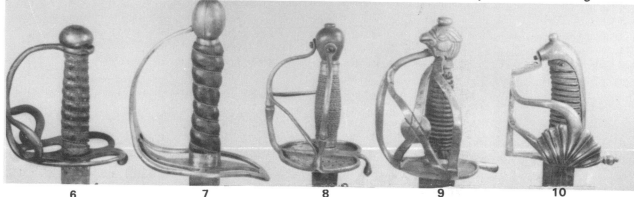

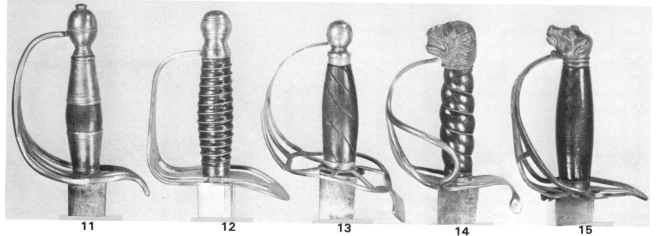

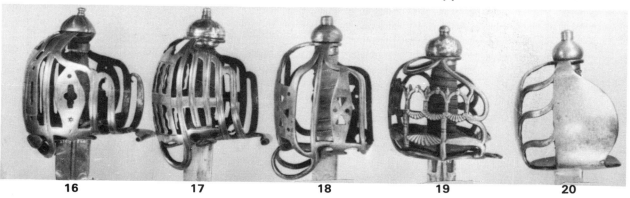

SWORDS (cont.) *Horseman Swords:* (1) Iron Hussar saber (curved 36″ blade) copied by much of Europe, c. 1765–1785. (2, 3) American iron-bound sabers. (4) Stirrup-hilt pattern with high dome pommel and spiraled wooden grip; American, c. 1775–1783. (5) Simple cast brass design incorporating an incised lion head; American; 35¼″ curved blade. (6) English light dragoon saber, c. 1759–1770; 37″ straight blade; iron hilt plus leather-covered grip. (7) British; c. 1768–1788; iron-mounted. (8) Early European "Walloon" pattern (iron) popular across continental Europe; c. 1700–1740, brass wire-wrapped grip. (9) German Prussian Model 1735; brass 37″ double-edged straight blade; 2.4 lbs. (10) German, c. 1750–1765; common side lobe and branch styling in brass; 39⅜″ overall; rope was wrapped around the wooden grip before the leather covering to create channels for outer wire rope binding. (11–15) *American light dragoon sabers* having brassbound hilts and wooden grips, single-edged straight or curved blades, c. 1777–1783. (16, 17) *Scotch Basket Hilts:* iron baskets and leather-wrapped wooden handles; typical double-edged straight blades, 34¾″ and 33½″; c. 1740–1760. (18–20) *British basket-hilted dragoon swords,* c. 1750; iron basket designs and straight blades; total lengths, 39½″ to 42″.

256

Sources: George C. Neumann.

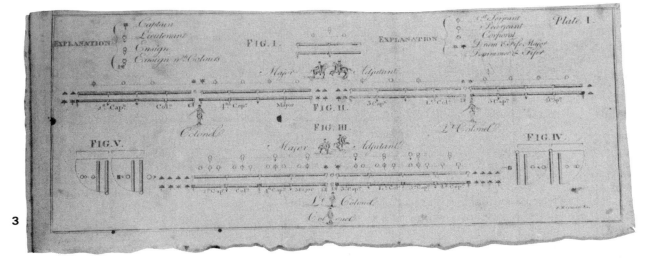

TACTICS, BATTLE (also see "Books," "Muskets"): The battle of the 18th century was devised to maximize the capabilities of the smoothbore musket and bayonet—while minimizing their shortcomings. Infantry fought in the open from long lines, two or three ranks deep. They would normally enter the field in column and rapidly deploy into lines facing the enemy. Artillery might accompany them in the line or be massed at strategic locations. Mounted troops were usually placed on the flanks or in the rear to attack at a critical moment. The places of honor among the regiments were on the flanks in the line of battle, in the advance during an attack, or at the rear in a retreat—and deeply felt rivalries attended the awarding of these positions. (2) A typical plan for a "Battalion in Firing Order." Each unit and officer had a specific location and followed precisely defined tactical procedures. (3) A formation guide from von Steuben's manual prepared for the American Continental Line. (cont.)

Sources: 1—Brigade of the American Revolution, photo by Richard Gerding; 2 ("Military Medley," Thomas Simes, London 1768); 3 (von Steuben Manual) George C. Neumann.

4

5

Order of Battle

Major General Marquis de la Fayette

Brigadier General Hans — *Brigadier General Poor*

Left Wing — *Right Wing*

Major General Arnold — *Major General Green*

Major Genl. McDougal — *Major General Howe* — *Major Genl. Lord Stirling* — *Major Genl. St. Clair*

Poor — *Starks* — *2d Massachts.* — *1st Massachts.* — *New York* — *New Jersey* — *2d Pennsylt.* — *1st Pennsylt.*

Glover — *Nickson* — *Clinton* — *Maxwell*

Major General Baron Steuben — *Brigadier General Parsons*

4th Massachusetts — *3 Massachusetts* — *2d Connecticut* — *1st Connecticut*

Learnard — *Patterson*

TACTICS, BATTLE (cont.): Because of the inaccuracy of the smoothbore muskets, firing speed was the critical factor (average 3–5 rounds per minute), and aiming was actually discouraged. The men stood shoulder to shoulder and fired together in volleys (by "pointing firelocks")—after marching across the field in good order with cadence (the drums immediately to their rear also sounded the commands). Having volleyed at close quarters, one of the two forces finally charged with the bayonet; thus cold steel and not the musket was the decisive weapon in the classic 18th century battle. The tactical objective was to break the opponent's line by frontal assault or, better yet, by attacking the flank or rear. All of this required iron discipline and control. Until the Continental Army received its thorough indoctrination in these European linear tactics at Valley Forge under von Steuben in 1777–1778, the Americans had little chance of winning. The tradition that the colonists finally won because they fired from cover at the exposed Royal troops has little historical justification. (4) An exercise from France's Marshal Saxe's "Reveries or Memories Upon the Art of War," reprinted in London 1757. It illustrates the classic maneuvering of straight lines of troops to the front and on the flanks. (5) An actual Order of Battle for the American Army on Aug. 1, 1780 at Peekskill when trying to challenge Gen. Clinton to emerge from New York City (he did not).

Sources: 4—George C. Neumann; 5—William H. Guthman.

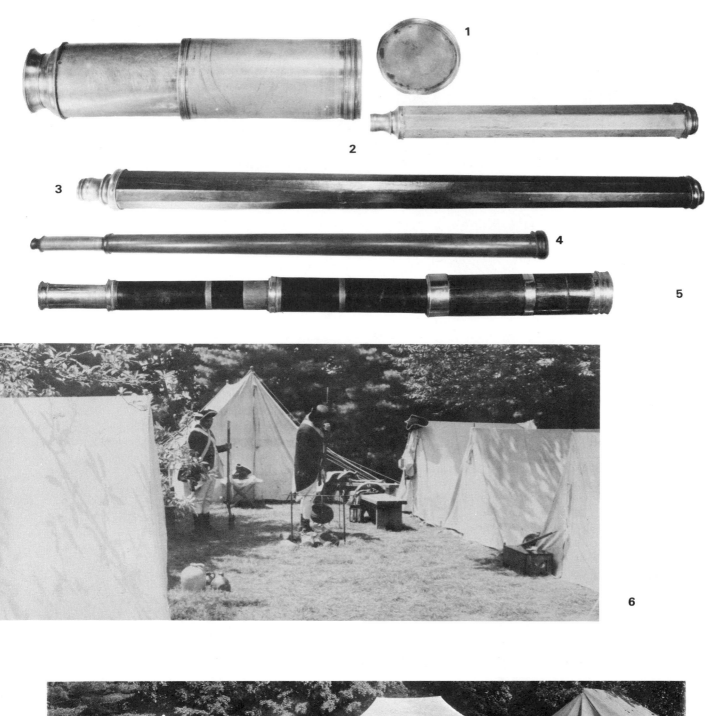

TAMPERS, PIPE (see "Smoking.") **TANKARDS** (see "Drinking ware.") **TELESCOPES:** Portraits of naval and military leaders in the early 18th century often include wooden telescopes of three feet or more in length. By the 1770s, shorter versions were also popular and carried by many officers during the Revolution. (1) A short brass pocket style with a screw lens cap (London) c. 1770–1810; 4½" closed, 6¾" open. (2) American, c. 1770–1810; of octagonal maple construction; 13½" closed, 22¾" extended. (3) Octagonal surface; 25¼" closed. (4) Round wooden frame and brass furniture; c. 1720–1750; 39" closed. (5) 4-section telescope used by Washington; lengths, 10½", 33". **TENTS** (also see "Camps"): Although the general styles of military tentage were established, many variations saw use. They were generally of linen canvas with the seams beeswaxed or painted for protection. Wagons transported them, and old tents were frequently cut up for clothing. (7) Tents used by Washington: (left) the sleeping tent roof is 8' in height; the officer marquee tent (center) has a 13½' ridge pole, 80' circumference, 5' 6" side wall; it is made of home-woven linen with a typical red flannel scalloped edge; the marquee tent fly is at the right. (cont.)

Sources: 1, 4—George C. Neumann; 2, 3—William H. Guthman; 5—Mount Vernon Ladies Assn.; 6—Brigade of the American Revolution, photo by Michael Cleary; 7—Smithsonian Institution.

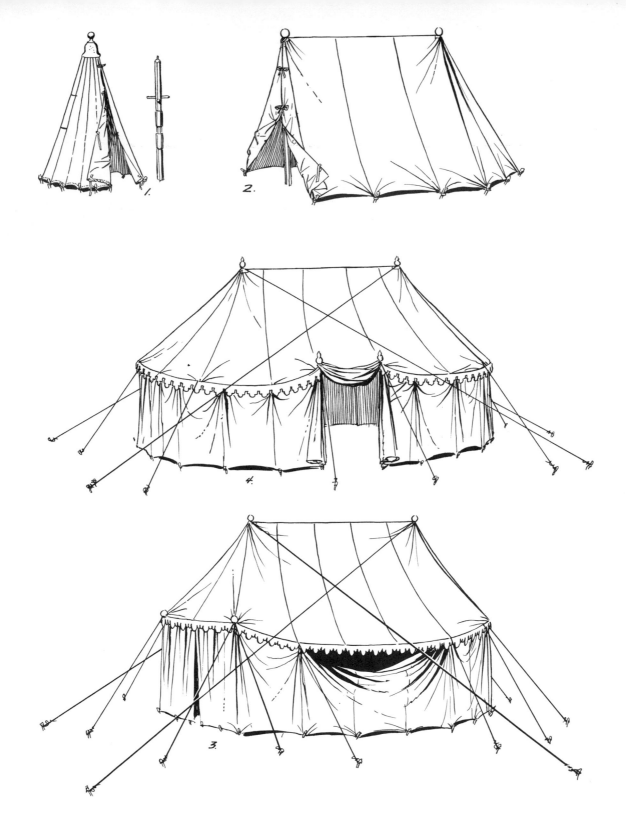

TENTS (cont.) (1) Bell of Arms for storing muskets (British and American); note its center pole with the crosspieces to support the firearms. The top cap is of painted leather and a regimental device was often reproduced on the tent's opposite side. (2) A private's tent for five men; 6½ feet square by 5 feet high; the round wooden balls atop the wooden poles were painted the regimental facing colors. (3) Officer's marquee tent, approximating 10½ feet x 14 feet x 8 feet high. (4) A colonel's or major's style of marquee; the scalloping would usually bear a colored edging.
THIMBLES (see "Sewing.")

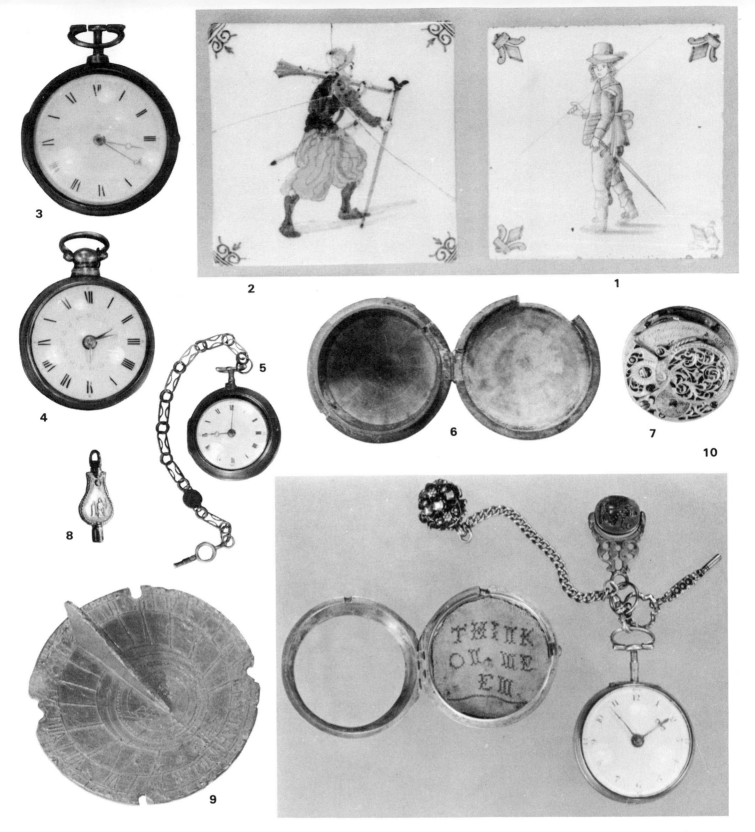

TILES: Dutch tiles were imported to America in the colonial period through British merchants or directly from similar English factories. The two illustrated here (1, 2) with military illustrations are of a type that adorned fireplaces in Dutch ethnic areas of the colonies and have been recovered from well established camps. Their corner designs were also distinctive; note the "bughead" and Fleur de lis motifs. **TIME KEEPING** (also see "Compasses, Pocket"): In camp the ordinary soldier kept time by the beatings of the drums signaling each activity of his established day. Most officers carried a pocket watch in their waistcoat—often with an elaborate chain which might hold the winding key and personal items such as seals. (3) A silver pocket watch in its outer silver case ("pair case"), London 1750–51. (4) Silver watch having a porcelain face with a third hand for its inner circle numbering the 31 days of the month; Bullingford, London 1758–59. (5) A silver watch that retains its winding key on a chain. (6) Protective wooden holding case with its opened watch at right exposing a typical elaborately pierced bridge—plus the chain drive mechanism beneath. (8) A winding key. (9) American portable cast sundial; it bears the initials "IM" believed to be Josiah Miller of Boston. (10) Pocket watch with an embroidered insert "THINK ON ME / EM"; the chain's provenance unknown. (cont.)

Sources: 1, 2, 6, 7—Frank J. Kravic; 3, 4—George C. Neumann; 5—Edward Charol; 8—Fort Ticonderoga Museum; 9, 10—William H. Guthman.

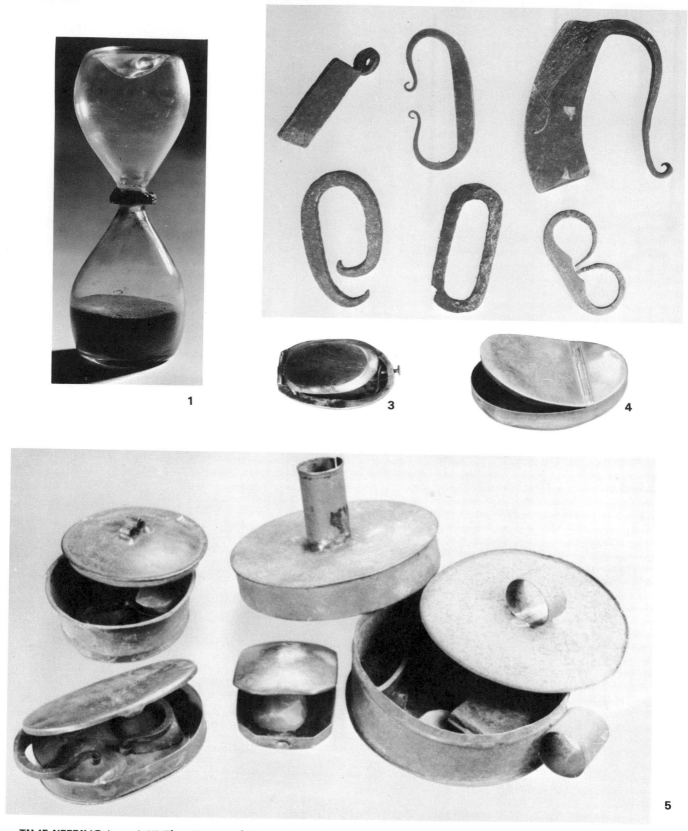

TIME KEEPING (cont.) (1) The 40 second "time glass" from the American gondola, "Philadelphia" (1776); note the typical seam at the center; its wooden frame is missing. **TINDER LIGHTERS** (also see "Lighting."): Just as with firearms, the manner of starting a fire in the 18th century was to strike flint on steel—either mechanically or by hand. Both home and traveler usually had a tinderbox containing a steel striker, a piece of flint, and charred cloth or tow ("tinder") to catch the sparks and burn. (2) Various steel strikers. (3–5) Typical tinderboxes including (#5 at right) a combination box and candle holder (a popular pattern c. 1760–1850). Most of these small tinderboxes were of tinned iron, brass, or pewter.

Sources: 1—Smithsonian Institution, Dr. Philip K. Lundeberg Collection; 2, 5—George C. Neumann; 3, 4—William H. Guthman.

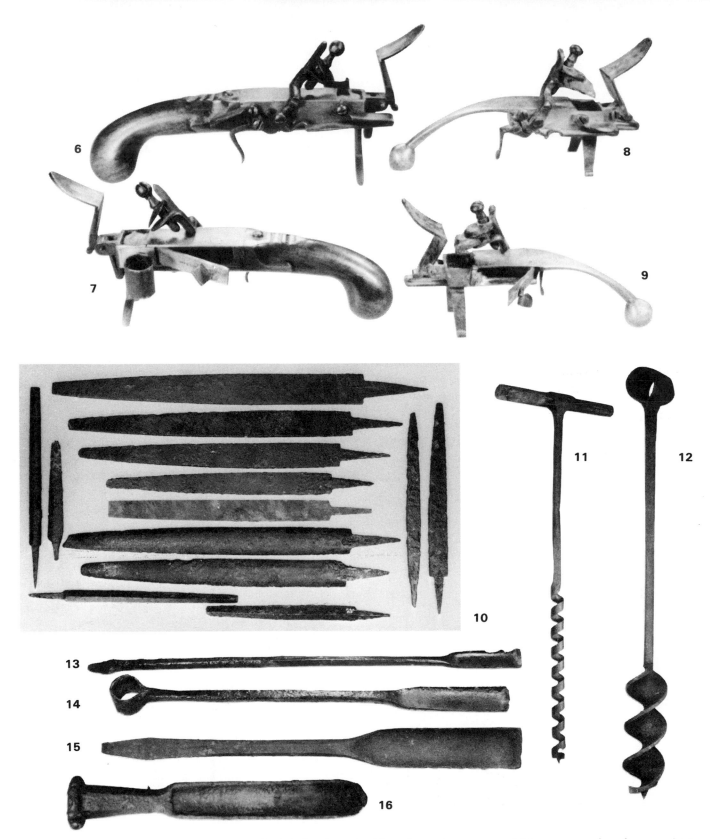

(6–9) Two mechanical tinder lighters (both sides shown) with a trigger, hammer, and frizzen as used on firearms (see "Flintlock, Action"); the sparks fell on tinder in the pan under the frizzen; note too the candle holder attachment on #7, and the small tinder storage compartments. (6, 7) English, c. 1760; (8, 9) German, c. 1750–1770. **TOBACCO** (see "Smoking.") **TOMAHAWK** (see "Axes.") **TOOLS, HAND** (also see "Axes," "Blacksmithing," Fascine Knives"): The form and design of modern hand tools reached its greatest development during the 18th century as America was rapidly settled and prior to the Industrial Revolution's shift toward mechanical methods. (10) All of these files and hasps have hand-cut crosshatched teeth and bear English makers' marks pressed into the tangs. Flat, half-round, and triangular blades are in this group—found buried in a wooden box at a British campsite of 1775. (11, 12) Spiral augers were used to drill holes in wood, usually for peg or metal pin construction; #12 from Champlain Valley camp, c. 1755–78. (13–16) Other augering tools used to carefully finish holes; from camp and hut areas, c. 1760–1780; the mushroomed handle on #16 indicates the heavy hammering it endured. (cont.)

Sources: 6–9, 11—George C. Neumann; 10, 12–16—Frank J. Kravic.

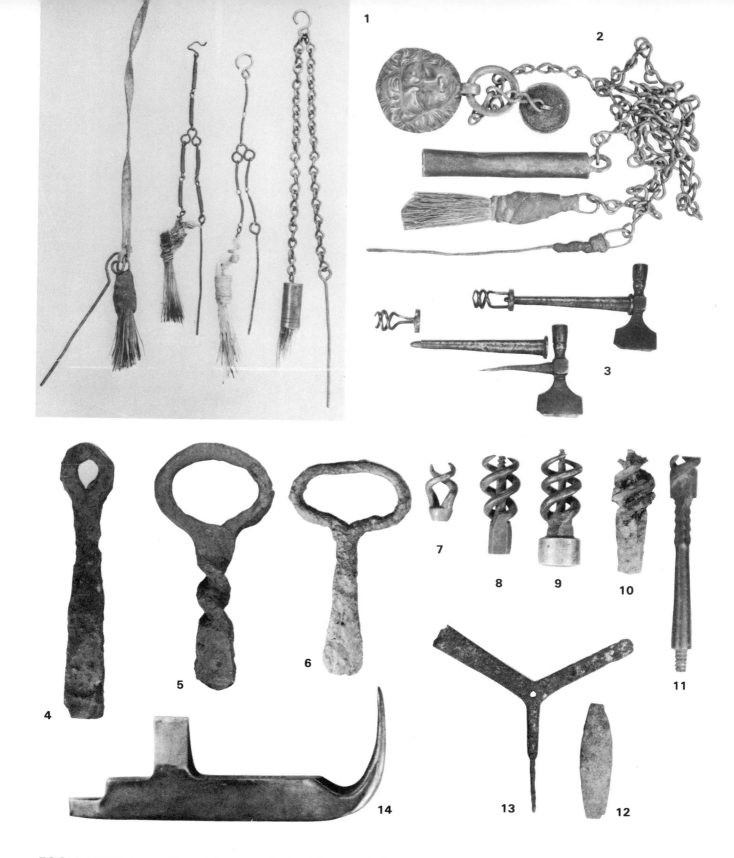

TOOLS, HAND (cont.) The soldier normally had three tools for his musket: a screwdriver to change flints; a pick ("pricker," "priming wire") plus brush to clear the touchhole and clean the pan; and, thirdly, a worm to screw on his rammer for cleaning the bore. (1) Various picks and brushes which usually hung in front by a chain or thong from his cross-belt (see #17). (2) This set also includes a cylindrical powder measure. (3) A small pocket combination tool, i.e. with a detachable worm, pricker, hammer, and flint knapper. (4, 5, 6, 12, 13) Screwdrivers; the #13 3-pointed tool included two screwdrivers and a threaded tip to hold a removable worm. (7–11) Types of worms; note that the middle three include a threaded ball puller in the center; #11 is from a c. 1775–1800 American rifle. (14) Reproduction of the steel combination tool recommended by Thomas Pickering (Salem Militia).

Sources: 1, 7, 8, 9, 12, 13—George C. Neumann; 2—Edward Charol; 3—William H. Guthman; 4, 5—Valley Forge Historical Society; Wm. Richard Gordon Collection; 6, 10—Frank J. Kravic; 11—Robert Nittolo.

(15, 16) A unique European pocket tool which combined a worm, pick, screwdriver, and corkscrew. (18–21) Mason trowels (handles missing) for brick and stone work; from a British fortified village in central New York, c. 1759–1775. (22) An auger with a screw tip (Pennsylvania troop camp, 1775–1776). (23) Small auger, c. 1760–1780. (24, 25) Excavated eye hooks for hauling with ropes (note rope guide ring on #24); #25 is from an American camp, c. 1775–1777, #24 was buried with a cache of iron objects, c. 1759–1780 site. (26) These various saw fragments with hand-cut irregular teeth came from military locations dating 1750–1778. Pit saws for cutting planks had long handles as shown at the bottom. One man stood in a pit below the log, and the other above—working the saw vertically. (cont.)

Sources: 15, 16—Edward Charol; 17—Brigade of the American Revolution, photo by Michael Cleary; 18–26 Frank J. Kravic.

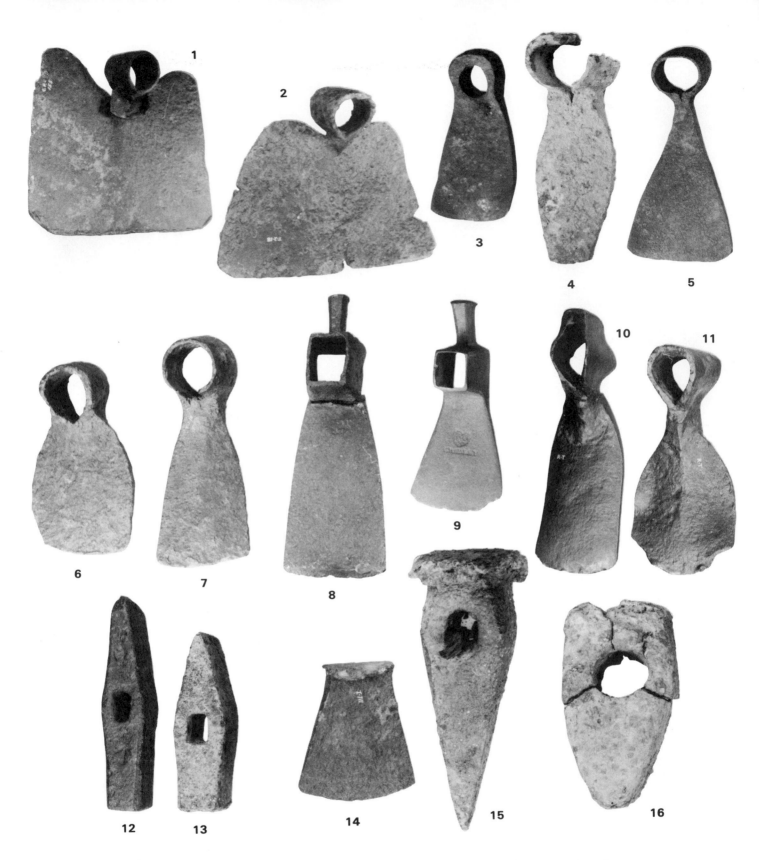

TOOLS, HAND (cont.) These hoes with their wide blades and crude handle sockets were found within a small entrenched camp. They may have been used for light digging or smoothing earthworks rather than agricultural crops; farm hoes were normally shorter than these; c. 1760–1780. (4–7, 10, 11) Mattocks, which were used to break up soil as well as to pry out rocks and roots; #4 is from a French site in northern New York, c. 1755–1759; 5–7 and 10, British sites 1760–1778; #11 was found in a 1775–1777 American camp. (3, 8, 9) Large beams were shaped from logs by these adzes which are more curved and sharper than mattocks (see above); excavated from English camps, c. 1760–1780. (12, 13) Small sledgehammers of a form favored by blacksmiths; these came from stone quarrying areas, c. 1760–1778. Note the British broad arrow deeply stamped into the face of the #12; many large tools were thus marked to identify them as British property. (14) When a tool was broken it often assumed new uses as with this axe blade that became a wedge; American site, c. 1775–1776. (15) A large sledge from a c. 1775–1776 American camp. (16) Sledge found in a British excavation c. 1760–1780.

Source:Frank J. Kravic.

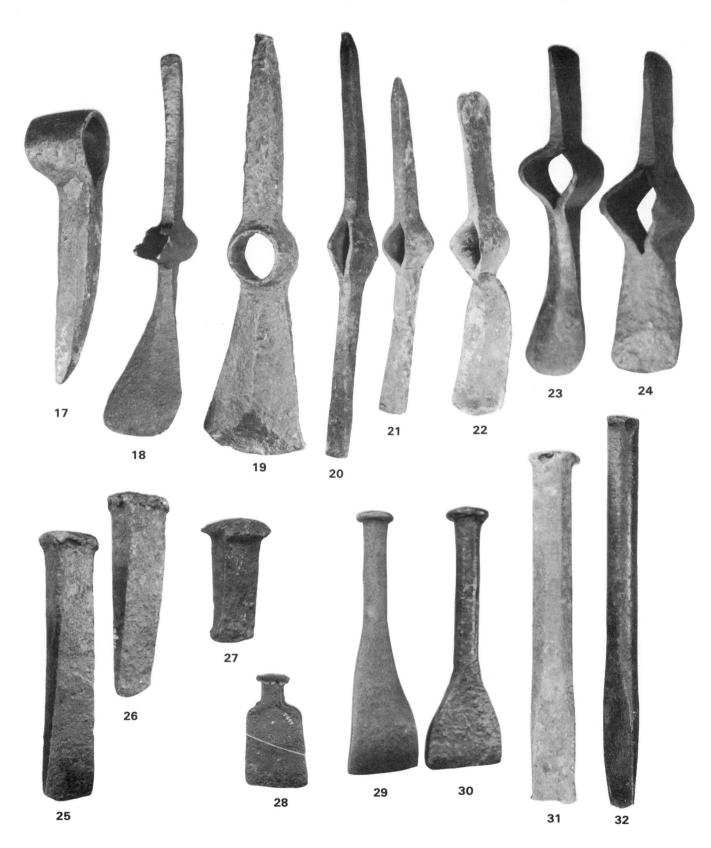

(17–24) The construction of earthworks, drains, and roads necessitated the employment of these tools; note that the top half was often varied to serve a secondary function; c. 1760–1780. (17) A half pick. (18) Pick mattock. (19) Pick mattock of a form commonly found on early Revolutionary or French and Indian War sites. (20, 21) Mattock axes which were useful for cutting roots as well as loosening soil. (22–24) Broad mattock axes with their blades at right angles to each other. (25–27) Wedges; #25 is a reused pick blade; c. 1760–1780. (28–32) Chisels: (28) A style used to shave wood for inletting, etc.; (29, 30) a type of chisel employed in caulking ships; these were recovered from camps associated with navigable water; c. 1750–1780. (31, 32) Stone chisels excavated out of a military quarry (upstate New York, c. 1760–1775); they split rock or drilled holes to be filled with black powder for blasting. (cont.)

Sources: 23, 24—George C. Neumann; remainder—Frank J. Kravic.

TOOLS, HAND, (cont.) Excavated spades and shovels: (1–4) These four spades all have slightly curved blades and sharpened edges, but little dishing as with modern shovels. (1) A spade made from two sheets of iron hammer-welded on the bottom third of the blade; the upper two-thirds was wood-filled, which extended through the short socket to become the handle; rivets passed through the blade to strengthen the bond between wood and iron; blade, 12½″ x 7″. (2) Another spade formed from two sheets of iron, but in this case hammer-welded over the entire blade except where the handle straps slid part way between them. One sheet was bent at a right angle over the other at the top to create a foot platform for digging; its blade measures 11½″ x 6½″. (3) A single sheet of iron was used for this spade; its handle socket is lap-welded; 9″ x 6½″. (4) A spade similar to #2, but made without extended straps for the handle; 13″ x 7″. (5, 6) Shovels constructed from one piece of iron with a socket cut from the sheet and lap-welded to shape. One rivet pierces the socket to secure its wooden handle. (7) A composite spade reformed from two broken ones. The parts were fitted, reheated, hammered and riveted together. The unusual blade shape is associated with early French settlements, c. 1750, but this specimen was excavated from an American campsite, c. 1775–1776 (Champlain Valley, N.Y.).

268   *Sources: 1–4, 6 Frank J. Kravic; 5—George C. Neumann; 7—Scott R. Bishop.*

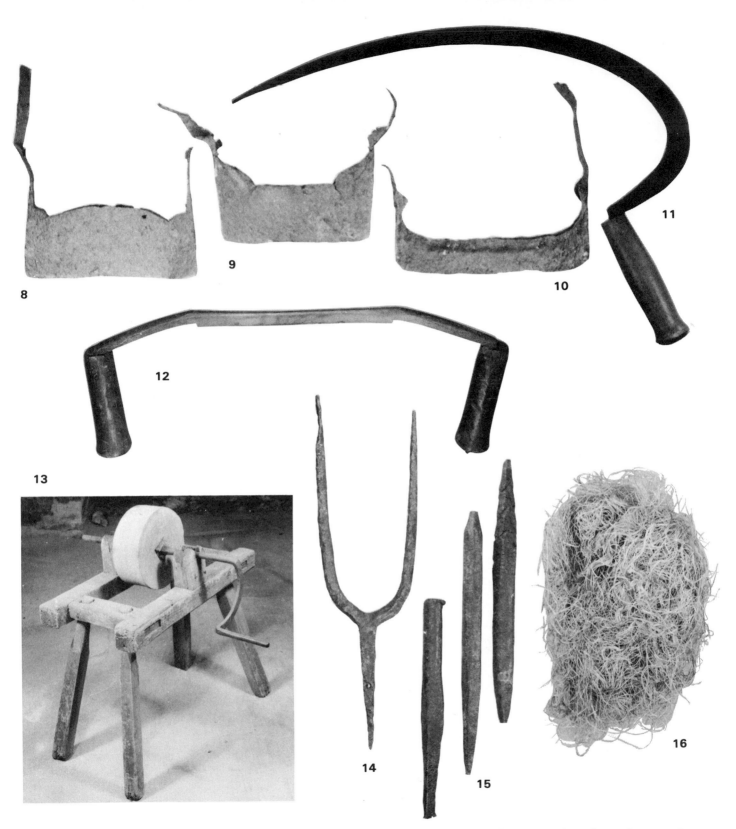

(8, 9, 10) The remains of "shod" spades; they used wooden blades plus the metal cutting edges shown here, and were more common in the French and Indian War than in the Revolution. Being rather fragile, they gradually extended their metal on the blade until achieving the form shown in #1, p. 268. (11) The long sweep of this sickle is a typical 18th century pattern; it was employed to keep camp areas neat, and defensive areas cleared. (12) A draw knife used to shave and shape wood by pulling it toward the operator. (13) A grinding wheel on a wooden frame. (14) This 2-tined hay fork could be used to remove brush from camp and cleared areas as well as to move hay; its pointed tang pierced the base of the wooden handle; from c. 1760–1780 entrenchments. (15) Inletting tools for driving nails or pegs flush or below the surface; found in a British camp site, 1760–1778. **TOW** (also see "Hunting Bag," "Tinder Lighters"): Tow was the coarse and broken unspun fiber of hemp and flax. (16) It served as a material for cleaning firearms and as wadding, or tinder with flint and steel: it also found use in making twine, rope, bags, and even caulking ships.

Sources: 8, 9, 10, 14, 15—Frank J. Kravic; 11, 12, 16—George C. Neumann; 13—Marvin K. Salls.

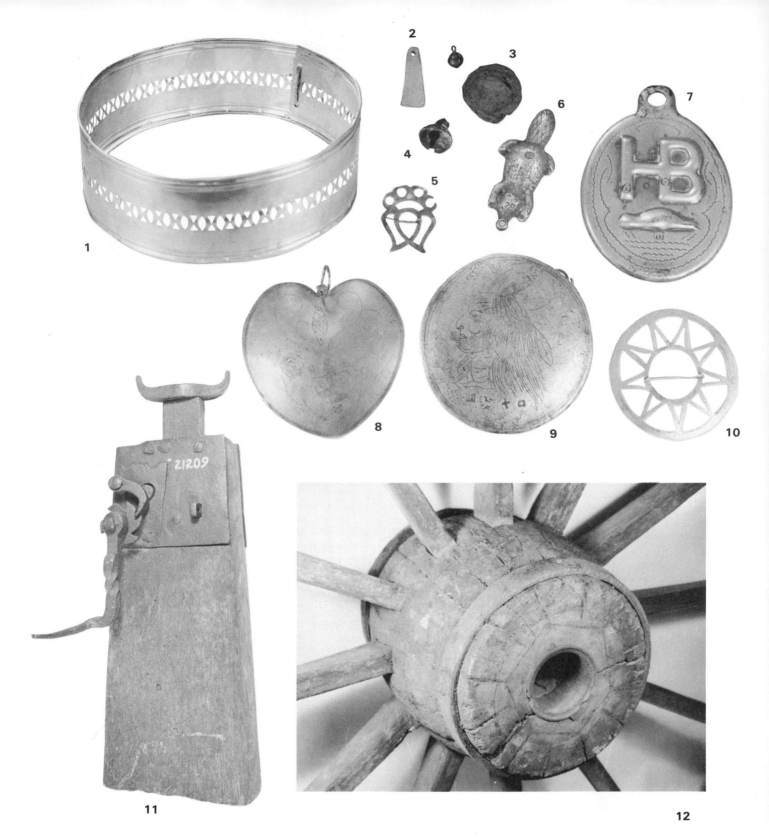

TRADE ORNAMENTS, INDIAN (also see "Beads," "Bells," "Crosses, Crucifixes," "Gorgets"): Trading with the American Indians in the 1700s was an enormous industry to the British, Dutch, French, and Americans; involved were a great variety of goods, sold, traded, or given away, e.g. guns, ammunition, axes, tools, blankets, kettles, paint, beads, gorgets, medals, agricultural implements, clothes, liquor, bottles, and ornaments. The ornaments involved a wide range of bright objects which could be worn with clothing or in their hair—much of it in silver ("trade silver"). (1) A silver crown usually sewn to a cloth turban; it is tied with a thong; 2⅜" high; c. 1760–1780. (2) A neck pendant of lead. (3) Small clay paint pot for face application. (4) Tiny ornamental bell; (#2, 3, 4 excavated in Champlain Valley, N.Y.). (5) A silver pin, 1⅜" high. (6) Silver beaver used for trade and a token of friendship; marked "IS" in a cartouche (Joseph Sasseville, Quebec 1776–1831); 2⅝" long. (7) Hudson Bay trade medal of pewter, c. 1720–1760; 4" length. (8) A silver trade medallion with a Scottish motif including a crown and thistle; the reverse side is flat with a raised heart; c. 1750–1765; 3" width. (9) Convex silver medal (2 hooks on the flat reverse side); note the engraved Indian head; by Louis Jackson, Montreal 1752–1769; 3¼" dia. (10) Silver star broach with a pin; 2⅜" dia., c. 1755–1765.

Sources: 1, 5–10—Edward Charol; 2–4—Frank J. Kravic; 11—Mercer Museum; Bucks County Historical Society; 12—The Conn. Historical Society.

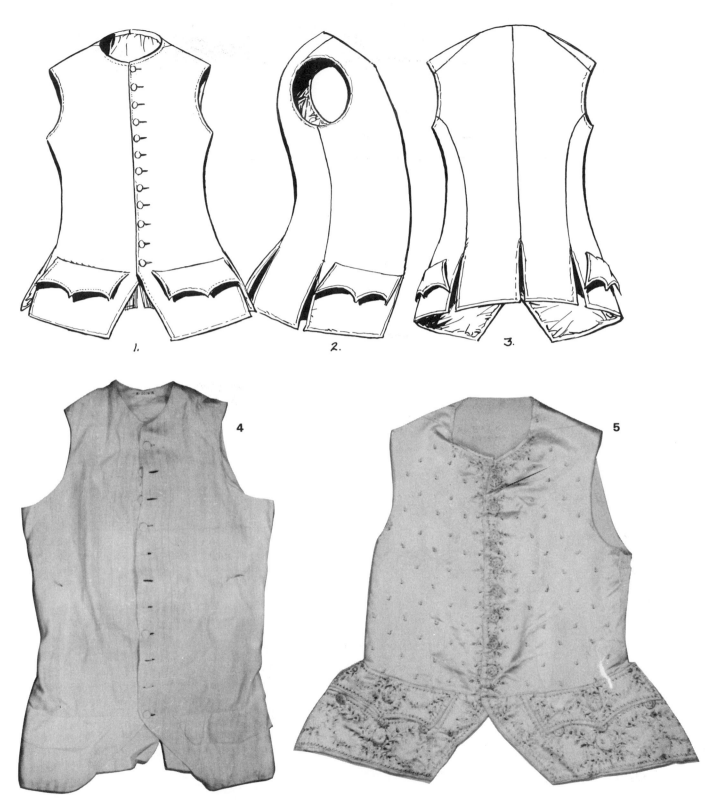

TROUSERS (see "Breeches.") **TRUNKS** (see "Luggage.") **UNIFORMS** (see "Breeches," "Coats," "Headgear," "Horsemen," "Infantry," "Marines," "Seamen," "Shirts," "Waistcoats.") **VESTS** (see "Waistcoats.") **WAGON JACK:** Wagons and occasionally sledges moved the heavy material of the armies. One source (Curtis), for example, states that between 1776 and 1780 Howe and Clinton averaged 739 wagons, 1958 horses, and 760 hired civilian drivers ("wagoners"). (11, on p. 270) A common wagon jack, c. 1770–1840. (12) Wheel hub construction of a wagon pressed into service to supply troops at Yorktown in 1781; its axle hole is 15" long; the outer wheel rim measures 4" across. **WAISTCOATS** (also see "Coats."): A formal article of both civilian and military dress, they extended well below the waist and usually omitted sleeves (which had been a popular form in the French and Indian War). The fighting man's version was usually of linen or wool and lined with lightweight fabric such as light linen, wool, muslin, or polished cotton. Pocket flaps for officers and noncoms showed holes and buttons; a private's flaps were plain. (1–3) The common soldier's waistcoat pattern. (4) A fine striped linen civilian example worn by militia Col. William Ledyard when killed by his own sword after surrendering it at Fort Griswold (Conn., Sept. 6, 1781). (5) A fine embroidered satin waistcoat as worn by civilians and officers on social occasions.

Sources: 4—The Connecticut Historical Society; 5—George C. Neumann.

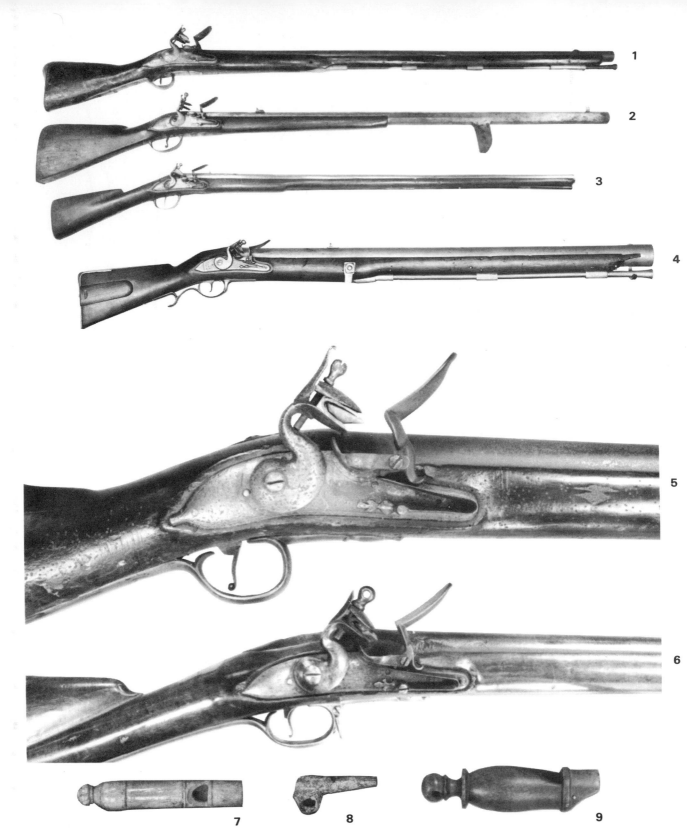

WALL GUNS (or "Amusettes," "Rampart Guns"): Fortified sites often used these large semi-shoulder firearms having a smooth or rifled bore. They were easier to produce and transport than light artillery and could carry across water or cleared land for impressive distances. Shorter versions were also mounted with swivels on ships' decks and longboats. (1) British; weight 32 lbs.; 1.05" bore in a 54" barrel; 6 feet overall. (2) Dutch, c. 1730–1740, iron furniture; 26 lbs.; 52" barrel of .94 cal.; total length 69". (3) A German-Swiss rifled rampart gun; 63" length; 16 lbs.; 47" octagonal barrel of .77 caliber. (4) American, made at the Rappahannock Forge about 1776. Its 44¼" barrel is rifled (12 grooves; 1.12" bore). Note the fixed "Y" swivel and wooden patch box; length is 61¼", the weight 53.5 lbs. (5, 6) Comparison of a British wall gun lock (5) with a standard musket size. (6) **WALLETS** (see "Purses.") **WATCHES** (see "Timekeeping.") **WATER BOTTLES** (see "Canteens," "Drinkingware.") **WHIPS** (see "Punishment.") **WHISTLES:** Whistles were apparently a common means of signaling and giving commands. Daniel Morgan even used a turkey call effectively to control his men at Saratoga. (7, 9) Whistle types of the period; they were commonly made of bone, pewter, antler, horn or wood.

Sources: 1, 2, 3, 5, 6, 9—*George C. Neumann;* 4—*West Point Museum;* 7, 8—*Fortress Louisbourg; Dept. of Indian and Northern Affairs, Parks, Canada.*

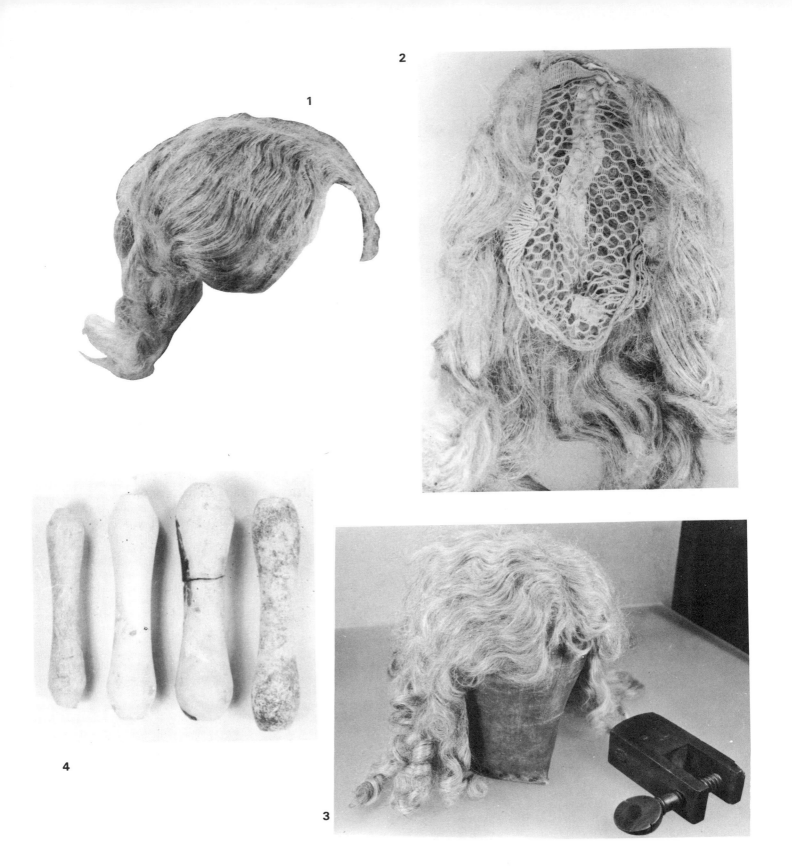

WIGS (also see "Combs," "Hair"): The practice of wearing wigs was losing favor by the time of the War for Independence, but it was still popular. Most used human hair, but many of the lower classes wore versions of horsehair, wool, and even tow. (1, 2) An American wig of coarse linen sewn to a cloth strip in the center which, in turn, is attached to a linen head net (2); the "hair" was tied in back and still retains much of its original form. (3) A full length wig of human hair on its original table stand (padded wooden center with a linen covering). The clamp originally held a missing base to the top of a table. (4) Made from pipe clay, these forms were used to produce the curls so fashionable in the 18th century. The hair was rolled around them with strips of damp paper, then tied and the wig baked. Wig curlers are narrow in the center to hold the curl material together while being rolled; they were often stamped with initials, numbers, and crowns on the ends to identify makers or contract lots. (cont.)

Sources: 1, 2—Frank J. Kravic; 3—Edward Charol; 4—Don Troiani.

WIGS (cont.) (1a, 1b) Wig curling irons which were heated and pressed over moist hair ends to form curls, c. 1750–1840. **WRITING IMPLEMENTS:** Most writing was done with ink and a quill pen (the sharpened end of a feather)—although lead pencils were available, and soldiers even hammered lead musket balls into long lengths for use in marking. (1) A European brass writing stand including a sander to sprinkle absorbent sand on wet ink, a quill holder, and an ink pot. (2) A larger stand with an added ink container, handle, and candle holder; both #1 and #2 date in the last half of the 18th century. (3) A soapstone ink holder. (4) An English basalt combination inkpot and quill holder; circa 1770s. (5, 8) Stone ink holders. (6) An excavated pewter ink well. (7) European pewter combination desk stand with a candle holder. (9) Wooden example holding a glass ink vial and holes for quill pens.

Sources: 1a, 1, 5, 9—George C. Neumann; 1b, 2, 4, 6, 7—Frank J. Kravic; 3—William H. Guthman; 8—Edward Charol.

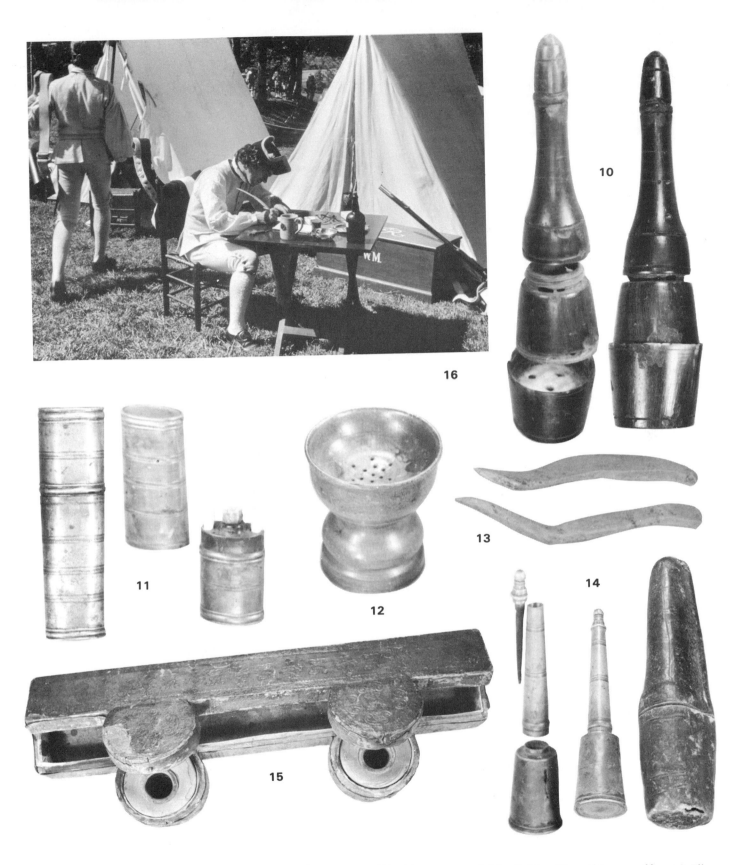

(10) Such small combinations of a sander, inkpot, and quill holder were useful for field writing; this one of horn is 7" high and dates c. 1780–1820. (11) A brass writing set with remains of two quill pens visible; the ink container was often of glass and handblown into the cavity created for it; 4¼" tall. (12) A wooden sander. (13) Two "pencils" made out of hammered musket balls (since bent); excavated from a 1775–1776 military camp. (14) A brass field writing kit with its original paper-mache case; note that in addition to the inkpot and long quill holder the tip holds a blade to sharpen the quills (which could also be reversed to use the stem as a handle). (15) An English writing case covered in tooled leather having a "GR" design; the two ink holders are backed by an open box area for quills and accessories, c. 1750–1780.

Sources: 10, 11, 12—George C. Neumann; 13, 14—Carroll V. Lonergan; 15—William H. Guthman; 16—Brigade of the American Revolution; photo by Richard Gerding.

Preserving Your Collection

Our present generation has embarked on such determined research into America's colonial heritage that many of the old interpretations are being re-evaluated and expanded. One of these areas of growing attention is the 18th century soldier. Early military collectors concentrated primarily on weapons and accoutrements, but interest is now spreading into a much wider spectrum—including the everyday living articles of a fighting man in the field.

The most accurate way to verify his personal environment is through items excavated from the original camps. Even small unattractive fragments can help to identify the proper styles, construction, and components of this equipment. Because of the random pilfering and continuing destruction of many of these sites, it is crucial that artifacts with proper verification be preserved by collectors for future study. The most common excavated metal to safeguard is iron, and an inexpensive method to protect it is described in most of this brief chapter. The proper care of

documents is also included because of their similar significance as an original source.

THE NATURE OF CORROSION

Metal occurs in nature as a mineral combined with non-metallic elements. It is then removed by man through the process of smelting. Yet, even after this treatment the stable state of a metal remains in its original mineral form, and a return to that more stable condition is what nature attempts through oxidation. Such combining of the metal with oxygen produces the various incrustations we see ranging from rust on iron to a green patina over copper.

Stabilization of the metal and often removal of incrustation is the goal of the conservator. Green colored copper or heavily pitted iron surfaces often make a more pleasing impression when not cleaned down to bare metal—so each object should first be carefully examined as to its state of deterioration, the presence of active corrosion, and the final appearance desired. Whether recovered from the soil, an attic, or a poorly maintained collection, the exposure to oxygen and moisture (including humidity) will lead to an item's deterioration.

In general, three conditions affect the rate of corrosion (especially of excavated objects): (1) acidity (or "pH"); (2) porosity of the object's surface; (3) presence of natural soluble salts. *Acidity:* the term, pH, refers to the degree of acidity which, in turn, is dictated by the balance of negative and positive ions in the soil. The greater the relative number of negative ions, the higher the acidity and the faster its rate of corrosion. Since the natural pH is regulated by the acidity of its minerals plus the decomposing organic matter present, geographic patterns emerge, e.g. eastern American soils are normally quite acid except in areas where limestone predominates. Thus most Revolutionary sites have earth that actively corrodes metal buried within it. Moisture, drainage, amounts of organic matter, disturbed soil—as well as the metal itself—also contribute to the rate of deterioration. *Porosity:* further, as an object corrodes it becomes pitted. This increases the amount of surface exposed and further accelerates the incrustation. *Salts:* since soils contain varying amounts of soluble salts that can conduct measurable electricity in the presence of moisture, this corrosion should also be thought of as an electro-chemical reaction.

TREATMENT OF METAL

Eighteenth century metals were seldom as pure as what we have today so that a metallic item could be composed of varying degrees of purity and structure, i.e. one area of it might corrode more rapidly than another. Moreover, Revolutionary War sites hold objects most often made of iron, tin, copper, and lead. Where these metals are alloyed together, such as tin and copper to make bronze, the rate of corrosion is usually greater than in either of its individual components. Thus the poor smelting methods of the 18th century can further accelerate deterioration.

The discarded equipment, lost items, and broken material in the camps typically ended up in trash heaps. These discard areas ranged from the far side of the nearest embankment to formally dug pits. Figure 1 illustrates a group of artifacts recently excavated from an 18th century military site. It indicates not only the wide range of materials found, but also the variety of items in use at the time. Most components that are organic in nature (i.e. made up of once living materials) usually rot away from bacteria and fungi in the soil. However, one buckle here still has remnants of its leather belt attached—although its iron "keeper" has corroded away. Nor should we expect to find just military objects—notice the liquor bottle fragments, pieces of a brick, a file, hook, ox shoe, sections of tinned iron, and even a cow bell. The military articles include musket balls, a sling buckle, broken musket butt plate, various buckles, and belt axes—one of which has rack numbers cut into it.

Metals buried together can further complicate a clear understanding of corrosion. When two dissimilar metals are adjacent in the soil, the "baser" one (i.e. lower in number on the Periodic Chart) will be preferentially corroded, with the more "noble" metal (higher on the Periodic Chart) experiencing less deterioration. The most stable of popular 18th century metals is gold, followed in order by silver, copper, lead, and iron. Thus iron, the most common Revolutionary War artifact metal, was the most easily corroded when in contact with the others (only alloys such as tin deteriorated more rapidly). Conversely, this principal can be extended by us to help remove incrustation from excavated iron by associating it with popular modern metals which, in turn, are more base and will attract most of the corrosive action to themselves. This is called "electro-chemical reduction."

Electro-Chemical Reduction

Any method involving chemical reactions must be started with a clear warning that the materials employed as well as the fumes emitted are dangerous and should be carried out with proper equipment and precautions. At no time should children or any person unfamiliar with the process be allowed near it.

Chemicals Required: Zinc, a readily available metal that is baser than iron, and can be used to transfer the corrosion to itself. "Mossy" zinc is the recommended form which may also be easily cleaned for reuse. *Caustic soda,* a commercial flake caustic soda that acts as the electrolyte once it is dissolved in water. The strength of the solution should not be less than ten percent (e.g. 2 ozs. to 1 pint of water) and may go up to twenty

Figure 1. A typical assortment of excavated material from a circa 1755–1779 campsite. Note the variety of items (see list in text).

Figure 2. Artifacts from Figure 1 after chemical and limited mechanical cleaning prior to the beginning of the preservation process.

percent—especially for heavily corroded items. This extremely active base must be handled very carefully. Contact by the skin with the flakes, the solution, or the fumes should be avoided. If an accident occurs, flood the skin with water and wash throughly as it can cause the skin to peel.

Wearing goggles and rubber gloves plus good ventilation are also necessary precautions.

Procedure: Artifacts of rugged construction such as axes and tools are put into a covered container

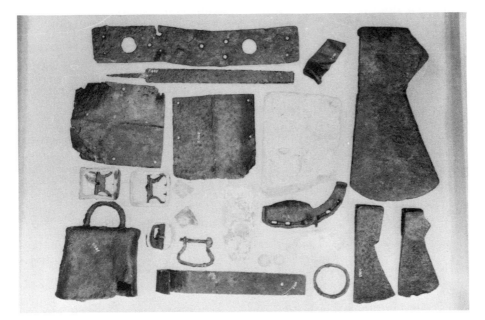

Figure 3. Campsite artifacts (see Figure 1) after application of the collection numbers and the preservative wax coating.

which should be iron or porcelain. Aluminum, for example, is a baser metal and would be broken down during the reduction. The flakes of mossy zinc are placed around each object to bury it (numerous items may be done at the same time in the container). Next, fill with the caustic soda solution until the artifacts and zinc are covered. The solution may then be boiled to speed up the reaction or allowed to proceed more slowly on its own. If heat is applied, about an hour will complete the process; otherwise it may require as many as four hours. You will note that hydrogen gas is produced and bubbles up to the surface (be careful to avoid boiling over).

The solution is then poured off and zinc saved for later reuse. The film of chlorides that have reacted with the zinc must now be removed. This is easily done by pouring a weak solution of hydrochloric acid over the zinc. When the bubbling ceases, wash the zinc with distilled water and touch pH sensitive paper to its moist surface to indicate if retreatment is required (the pH paper should show a red color for a satisfactory condition). In this manner some zinc is lost, but most can be recovered and used many times.

Your next step is to place the artifacts in mild soapy water and scrub them. A table knife may be scraped along surfaces of objects that still have a solid core of metal to loosen heavy incrustation and then bristle brushes can be used to help take off the remainder. For the sake of appearance, it may not be desirable to remove all of this coating as ugly pits will be visible in the surface (although any remaining corrosion contains chlorides which might cause trouble in the future).

At this stage, the surface is filled with many tiny pores still holding chlorides so a series of soakings in first hot and then cold water will open and close them in a flushing action. Distilled water is recommended.

Following these rinsings, the artifacts may be immersed in a mild solution (10%–20%) of phosphoric acid. This will remove any excess base still present and bring the surface pH to about a neutral pH-7. As distilled water has a pH of "7" the objects should have a neutral pH by the end of the washing process. Several soakings ought to follow the phosphoric acid treatment. Again, this acid should be handled carefully although dilute solutions are not overly reactive.

Next, remove the articles from a hot soak and allow them to dry (the hot surface increases evaporation and speeds drying). Those items needing another treatment (i.e. still showing excess adhering corrosion) may be sent through the entire process again. The great advantage of this reduction method is that no complicated or expensive apparatus is required. Final techniques for checking the presence of any residual chlorides are not difficult and can be found in the more technical works cited in the bibliography.

With delicate objects or items still retaining tiny bits of rust, small picks such as dentists use are helpful. Since these picks exert a strong pressure at the point of contact, care must be used. An inexpensive dissecting microscope can also be employed during this process to permit added control. When the artifacts are at the desired state of cleanliness they are ready for preservation.

PRESERVATION OF ARTIFACTS

If the collector has a numbering system for identifying his items, the figures can be printed directly on the object with a pen and white india ink at this stage. For an encrusted surface the writing may be done over dry nail polish.

One of the best preservatives is ceresin wax. This microcrystalline material is a petroleum product of consistent purity vs. alternatives such as beeswax which is a natural product that turns opaque on its surface, or paraffin that is highly flammable.

In this procedure the object is pre-heated in an oven (e.g. a small rotisserie oven) until hotter than the wax's melting point (150 degrees) to drive out any residual moisture and to help the wax penetrate its porous surface. It is then immersed in the melted wax and remains there till bubbling ceases. The object should be warm enough so that the wax remains liquid on its surface. A pair of laboratory tongs can be used to lift the artifact from the wax for placement on a newspaper to cool. As excess wax drains off, the object should be moved to dry paper to prevent sticking. Surplus wax may be rubbed off with a cloth, but for storage and handling it is best left with the thicker coating.

The cooled artifact will take on a darker shade. There is no shiny surface or dulled visibility to hamper close study and—most important—simple heating can remove the wax coating for later cleaning or renewed preservation. Occasional inspection of items treated in this manner will also indicate the continuing stability of the corrosion. Brown liquid bubbles on the surface or whitened areas in the wax show that deterioration is continuing and the item should be reprocessed. If this activity is not visible, it can be assumed that your object remains stable. The microcrystalline nature of this wax not only prevents water from penetrating, but allows air to enter free of its water vapor. Thus, variations in temperatures and the resultant changes in the object will not cause cracking of the wax surface as is common when shellacs or varnishes are used.

Summary

This electro-chemical method for preserving iron objects involves these steps:
1. Wash the artifact to remove loose corrosion and dirt.
2. Carry out surface reduction with caustic soda and zinc.
3. Wash with mild soapy water and then rinse in hot and cold water.
4. Immerse in dilute phosphoric acid.
5. Wash thoroughly in hot and then cool water.
6. Rinse in distilled hot water and let cool.
7. Remove and dry thoroughly.
8. Apply your collection numbers with india ink.
9. Heat the artifact and immerse it in ceresin wax till all bubbling ceases.
10. Remove, drain, and let cool.
11. Store in a dry place.

PAPER PRESERVATION

Many collectors are surprised at the durability of 18th century paper when they see how quickly most modern paper fades, yellows, and becomes brittle. Today's product is commonly made of wood pulp, but at the time of the Revolutionary War paper was normally produced from linen scraps and rags. Their fibers were separated in water to create a slurry which was then poured over a screen and allowed to dry. Often a special design was incorporated into this screen—transferring itself as a watermark to the paper to identify the maker or quality of the stock. Paper produced in this manner was relatively free from the strong acids used to separate wood fibers in modern manufacture, and actually differed little in substance from linen cloth. Nevertheless, because of the organic composition it is subject to deterioration if not properly handled and stored.

Care Of Documents

Since the ink originally used has stained the paper, a wrinkled document may be safely washed in lukewarm water and pressed between absorbent cloth or paper to flatten and remove surface dirt. If it has been stored in association with modern wood pulp paper or folders, the early document has probably acquired a somewhat acid pH by transfer. A mild solution (about 5%) of a commercial home laundry bleach with water can be used to rinse the sheets, but care must be taken not to overclean and cause fading or bleaching of the ink. Once dry, the paper should be stored flat in an acid-free folder (available from document dealers) where the humidity is below 60% and the temperature averages 65–70°.

Pieces that have been wet and not quickly dried may be attacked and rotted by organic mildews. These appear as a fuzzy growth capable of rapid spreading by the release of thousands of spores to infect other areas. Fresh air and light will stop their growth, and the maintenance of less than 60% relative humidity should prevent recurrence. Keep in mind too that in the long run both sunlight and fluorescent light can fade documents.

The repair of tears should be done only with wettable book tapes (never use permanently sticky adhesive ones). Should you encounter a permanent type on a document an acetone mixture can be used to dissolve the adhesive tape and a scalpel carefully employed to scrape away any excess adhesive. Good results have been obtained by using 1 part acetone, 3 parts of alcohol, and 3 parts of toluene. These three ingredients are highly flammable either separately or together, and adequate ventilation must be provided.

Small insects also attack paper; the presence of moth crystals or sodium fluoride provide a good control against them.

Our true knowledge of the men who fought to win America's freedom depends in part on the preservation of these original items. Even if you possess only a few it is your obligation to properly insure their protection for future generations. More detailed information can be obtained from the relevant sources listed in the bibliography.

Bibliography

Not all sources employed in the preparation of this book are included in this list. It is intended only as a presentation of the major references and an indication of the range of material studied.

I. TEXTS

Albert, Alphaeus H., *Record of American Uniform & Historical Buttons*. Boyertown Publishing Co., Boyertown, Penn., 1969.

American Heritage Book of the Revolution. American Heritage Publishing Co., Inc., New York 1958.

American Heritage History of Colonial Antiques. American Heritage Publishing Co., Inc., New York, 1967.

Annis, P.G.W., *Naval Swords*. Stackpole Books, Harrisburg, Penn., 1970.

Aylward, J.D., *The Small Sword in England*. Hutchinson & Co., Ltd., London, 1960.

Barnes, Major R. Money, *A History of the Regiments and Uniforms of the British Army*. Seeley Service & Co., London, 1962.

Blackmore, Howard L., *British Military Firearms*. Arco Publishing Co., Inc., New York, 1962.

Blair, Claude, *European and American Arms*. Crown Publishers, Inc., New York, 1962.

Bland, Humphrey, *A Treatise of Military Discipline*, London, 1746.

Boatner, Mark M. III. *Encyclopedia of the American Revolution*. David McKay Co., Inc., New York, 1966.

Bolton, Charles Knowles, *The Private Soldier Under Washington*. Kennikat Press Inc., Port Washington, N.Y., 1964.

Boudriot, Jean, *Armes a Feu Francaises*. Paris, 1961.

Brigade of the American Revolution, *The Soldiers Manual*, 1974.

Brown, Rodney Hilton, *American Polearms 1526–1865*. N. Flayderman & Co., New Milford, Conn., 1967.

Burke, Joseph and Caldwell, Colin, *Hogarth*. Harry N. Abrahams, Inc., New York.

Butler, David F. *United States Firearms The First Century 1776–1875*. Winchester Press, N.Y. 1971.

Chaffers, *Marks and Monograms on Pottery and Porcelain*. Lowe & Brydon Ltd., London.

Chapelle, Howard I., *The History of the American Sailing Navy*. Bonanza Books, New York, 1949.

Cobban, Alfred, *The Eighteenth Century, Europe in the Age of Enlightment*. McGraw-Hill Book Co., New York, 1969.

Coggins, Jack, *Ships and Seamen of the American Revolution*. Stackpole Books, Harrisburg, Penn., 1969.

Cotterell, Howard Herschel, *Old Pewter Its Makers & Marks*. Charles E. Tuttle, Rutland, Vt.

Curtis, Edward E., *The Organization of the British Army in the American Revolution*. Yale University Press, New Haven, Conn., 1926.

Curtis, John Obed and Guthman, William H., *New England Militia Uniforms and Accoutrements*. Old Sturbridge Village, Sturbridge, Mass., 1971.

Darling, Anthony D., *Red Coat and Brown Bess*. Museum Restoration Service, Ottawa, 1970.

Dawney, Major N.P., *The Distinction of Rank of Regimental Officers, 1684 to 1855*. The Society For Army Historical Research, London, 1960.

Diderot, Denis, *L'Encyclopedie, ou Dictionnaire Raisonne des Sciences, des Arts et des Metiers*, 1763.

Dillon, John G.W., *The Kentucky Rifle*. Ludlum & Beebe, New York, 1946.

Earle, Alice Morse, *Costume of Colonial Times*. Empire State Book Co., 1924.

———, *Home Life in Colonial Days*. The Macmillan Co., New York, 1926.

Exploring Rogers Island. The Rogers Island Historical Assn., Fort Edward, N.Y., 1969.

Ferguson, Homer L., *Salvaging Revolutionary Relics from the York River*. The Mariners' Museum, Newport News, Va., 1939.

Ffoulkes, Charles, and Hopkinson, E.C., *Sword, Lance, and Bayonet*. Arco Publishing Co., Inc., N.Y., 1967 (originally 1938).

Fuller, Col J.F.C., *British Light Infantry in the Eighteenth Century*. Hutchinson and Co., London, 1925.

Glendenning, Ian, *British Pistols and Guns 1640–1840*. Cassell & Co., Ltd., London, 1951.

Godden, Geoffrey A., *An Illustrated Encyclopedia of British Pottery and Porcelain*. Crown Publishers, New York, 1967.

Gooding, S. James, *An Introduction to British Artillery in North America*. Museum Restoration Service, Ottawa, 1965.

Gould, Mary Earle, *The Early American Wooden Ware*. Charles E. Tuttle Co., Inc., Rutland, Vt., 1962.

———, *The Early American House*. Charles E. Tuttle Co. Inc., Rutland, Vt., 1965.

Grancsay, Stephen V. *American Engraved Powder Horns*. Ray Riling Arms Books Co., Philadelphia, Penn., 1965.

Graymont, Barbara, *The Iroquois in the American Revolution*. Syracuse University Press, Syracuse, N.Y., 1972.

Greathouse, Glenn A., and Wessell, Carl John, *Deterioration of Materials: Causes and Preventive Techniques*. Reinhold Pub. Corp., 1954.

Grimm, Jacob L., *Archaeological Investigation of Fort Ligonier 1960–1965*. Carnegie Museum, Pittsburgh, Penn., 1970.

Grose, Francis, *Military Antiques, a History of the English Army (Vols. I, II)*. London, 1801.

Guldbeck, Per E., *The Care of Historical Collections*. The American Assn. for State and Local History, Nashville, Tenn., 1972.

Hardin, Albert N., Jr., *The American Bayonet 1776–1964*. Riling and Lentz, Philadelphia, Penn., 1964.

Hayward, Arthur H., *Colonial Lighting*. Dover Publications, New York, 1962.

Heizer, Robert F., *A Guide to Archeological Field Methods*. The National Press, Palo Alto, Calif., 1962.

Held, Robert, *The Age of Firearms*. Harper & Brothers, New York, 1957.

Howell, Edgar M., and Kloster, Donald E., *United States Army Headgear to 1854*. Smithsonian Institution Press, Washington, D.C., 1969.

Hughes, Major-General B.P., *British Smooth-Bore Artillery*. Stackpole Books, Harrisburg, Penn., 1969.

Hume, Ivor Noel, *Archaeology and Wetherburn's Tavern*. Colonial Williamsburg, 1969.

———, *Excavations at Tutter's Neck*. Smithsonian Institution, Govt. Printing Office, 1966.

———, *A Guide to Artifacts of Colonial America*. Alfred A. Knopf, New York, 1970.

———, *The Wells of Williamsburg*, Colonial Williamsburg, 1969.

Hummel, Charles F., *With Hammer in Hand*. The University Press of Virginia, Charlottesville, Va., 1968.

Jackson, C., *A Complete System of the Military Art*. Dublin, 1780.

Kane, General, *A System of Camp-Discipline*. London, 1757.

Kauffman, Henry J., *Early American Gunsmiths 1650–1850*. The Stackpole Company, Harrisburg, Penn., 1952.

———, *Early American Ironware*. Charles E. Tuttle Co., Rutland, Vt., 1966.

Kehoe, Vincent J-R, *The Officer's Guide, 10th Regiment of Foot*.

Kindig, Joe, Jr., *Thoughts on the Kentucky Rifle in Its Golden Age*. Trimmer Printing, Inc., York, Penn., 1960.

Klinger, Robert L., and Wilder, Richard A., *Sketch Book 76*. Cooper-Trent, Arlington, Va., 1967.

Langdon, William Chauncy, *Everyday Things in America 1607–1776*. Charles Scribner's Sons, New York, 1937.

Latham, R.J. Wilkinson, *British Military Bayonets From 1700 to 1945*. Hutchinson of London, 1967.

Lawson, Cecil C.P., *A History of the Uniforms of the British Army (Vols. I–IV)*. Norman Military Publications, London, 1940, 1942, 1961, 1966.

LeBlond, Guillaume, *A Treatise of Artillery*. London, 1746.

Lefferts, Charles M. *Uniforms of the American, British, French, and German Armies in the War of the American Revolution 1775–1783*. New-York Historical Society, 1926.

Lewis, Berkeley R., *Small Arms and Ammunition in the United States Service 1776–1865*. Smithsonian Institution, Washington, D.C., 1956.

Lewis, Waverly P., *U.S. Military Headgear 1770–1880*. 1960.

Lezins, Martin, *Das Chrenfleid des Soldaten*. A.G. Ullstein, Berlin, 1936.

Lichtenberg, *The World of Hogarth*. Houghton Mifflin Co., Boston, 1966.

Lindsay, J. Seymour, *Iron & Brass Implements of the English House*. Alec Tiranti, London, 1964.

Lowell, Edward J., *The Hessians*. Kennikat Press Inc., Port Washington, N.Y., 1965.

Martin, Joseph Plumb, (Edited by George F. Scheer), *Private Yankee Doodle*. Popular Library, New York, 1963.

May, Cmdr. W.E., and Annis, P.G.W., *Swords for Sea Service (Vols. I, II)*. Her Majesty's Stationery Office, London, 1970.

McClinton, Katharine Morrison, *Antique Collecting for Everyone*. Bonanza Books, New York, 1951.

McDowell, Bart, *The Revolutionary War, America's Fight for Freedom*. The National Geographic Society, Washington, D.C., 1967.

Mercer, Henry C., *Ancient Carpenters Tools*. The Bucks County Historical Society, Doylestown, Penn., 1921.

Miller, A.E. Haswell, and Dawnay, N.P. *military Drawings and Paintings in the Royal Collection (Vols. I, II)*. Phaidon Press Ltd., London, 1970.

Miller II, J. Jefferson, and Stone, Lyle M., *18th Century Ceramics from Ft. Michilimackinac*. Smithsonian Press, 1970.

Mitchell, Lt. Col. Joseph B., *Discipline & Bayonets*. G.P. Putnam's Sons, New York, 1967.

Montross, Lynn, *Rag, Tag, and Bobtail*. Harper & Bros., New York, 1952.

Moore, Warren, *Weapons of the American Revolution*. Funk & Wagnalls, New York, 1967.

Mount Vernon Ladies Assn., *General Washington's Military Equipment*. Mount Vernon, Va., 1963.

Muller, John, *A Treatise of Artillery*, London, 1780.

Neumann, George C., *A History of Weapons of the American Revolution*. Harper & Row, New York, 1967.

_____, *Swords, and Blades of the American Revolution*. Stackpole Books, Harrisburg, Penn., 1973.

Norman, A.V.B., *Small Swords and Military Swords*. Arms and Armour Press, London, 1967.

Peterson, Eugene T., *Gentlemen on the Frontier*. Mackinac Island State Park Commission, Mackinac Island, Michigan, 1964.

Peterson, Harold L., *American Indian Tomahawks*. Museum of the American Indian, New York, 1965.

_____, *The American Sword 1775–1945*. The River House, New Hope, Penn., 1954.

_____, *Arms and Armor in Colonial America 1526–1783*. Stackpole Books, Harrisburg, Penn., 1956.

_____, *The Book of The Continental Soldier*. Stackpole Books, Harrisburg, Penn., 1968.

_____, *Daggers and Fighting Knives of the Western World*. Walker & Company, New York, 1968.

_____, *Encyclopedia of Firearms*. E.P. Dutton & Co., New York, 1964.

_____, *Round Shot and Rammers*. Stackpole Books, Harrisburg, Penn., 1969.

Phipps, Frances, *Colonial Kitchens, Their Furnishings, and Their Gardens*. Hawthorn Books, Inc., New York, 1972.

Plenderleith, H.J., *The Conservation of Antiquities and Works of Art*. Oxford University Press, London, New York, 1966.

Pratt, Peter P., *Oneida Iroquois Glass Trade Bead Sequence 1585–1745*. Fort Stanwix Museum, Rome, N.Y., 1961.

Quaife, Milo M., and Weig, Melvin F., and Appleman, Roy E., *The History of the United States Flag*. Harper & Bros., New York, 1961.

Riling, Joseph R., *Baron Von Steuben and His Regulations*. Ray Riling Arms Books, Co., Philadelphia, 1966.

Riling, Ray, *The Powder Flask Book*. Bonanza Books, N.Y. 1953.

Robbins, Roland Wells, and Jones, Evan, *Hidden America*. Alfred A. Knopf, New York, 1959.

Rogers, Col. H.C.B., *Weapons of the British Soldier*. Seeley Service & Co., Ltd., London, 1960.

Russell, Carl P., *Firearms, Traps, and Tools of the Mountain Men*. Alfred A. Knopf, New York, 1967.

Savage, George, *The Art and Antique Restorer's Handbook*. Frederick A. Praeger, New York, 1967.

Saxe, Field Marshal Count, *Reveries on Memories Upon the Art of War*. London, 1757.

Scheer, George F., and Rankin, Hugh F., *Rebels and Redcoats*. The World Publishing Co., New York, 1957.

Schermerhorn, Frank Earle, *American and French Flags of the Revolution 1775–1783*. Penn. Society of Sons of the Revolution, Philadelphia, Penn., 1948.

Simes, Thomas, *The Military Medley*, London, 1768.

_____, *The Regulator to Form the Officer.*, London, 1780.

Sloane, Eric, *A Museum of Early American Tools*. Wilfred Funk, Inc., New York, 1964.

_____, *A Reverence for Wood*. Funk & Wagnalls, N.Y. 1965.

Smith, Elmer L., *Early Tools and Equipment*. Applied Arts Publishers, Lebanon, Penn., 1973.

Smith, Captain George, *An Universal Military Dictionary*. J. Millan, London, 1779.

Stone, George Camerone. *A Glossary of the Construction, Decoration and Use of Arms and Armor*. Jack Brussel, New York, 1961.

Todd, Frederick P., and Kredel, Fritz, *Soldiers of the American Army 1775–1954*. Henry Regnery Co., Chicago, 1950.

Towner, Donald, *The Leeds Pottery*. Taplinger Publishing Co. Inc.

Tunis, Edwin, *Colonial Craftsmen*. The World Publishing Co., New York, 1965.

_____, *Colonial Living*. The World Publishing Co., New York, 1957.

Von Krafft, Lt. John C.P., *Journal 1776–1784*. New-York Historical Society, New York, 1882.

Wallace, John, *Scottish Swords and Dirks*. Stackpole Books, Harrisburg, Penn., 1970.

Ward, Christopher, *The War of the Revolution (Vols. I, II)*. The Macmillan Co., New York, 1952.

Watney, Bernard, *English Blue and White Porcelain of the 18th Century*. Thomas Yoseloff, New York.

Welsh, Peter C., *Woodworking Tools 1600–1900*. The Smithsonian Institution, Washington D.C., 1966.

Wilbur, C. Keith, *Picture Book of the Continental Soldier*. Stackpole Books, Harrisburg, Penn., 1969.

_____, *Picture Book of the Revolution's Privateers*. Stackpole Books, Harrisburg, Penn., 1973.

Wilkinson, Frederick, *Edged Weapons*. Doubleday & Co., Inc., Garden City, N.Y., 1970.

Williamsburg Craft Series, *The Leatherworker in Eighteenth-Century Williamsburg*. Colonial Williamsburg, 1967.

Windham, William, *A Plan of Discipline for the Use of the Norfolk Militia*. London, 1759.

Woodward, Arthur, *Indian Trade Goods*. Binfords & Mort, Portland, Oregon, 1965.

Wright, Col. John Womack, *Some Notes on the Continental Army*. National Temple Hill Assn., Vails Gate, N.Y., 1963.

Wyler, Seymour B., *The Book of Old Silver*. Crown Publishers, New York, 1937.

II. PERIODICALS

American Pole Arms or Shafted Weapons, Bulletin of the Fort Ticonderoga Museum, Vol. V, July 1939.

Atkinson, Capt. C.T., *Grenadier Companies in the British Army*, Society for Army Historical Research Journal, London, Oct. 1931.

Berkebile, Don. H., *The Military Rifle Pouch*, Journal of the Company of Military Historians, Spring 1960.

Blackmore, Howard L., *British Military Firearms in Colonial America,* American Society of Arms Collectors Bulletin #25, Spring, 1972.

Brewington, M.V., *The Sailmaker's Gear,* The American Neptune, Oct., 1949.

Brown, Margaret Kimball, *Glass from Fort Michilimackinac,* The Michigan Archaeologist, Sept.–Dec. 1971.

Caroll, George P., *The Band of Musick of the Second Virginia Regiment 1779–1783,* The Brigade of the American Revolution "Dispatch," March 1966.

Chard, Jack, *Historic Ironmaking,* Journal of the Council for Northeast Historical Archaelogy, Vol. 1, No. 1, 1971.

Chernoff, Arnold Marcus, *Early American Powder Horns,* Guns & Ammo, Sept., 1969.

Cleary, Michael, *The Continental Pioneer,* The Brigade of the American Revolution "Dispatch," October–November, 1974.

Cornwell, William S., *The Museum's Collection of Military Canteens,* Museum Service Bulletin of the Rochester (N.Y.) Museum of Arts & Sciences, June 1964.

Daniels, Wayne M., *A Survey of Musket Powder Horns,* The Brigade of the American Revolution "Dispatch," Oct. 1968, and Feb. 1969.

_____, *The Forms of Musket Powder Horns,* Brigade Dispatch, August 1969.

Darling, Anthony D., *Staff Weapons of the British Army,* The Canadian Journal of Arms Collecting, Vol. 9, No. 1.

_____, *The British Basket Hilted Cavalry Sword,* Vol. 7, No. 3.

_____, *The British Infantry Hangers,* Vol. 8, No. 4.

Davis, Ogilvie H., *Directional Time Tellers of the French and Indian Wars,* Muzzle Blasts, October 1969.

_____, *The Frontier Knife,* Muzzle Blasts, Nov. 1965.

Elgin, George, *Powder Men of the Brandywine,* Muzzle Blasts, May 1965.

Frayler, John M., *Corps of Sappers and Miners Continental Army 1780,* Tradition Magazine, No. 69.

Good, Mary Elizabeth, *Fort de Chartres: French Stronghold on the Mississippi,* Muzzle Blasts, Feb. 1972.

Haarman, Albert W., and Holst, Donald, *The Friedrich Von Germann Drawings of Troops in the American Revolution,* Journal of the Company of Military Historians, Vol. XVI, No. 1, 1964.

Hagerty, Gilbert, *The Iron Trade-Knife in Oneida Territory,* Penn. Archaeologist, Vol. XXXIII, July 1963, Nos. 1–2.

Holst, Donald W., *18th Century Accoutrements of the Royal Artillery,* Journal of the Company of Military Historians, Vol XVIII, No. 2, Summer 1966.

Kehoe, Vincent J-R, *The Pioneer in the British Foot Regiments in the 1770–80's,* Crown Forces Bulletin #1, 20, Nov. 1972.

Knoetel, Herbert, *Hesse Cassel Fusilier Regiment Von Ditfurth 1776–1782,* Journal of the Company of Military Historians, Vol. II, No. 1, March 1950.

Leliepvre, Eugene, *French Soissonnois Infantry 1780–1783,* Journal of the Company of Military Historians, Vol. XVI, No. 4, Winter 1964.

Lunn, John, *Louisbourg—The Forgotten Fortress,* Antiques Magazine, June 1970.

Martin, Dennis, and Katcher, P.R.N., Seaman, *Pennsylvania Armed Boats, on the Jersey, 1781,* The Brigade of the American Revolution "Dispatch," Nov.–Dec. 1971.

Montgomery, Charles F., *A History of American Pewter,* Antiques Magazine, October 1973.

Mulligan, Robert E., *American Engineer—1776,* The Brigade of the American Revolution "Dispatch," August 1970.

Neumann, George C., *Common Pike Heads of the American Revolution,* The Brigade of the American Revolution "Dispatch," Vol. IV, No. 4.

_____, *Firearms of the Revolution* (4-part series), The American Rifleman, July to October 1967.

_____, *Revolutionary War Rifles,* The American Rifleman, October 1973.

_____, *Stone Bullet Molds,* The Brigade of the American Revolution "Dispatch," July-August 1971.

Norman, A. V. B., *Early Military Dirks in the Scottish United Sciences Museum, Edinburgh,* The Journal of the Arms & Armour Society, Vol. IV. No. 1, March 1962.

Peal, Christopher, *An English Pewter Collection,* Antiques Magazine, August 1969.

Peterson, Harold L., *Hessian Cartridge Box Plates,* Journal of the Company of Military Historians, Vol. II, No. 2, June 1950.

_____, *John Paul Jones' Corselet,* Journal of the Company of Military Historians, Vol. III, No. 2, June 1951.

Peterson, Mendel L., *American Epaulettes 1775–1820,* Journal of the Company of Military Historians, Vol. II, No. 2, June 1950.

Ray, Fred, Jr., and Todd, Frederick P., *British 42nd (Royal Highland) Regiment of Foot, 1759–1760,* Journal of the Company of Military Historians, Vol. VIII, No. 2, 1956.

Sabine, David B., *Medicine in the Revolution,* American History Illustrated, June 1973.

Todd, Frederick P., *Preliminary Study of Continental Army Flags and Colors,* The National Temple Hill Assn., 1964.

Todd, Frederick P., and Knoetel, Herbert, *Hesse Cassel Field Artillery 1776–1782,* Journal of the Company of Military Historians, Vol. VI, No. 3, Sept. 1954.

Webster, Donald B., Jr., *American Wall Guns,* The American Rifleman, August 1963.

Whitelaw, Charles E., *Notes on Swords with Signed Basket Hilts by Glasgow and Stirling Makers,* Glasgow Archaeological Society New Series, Art. VIII, Part IV, Supplement 1934.

Wigham, William, *The Frock: A Revolutionary War Fatigue Shirt,* The Brigade of the American Revolution "Dispatch," May–June 1971.

Wolf, Paul J., *How Powder Was Put to the Test,* The American Rifleman, December 1971.

_____, *Powder Testers,* The American Arms Collector, Oct. 1958.

Woodward, Arthur, *Some Notes on Gun Flints,* Journal of the Company of Military Historians, Vol. III, No. 2, June 1951.

Wright, Edwin S., *The Gun Flint in the American Revolution,* The Brigade of the American Revolution "Dispatch," January 1967.